Love Itself is Understanding

Love Itself is Understanding

Hans Urs von Balthasar's Theology of the Saints

Matthew A. Rothaus Moser

Fortress Press
Minneapolis

LOVE ITSELF IS UNDERSTANDING

Hans Urs von Balthasar's Theology of the Saints

Cover image: Adoration of the Trinity, Albrecht Dürer (16th c.)/Wiki

Cover design: Laurie Ingram

Library of Congress Cataloging-in-Publication Data

Print ISBN: 978-1-4514-9959-9

eBook ISBN: 978-1-5064-1899-5

Manufactured in the U.S.A.

This book was produced using Pressbooks.com, and PDF rendering was done by PrinceXML.

To Robert W. Johnston (1917–2012):

In communione sanctorum, in luce aeterna

And to Kaitlyn:

*"Mille disiri più che fiamma caldi
strinsermi li occhi a li occhi rilucenti,
che pur sopra 'l grifone stavan saldi."*

—Dante, Purgatorio XXXI.118–120

"He knew now at the end there was only one thing that counted—to be a saint."

—Graham Greene

Contents

Contents

Acknowledgements

No book is written in a vacuum. In my study of theology so far, I have been accompanied by a host of friends and colleagues to whom I am indebted. During my years at Baylor University, I was fortunate to encounter several people who challenged and enriched my thinking about theology, philosophy, art, and ministry. Special thanks to Ralph Wood for nearly a decade of intellectual friendship and debate. Thank you to my other professors and mentors from Baylor University, Phillip Donnelly, D.H. Williams, and Jonathan Tran, for taking time to challenge and encourage the current project. Most especially, I offer my thanks to my *Doktorvater* and friend, Peter M. Candler. I am grateful to Pete not only for his patient and thoughtful mentorship of this project when it was a PhD dissertation, but also for the consistent reminder that I should not endeavor to write on prayer without also learning to pray, nor about the saints without journeying toward sanctity.

I am fortunate to have excellent colleagues at Loyola University Maryland who have given up their time to read, critique, and edit this manuscript. I am especially grateful for the keen theological insight of Fritz Bauerschmidt, Steve Fowl, Jim Buckley, Rebekah Eklund, Dan McClain, and Matthew Moran. These colleagues have reminded me that theology must be done in and with the Church, that there is no theology outside of prayer, and that the vocations of professor and priest may not be as exclusive as is commonly assumed. My thanks to them.

Finally, to my family and friends, who have encouraged and supported me through the long years of researching, writing, and editing this book, I'm afraid I have only inadequate words with which to offer my gratitude. Thanks to my mother, Karen Moser, for her Christ-like self-giving; to my father, Larry, and Jeanette, for their ongoing support and encouragement; to Rob, Wendy, Ryan, and Jordan for laughter and play; and to my grandmother Alzada Johnston, whose love knows no bounds. My affection and thanks to dear friends: David and Molly Wilmington, Dan and Carrie Marrs, Daniel and Kate McClain, Will and Lesley-Ann Williams, Jenny and Eric Howell. Thank you for challenging me intellectually and spiritually, for keeping my speculative mind grounded in the concrete practices of the Christian life, and for a thousand conversations that formed me as a friend, theologian, and lover of God. Special thanks also to my friends and former professors, Dr. Christopher Hall and Dr. Steven Boyer, who first introduced me to theology and who taught me how to pray. I am a better man, theologian, and disciple of Christ because of all of you. If there is any wisdom in the pages that follow, it has its source in you.

This book is dedicated to two people. First, to my grandfather, Robert Johnston, who passed away during its composition. While writing his eulogy, I realized that the communion of saints I was writing about was not an abstract, academic idea, but a living reality of which he is now a part. May light perpetual shine upon you, Gramps. Pray for us here below. Second, to my wife, Kaitlyn, who has been for me a deep well of grace, patience, and understanding. Thank you, Kait, for the way that you see me, know me, and love me. If Balthasar is right that love is the truth of all things, then you have taught me more truth than ten thousand books ever could.

Despite all the assistance provided by colleagues and friends, I alone am responsible for what follows, including any errors, omissions, or redundancies that might inadvertently remain.

Matthew A. Rothaus Moser

Feast of All Saints

November 2015

List of Abbreviations

Abbreviations of Primary Texts by Hans Urs von Balthasar

CL   *Cosmic Liturgy: The Universe According to Maximus Confessor*

ET 1-5   *Explorations in Theology*, vols. 1-5

GL 1-7   *Glory of the Lord*, vols. 1-7

LA   *Love Alone is Credible*

MW   *My Work: In Retrospect*

PT   *Presence and Thought*

TD 1-5   *Theo-Drama*, vols. 1-5

TKB   *The Theology of Karl Barth*

TL 1-5   *Theo-Logic*, vols. 1-3

Complete reference information for all of these works can be found in the bibliography.

Introduction

"The only sadness today," Léon Bloy once wrote, "is not being saints."[1] Modernity is plagued by a sadness that emerges in the absence of lives of sanctity and love. Decades after Bloy, Alexander Schmemann argued that modern secularism is the fruit of a problem at the heart of theology, underscoring that "the ultimate problem of theology is that of knowledge, and more precisely, of the possibility and nature of knowledge of God."[2]

While at first blush it would seem that Bloy and Schmemann identify two different issues troubling the modern world, Hans Urs von Balthasar (1905–1988) sees them as two sides of the same coin. The problem of the knowledge of God that haunts modern theology and contemporary culture *is* the loss of the saints that Bloy laments. The following essay is devoted to parsing out this relationship between theological epistemology and the saints, and presenting Balthasar's own solution to the metaphysical and spiritual malaise plaguing modernity.

Balthasar was convinced that the loss of the saints that Bloy describes has caused a shattering of truth, what Balthasar defines as the "living exposition of theory in practice and of knowledge carried into action."[3] The consequence of this shattering is the impoverish-

---

1. *La femme pauvre* (Ebooks libres et gratuits, 2010), 260: "Il n'y a qu'une tristesse . . . c'est de n'être pas des saints."
2. Alexander Schmemann, *For the Life of the World* (Crestwood, NY: St Vladimir's Seminary Press, 1973), 140.

ment of truth itself. The loss of the saints introduces a crisis in theology, and, attendant upon that, crises in epistemology and metaphysics. Balthasar's saints are something more than pious figures of Catholic kitsch. They are agents of theological and metaphysical truth, images of divine love in the world, and, as such, living exegetes of Being. Such is admittedly a lofty claim, but it will be the principle burden of the following essay to justify it.

There are two main agendas at work in the current project. The first is to exposit and interpret Balthasar as a thinker whose intellectual ecosystem is shaped by an Ignatian theological vision. This side of the project is explored through a close reading of Balthasar's theology of truth in his *Theo-Logic* and what he calls a "theology of the saints." Through this analysis, I develop what we might call Balthasar's sacramental epistemology—the relationship between Christ as the truth (John 14:6) and the truth of the created world (what Balthasar calls "creaturely truth"). Balthasar's exploration of this draws on his metaphysics, aesthetics, and Trinitarian theology most especially. But as we shall see, this relationship cannot adequately be explored without recourse to what is commonly called "spirituality." Balthasar's account of truth is developed in an Ignatian register as the interplay of knowledge and love for understanding truth.

I identify Balthasar's attempt to overcome this divorce between theology and spirituality by arguing that the "truth of Being" is most fundamentally the love revealed by Jesus Christ, and is therefore best known through participation and dialogue—or, by being what Balthasar calls a saint.[4] More specifically, I show how Balthasar's attempted re-integration of speculative theology and spirituality through his theology of the saints serves as his critical response to the metaphysics of German Idealism that elevated thought over love. Such a philosophy loses the mystery and giftedness of Being and turns humans into "masters and possessors" of the world—as titanic strivers

---

3. Hans Urs von Balthasar, "Theology and Sanctity," in *Explorations in Theology*, vol. 1: The Word Made Flesh, trans. A.V. Littledale with Alexander Dru (New York: Herder and Herder, 1964), 181.

4. Balthasar's particular understanding of the saints as representative and customary is explored below.

after "absolute knowing" and absolute control. Balthasar constructively responds to this problem by re-appropriating the ancient and medieval spiritual tradition of the saints, as interpreted through his own theological master, Ignatius of Loyola. He develops a Trinitarian and christological ontology and a corresponding pneumatological epistemology that is performed most truthfully by the saints at prayer.

Enmeshed within this scholarly project, however, is a more decidedly theological one. Through the study of Balthasar, this book revisits the relationship between theology and philosophy, but with an expanded form of theology: one that includes the spiritual practices of prayer and contemplation. Balthasar's scandalous claim that *saints* are the truest philosophers extends the relationship between theology and philosophy beyond the typical rationalistic terms in which the relationship is usually framed. By focusing on the question of truth, Balthasar helps reinterpret theology and philosophy from two intellectual or academic disciplines to the relationship between living "words about God" and the "love of wisdom."

Balthasar emphasizes that truth is known through *dialogue*, which for him is the rhythm of expression and response, donation and receptivity, kenosis and obedience. The dialogical emphasis of Balthasar's project opens the door to consider the way that theology and, more surprisingly, prayer—dialogue *par excellence*—bears on metaphysics. As such, this essay is an exercise in theological method, but in a Balthasarian key. Despite Jeffrey Stout's claim that preoccupation with methodology is akin to throat-clearing, and thus, devoid of any substantial content, to speak of method with Balthasar is to speak of Christ, the *methodos*, the way (John 14:6), of all Christian thought.[5]

This is not, of course, a book of constructive theology. Whatever constructive claims are made about theology and philosophy are necessarily tentative and heuristic. This is a project about Balthasar and his thought. Yet, any project about Balthasar, if it is to honor the

---

5. Balthasar, *TL* 2, 363. Cf. Jeffrey Stout, *Ethics After Babel* (Princeton: Princeton University Press, 2001), 163.

spirit of its subject matter, cannot be content with exegesis alone. As Charles Péguy once described St. Thomas Aquinas, Balthasar himself is "A great and estimable doctor, renowned, authoritative . . . and very much dead and buried."[6] We must approach Balthasar afresh with the questions of our own day, and allow him to speak to today's church, to our contemporary context, to the questions that challenge us in the present moment. And so we will, by interrogating Balthasar on *his* terms, thereby allowing him to interrogate *us* in *ours*. Such a method fits well with the spirit of this important, controversial, and challenging figure.

Terms

Balthasar's language is often specialized and cumbersome with its reliance on metaphysical jargon. While I have done my best to render Balthasar's idiom into more accessible language throughout this study, it may be useful to clarify up front the Balthasarian flavor of certain terms.

Truth

For Balthasar, "truth" is shorthand for the "truth of Being." It is therefore a theological and metaphysical term. Throughout this study, we will sometimes distinguish between "creaturely" and "divine" truth, the former having created Being as its primary referent, while the latter is primarily concerned with the truth of God.

Metaphysics

Balthasarian metaphysics has to do with the study of Being *qua* Being, though this is inseparable from theological claims about Being. We will see the way that Balthasar makes theology a constitutive element of metaphysics, but we must understand from the outset that Balthasar

---

6. See the quote in Hans Urs von Balthasar, *Presence and Thought: An Essay on the Religious Philosophy of Gregory of Nyssa*, trans. Marc Sebanc (San Francisco: Ignatius Press, 1995), 10. Henceforth identified as *PT*.

does not conceive of metaphysics as bearing absolute disciplinary autonomy.

Epistemology

This is perhaps one of the slipperiest of philosophical concepts in Balthasar's writing. He is concerned about epistemology, especially as it emerges in post-Kantian thought, but he is less interested in developing a "science of knowledge" as some critics have suggested.[7] Balthasar, by and large, is a metaphysical realist—and thus an epistemological optimist—in the Thomistic sense, but his own work is devoted to developing a performative rather than an intellectualist or exclusively noetic account of knowledge.

There is an important Heideggerean distinction at work in Balthasar's epistemology. Like Heidegger, Balthasar operates according to the distinction between "knowledge" (*Wissen*) and "understanding" (*Verstehen*). The former is propositional knowledge while the latter is more akin to an intuitive or inarticulate understanding of the whole.[8] These two are not polar opposites for Balthasar, but he does insist that truth transcends mere *Wissen*. There must be a form of knowing that corresponds to, rather than eradicates, the mystery of Being.

Love

Balthasar interprets love as a "mode of being" or a "form of life" rather

---

7. Victoria S. Harrison, "Putnam's Internal Realism and Von Balthasar's Religious Epistemology," *International Journal for Philosophy of Religion*, vol. 44 (1998): 89. Harrison is largely critical of Balthasar's saintly epistemology. She accuses it as being underdeveloped and in need of a robust *philosophical* completion, which, she argues, can be offered by Putnam's realism. Harrison's essay is a decidedly nontheological and nonspiritual reading of Balthasar's use of the saints, and therefore, sees the lack of a rigorous, systematic epistemological theory as a significant failure. While there are deficiencies in Balthasar's theology of the saints, the lack of a systematic epistemological theory is not one of them. The saints represent a distinctly *theological* way of knowing *truth* through their *lives*. The only methodology appropriate for them is a christological one. Saints know by following the method of the one who is "the way, the truth, and the life" (John 14:6). Balthasar acknowledges that his christological account of truth may be accused of being methodologically sloppy. But he embraces this accusation, claiming that there is no other way that a genuine account of truth could be.

8. Cf. Martin Heidegger, *Being and Time*, trans. John Macquarrie and Edward Robinson (New York, Harper & Row, 1962), 182–85.

than as an affective state. The description of love that Balthasar commonly adopts is "being-for-another." Love is an ecstatic form of life, or what the classical tradition called *caritas* or charity. But Balthasar does not neglect the erotic dimension of love. Love is the fruitful interplay of desire and grace, *eros* and *agape*. Both dimensions of love are necessary for it to be a truly ecstatic form of life.

Saints

Perhaps no term is more important to this study, and yet, ripe with more potential for confusion, than Balthasar's use of the title "saint." He nowhere gives a clear-cut definition of sainthood, offering, at best, intimations of what or who a saint is: a lover of God who, marked by holiness, is commissioned by God for specific tasks in the world.

For Balthasar, there are two types of saints. There is what he calls "customary" sanctity, or the holiness of ordinary life. This is the vocation of every Christian, to "fulfill his vocation through the normal, unspectacular round of the Church's life."[9] Every Christian can and should be a saint in this sense, and this will be the image of the saint that we develop in the following pages. In addition to this, however, there is "representative" sanctity "by which God singles out some individual for the good of the Church and the community as a model of sanctity."[10] The difference between the customary and the representative saint lies neither in the quality of their holiness nor in their ecclesial importance. It lies only in the type of mission to which they are called. Sanctity is determined by the extent to which one hands oneself over to one's missional vocation. This understanding of the saints is chiefly derived from Balthasar's Jesuit training; it is the

---

9. Hans Urs von Balthasar, *Two Sisters in the Spirit: Thérèse of Lisieux and Elizabeth of the Trinity*, trans. Donald Nichols, Anne Elizabeth Englund, and Dennis Martin (San Francisco: Ignatius Press, 1992), 22.

10. Ibid. On Balthasar's emphasis on the customary saint, see Jacques Servais, "The Lay Vocation in the World According to Hans Urs von Balthasar," *Communio*, vol. 23, no. 4 (1996): 656–76. Balthasar's insistence on the importance of lay sanctity lead him to leave the Jesuits in 1950 in order to found, with Adrienne von Speyr, the Community of St. John for laypersons interested in adopting a ruled life in the midst of their "secular" vocations.

figure of Ignatius of Loyola who fundamentally determines the shape and character of Balthasar's theology of the saints.

Plotting Balthasar's Theology of the Saints

At this point, Balthasar's precise meaning of a "theology of the saints" may be unclear. He is not referring to the specific theologies, the particular intellectual representations, of any given saint. Balthasar's theology of the saints is concerned with the theology that the saints' lives *are* rather than the particular theologies that the saints may hold.

Balthasar's theology of the saints has both an objective and a subjective form. In the former, the saints act as an object of theological reflection. Their lives present to the world a sensible image of an authentic theological existence. Subjectively, the theology of the saints is concerned with the *manner in which* the saints carry out the theological task. It is concerned with the style of saintly knowing, theologizing, and philosophizing.

What little scholarship has been done on Balthasar's account of the saints has generally focused on their objective purpose. While this objective dimension is an essential aspect of Balthasar's theology of the saints, the current project focuses on the relatively unexplored subjective form of saintly knowing.[11] Before turning to the central task of this project, let us briefly explore the objective form of the saints; we shall situate our subsequent subjective account of the saints within this larger context of their objective mission in the world.

In his attempt to define precisely how the saints function objectively in Balthasar's theology, David Moss draws attention to one of Balthasar's tantalizingly dense descriptions. Balthasar argues for "a sort of supernatural phenomenology" of the saints. The purpose of theology, then, is "to discern in the lives of the saints the '*intelligibile in sensibili*', where the *intelligibile* is precisely something supernatural."[12]

---

11. For a study that develops a saintly epistemology *in light of* Balthasar, see David L. Schindler, "Sanctity and the Intellectual Life," *Communio*, vol. 20, no. 4 (1993): 652–72.

12. David Moss, "The Saints" in *The Cambridge Companion to Hans Urs von Balthasar*, eds. Edward T. Oakes, S.J., and David Moss (Cambridge: Cambridge University Press, 2004), 85. The saintly *traditio* finds its exemplar in Gethsemane, in Christ's handing his life and will over to the Father.

That is, the lives of saints are observable forms that manifest by making present a supernatural reality. The saints are *symbols* or *epiphanies* of divine truth. Moss identifies three phenomenological reductions that he finds present in each of Balthasar's treatments of the saints: theological unity, christological obedience, and Marian fruitfulness. As Moss rightly notes, these three dimensions always attend divine love (John 15:12).

Because the saints are defined by a particular mission (*Sendung*), they become models of the unity of the divine life, which Balthasar defines as "being-for-another," an otherness-in-unity. Saintly lives reveal the life of God "in its unfathomable dispossession and giftedness" that actually constitutes the unity of God. The saint does not exist for herself alone. She exists for her mission of "self-giving" to the church, as an image of the kenotic life of God. This kenotic act involves participating in the radical obedience of Christ. Obedience here is the "creaturely analogue of the divine being-for-one-another," the act of handing oneself over (*traditio*) to one's calling and mission. It is "an objectifying and deprivatizing obedience."[13]

This "objectifying and de-privatizing obedience" results in Moss' third reduction, fruitfulness. Here, Mary is the central figure whose physical fruitfulness in bearing Christ is bound to her spiritual fruitfulness as the mother of all believers, as the church. Mary makes clear what Balthasar means by obedience. Mary's divine vocation is to exist no longer for herself, but to birth the church.[14] The saints (of whom Mary is the highest) allow their *subjective* calling, through the process of de-privatization, to nourish (perhaps even become a part of) the objective revelation of God. Their obedient fruitfulness is their handing on (*tradere*) of divine truth in the church.

Moss' three characteristics of the saints, their unity with God, the obedient conformity to Christ, and their spiritual fecundity, are particularly helpful ways of making sense of Balthasar's varied

13. Moss, 88.
14. See Hans Urs von Balthasar, *Razing the Bastions*, trans. Brian McNeil (San Francisco, Ignatius Press, 1993), 40.

treatment of the saints throughout his work. These three themes will recur throughout the pages that follow.

We should be clear that Balthasar never separates form from content. Indeed, what Balthasar fears being lost in the church is not only the form, but also the content of Christian truth due to the limitation of the saints to the realm of "spirituality." Balthasar believes that the theological form of the saints' lives enriches the objective teaching of the church. The saints function as the form of theology as well as offering specific insight into the content of revelation.[15] Only by being both does the saint illumine truth.[16]

What then is the subjective form of the saints' knowledge? For Balthasar, the saints know as lovers do, that is, by loving. Love is a disposition of receptivity, surrender, and obedience, an ecstatic charity toward something beyond the self. Balthasar, as we shall see, identifies this "something" as Being, which, he will argue, is love. Because Being is co-extensive with love, knowledge of truth—of Being—can come only through love. As Balthasar said, and as I will repeatedly insist throughout this study, "the inner reality of love can be recognized only by love."[17] By loving, the saints are conformed or attuned to truth. Their entire existence is adequated to the truth of Being, and their knowledge arises from this adequation. Love is the logic of the saints.

As this book shall argue, a critical component of both knowledge and love is dialogue. And so, the form (*Gestalt*) of the saints' loving

---

15. Moss recognizes this when he writes that "Balthasar will in turn let the dogmatic construal of these two central mysteries [the Trinity and the Incarnation] *stand under* the unique experience of the saints, thereby giving to Church dogma what he claims to be its truly existential depth. For example, in order to indicate how we are to understand Christ's cry of dereliction on the Cross—however feebly and inadequately—Balthasar will direct our attention to the 'dark night' experience of certain saints and mystics" (82). Moss is overstating the case a bit. Balthasar never allows dogma or doctrine to "stand under" or be determined by the experiences of the saints. What he will say instead is that the saints inhabit the objective mystery, enlarging it and enriching it through their subjectivity. The "ecclesial vocation" of the saints and mystics is the enlargement or the "existential deepening" of the truth of revelation—what Balthasar calls "enlarging the cathedrals."

16. For appreciative criticisms of Balthasar's apologetic use of the saints, see Victoria S. Harrison, *The Apologetic Value of Human Holiness: Von Balthasar's Christocentric Philosophical Anthropology* (Dordrecht: Kluwer Academic Publishers, 2000); and Mark Van Steenwyk, "Defending von Balthasar's Apology of Holiness," in *Quodlibet Journal*, vol. 7, no. 2 (2005): http://www.quodlibet.net/articles/vansteenwyk-holiness.shtml (accessed March 12, 2013).

17. Hans Urs von Balthasar, *Love Alone Is Credible*, trans. D. C. Schindler (San Francisco: Ignatius Press, 2004), 75. Henceforth abbreviated as *LA*.

knowledge is prayer. For the saint, prayer is union with God in Christ who, as the incarnate one, *is* truth, both of God and the God–world relationship. As such, prayer acts as an existential modality of the speculative knowledge of this relation. The dialogue of prayer decodes the truth of the world in its analogical bond to the truth of God by means of its inhabitation in this relationship. In other words, for the saints, Christ is the truth of the world, and prayer is union with Christ. In this union, Christ unveils truth. Those dimensions of the truth of Being, the subject–object relation, the inter-subjectivity of worldly consciousness and knowledge, are all illumined within the participative, dialogical dynamic of the saint at prayer. In short, prayer is metaphysics in act.[18]

The Need for This Project

The present chapter addresses three principle needs. First, the current book bridges the gap between the "two sides" of Balthasar's *oeuvre*: the intellectual, metaphysical project (associated with his fifteen-volume Trilogy) and the pastoral project (associated with his sermons, devotional writings, and spiritual direction).[19] Rejecting the false dichotomy between these two dimensions of Balthasar's thought, this book offers a more comprehensive vision of Balthasar as a priest whose intellectual project was formed by Ignatius of Loyola's injunction to "find God in all things." This project reclaims Balthasar's intellectual and dogmatic project as an outworking of his Ignatian concerns.[20]

---

18. ". . . Being and the subject are always richer and deeper in their appearing than that which can appear and that the historicity of the truth and its element of perspective, which are conditioned in this way, and its dialogical essence are ultimately a dialogue that has been going on from the very outset between Creator and creature and that the human act of seeking is enclosed a priori in the state of being safe in God and of having been found by God . . . More and more, everything tends toward the indivisible act of hearing the word [that is the Word, the concrete first Idea of the creating God and thereby the goal of the world] which is at the same time an act of prayer. . ." (*My Work: In Retrospect*, 22, 24–25). Henceforth identified as *MW*.

19. A notable exception to this is Mark A. McIntosh, *Christology from Within: Spirituality and the Incarnation in Hans Urs von Balthasar* (Notre Dame: University of Notre Dame Press, 2000). McIntosh gives a thorough account of Balthasar's dramatic Christology, highlighting the way that Balthasar sourced the mystical tradition for his insights.

20. Part of this involves Balthasar's Ignatian concern for mission to the prevailing intellectual culture. On Balthasar's relationship with philosophical modernity, Cyril O'Regan has published the definitive texts in his two-part *Anatomy of Misremembering: Von Balthasar's Response to Philosophical*

Second, there is a noticeable lacuna in Balthasar scholarship. While commentary abounds on his theological aesthetics and dramatics (the first two of his three-part Trilogy), there is very little English-language scholarship on his final series, the three-volume *Theo-Logic*. What has been published is embedded in summary and exposition of Balthasar's entire systematic Trilogy with very little critical assessment of the *Theo-Logic* itself. Through close reading of each volume of the *Theo-Logic*, this book provides a deeper level of analysis of these texts than these summarizing volumes allow.

Finally, and more constructively, there is a growing concern in theological circles to overcome the dichotomy between "academic" and "pastoral" theology. Theologians with this concern often look to Balthasar as an eloquent but enigmatic resource for addressing this problem. This book offers an interpretation of Balthasar's re-integration of speculative, academic knowledge and Christian practices of prayer, assessing both its strengths and weaknesses for the contemporary project of bringing together a "theology at the desk" and a "theology at prayer."

The Pervasive Question

At the heart of Balthasar's theology is the pervasive question of the God–world relationship. This question was especially prevalent for the theologians of modernity.[21] While this question has always been present in Christian theological reflection, it took on a special urgency with the advent of modernity when "cosmos" was replaced by

---

Modernity (New York: Herder & Herder, 2014). The first volume focuses on Balthasar's critical engagement with Hegel (a topic we will explore in the following pages). The second volume will address Balthasar and Heidegger. Both volumes take seriously Balthasar as a theologian critically engaged with the philosophical questions of German and modern culture, though O'Regan is not as concerned to address the Ignatian, spiritual, and orantic dimensions of Balthasar's critique of modernity as the present essay is.

21. Cf. *Mapping Modern Theology*, eds. Kelly M. Kapic and Bruce McCormack (Grand Rapids, Baker Academic, 2012). Other significant theological concerns of the twentieth century, related to this, are the nature–grace relationship as well as a renewed interest in Christo-centric theological anthropologies. Cf. Stephen Duffy, *The Graced Horizon: Nature and Grace in Modern Catholic Thought* (Collegeville: Liturgical Press, 1992) and Fergus Kerr, *Twentieth Century Catholic Theologians* (Oxford: Blackwell Publishing, 2007).

"nature," metaphysical realism was confronted with nominalism, rationalism, and idealism, and theology was reduced to anthropology.[22]

The urgency of this question becomes acute in twentieth-century theology, especially in the debate between Karl Barth and Erich Przywara over the *analogia entis* and, within Roman Catholicism, in the controversial re-narrating of the nature–grace relationship in Henri de Lubac's *Surnaturel* (1946). Balthasar himself was caught up in both of these debates. Similar to Barth and the later Pryzwara,[23] Balthasar sought to address the God-world relationship in a distinctly christological and "dramatic" way.[24] To engage this question with Barth, Pryzwara, and de Lubac, Balthasar takes on the challenge of constructing a theological project with the drama of the God–world relationship at its center. This involves treating the great questions of metaphysics, epistemology, and theology in a distinctly new way.

But Balthasar's new way of addressing the God–world relationship should not be understood as sheer invention. Balthasar is a *ressourcement* thinker, and thus attends to the question of the God–world relationship (and its sub-themes: metaphysical analogy, knowledge of God, the truth of the world, etc.) *via* a retrieval of ancient and medieval theology, especially the Christian mystical tradition.[25] His unique contribution to this question comes in his construction of his theology of the saints, as the union of the speculative and affective, the objective and subjective dimensions of Christian knowledge.

The Procedure of This Book

The task of this book is to illuminate Balthasar's theology of the saints

---

22. On this, see Louis Dupré, *Passage to Modernity* (New Haven: Yale University Press, 1991), 15–64. See also the first two chapters of Balthasar's *LA*, 15–50.
23. Most especially in his later works published after his landmark *Analogia Entis* (1932).
24. D. C. Schindler offers a helpful summary of Balthasar's concept of *Dramatik*: "The term *drama* refers, in the literal sense, to the form of art created in Attic Greece, in distinction from the lyric and epic forms of poetry that are also due to the Greeks. What makes drama unique in relation to these other forms is, in the first place, that it is essentially *dialogical*, involving the interaction of relatively autonomous characters. Second, drama is not merely recited but *performed* and, indeed, performed before an audience." D. C. Schindler, *Hans Urs von Balthasar and the Dramatic Structure of Truth* (New York: Fordham University Press, 2004), 17.
25. On the impropriety of the term "mystical tradition," see Andrew Louth, *The Christian Mystical Tradition: From Plato to Denys* (Oxford: Oxford University Press, 2007), 200–214.

as it bears on his theology and his Ignatian mission of evangelization of his contemporary German intellectual culture.

The first chapter accomplishes three things. First, it introduces Balthasar, paying special attention to his vocation as a Jesuit and a priest. Second, it explores the role Ignatius plays in Balthasar's theological project. As this section shows, Balthasar's mind was deeply shaped by his Jesuit spirituality. Although Ignatius does not appear regularly in Balthasar's writings, he nevertheless helps bridge what critics have described as the two distinct "realms" of Balthasar's thought: the pastoral and the speculative. Third, this chapter introduces the uniquely Ignatian flavor of Balthasar's interpretation of the saints as models of a subjective form of knowing the metaphysical truth of Being. For Balthasar, the saints are those who best fulfill the Ignatian dictum to "find God in all things," and thus apprehend the truth of God and the world.

The second chapter extends the Ignatian interpretation of Balthasar's work by highlighting Balthasar's missional concerns. These first two chapters ground my assertion that the Balthasarian project is a distinctively Catholic—more specifically, Ignatian—counter to the dominant (and dominating) metaphysical epistemology of German Idealism. Interpreting Balthasar as a missional theologian situates his account of truth in the *Theo-Logic* as his contribution to a distinctively Catholic form of knowledge in response to German Idealism and the perceived muddling of Catholic identity in the wake of the Second Vatican Council.

The third chapter outlines Balthasar's "genealogy of modernity" as it bears on his theology of the saints. This genealogy is the foundation for his constructive, theological re-narration of metaphysics and epistemology. While Balthasar is not unique for developing a genealogy of modernity, the significance of his genealogy lies in the way he identifies modernity's malaise as a spiritual pathology. He interprets the "shattering of Christian truth" as the "loss of the saints" from the intellectual world of the late medieval and early modern periods. This chapter accomplishes three things. First, it traces

Balthasar's account of the disintegration of dogmatic theology, spiritual practices, and metaphysics. Second, it diagnoses Idealist epistemologies as the fruit of a significant shift in late medieval metaphysics that Balthasar attributes to Duns Scotus, William of Occam, and Meister Eckhart. Balthasar sees in them the problematic elevation of knowledge over love as the result of a distorted spirituality. Finally, this chapter gives an overview of the way Balthasar sets out to correct these proto-Idealist trajectories through a creative re-appropriation of the Church's contemplative tradition.

The fourth chapter marks the opening of the second part of the book by shifting the focus from a general view of Balthasar's project to a more focused study of his *Theo-Logic*. In the fourth chapter, I consider the first volume of the *Theo-Logic: The Truth of the World*. This chapter accomplishes three things. First, I interpret Balthasar's understanding of truth as a property of Being (metaphysics) and knowing (epistemology). Truth as a concept belongs to both worlds and cannot be reduced to epistemology alone, for which Balthasar criticizes Idealism, nor metaphysics, for which Balthasar criticizes neo-scholasticism. To isolate truth to either one or the other is to mistake the fundamental nature of truth. From this I go on to argue that Balthasar presents truth as a form of love. Since truth is love, Balthasar insists that both Being and knowing must also be understood together as love. I therefore consider Balthasar's account of knowledge as a dialogue of love between subject and object. Finally, I argue that Balthasar's philoso-phical argument in *Theo-Logic* 1 is implicitly and necessarily theological (thus, its inclusion in a "theo-logic"). I highlight the way the theological truth of God is both the beginning and the end (*principium et finis*) of the truth of the world. This helps us reconcile the natural world as always and already graced, and therefore, open to the truth of God. This demonstrates Balthasar's Ignatian desire to find God in all things. Balthasar's phenomenology in the first volume of the *Theo-Logic* paves the way for an explicitly theological understanding of truth because God is implicitly known in every act of knowing.

Chapter five explores Balthasar's Christology and its relationship to truth. I argue that it is through his Christology that Balthasar most convincingly presents truth as love. My argument falls into two main sections. In the first, I interpret Balthasar's Christology through the category of truth; in the second, I argue that Christ's identity as truth manifests itself as love. This chapter therefore locates the relationship between truth and love in the incarnate person of Jesus Christ. In the first section, I consider the way Christ fulfills the philosophical description of truth from *Theo-Logic* 1. For Balthasar, Christ's life is the expression of his truth. Here, I argue that Balthasar's Christology takes an especially Ignatian character as he interprets the life of Christ as kenosis, receptivity, and obedience. Through the performance of his truth through his actions of love, Christ overcomes the moral and ontological distance between God and world, re-establishing the right relationship between the truth of God and the truth of the world. I conclude by arguing that for Balthasar, Christ's loving performance of truth transfigures the God–world relation, reuniting heaven and earth, making possible the contemplative knowledge of the truth of Being.

According to Balthasar, truth is most fully known through the participation of the subject in the object known. This participation is accomplished by the Spirit. The sixth chapter explores this claim by expositing what Balthasar means when he refers to the Spirit as the "Spirit of Truth" (*Geist der Warheit*). I first explore Balthasar's account of the Spirit as the expositor of Christ's truth. This section explores the Spirit as the subject of divine knowing, both in the life of the Trinity and in the lives of the saints. The Spirit's perfect knowledge of truth is possible because he explores "even the deep things of God" (1 Cor 2:10) as the Spirit of Love. For Balthasar, the Spirit knows because the Spirit is love. The Spirit is the love that flows within the eternal dialogue of Father and Son. Second, I consider the way the Spirit works as the illumination of Christian understanding. The saints understand the objective truth as revealed in Christ by means of the subjective illumination of the Holy Spirit. This section explores the Spirit's identity as the Spirit of Pentecost, who gathers together the myriad of truths in the world and enfolds them into the encompassing truth of God.

Chapter seven marks the beginning of the final section of the book. In this chapter, I consider how Balthasar's theological account of truth in the *Theo-Logic* demands a transformed epistemology. Balthasar insists that genuine understanding of the truth can only come through existential encounter with the object of knowledge. Epistemology, in Balthasar's theological account, is participatory. For Balthasar, it is the saint who most faithfully actualizes this form of knowledge. It is the saint whose life is conformed to Christ who apprehends the truth of Being. Her knowledge comes not primarily as an intellectual achievement, but rather, through her contemplative participation in the truth through the Spirit. For Balthasar, understanding theological truth is ultimately the fruit of the contemplative dialogue of prayer. Here, we see Balthasar's final attempt to confront the legacy of Idealism. By arguing that truth is known through the humble receptivity of love and obedience, Balthasar rescues the saints from mere devotion, and contemplation from an Idealist, intellectualist hegemony. Truth is known by being performed, that is, through existential participation in the reality known. This is Balthasar's spiritual epistemology of the saints, a theological re-appropriation of the tradition of Ignatian contemplation that knows and understands all things theologically.

The eighth chapter turns to a concrete examination of a specific figure as a concrete example of Balthasar's saintly epistemology. This figure is the controversial mystic and Balthasar's spiritual directee, Adrienne von Speyr. In this chapter, I offer a Balthasarian interpretation of her life and thought, highlighting the connections between the sanctity of her life, the form of her spirituality and prayer, and the theological and metaphysical fecundity of her spiritual understanding.

The concluding chapter summarizes and assesses Balthasar's theology of the saints, looking forward to ways that analysis of Balthasar's work can be extended after the work done in the present book. By identifying divine love as the truth of all things, Balthasar issues a clarion call for the renewal and revitalization of the discipline of theology through the resurgence of prayer, contemplation, and the saintly form of life.

1

Balthasar, the Ignatian Theologian

Of all the figures from the history of the church that Balthasar studied (and they are legion), few have played as determinative a role in shaping his thought as St. Ignatius of Loyola (1491–1556).[1] Balthasar was, according to Henri de Lubac, a "fervent disciple" of St. Ignatius for most of his adult life, maintaining his "spiritual association" with Ignatius even when he left the Society of Jesus in 1950. Throughout his life, Balthasar maintained private vows of poverty, chastity, and obedience at the Benedictine Abbey of Maria Laach "under the guidance of Ignatius."[2]

All secondary scholarship on Balthasar acknowledges the importance of Ignatius for Balthasar's theological and priestly formation. The present chapter goes a bit further by suggesting that Balthasar articulates his own mission as a theologian in Ignatian terms. Ignatius and Ignatian spirituality provide a useful hermeneutic for interpreting Balthasar's theology of the saints. This chapter highlights

1. See Jacques Servais, "Hans Urs von Balthasar and the Continuing Youthfulness of the *Exercises*," *Communio*, vol. 21, no. 2 (1994): 331–43. See also, Jacques Servais, *Théologie des Exercices spirituels: H.U. von Balthasar interprète saint Ignace* (Bruxelle: Culture et vérité, 1996).
2. Werner Löser, "The Ignatian Exercises in the Work of Hans Urs von Balthasar," lecture at Boston College, January 28, 1999.

the Ignatian flavor of Balthasar's theology of the saints, arguing that Ignatius provides a helpful lens for interpreting the intersection between Balthasar's metaphysics and his spirituality in his account of truth.[3]

Balthasar's Ignatian Conversion

That he should become a Jesuit surprised even Balthasar himself. His decision to enter the Order came in 1927, shortly before he completed his doctoral dissertation. Seemingly on a whim, Balthasar attended an Ignatian retreat lead by Fr. Friedrich Kronseder at Whylen, not far from Basel. He would later recall this life-altering event:

> Even now, thirty years later, I could still go to that remote path in the Black Forest, not far from Basel, and find again the tree beneath which I was struck as by lightning. . . . And yet it was neither theology nor the priesthood which then came into my mind in a flash. It was simply this: you have nothing to choose, you have been called. You will not serve, you will be taken into service. You have no plans to make, you are just a little stone in a mosaic which has long been ready. All I needed to do was "leave everything and follow", without making plans, without wishes or insights. All I needed to do was to stand there and wait and see what I would be needed for.[4]

It is important to note here at the outset that Balthasar's conversion arose from an attitude of receptivity. Balthasar characterizes his conversion as the response to a call and not the result of a personal ambition to join the Jesuits. He simply heard, responded to, and obeyed the voice that called him. As Henrici points out, Balthasar compared his conversion to that of Levi the tax collector and St. Paul: men "to whom Christ's call went out in a totally unmistakable way, not because of their merits but because of their ignorance."[5] Balthasar's responsibility

---

3. Ignatius himself was deeply influenced by the saints whom he read about in *Legenda aurea* by the Dominican priest Jacobus de Voragine (d. 1298). Ignatius was probably familiar with the Spanish translation of this work, *Flos sanctorum* ("Flowering of the Saints"). Ignatius was most taken by the accounts of St. Francis and St. Dominic. The distinctively Ignatian approach to the discernment of spirits took root as he meditated on these saints.

4. Quoted in Henrici, "A Sketch of von Balthasar's Life" in *Hans Urs von Balthasar: His Life and Work*, ed. David L. Schindler (San Francisco, Ignatius Press,1991), 11. Note the role of passivity in Balthasar's narration. This passivity will play an important role in Balthasar's theology of the saints.

in the face of his call was simply "to surrender myself . . . to put myself entirely at the disposal of God."[6] Receptivity and obedience serve as the chief cornerstones of Balthasar's appropriation of Ignatius, and so it is unsurprising that we see these themes at play in the dynamics of Balthasar's own life.[7]

Balthasar entered the novitiate of the Jesuits in 1929, shortly after completing his doctoral studies. Though my concern in this chapter is primarily Balthasar's relationship with Ignatius, it seems appropriate to highlight briefly Balthasar's conflicted relationship with the Jesuit order. Though Balthasar left the Jesuits in 1950 to form the Community of St. John with Adrienne von Speyr, he continued to consider the order as "his most dear and self-evident home."[8] But, like any home, Balthasar's relationship with the Jesuits was not an easy one. He underwent six years of training; two years of philosophical training at Pullach, and four years of theological education at Fourvière. Balthasar's dismay during these years is well-known. As he grimly describes it:

> My entire period of study in the Society was a grim struggle with the dreariness of theology, with what men had made out of the glory of revelation. . . . I could have lashed out with the fury of a Samson. I felt like tearing down, with Samson's strength, the whole temple and burying myself beneath the rubble.[9]

But this time also challenged and formed his character to align more closely to the spirit of Ignatius. The quote continues:

> But it was like this because, despite my sense of vocation, I wanted to carry out my own plans, and was living in a state of unbounded indignation.

---

5. Ibid.

6. Hans Urs von Balthasar, *Pourquoi je me suis fait prêtre*. Témoignages recueillis par Jorge et Rámon sans Vila, ed. San Centre Diocésain de Documentation (Tournai, 1961), 22.

7. What this signifies above all else is that Balthasar's project, insofar as it drinks from an Ignatian well, remains incomplete unless it is brought to fruit in the actuality of human life. Balthasar, brilliant though he was, never stops insisting that genius too must be characterized by obedient discipleship.

8. There is an undercurrent of irony in what follows. Balthasar makes much of obedience as a key characteristic of the saints, but his split from Jesuits arose in a conflict of obedience between what he believed to be God's calling and the demands of his superiors.

9. Quoted in Kevin Mongrain, *The Systematic Thought of Hans Urs von Balthasar: An Irenaean Retrieval* (New York: Crossroads, 2002), 2.

I told almost no one about this. Przywara understood everything; I did not have to say anything. Otherwise, there was no one who could have understood me. I wrote the "Apocalypse" [his doctoral dissertation] with a dogged determination, resolved, whatever the cost, to rebuild the world from its foundations. It really took Basel, especially the all-soothing goodness of the commentary on St. John to lead my aggressive will into true indifference.[10]

Yet, it was at Fourvière under the direction of Henri de Lubac that Balthasar discovered the patristic and medieval writers, finding in them the true "glory of theology" that had been lost in the ugly and arid manuals of his neo-scholastic training.[11]

Balthasar also discovered theology's glory in works of French Catholic literature—most notably Claudel, Bernanos, and Péguy. These men, though neither philosophers nor theologians, captured a fuller picture of Christian truth than Balthasar had seen in his formal training. They presented theology in a way that resonated with Balthasar's Ignatian soul: their poetry captured what Balthasar will later call an existential theology—the meeting place of theological and doctrinal speculation with the living reality of the Christian faith.[12]

In 1939, Balthasar was offered a choice for the next stage of his life. He was offered a professorship at the Gregorian University in Rome—a notable and impressive position. But he was also offered a student chaplaincy at Basel. Balthasar opted to become a chaplain. According to Henrici, and quite important for our portrayal of Balthasar, his decision reveals that "pastoral work was closer to his heart than lecturing."[13] Balthasar unquestionably would have succeeded with a brilliant career at the Gregorian, but that he opted instead for chaplaincy shows that Balthasar saw himself called to direct pastoral, rather than academic, work. That Balthasar is almost exclusively the

---

10. Adrienne von Speyr, *Erde und Himmel. Ein Tagebuch. Zweiter Teil II: Die Zeit dergrosser! Diktate*, ed. and with an introduction by Hans Urs von Balthasar (Einsiedeln: JohannesVerlag, 975), 195ff.

11. In one delightful anecdote, Balthasar reportedly read through the complete works of Augustine while sitting in lectures. He could concentrate on the words of the Bishop of Hippo more easily because he had plugged his ears to drown out the droning of his teachers.

12. As we shall see in the next chapter, "speculation" and "life" are the two components of Balthasar's vision of "Christian truth." Bringing these two together is the task of the saint. That these artists can embody this holism, despite not being canonical saints, will be explored in chapter 8.

13. Henrici, 14.

territory of academic interest misses this central characteristic of his entire life. We will return to this Ignatian character of Balthasar's life at the end of this chapter. We must examine the way Balthasar interprets Ignatius before we can consider what it means to call Balthasar an Ignatian theologian.

Balthasar's Interpretation of Ignatius

The heart of St. Ignatius' thought and spirituality is doubtless his *Spiritual Exercises*, begun in 1522 and published in 1548. The *Exercises* are neither a treatise on the spiritual life nor an explicitly dogmatic theology, though Balthasar argues quite ardently that they are implicitly dogmatic. They are, rather, a thirty-day exercise in contemplation, an extended meditation that endeavors to conform and unite, the retreatant with Christ. Over the course of four weeks, the retreatant is guided through a process of purgation from sin, virtuous illumination in imitation of Christ, and the unitive practices that habituate one to Christ by sharing his suffering and joys. Each of the disciplines associated with the weeks serves to realize the purpose of human existence: "Human beings are created to praise, reverence, and serve God our Lord, and by means of this to save their souls."[14]

The opening of the *Exercises* leads to the common interpretation that the retreat is primarily an ascetic discipline, focused on overcoming one's passions and reordering one's life to holiness. The *Exercises* were written to "conquer oneself through any affection that is disordered." The ascetic interpretation ran into a number of challenges, both internal to the Order and external, especially from the Dominicans and Carmelites. The Dominican Reginald Garrigou-Lagrange was especially critical of the Jesuits for being an active—rather than contemplative—Order.

Eventually, the Jesuits of Balthasar's time moved away from a strictly ascetic interpretation of the *Exercises* and a more mystical

---

14. See the opening of the First Week, chapter 23, in Ignatius of Loyola, "The Spiritual Exercises," in *Ignatius of Loyola: Spiritual Exercises and Selected Works*, ed. George E. Ganss, S.J. (New York: Paulist Press, 1991), 130.

approach began to emerge. Father Albert Steger is one of those chiefly associated with the mystical interpretation of the *Exercises*.[15] Steger played a formative role in the spirituality and theology of Balthasar and Karl Rahner. He taught at Pullach and was Balthasar's mentor upon the latter's return to Pullach in 1939.

Steger's interpretation of the *Exercises* was formative for Rahner, but Balthasar saw certain limitations in the mystical interpretation. For Balthasar, a purely mystical interpretation of the *Exercises* would reduce them to a vaguely Neoplatonic imitation. They would become a form of meditation on the world, on nature, and on God. And though meditation is by no means a bad thing, it does neglect the distinctly Ignatian emphasis on action, freedom, and obedience. Instead of an ascetic or mystical interpretation, Balthasar develops what we might call a "dramatic" interpretation. According to Werner Löser,

> A dramatic theology understands the whole of reality as a great and serious drama that, thanks to God's action, culminates in the heavenly Jerusalem. And every human person is called to play his or her unique, inalienable part. The point of the Ignatian *Exercises* is to help people discover their role and make it their own. They do this by letting themselves be called, letting themselves be sent.[16]

For Balthasar, it is the *Contemplation to Attain Love* that provides a sketch of the whole of Ignatian spirituality.[17] Balthasar's Ignatius is focused less on a moral perfection through *askesis* or mystical union with the divine, and more on the contemplative *traditio* of handing oneself over to God. Ignatian contemplation is the action of living *within* God's activity in the world by means of prayer and love. Through this kind of divine living, God illumines one's understanding and orders one's life. But these mystical and ascetic graces occur within one's life of openness and receptivity before God. This is the heart not only of

---

15. Albert Steger, "Primat der göttlichen Gnadenführung im geistlichen Lebel nach dem Ignatius von Loyola," *Geist und Leben* 21 (1948): 94–108.
16. Werner Löser, "The Ignatia *Exercises* in the Work of Hans Urs von Balthasar" in *Hans Urs von Balthasar: His Life and Work*, ed. David L. Schinder (San Francisco: Ignatius Press, 1992), 117.
17. Ibid., 130.

Balthasar's reading of Ignatius, but also of his own theology of the saints.

Balthasar believes that the "purpose and foundation" of the *Exercises* and the four points of the *Contemplation* tie Ignatius to some broader philosophical and theological concerns of modernity. Ignatius' importance, therefore, is not limited to the realm of spirituality. There is a significant metaphysical injunction latent in the *Exercises* and the *Contemplation*, namely, in the Prayer of *Examen*, to "find God in all things."[18] The goal of *Examen* is to recollect your day and identify the presence of God within it.[19] According to Balthasar, this contemplative practice is inherently metaphysical, insofar as it is an existential form of the cosmic question of the God–world relationship. The retreatant prays her personal prayer within the cosmic, christic drama of God's presence in the world. Thus, the spirituality of the prayer is also a form of metaphysical inquiry, a foray into the truth of the world as it stands in relation to God.

The four points of the *Contemplation* highlight the metaphysical drama in which the retreatant finds herself.[20] There is a certain

---

18. See *Exercises*, chapters 233, and 235. See also his *Constitutions of the Society of Jesus*, III.1.26: "Further, [members of the society] should often be exhorted to seek God our Lord in all things" in ibid., 292. This phrase, however, does not seem to belong properly to Ignatius himself.

19. The five steps of *examen* are as follows: 1) recall that you are in the presence of God; 2) look at your day with gratitude; 3) ask for guidance in contemplation from the Holy Spirit; 4) review your day in the light of God's presence, both your failings and successes in loving and serving God; 5) reconcile and resolve. Note here how the *sanctity* of one's life is tied to the *missional* dimension of one's existence—to know and serve God by loving him. In Balthasar's interpretation, this call to know and to serve is both existential and metaphysical, as we shall see throughout the following pages.

20. The four points of the *Contemplation* are as follows:

1) to call into memory the benefits received of creation, redemption and special gifts, by considering with great commitment what a great thing God our Lord has done for me and how much He has given me of what He possesses, and consequently how much the same Lord desires to give Himself to me, limited only by how much He can in accordance with His divine condescension. And then to think back on myself, and consider with much good reason and justice what I from my side by virtue of debt must offer and give to His Divine Majesty, namely everything I have, and myself with it, just like one who offers, with great generosity: Take to yourself, Lord, and receive all my freedom, my memory, my understanding and my entire will, all that I have and possess. You have given it to me; to you, Lord, I return it. It's all yours. Dispose entirely according to your will; give me your love and grace, that's enough for me. (Exx 234)

2) to consider how God is dwelling in creatures: bestowing in the elements existence, in plants growing life, in animals sensory feeling, in human beings conscious awareness. And so too in me: how He is giving me existence, animating me through and through, awakening senses for me, and giving conscious awareness—how He, so to speak, is making a temple of me, since I am created to an image and likeness of His Divine Majesty. And once more to think of myself, in the way said in

aesthetic element at play, especially in the first two points. The retreatant must look back at her world and see it, not according to her natural vision, but with the eyes of faith.[21] More significantly, though, this contemplative vision—"finding God in all things"—also involves offering up the world to God. To see the world in this way is to return the world to its source in divine love. This is done through prayer. We could see this as an Ignatian riff on Aquinas' understanding of *sacra doctrina*: as seeing God and all things as they relate to God, and then, offering them up as such. For Balthasar, this is contemplative prayer.[22] It is, moreover, the Ignatian form of genuine knowledge of truth: the receptive, self-offering of all things in love to God.

There is a particular anthropology at work in the *Contemplation* that is important for Balthasar's theology of the saints. The second point of the *Contemplation* places the retreatant in a cosmos. She is not isolated or alienated from the world around her; to be human is to be a cosmic figure. Moreover, she is a doxological figure: she is made into a temple where heaven and earth meet. We will see this Ignatian emphasis on doxology in Balthasar's use of the term "adoration" [*Anbetung*] at critical junctures in his *Theo-Logic*. From this point, Balthasar develops a meta-anthropology: a doctrine in which humanity is the summit of the natural realm and the avenue for the cosmos' elevation to God. The ontological status of humanity is also its mission: humanity is *from*

---

the first point, or in another way if I feel this to be the better. And let it happen in the same way with each of the following points. (Exx 235)

3) to consider how God exerts Himself and takes pains for my sake in all created things in the world, that is, He behaves as one who undertakes strenuous work. So in the skies, elements, plants, fruits, herds, etc., by giving and conserving their existence, giving them growth and sensory life, etc. Then to think back upon myself. (Exx 236)

4) to look at how everything good and all gifts come down from above—so as also my limited power from the highest and infinite above; and so too our justice, goodness, piety, mercy and so on, as the rays come down from the sun, from the source the water, and so on. Then finally to look back into myself in the way said. To finish with a colloquy and an Our Father. (Exx 237)

21. Löser, 122.

22. As Löser puts it, "In this second variation on his theme, Ignatius expresses the embeddedness of the self in the cosmos, and the inclusion of the cosmos in the self. God's self-gift is not directed just towards the individual, but towards the whole of reality, of which nevertheless the individual is a part. Moreover, it touches not just the person's deepest interiority, but their whole self at every level. Conversely, the person's handing themselves over to God is not a purely interior, unworldly affair; it involves the whole range of the personality. Nothing is to be held back. The very cosmos needs to be brought into the movement of self-giving. The person of prayer returns everything to God, their Lord: their freedom, their memory, all that they have and possess" (124).

above, but *for* below. Humanity's vocation is to stand in the heart of the God–world relation, representing God to the world and the world to God. Ignatius' cosmic positioning of humanity means that the human is a "metaphysical Janus," with one face looking toward heaven and one looking back to earth. This is what makes her a naturally contemplative creature. Beholding the light of God also illuminates her understanding of all Being; knowledge of God issues in knowledge of the world. Balthasar's Ignatian, sacramental metaphysics turns on this point.

A corrupted form of this idea is possible, however. When God becomes the *means* by which man achieves knowledge of Being, then God is no longer the *goal* of knowing, but only the instrument. "When this happens, man becomes the measure of all things, theology becomes anthropology."[23] Balthasar sees this as the chief temptation of modernity, especially in forms of liberalism and Idealism.[24] He sees this temptation at work even in some medieval thinkers who struggle to find the balance between the *eros* of knowledge and the *agape* of the descent of revelation. This problem is especially pronounced in mystical figures such as Meister Eckhart (1260–1327), whom Balthasar sees as being more concerned with the human's divine knowing than with the union of love that comes through the descent of the *Logos* in the economy of history.[25]

Ignatius' major contribution to theology is the balance he strikes between *eros* and *agape*. The erotic longing for salvation and blessedness that is the destiny of humanity arises only after the prior descent of God, to which the only proper response is praise and loyal service. Ignatius envisions blessedness not as a contemplative escape from worldly concerns, but as "right living"—that is, living in harmony within the "descending line" of incarnation and cross. "Ignatius clearly gave first place to the theology and anthropology that think in terms of descending *agape*, and he gave the subordinate place to the theology

23. See Balthasar's introduction to Henri de Lubac, *The Drama of Atheist Humanism*, trans. Edith M. Riley and Anna Englund Nash (San Francisco: Ignatius Press, 1995), 9–10.
24. Ibid.
25. See Cyril O'Regan, "Balthasar and Eckhart: Theological Principles and Catholicity," *The Thomist*, vol. 60, no. 2 (1996): 203–39.

and anthropology of *eros*."[26] What is significant is that Ignatius does not remove the erotic epistemological and metaphysical elements from spirituality, but integrates them within the larger, descending movement of divine love.[27] The proper way of living within the reality of *agape* is by living "in praise, reverence and service and [by letting] [oneself] be sent, at the same time, with Jesus into serving others."[28] Living truthfully in the reality of Christ involves the active response to the call of Christ to a particular mission that participates in Christ's own mission of love. This is Balthasar's understanding of the theological task of the *Exercises*. It is also the heart of Balthasar's theology of the saints.

The *Exercises* accomplish this task by meditating on the "call of Christ" as the prior "deed word" to which the Christian is called to respond.[29] This response involves the Christian's obedient receptivity to the call from Christ. This obedience may manifest itself in one of two states of life. The first is the state of the commandments: the obedience of regular, non-religious life. The model for this state of

---

26. Löser, 11.

27. According to Balthasar, Ignatius attempts "to reach a balance between the biblical glorification of God and the blessedness of God in antiquity. Ignatius is distinct from this balance inasmuch as he pinpoints 'praise, reverence and service as the goal of creation,' even in the final sentence of the 'foundation' according to which one must choose with indifference, 'lo que mas nos conduce para el fin que somos criados' (that which brings us most to the goal for which we were created). Only in a short final phrase and as if by the way does he mention that one thereby 'saves one's soul' and reaches salvation. It must also be noted that Ignatius demands from the beginning the transcending of all selfish strivings for the sake of reaching that indifference which is the presupposition of pure praise and pure reverent service, and that this effort throughout the *Exercises* has as its aim that I make what God has chosen for me my own choice (no. 135), and thus that I choose 'praise, reverence, and service' from 'generous' love of God as the goal of my life. For this reason he can juxtapose and mention in one breath, almost by the way, 'amor y alabanza' (no. 15), 'amor y servir' (no. 233), 'en todo amor y servir' (no. 363). Just as the Psalmist who praises and serves God has the *Shema*, the main commandment, in his ear, so in Ignatius, throughout the *Exercises*, the love of God is present in a hidden and nevertheless effective way, in such a way, however, that he thinks and especially acts always for God and his glory (for all forms of prayer and choice in the Exercises are in an eminent sense action, which becomes clear already from the comparison with the bodily exercise in the first preliminary remark). Love finally emerges thematically in the 'meditation for obtaining love' (Nos. 230–237) while the concept of 'blessedness' still remains unmentioned; this concept need not be mentioned, because the entire blessedness of the person clearly lies already in the *Suscipe* (no. 234) which answers God's abounding love. If one has given all one's own to God, because one returns what one has received, what more can one ask for? 'Give me your grace and your love and that is enough for me.'" "*Homo creatus est*," in *ET* 5, 23–24.

28. Löser, 11.

29. See Balthasar's lengthy commentary on this point in the *Exercises* in his *Christlicher Stand* (Einseideln, Johannes Verlag, 1977).

obedience is Jesus's obedience to his parents—his fulfillment of the fifth commandment. The second state of obedience is what Balthasar calls "the perfection of the Gospel." It is the obedient surrender to the will of the Father. It is the obedience to being sent on a particular mission. The core event of the *Exercises* is thus a christic one, "the self-abandonment to God's call, in choosing God's choice."[30] The heart of the *Exercises* is choosing to share in the kenotic obedience of Christ. By developing this theology of choice, Ignatius surpasses the medieval ascending "ladder of perfection" that attempts to attain to God apart from God's call. Instead, Ignatius posits a theology of spiritual *response* as an "ever-actual event of freedom and love." It is the freedom that chooses to love in response to love.

The proper disposition of the creature in this "theology of choice" is what Ignatius labels *indiferencia*: disponibility or self-abandonment.[31] Balthasar uses the language of receptivity to capture this idea. For Ignatius, *indiferencia* is not pure passivity, but rather, an "active indifference" to receive *and* to obey, to be sent into mission.[32] For Ignatius, this abandonment is not, as it was for some medieval writers (Meister Eckhart, again), an absolute emptiness that results in transcending everything creaturely in order to be immediately present to God. It is rather an active cooperation with God. What Ignatius posits is an *analogia libertatis* in the God–world relation. Balthasar argues that

> [i]t is absolutely decisive that Ignatius, when he followed out the idea of indifference in all its Christian radicality, did not take over its

---

30. Löser, 5. Cf. *Lumen Gentium*, V–VI for a reprise of the ancient distinction between commandments and evangelical counsels: "In all the various types and duties of life, one and the same holiness is cultivated by all who are moved by the Spirit of God, and who obey the voice of the Father, worshiping God the Father in spirit and truth. These souls follow the poor Christ, the humble and cross-bearing Christ, in order to be made worthy of being partakers in His glory. Every person should walk unhesitatingly according to his own personal gifts and duties in the path of a living faith which arouses hopes and works through charity" (*Lumen Gentium*, V.41).

31. See Balthasar's summary of Ignatian *indiferencia* in his essay "Drei Formen der Gelassenheit" in *ET* 5, 31–37.

32. This active indifference involves what Ignatius labels the *applicatio sensuum* (the use of the senses) in meditation (this is itself an aspect of the *Lectio Divina* tradition, especially the practice of *meditatio*). The role of the senses in the *Exercises* "intends to familiarize the person (who is going through the *Exercises* and choosing) in all layers of his being with the character of Jesus Christ, so that the choice can concretely orient itself by Jesus Christ." There is thus a distinctly aesthetic dimension to the *Exercises*.

metaphysical formulation by the Germans, especially Eckhart. Even when it is thought and lived without any subtraction, Christian indifference does not imply the hylomorphic schema of antiquity: form (God) and matter (creature). In this way, indifference need not be practiced in the direction of the annihilation of the creature's own being and will, a direction that, with more or less strength, has been given to spirituality from Eckhart to Fenelon, hidden monothelite, not to say oriental-pantheist parameters. By contrast, the true mystery of God, namely, "God in all", "I live, yet not I, Christ lives in me", may be sought as God's universal causality in the creature's active cooperation—in indifference, abandonment, and service. This cooperation cannot remain in the condition of indifference as mere "letting it happen"; rather, God's particular will, which is actively to be grasped and realized, must also actively be sought. For this reason, indifference, which stands at the end of Rhineland mysticism, stands at the beginning in Ignatius and heightens itself in the Second Week of the Exercises through the central event of the "choice." In the analogy of freedom between God and the creature, *man chooses what God our Lord gives us to choose*; he freely and spontaneously consents to the particular choice that has been made for us in God's eternal freedom.[33]

This freedom is the freedom of obedience and love. Ignatius thus represents for Balthasar the saintly rhythm of gift and receptivity, call and response, vocation and obedience. These rhythms occur as the ascending love of the saints responds to the prior descending love of God. Ignatius moves the question of the God–world relationship from a strictly metaphysical, speculative domain, toward spiritual interpretation via an analogy of freedom. This Ignatian *analogia libertatis* marks a reinterpretation of the questions of Western metaphysics and the emergence of metaphysics of freedom in which receptivity, obedience, and mission make present the truth of Being unveiled as love. We will make much of this Ignatian revolution in what follows.

Ignatian Metaphysics

Balthasar believes that Ignatian spirituality is inherently metaphysical. But he sees more in Ignatian metaphysics than a fascinating theoretical

---

33. *GL* 5, 102. Emphasis added.

vision. He sees a charismatic theology of revelation capable of offering an "unsurpassed answer to all the problems of our age that terrify Christians."[34] As we shall see in chapter three, Balthasar saw the metaphysical and intellectual malaise of modernity as the result of "spiritual pathologies"—breakdowns in the God–world relation.[35]

This was not a popular interpretation of Ignatius in Balthasar's day. In his article "Exerzitien und Theologie," Balthasar laments the dualism among his fellow Jesuits between a "theoretical philosophy and theology with a specifically pre-Ignatian form . . . and an Ignatian pastoral method."[36] In what I take to be a melancholy tone, Balthasar says, "A great number of Jesuits, by the way, are Thomists, either of the old or newer form."[37] Balthasar laments that the "riches of teaching"—dogmatic and metaphysical—found in Ignatius remained undiscovered by his Order, and by Catholic theology in general.

This neglect is partially explained by the fact that the *Exercises* were predominantly interpreted ascetically.[38] According to Balthasar, this ghettoization of Ignatius to the world of devotion and practical spirituality missed two fundamental things. First, it makes a general categorical error by assuming that a "practical" guide cannot also bear theoretical weight. As we shall see, Balthasar refuses to draw a hard-and-fast line between the "practical" and the "theoretical/ speculative," or the "spiritual" and the "theological." Second, such neglect misses that the *Exercises* express an entire theological and metaphysical vision which ignores the common dichotomy of "contemplative" and "active;" "spiritual" and "dogmatic;" "practical" and "theoretical." In fact, one of Ignatius' chief gifts to the church is his distinctively Catholic metaphysic. As we shall see, Balthasar uses this

---

34. *MW*, 21.
35. See Kevin Mongrain, "Poetics and Doxology: Von Balthasar on Poetic Resistance to Modernity's Turn to the Subject," *Pro Ecclesia.* vol. 16, no. 4 (2007): 385.
36. Quoted in Löser, 106.
37. Ibid.
38. "The flood of literature on the *Exercises* remains almost entirely stuck in pastoral and ascetic aspects; only few had the idea that the *Exercises* must contain decisive pointers and points of departure for theoretical theology as well. Suarez attempted in his time to construct a sort of theological spirituality of the Society; most recently Erich Przywara has undertaken the same synthesis in his monumental work, *Deus semper maior: Theologie der Exerzitien. . .*," ibid.

Ignatian metaphysic to counter the emerging "secular" metaphysics of modernity. Since the current book argues that it is this Ignatian metaphysic that shapes Balthasar's own work, it is important to give at least a cursory summary of it here at the outset. We shall fill in more details as this book proceeds.

The most sustained attention Ignatius receives in Balthasar's Trilogy comes in the fifth volume of *The Glory of the Lord*.[39] As we shall see in chapter three, Balthasar sees a spiritual malaise at the heart of modernity. This malaise is the result of the ghettoization of the saints to the realm of subjective devotion. He sees a tragic conflation of metaphysical nominalism and mystical subjectivism that fragments the unity of Christian truth. This imperils Christian metaphysics and results, Balthasar claims, in the idolatrous speculations of Idealist philosophy.

It is in the context of this spiritual and metaphysical fragmentation that Balthasar develops his "metaphysics of the saints" through the figures of Tauler, Suso, the Rhineland mystics, and especially, Ignatius of Loyola. Balthasar identifies Ignatius as one in whom a metaphysics of divine glory is maintained, both theologically and spiritually. The "metaphysics of the saints" is the idea that the Christian relates to God in such a way that the relation is mediated through the cosmos that God creates. A saintly metaphysic reads the world as the sacramental display of God's glory. For Ignatius specifically, it means "finding God in all things."[40]

Ignatius' injunction to find God in all things ties him, Balthasar claims, to the sacramental metaphysics of the ancient Christians, especially Dionysius the Areopagite. Both Ignatius and Dionysius believe that knowledge of God (and therefore, union with God) is mediated through a series of "sacred veils" that disclose the divine. The final meditation of the Ignatian *Exercises* echoes the Dionysian

---

39. Volume 2.2 of *Herrlichkeit*.
40. This is at least how Balthasar interprets this doctrine in *GL*. In his essay, "Finding God in All Things," Balthasar interprets this injunction in terms of mission and obedience: "If we are the fruit of God's own deed of love, then it is only by doing love's work that we can 'find him in all things'" (*ET* 5, 462).

metaphysic where creation is seen as a theophany.[41] The *Exercises*, for Balthasar, involve a performance of metaphysical understanding: of seeing God immanently present in created things.

Ignatius' metaphysic turns on four main theological claims. First, that God is creator. Such a claim makes Christianity a *de facto* metaphysical religion. From the opening claim of Genesis 1, the God–world relationship is thrust to the center of Christian teaching. One cannot rightly speak of the world in an non-theological way. For Balthasar, to speak of the world at all is, at least implicitly, to speak of God.

Second, God is the indweller of creation. Divine transcendence does not remove God absolutely from the world, but instead, divine otherness allows God's closeness and proximity to his creation. God is present in all things: "in being as the source of being, in life as the source of life, in sense as the archetypal sense, in thinking and willing spirit as primordial Spirit."[42] There is for Ignatius, as for Balthasar, no such thing as *natura pura*, a nature that is *absolutely* closed off to God. Instead, God is ever-present in the world; or, perhaps better, the world is present, enfolded, embraced, within the divine life.

Third, God is present in the world as the "one who labors" on the world's behalf. Ignatius' God is neither uninvolved nor disinterested. For Ignatius, as for Balthasar, creation is a divine action in which creating and sustaining are of a piece. One knows God in creation not only as the source and the goal (*principium et finis*) of creation, but also as the vital, dynamic, sustaining presence within it.

Finally, God is the Father of lights who in his creative indwelling shines forth in creation. Here, we hear an echo of Balthasar's account of theological aesthetics as luminosity and splendor.[43] Ignatius' God wills to be known through the world. All spiritual subjects are therefore illuminated and illuminating.

What Balthasar sees Ignatius offering to modernity is a way of re-

41. Balthasar derives this interpretation of the *Exercises* from Przywara's own theological interpretation. Cf. *Deus Semper Maior*, 369–407.
42. *GL* 5, 109.
43. *GL* 1, 20.

theologizing the cosmos, freeing it from totalizing philosophical vision. According to Werner Löser, "Ignatius is decisively important in the attempt to find a correct mediation between Western metaphysics and Christian theology inasmuch as Ignatius freed theology and anthropology again from the embrace of philosophy, not by abandoning philosophy, but by inserting it into the primarily theological overall picture."[44] Here, we see Balthasar's riff on the "mystical" interpretation of the *Exercises*.

Yet, as we've stated, Balthasar does not want to reduce Ignatius to either an ascetic or a mystical interpretation, nor to an exclusively intellectualist interpretation. Balthasar's interpretation of Ignatius is also dramatic, bringing metaphysics together with human action, whether that action is belief, service, or discipline. Ignatian metaphysics, Balthasar avers, is a dramatic metaphysics.

Drama requires an actor. Balthasar thus insists that Ignatian metaphysics cannot be understood apart from a specific form of life. Ontology must correspond with anthropology. A distinctively Christian metaphysics yields a distinctively Christian form of life. For Balthasar, following Ignatius' lead, this form of life is that of the saint.

According to Balthasar, Ignatius' anthropology hangs on the practice of *indiferencia*. Ignatian indifference is continuous with the Christian tradition of abandonment, though Balthasar insists that Ignatius resists some of the metaphysical formulations behind late medieval theories of abandonment, especially those of Meister Eckhart.[45]

Ignatian *indiferencia* is not the annihilation of a person's being and will; it is not absolute passivity. According to Balthasar, the Christian life is active rather than passive. Or, perhaps better: it is an active passitivity, willed openness, receptive obedience—being at the disposal of God's grace.[46] In Balthasar's interpretation of Ignatius, to be truly human is to have your will utterly handed over to God. But unlike the

---

44. Werner Löser, "The Ignatius Exercises in the Work of Hans Urs von Balthasar," in *Hans Urs von Balthasar: His Life and Work*, ed. David L. Schindler (San Francisco: Ignatius Press, 1991), 103–20.

45. *GL* 5, 104. Eckhart features prominently in Balthasar's genealogy of modernity, which we will explore in chapter three.

46. Ibid., 105.

Rhineland mystics, for example, for whom abandonment is the summit of the Christian life, Ignatius makes it the principle and foundation, not just of the *Christian* life, but of *human* life.

Balthasar sees Ignatius' anthropology as a fundamentally contemplative one. But contemplation here is not exactly synonymous with classical *theoria*. Balthasar finds in Ignatius a "receptive contemplation" that is not limited to a cloistered monasticism, but can be translated into an "active apostolate of service to neighbor." Contemplation, which has for Ignatius a metaphysical and gnoseological dimension, must be *performed* by a human life. The practice of Ignatian contemplation is, as seen in the *Contemplation to Attain Love*, representational:

> The imitator of the Lord places himself, in total "indifference", at the disposal of his Master's will and command, without ceasing, for all that, to be a spontaneous and free human subject. For himself and for others he is still only the agent, the representative of his Lord, like a viceroy, who more perfectly represents the king the more absolutely he places his personal, intellectual and creative powers at the service of the thought and will of his monarch.[47]

We see here the way that Balthasar unites the objective and the subjective, that is, the objective truth of God and the subjective understanding and performance of that truth, in the act of contemplative obedience. Moreover, the activity of service is something more than religious social work. Contemplation is the loving handing over of the self to divine truth, and is also a way of knowing. For Ignatius and Balthasar, contemplation is the spiritual action of love in its fullness; that is, in its missional, metaphysical, and epistemological dimensions.

By transforming contemplation into a representation of truth, Balthasar sees Ignatius integrating the two worlds of medieval scholasticism and mysticism. Ignatian *indiferencia* relies, Balthasar claims, on the Thomistic metaphysical doctrines of secondary causality and the *analogia entis*: the contemplative, or the saint, is a vessel that

---

47. Ibid., 106.

analogically manifests the divine glory. Contemplation so understood becomes the performance of Ignatian metaphysics: "the idea of representation thus brings about a new awareness of the manifestation of divine glory in the world. For now this glory finds a receptacle, in and by which it manifests itself . . . this is a receptacle in which it can stand out clearly as the real glory of the Lord, the manifestation of absolute sovereignty."[48] For Ignatius, the contemplative's existence is lived *ad maiorem Dei gloriam*, for the greater glory of God.

Balthasar interprets this Jesuit motto as emphasizing the *Deus semper maior* of Lateran IV.[49] Balthasar's entire doctrine of metaphysical analogy hinges on this concept. It is no coincidence that he sees this concept embodied existentially in Ignatian spirituality.

Balthasar as an Ignatian Theologian

Let us return to Balthasar's biography. This chapter has set out to highlight Ignatius of Loyola's significant influence on Balthasar's thought and work. I am certainly not alone in seeing Ignatius as an important source of Balthasar's thought, but we must press a bit further. Balthasar is not simply drawing on ideas or concepts from Ignatius. Balthasar himself can be characterized as an Ignatian theologian. But immediately the question arises: what exactly does it mean to call Balthasar an "Ignatian" theologian? We could divide an answer into "theological" and "priestly" forms of Balthasar's Ignatian character, but to do this would be artificial and would, in fact, undermine the unity of speculative thought and lived spirituality that Balthasar attempts to re-establish.

Calling Balthasar Ignatian is not meant as a kind of hermeneutical key to "figuring out" Balthasar. There have lately been a number of publications that argue for a single, dominant figure that characterizes Balthasar's work.[50] The present book should not be misunderstood as

---

48. Ibid., 107.
49. "*in tanta similitudine maior dissimilitudo.*" ("in every similarity [between God and world], there is an ever greater dissimilarity.")
50. Two examples of these kinds of studies are Mongrain, *Systematic Thought of Hans Urs von Balthasar* and Junius Johnson, *Christ and Analogy: The Christocentric Metaphysics of Hans Urs von Balthasar*

making a similar case about Ignatius' role in Balthasar's work. The list of Balthasar's influences is vast, and there is no way to identify *the* chief source of Balthasar's theological imagination. Ignatius stands as one of many significant voices from the Christian tradition that bear on Balthasarian theology. In presenting Balthasar as an Ignatian theologian, I am arguing that Ignatius is not just one influence among many, but that Ignatius plays a substantially formative role in Balthasar's theology.

But we can go a bit further still. To call Balthasar an Ignatian theologian is to highlight the distinctively missional thrust of Balthasar's work. That is, Balthasar saw his own mission as a priest and a theologian in Ignatian terms. We see this quite clearly in his 1955 retrospective, "A Short Guide to my Works."[51] In that essay, Balthasar outlines the three main topics that structure his theological investigation: the revelation of God in Jesus Christ, the church as the fullness of Christ, and the mission of the church in the world. Balthasar frames each of these topics in Ignatian terms.

Balthasar's theology of revelation is grounded in the "spiritual space" between the Apostle John, who discloses Christ as the full unveiling of the truth of God, and Ignatius who leads, through the contemplative discipline of the *Exercises,* to the encounter between God and man.[52] This is why Balthasar's Trilogy begins with a theological aesthetics rather than with philosophical prolegomena. Theology begins, he avers in the spirit of Ignatius, with the encounter between the Christian and Christ.[53] What is significant about Balthasar's theology of revelation for our purposes is not that it is christocentric,

---

(Minneapolis: Fortress Press, 2014). Mongrain gives an Irenaean reading of Balthasar's theology, while Johnson notes the characteristically Bonaventurean orientation of Balthasar's metaphysical thought.

51. *MW,* 17–45. It is worth noting that this retrospective was written in 1955, and, therefore, between two distinct stages of Balthasar's theological career. Balthasar left the Jesuit Order in 1950 in order to develop the Community of St. John with Adrienne von Speyr. In the 1960s, while many of his friends and colleagues were attending the Second Vatican Council, Balthasar began writing his *Herrlichkeit,* the first part of his Trilogy. This retrospective thus lies between Balthasar's Jesuit stage and the stage of Trilogy.

52. *MW,* 20.

53. You can contrast Balthasar's starting point with that of Karl Rahner. The latter's theology, Balthasar says, begins with Kant and transcendental philosophy rather than with the concrete encounter with the form (*Gestalt*) of Christ. Cf. *MWC,* 100–113.

but that he frames this christocentrism in Ignatian terms. It is through Ignatius that Balthasar develops a "wide-ranging theology of the Word" that frames the theological endeavor as the ongoing dialogue between Christ and Christian in the church.[54]

In this way, Balthasar puts Ignatius to use to address a lacuna in contemporary theology. Ignatius' *Exercises* have, Balthasar laments, "functioned far too little as the charismatic kernel of a theology of revelation."[55] Ignatius is an untapped resource, not just for spirituality, but for the discipline of theological and metaphysical thought.

Balthasar's Ignatian christocentrism leads him to articulate the church as an extension of Christ himself, as the Body of Christ. As the living members of Christ, the church exists as the fullness of Christ in the world, and thus participates in Christ's reality. For Balthasar this means that mission constitutes the church.[56] The subjective charisms of the church—mysticism, contemplation, etc.—are rerouted into an objective and ecclesial form. Balthasar sets out to reinterpret the "history of Christian mysticism and spirituality as a whole under the leitmotiv of mission"—a decidedly Ignatian move.[57]

This leads directly into the final theme that structures his theological project, as Balthasar understood it in 1955: the church's contemplative union with God in Christ manifests itself in obedience and mission in the world. Balthasar sees the church as the "sacrament of the redeemed cosmos."[58] As such, the church must move beyond

---

54. *MW*, 31.

55. Ibid., 21. He continues in a footnote: "I have often given lectures at conferences on the idea of the *Exercises*, their fundamental philosophical and dogmatic bases, about the encounter between the thought of Ignatius and modern thought in a theology of election."

56. Ibid., 30.

57. This move that Balthasar makes is part of a larger debate between the Jesuits and Dominicans such as Reginald Garrigou-Lagrange. This debate focused on whether or not the Jesuits were a "contemplative" or an "active" order. According to Garrigou-Lagrange, the Jesuits lacked a substantial contemplative dimension and were, instead, exclusively an active Order, and thus, intellectually hollow. Balthasar, in response, tries to reframe the debate by re-contextualizing contemplation as being in service to ecclesial mission: "None of this is meant to lead to a devaluation of Christian interiority: all that is ever intended is to break open hollow human subjectivity to the clear fullness of the Church, which is the one Bride, in whose mystery everyone who loves must participate" (*MW*, 37). This is also part of Balthasar's larger criticism of the subjectivization (or privatization) of spirituality and the failure of the church to integrate the mystic into an ecclesial form of life.

58. *MW*, 38.

the fortress mentality of neo-scholasticism and the Modernist controversy. It must raze the bastions that surround the church and once again sally forth into the world in a cultural mission. Balthasar, especially in his pre-conciliar writings, is clear that the church cannot afford to be sectarian, but rather must engage the cultural in "dialogue with the thought of the age."[59]

Balthasar's insistence on the church's engagement with the world adopts an Ignatian character. It is important to note that Balthasar sees the church's engagement with the world occurring on two levels: an intellectual and cultural level and an existential level in particular, sanctified forms of life.[60] For Balthasar, the church's engagement with the world's intellectual culture had to move beyond "literary chatter"—because ideas alone, no matter their power, could not ultimately transform the world. Instead, the Christian idea had to take on flesh in the lives of Christians. It was at this point that Ignatius pushes Balthasar toward his "life work"—the spiritual development of the laity.

Balthasar, anticipating the emphases of Vatican II's *Lumen gentium*, believed that the "hour of the laity" had come. His vocation as priest was to enflame the love for God among lay people, equipping them for mission in the world. The form this mission took was the *Johannegesmeinschaft*, the Community of St. John. This was the secular institute that Balthasar co-founded along with the mystic Adrienne von Speyr that precipitated Balthasar's conflict with the Jesuits in the late 1940s. His superiors did not accept the formation of the community as Balthasar's vocation. Frustrated and conflicted, Balthasar ended up leaving the Jesuits in 1950. Despite his formal break with the Jesuits, the Community of St. John—Balthasar's self-described life work—was decidedly Ignatian in character. According to Balthasar, "[w]hat Ignatius had intended in his time meant henceforth for me

---

59. Ibid., 40.
60. The first level is Ignatius interpreted through Erich Przywara; the second is Ignatius interpreted through Adrienne von Speyr. This is not to suggest that the Jesuits have cornered the market on Christian engagement with the world, but only highlighting the way Balthasar frames the church's engagement in a distinctively Ignatian tone.

a 'secular institute.'"[61] The community adopted a rule of obedience and a vocation of mission, both articulated in Ignatian terms.[62] The Community was grounded in this idea of obedience and surrender, especially as it was performed in the regular act of praying the *Suspice*: "take, Lord, and receive my liberty." Martha Gisi, an early member, once described the Ignatian character of the community:

> I believe what the Herr Doktor's [Balthasar's] and Adrienne's [von Speyr's] reflections had in common with the view of St. Ignatius lies in the idea of obedience as following the obedient Christ. This is really the central idea. And when one speaks in this context about our community one can understand obedience only in the light of this theology: obedience as following the crucified Lord. This is what was alive in him and Adrienne as something coming from Ignatius, and it is here that one can see the true core of their Ignatian thinking and faith.[63]

The Community of St. John is the heart of Balthasar's theological project. All of his writing is, on his own testimony, ancillary to the Ignatian mission of this lay community.[64] Indeed, as Balthasar describes his own theological project in his reflections of 1955, where the *lived* Christian life serves as the necessary summit and completion of his literary work: "All this would remain merely literary chatter were it not at the service of, and obedient to, an ecclesial action that has been assigned to me, which I myself have not chosen": the secular institute, the "unnameable ideal of the Christian: to follow the counsels of Jesus in the midst of the world, without abandoning one's post."[65] What Balthasar's written theology does, we might say, is provide a "comprehensive theological horizon" for the dramatic performance of Christian truth in the lives of the lay community.[66]

---

61. *MW*, 89.
62. For the entire rule, as well as the theological grounding of the community, see Balthasar, *Unser Auftrag: Bericht und Entwurf* (Einsiedeln, Johannes Verlag, 1984).
63. Maximilian Greiner, "The Community of St. John: A Conversation with Cornelia Capol and Martha Gisi," in *Hans Urs von Balthasar: His Life and Work*, trans. Michael Waldstein, ed. David L. Schindler (San Francisco: Ignatius, 1991), 94. Gisi's comment is perceptive. For Balthasar, obedience (as well as receptivity) are ultimately *christological* characteristics. Ignatius serves as a guide into the richness of a Christic existence or what Balthasar will call a *saintly* one.
64. See *MW* 58–59. For Balthasar, the saintly form of life—that will be evangelical and thus missional—takes ecclesial shape in institutes such as the Community of St. John.
65. Ibid., 43.
66. I derive this phrase from Balthasar, *Test Everything: Hold Fast to What Is Good*, trans. Maria Shrady

Finally, to call Balthasar Ignatian is to highlight the structural role played by the themes of *receptivity* and *obedience* throughout both his written and pastoral work. These two themes are derived from Ignatius and structure every major doctrine in the Balthasarian corpus. Balthasar will, as we shall see, structure his account of knowledge, his metaphysics, his Christology, and his spirituality on these two ideas.[67] Balthasar's written theology can therefore be seen as an attempt to derive a theology from the underutilized depths of Ignatian reflection.

Ultimately, Balthasar is an Ignatian theologian because, for him, theology is the act of receiving the Word and responding to it in the obedience of love. To call Balthasar an Ignatian theologian is to acknowledge the way Balthasar's theology exists for the service of love and mission, a saintly life of contemplation, prayer, and obedience.

A speculative theology that remains merely speculative fails to be theology in its truest sense. Theology is the language of *encounter*, the language of love. As we shall see, for Balthasar, "theology" is ultimately the divine person of Christ—the Word of God. Human theology arises from the encounter with Christ through revelation. For Balthasar, it is Ignatius who best leads the Christian into the personal encounter with Christ.[68] This encounter transforms the nature of theology. It is not only the language of intellectual speculation, but also, becomes the orantic language of worship and charity. Theology, for Balthasar, is the *Suspice*; to theologize is, ultimately, to pray, to offer oneself in receptivity and obedience. It is, as we shall see, to imitate Christ. This is why, for Balthasar, theology (and therefore metaphysics) is most truly performed by the saints.

(San Francisco: Ignatius, 1989), 88. The phrase originally referred to Balthasar's theology as the horizon for Adrienne von Speyr's mysticism, but it fits the Community of St. John as well.

67. Beyond these, Balthasar also adopts receptivity and obedience to structure his Trinitarianism, Mariology, mysticism, and so on. Much of this emphasis comes through the influence of Adrienne von Speyr. See Matthew Lewis Sutton, *Heaven Opens: The Trinitarian Mysticism of Adrienne von Speyr* (Minneapolis: Fortress Press, 2013) for a summary of Speyrian mysticism and its influence on Balthasar.

68. *MW*, 20–21.

2

Balthasar on Mission

As an Ignatian theologian, Balthasar endeavored to see his work not as an expression of genius, but as obedience to a mission to which he had been called. This mission was twofold. It involved, first, "enlarging the chapels" by deepening and enriching the church.[1] The second dimension of his mission involves an interpretation, critique, and redemption of the broader culture. Balthasar was a man who actively criticized the church for holing up away from the world, for taking flight from it. He believed that the church must be actively engaged with the world; the church's social situation in history demanded it. More importantly, however, the *Christic* nature of the church requires openness to the world. If Christ could eat with publicans and sinners, the church has no right to hide away in narrow religious parochialism. To be the church is to be a church on mission.

Razing the Bastions

Balthasar's most compelling writing on the situation of the modern

---

1. *First Glance at Adrienne von Speyr*, 71. Balthasar believes that the *Spiritual Exercises* are the most promising way that the modern church can be theologically and spiritually expanded and enriched. Cf. *MW*, 51.

church is his 1952 book, *Schleifung der Bastionen: Von der Kirche in Dieser Zeit.*[2] What Balthasar calls a "most programmatic little book," *Razing the Bastions* argues for a missional openness of the church to the world, the tearing down of the walls of the "fortress mentality" of anti-modernist fears, and the careful articulation of Christian truth amidst the clamor of a myriad of philosophies and theologies of the world.

Balthasar's conviction throughout *Razing the Bastions* is that the time has come for the church to understand itself as existing for the sake of the world rather than for itself. The problem with neo-scholasticism and the so-called fortress mentality of the church was that it enclosed and ossified the living heart of faith. Neo-scholasticism was, for Balthasar, a "bed of historical sleep" that kept the church from the "deed of today."[3] The deed of today witnesses to Christ, but only through a church that has "interpreted, understood, and responded to the signs of the times" and learned to articulate its message "in a new and different way."[4] The church cannot simply offer a represtinated medievalism. A merely historical Aquinas, or Augustine, or Bonaventure, or Pascal, or Newman, or even an Ignatius, will fail to engage the contemporary world as it needs to be addressed.

According to Balthasar, the contemporary world has issued a challenge for the church to re-think its self-understanding. Is the church meant as a bulwark of timeless truths over which history passes without leaving a trace? "Or should one say that the truth, even the truth that endures, ought not at all to be compared to rigid stone, but itself possesses a fullness of interior life that can present itself ever anew without denying the past?"[5]

Balthasar is no relativist. He does not see the historical truth claims of Christianity as something to be dispensed with for the sake of

2. Published in English as *Razing the Bastions: On the Church in this Age*, trans. Brian McNeil (San Francisco: Ignatius Press, 1993). It is worth noting that the cover art of the English version is the *Conquest of Jericho* by S. Maria Magiore, though the book bears little resemblance to the theology of that Old Testament event. The church is not Jericho, conquered from without. Instead, the church is called to pull down its own defenses against the world so as to offer itself up in vulnerability to the world.
3. Ibid., 37.
4. Ibid.
5. Ibid., 47.

aligning the church and the world. But neither is he a dogmatic positivist or one who claims that the truths of Christianity descended to the church in a completed form and need only to be articulated the same way over and over, regardless of the cultural context. Balthasar instead understands the church as the church *in the world*; the church as both an image of the timeless kingdom of God *and* a historically located institution. "The truth of the Church is always the same, but the onward march of the world's hour puts it into a new light, into altered relationships that allow something new, something altered, to become visible in the truth itself."[6]

For Balthasar, the church is *supra-*, but not *a*-temporal. Just as Christ was a human being who grew from an embryo to a mature man, so too the church is caught up in the course of history. The church is therefore a dramatic body, engaged and engaging the world as the world finds itself in this present moment.

Balthasar is confident that the church has been given the full deposit of divine truth in Christ. But he is equally confident that this truth does not hover above time. Instead, "the onward march of the world's hour puts it into a new light, into altered relationships that allow something new, something altered, to become visible in the truth itself."[7]

Solidarity with Humanity

The change in epoch to the modern world means that the relationship between the church and the world has changed. The church now exists in horizontal solidarity with the whole of humanity.[8] The church is now one social institution among many. The neo-scholastic retreat into a fortified stronghold was a futile attempt to maintain an ecclesial purity and superiority in a world that no longer recognized it. For Balthasar, to speak of the church is to speak of the church that is sent into the world.[9] The way the church enters the world requires that she

6. Ibid.
7. Ibid.
8. Balthasar's assessment of the church's situation in the modern world, especially as he develops it in terms of solidarity, shows his clear reliance on Henri de Lubac's *Catholicism*, which Balthasar translated into German.

"find an intellectual language that can in principle be understood by the present period."[10]

He identifies two temptations that the church must avoid in order to be a successfully missional presence in the world. The first is an "absolutism" of truth that fails to acknowledge the solidarity of the church with the world. This fortress mentality refuses the church's mission and is therefore a rejection of Christ's call. It is, moreover, a rejection of the christic identity of the church herself.

The second temptation is religious relativism. Balthasar sees this as the fallout of the Enlightenment and an unavoidable reaction to medieval and neo-scholastic absolutism. After the Council, Balthasar might identify this temptation in people such as Hans Küng and the other Catholic progressives.

If the contemporary church is to avoid both temptations, the path between them cannot merely be a compromise. Instead, the church must "bring to the surface a truth and an attitude that, as Catholic truth and attitude, display to the world a clear, defined and unmistakable countenance."[11] Balthasar will later characterize this as a "distinctively Catholic" approach to truth. The church is called to be in dialogical, rather than sectarian, relationship with the world. The church does this primarily through "interpretation and transposition" that bring the distinctively Catholic content of Christianity into fruitful dialogue with the thought of the world. Balthasar cites Erich Przywara and Joseph Maréchal as the chief models of this in his day.[12]

Balthasar's pre-conciliar program for the church relies on de Lubac's construal of the relationship between nature and grace. Neo-scholasticism's conceptual walls pulled apart creation and redemption —God and world—and erected impermeable walls between them. It used to be the case, Balthasar claimed, that in order to attain to God, one "had to turn away from the world for a time and for ever."[13] But

---

9. *MW*, 40.
10. Ibid. Balthasar makes the same claim in *Razing the Bastions*, 51.
11. *Razing the Bastions*, 52.
12. Ibid., 53. He also mentions his own "forgotten" *Apocalypse of the German Soul* as a model of this kind of dialogue. More on this below.
13. Ibid., 103.

that understanding is collapsing because "God himself broke down yet higher separating walls when his Son appeared, 'in order to make out of the two one new man in himself, establishing peace' (Ephesians 2:15)."[14]

God's activity makes it possible for the church to engage in the Ignatian discipline of finding God in all things.[15] This is not an invitation to relativism or to the mistake of enfolding God into the world. It is instead invites us to reimagine all things theologically. We see here again the Ignatian thrust of Balthasar's construal of the church's mission in the modern world, to restore to theology its cosmic dimension.[16]

Razing the bastions of the church is risky business, as Balthasar learned after Vatican II.[17] But such risk is worth it, because it is only when the walls tumble down that the church is truly herself. "Tumbling walls can bury much that seemed alive as long as they protected it; but the contact with the space that then comes into being is something greater."[18]

Balthasar's Cultural Critique

Balthasar was a man attuned to the prevailing cultural movements of his day, especially as they were expressed in the intellectual legacy of his German heritage. Balthasar is often pegged as a theologian and a philosopher—which he no doubt was—but his early intellectual training was as a Germanist. His mammoth first book (based on his doctoral dissertation) was a study of what the German literary tradition reveals about the final standing of the human soul before God. It is Balthasar's first eschatological project, and moreover, a sustained work of cultural criticism.[19] It is important to note that this

14. Ibid.
15. Ibid.
16. *MW*, 22.
17. Despite the danger of relativism and the watering down of Catholic identity that Balthasar saw in the post-conciliar period, he nevertheless reaffirms this stance as late as 1987: "We have said already that it should be the Church's defenseless exposure of herself to the world, the dismantling of bastions and the leveling of all bulwarks to boulevards" (*MCW*, 136–37).
18. *Razing the Bastions*, 103.
19. For a summary of this text see Aidan Nichols, *Scattering the Seed: A Guide through Balthasar's Early*

criticism takes on a theological dimension. Though it is not as developed as his later theological critiques of culture, we do see that Balthasar from the beginning saw his intellectual mission as involving sustained interaction between the faith once delivered to the saints and the dominant legacies of Idealism, Romanticism, and other modern schools of thought.

Since Balthasar's critique of Idealism lingers in the background of the current project, it is useful to consider his early critique of the Germanist heritage in general before turning to a more specific reading of Balthasar's main Idealist interlocutor, G. W. F. Hegel.

***

It often surprises people to learn that Balthasar was not formally trained in theology or philosophy. Though he received some theological and philosophical training as part of his Jesuit formation at Pullach and Fourvière, his main academic expertise was as a Germanist, a scholar of German culture and literature. Yet, from the very beginning of his intellectual career, he was engaged in distinctly theological critique of German culture.

Przywara and a Theology of Culture

We cannot rightly understand Balthasar's cultural mission without reference to his fellow Jesuit, Erich Przywara. While Przywara was not one of Balthasar's formal instructors,[20] Balthasar nevertheless cites him as "the greatest spirit whom I have been permitted to meet" and deliberately ties his own project to that of Przywara.[21] Much of Balthasar's understanding of the Jesuit vocation of mission to the culture bears the stamp of Przywara's influence. Much of this influence

---

Writings on Philosophy and the Arts (Washington DC: The Catholic University of America Press, 2006), 33–44. For a critical assessment of Balthasar's eschatological thought, see Nicholas Healy, The Eschatology of Hans Urs von Balthasar: Being As Communion (Oxford: Oxford University Press, 2005).

20. Unlike Karl Rahner who is often—though perhaps artificially—portrayed as the successor of Przywara's theological legacy. See Thomas O'Meara, Erich Przywara: His Theology and His World (Notre Dame: The University of Notre Dame Press, 2009).

21. MW, 10.

came through Przywara's "theological interpretation" of the *Spiritual Exercises*. It was Przywara who helped Balthasar see the cosmic and cultural dimensions of Ignatian spirituality.

Przywara's focus is on the metaphysics of lived life, that is, bringing spirituality into conversation with philosophy of culture, art, and music. We might call him a theologian of culture. He believed that modern culture manifests a thirst for God in both its cultural forms and its hidden metaphysical assumptions. Przywara's theological project was to highlight the hidden mystical contours of human existence in prevailing cultural forms. His major project, *Analogia Entis*,[22] is a landmark study, which—among many other things—identifies touchpoints between God and the world through the lens of "Ignatian evangelization."[23] Przywara, like Balthasar, approaches theology and metaphysics in an Ignatian register, developing what O'Meara calls a "mysticism of open eyes." Theology, metaphysics, and spirituality are all a "life-long exercise in seeing."[24] The task of Ignatian evangelization of the culture is to find God in all things, which is to say that the theologian of culture identifies the analogies between God and world, identifying the implicit *theologumena* in each cultural form.[25]

Przywara not only shaped Balthasar's understanding of Ignatian evangelization of the culture, he also deepened the way Balthasar approached and interpreted the German intellectual tradition. Przywara was a great reader of the Idealists, especially Hegel, Heidegger, and Scheler. Balthasar had already engaged these thinkers from a critical Catholic perspective in his PhD dissertation in 1927, but

---

22. Erich Przywara, *Analogia Entis I. Metaphysik. Ur-Strukur und All-Rhythmus.* (Einseideln, Johannes Verlag, 1962).

23. O'Meara, 27.

24. O'Meara, 31.

25. O'Meara helpfully summarizes Przywara's theology of culture: "There always exists a remarkable interplay between the practical face of an age, that is, its visible surface expressing itself in various political and social movements, and its metaphysical core, its invisible spirit. The practical face of a time can be read in the great controversies occupying it from day-to-day. The metaphysical core reveals itself in philosophies and theologies which emerge from it. The observers and interpreters of the age should neglect neither of these, for what is of decisive import for the knowledge of God in particular also has its proper meaning for the temporal flow of this age. The invisible is recognized in the visible" (26).

his subsequent encounter with Przywara helped him develop a more robustly *christological* critique of German culture.[26]

A cultural, theological, and specifically christological interpretation of Ignatian evangelization are the main ways Przywara shaped the way the young Balthasar approached his own work. We can see Przywara's influence on Balthasar's analysis of the German soul and the way he develops a distinctively Catholic form of intellectual and cultural engagement.

The German Soul

We can see Balthasar's concern for a theological interpretation and criticism of culture in the revised form of his dissertation, *Apokolypse der deutschen Seele*, or *The Apocalypse of the German Soul*. It was a massive three-volume work that consisted of a series of minor monographs on particular German literary thinkers, including philosophers, artists, novelists, and poets. The intention of the project was to let the German literary tradition reveal its own eschatological understanding of the human soul. The project was ambitious, clearly, and neither Balthasar nor his first readers knew what to make of it.

Regardless of what we make of the quality of the project, its very existence reveals something telling about Balthasar: he was, from the first, a firm believer in the intersection of Catholicism and the prevailing intellectual and literary culture of his day. His was no closed Catholicism; there was no parochialism in his faith, no fearful flight from the world. This engagement with the world characterizes Balthasar throughout his life as a priest, a theologian, and a writer.

The Apocalypse of the German Soul is a work of literary criticism and theological critique. Balthasar's analysis of German culture operates under two main typologies: the Promethean and the Dionysian.[27] Each

---

26. Przywara's influence on Balthasar's Christology was primarily a negative one. Early in his writing career, Balthasar criticized Przywara for failing to be sufficiently christological. It is only later, in the 1950s, that Balthasar sees Przywara beginning to develop a christological understanding of analogy.

27. We see already the shadow of Nietzsche lurking in the background of Balthasar's thought. The typology of Balthasar's *Apocalypse* echoes Nietzsche's own in Apollo vs. Dionysian in *The Birth*

of these asks of humanity: what is your meaning? How do you stand in relation to infinite Being? Balthasar uses these questions to begin his interrogation of each type and the thinkers associated with them.

As a general trend, the figures of the Promethean type are the Idealist thinkers that dominated the philosophical landscape of Balthasar's day.[28] The net result of the Promethean type is monism, the breakdown of the *distinctio realis*—the "real difference"—between infinite and finite (or, theologically speaking, creator and creature). The Promethean thinkers, primarily Idealists, conflate "self" with the "absolute." Idealism absolutizes subjectivity. It is a Luciferean agenda, setting out to undermine ontological distinction, absorbing the absolute into the I. Throughout his works, Balthasar calls Idealism a "titanic" philosophy whenever it strives to dominate and control all things under the auspices of the self. The Prometheans are monists whose principle is the "creative negation as the dynamic middle-point between the 'one' and 'all.'"[29] We might call the Promethean a kind of gnostic deification, an echo of Neoplatonic philosophies of identity.[30] It rejects paradox in favor of a dialectically determined system. Metaphysically speaking, Promethean monism annihilates Being by enfolding it into the self. It is one of the great temptations of modernity, and like the gnosticism of the second century, one of the greatest threats to the Catholic faith.

Developing from the Promethean, however, is the Dionysian. This is the philosophy of life; a kind of *Lebensphilosophie* that draws figures such as Bergson, Rilke, George, and finally, Nietzsche into confrontation with the titanic ideals of the Promethean.[31] This group

---

of Tragedy (1872). Balthasar's method of cultural criticism, namely his genealogical method, attempts to out-narrate Nietzsche's own genealogy.

28. It is worth noting that Balthasar maintains this category throughout his life. He claims in *TD 2* (first published in 1976) that "the whole age is under the sign of 'the Prometheus principle'" (420). Though Balthasar is critical of the Prometheans, he acknowledges that the principle derives from a misreading of Christian anthropology.

29. *Apokalypse der deutschen Seele* I: *Der deutschen Idealismus* (Einsiedeln, Johannes Verlag, 1998), 147.

30. Later in his career, Balthasar will respond to this ontological monism with his robust doctrine of the *analogia entis* as the theological counter to pagan philosophy. We can catch a first glimpse of that later argument in Balthasar's reading of Kierkegaard at the end of *Apocalypse*.

31. "It is possible to see with one's eyes how the Promethean tendency, which was primarily concerned with spiritualization (the union of the limited 'I' with the absolute 'I'), logically turns

also includes Existentialists, especially Scheler, Heidegger, and the hero of the narrative, Søren Kierkegaard. The Dionysians undermine the powerful dialectic and synthesis of the Private with their portrayal of the heroic life living amidst the contradictions of reality. The tragedy of modernism, caught as it is between "Prometheus bound" and "Dionysius crucified," is the metaphysical contradiction that runs through them. Promethean Idealism offers the "complete transfiguration of the world, the divinizing of the earth," and Dionysian *Lebensphilosophie* and existentialism offer only the "pure falling, the path into nothingness and judgment."[32] Negativity becomes positivity.[33] Balthasar sees these two principles as the main intellectual convictions of modernity. Their bitter fruit—and here, we see the stakes of Balthasar's analysis—was World War I.

Yet for all of that, Balthasar does not reject modernity outright. Though he is often depicted as a severe critic of modernity, his relationship with the modern project is much more subtle and sophisticated. *Apocalypse* is not a correlationalist project by any means, but Balthasar does find important points of contact between philosophical modernity and his Catholic theology. Perhaps the best term to describe the relationship between the two comes from Alois Haas: Balthasar sees in the Promethean and the Dionysian, a *"reductio ad crucem,"* a reduction or return to the cross. The unveiling—the apocalypse—of both Prometheus and Dionysius reveals their cruciform nature. Balthasar sees both as secular parodies of the true myth of Christ crucified. Here we see the theological endgame of Balthasar's first intellectual project, a shadow of things to come:

> After this reduction of the crucial myths of German intellectual history to the myth of the Cross, one must see the sense in which this myth is the final form (*Gestalt*) of the world and therein provides the parameters of the final human attitude. For it does not seem self-evident that an

into the Dionysians, because the absolute 'I' possess a suprarational, natural vitality to which the *ratio*, together with consciousness in its limitedness, must surrender" (TD 2, 422).

32. Quoted in Alois M. Haas, "Hans Urs von Balthasar's 'Apocalypse of the German Soul': At the Intersection of German Literature, Philosophy, and Theology," in *Hans Urs von Balthasar: His Life and Work,* ed. David L. Schinder (San Francisco: Ignatius Press, 1991), 53.

33. Ibid.

"accidental" historical event like the crucifixion of a "man" in a corner of the Roman Empire antecedently conditions and determines not only the entire course of world history, but, more profoundly, the inner reality of *every* human being, in fact, the entire ontological structure of every person. If that is correct, then all being and all possible thought proves to be Christian. . . .[34]

Balthasar's theological critique of culture is, therefore, a kind of apocalyptic reading of the German intellectual culture through a method of integration. This method requires a careful exposition of culture, reading it in such a way that both its positive and negative relation to Christianity becomes clear. Balthasar does not shy away from pointing out the contradictions, consequences, and limitations of culture, but he does so with a keen and sensitive eye to the way culture reveals genuine, even if partial, truth. *Apocalypse* sets the stage for Balthasar's intellectual mission as both a critique of culture and constructive reinsertion of that culture into the fullness of Christianity. It is a "monstrous" book, but it nevertheless reveals Balthasar's first sustained attempt at finding an intellectual language for the church's evangelistic dialogue with the world.[35]

Haas rightly identifies Balthasar's methodological *stragem* in *Apocalypse* as Ignatian in character. Balthasar interrogates the Prometheans and Dionysians to a very particular set of questions that are meant to extract the "final attitude" of each to transcendence. According to Haas, "this question expresses a genuinely Jesuit motif of the Ignatian *Spiritual Exercises* that lets all reflection on the world and on humanity result in helping one decide for God's ever-more [*Magis*]—which must be given honor before all, precisely because of its transcendence over all."[36] Balthasar's earliest work is already colored by an "Ignatian aesthetics" that finds God in all things, even in the Promethean and Dionysian. In the next two sections, we give a brief overview of Balthasar's appreciation and more fundamental critique of these two trajectories, setting the stage for our account of intellectual

---

34. Quoted in Haas, 54.
35. *MW*, 41.
36. Haas, 51.

mission that Balthasar sees for the church and the saints in the modern world.

The Diabolical Reductions of Modernity

Balthasar believes that modernity is an era in crisis. Modern Europe has reached a point where a decision must be made between a "philosophy of identity"—the legacy of Plotinus that culminates in Hegel—or the "suspended adventist character" of Being.[37] He sees the Promethean, or Idealist, trajectory as having dominated modern philosophy and fears that it results ultimately in a reduction that undermines the beauty, freedom, and gratuity of Being.

For Balthasar, the question of truth is ultimately the question of the God–world relationship—a question whose validity has been fundamentally called into question by the legacy of Cartesian rationalism and Kantian Idealism.[38] Balthasar attempts to re-engage this question in the wake of the rise of titanic Idealism—which, as we have seen, reduces Being to the Absolute I where thought conquers Being, and world is known only as "I." Idealism's knowledge is titanically possessive, stripping knowledge of its reality, its givenness, and its mystery. Balthasar sees titanic Idealism as the philosophical child of Babel.

Balthasar sets out to rescue modernity from its crisis by countering two reductions that he identifies as emerging from the philosophical commitments of modernity.[39] Balthasar fears that without a proper initiation into the irreducible mystery of Being, truth is threatened by a twofold reduction. This reduction can be either cosmological (what Balthasar calls a "cosmic monism") or anthropological (an "anthropro-

---

37. Henrici, 157.
38. Cf. Louis Dupré, *Passage to Modernity: An Essay in the Hermeneutics of Nature and Culture* (New Haven: Yale University Press, 1993), 87.
39. Descartes is emblematic here. "[Descartes'] thought began by transforming philosophy from a science of first things into an epistemological investigation of the first principles of knowledge . . . all being, insofar as it must be represented by the mind, comes to depend on a single metaphysical principle—the thinking substance," Dupré, 80ff. Cf. Jean-Luc Marion, *Sur le prisme métaphysique de Descartes* (Paris: Presses Universitaires de France, 1986), 110ff.

monism"), but both are deadly to the question of truth—an account of the world and its relation to God.[40]

The cosmological reduction arises in the development of "nature" as something distinct from "supernature."[41] Nature, according to this line of thought, exists in and for itself, and is epistemologically accessible to autonomous rationality. What emerges is a distinction between a "natural religion" and a "positive religion." For many of the religious thinkers of modernity, an immanentized version of Justin Martyr's *logos spermatikos* gains prominence in which the particularity of Christian truth draws all other religious truth ("religion" now being a general sociological concept) into itself.[42] Christianity "represents the concluding stage of 'the phenomenon of revelation in general'."[43] Leibnizian philosophy then sets the stage for the cosmological reduction of Idealism (and German Romanticism) by absorbing Christianity into the cosmological totality of the monad. Herder, Hegel, and Drey are swift to follow. In them, the problem of the relationship between God and world is solved at the expense of both: a metaphysic of identity is ultimately the destruction of difference, and thus, of metaphysical meaning. In this reduction, objective reality can only be objectively realized. The human, dramatic subject can only play an insignificant role within this scheme.[44]

The second reduction is anthropological and more often than not, the temptation of modernity. This reduction distorts the ancient anthropology of the human as the "microcosm" of the world, and thus, as the mediator between God and world. Enlightenment thought, especially as summed up in Kant, builds upon this ancient idea but ends up making man into the author of the structure of the cosmos,

---

40. Balthasar's solution to this question will ultimately be christological—where "Christ and the paschal mysteries become the focal point of any contact between God and man." The revelation of Christ will give the fullest account of the God-world relation, but one can only arrive at such a conclusion "in the fullness of time." Joseph Palakeel, *The Use of Analogy in Theological Discourse: An Investigation in Ecumenical Perspective* (Rome: Editrice Pontificia Università Gregoriana, 1995), 75.
41. Dupré, 15–63.
42. Balthasar sees this same tendency even in some Renaissance figures. Nicholas of Cusa is a prime example: *LA*, 15–19.
43. *LA*, 29.
44. Countering this prevailing idea, Balthasar will insist that what is objectively given must be subjectively received and appropriated.

"a cosmos he transcends through his reason."[45] For Kant, "everything that is humanly knowable . . . is restricted to the synthesis of sensible intuition and concept,"[46] while anything lying beyond this phenomenal realm only serves as the practical possibility of ethical practice. This same tendency can be seen in Schleiermacher, who reduces religion to the human capacity *for* that religion—the universal experience of *Gefühl*, the feeling of absolute dependence. The meaning of the world, the meaning of the God–world relationship, can be accounted for by some purely natural human capacity. Feuerbach's "theology is anthropology"[47] is not far away. For Balthasar, "the central presupposition of modernism, in a nutshell, is that every objective dogmatic proposition must be measured in terms of its suitability to the religious subject, in terms of its positive effects on and capacity to complete and fulfill that subject." Modernity's anthropology reduces Being to that which is suitable to the rational and moral needs of the human being. Balthasar fears that this will lead to the annihilation of the human and the world in the "gnostic elevation" of humanity.[48]

For Balthasar, neither of these reductions adequately accounts for the mystery of Being. A third option is needed—one which maintains the integrity of both God and world, that expresses the necessary rhythm of the objective gift and its subjective reception. This is what Balthasar calls the third way of love—the way of Jesus Christ and the way of the saints.[49] It is only love that reveals and preserves Being *and* beings.

It is the anthropological reduction and its inherent nihilism that

---

45. *LA*, 31.
46. Ibid., 33.
47. In an interesting twist, Balthasar will say that Feuerbach was, in a way, correct: theology *does* become anthropology because God becomes human in the incarnation.
48. See *TD* 2, 417ff. The consequence of this reduction is nihilism: "With this [reduction], metaphysics comes to an end and, at the same time, all metaphysical love. There remain at best the substitute forms of a love within the world and a love among men. And because the former must be increasingly dissolved within the latter, as man himself takes control of the world, for which a transcendental and evolutionistic philosophy furnishes the justification to salve his conscience; because he himself has the world in and beneath himself, there remains for him—like the last of his emergency rations—only love among men" (*GL* 5, 643). But even this love cannot remain for long. For without any metaphysical grounding, both the I and the Thou necessary for love are disconnected from any mooring in Being, and thus, existence itself becomes phantasmic.
49. *LA*, 12–13.

hovers in the background of Balthasar's theology of the saints. According to Balthasar, the unrestrained divinization of the human person via subjective reason to a position above Being—even above God—brings about a twofold consequence: the annihilation of the mysterious depth of Being (expressed most succinctly in the common saying, "A is nothing other than . . .") and, inseparable from this, the annihilation of the human person as such. The person who *should* be constituted by her receptivity of existence from the depth of Being is constituted, instead, by her striving after power. Her existence is "a gift that now belongs to [her] entirely."[50] Her receptive humanity is replaced by titanic striving:[51]

> Ever since Nietzsche [who is, for Balthasar, the culmination of Kant], this hollowing out of the transcendentals has been justified by the degradation that man's freedom has been able to inflict upon them: falsehood, malice, ugliness, and the elevation of a violent dualism to the level of a first principle seem to dominate man's world so thoroughly that anyone who can look all of this in the face . . . must dismiss the idea that being is true, good, and beautiful as a hopeless illusion. Existence is governed by the will to power, which uses the transcendentals to its best advantage: truth, *pravda*, is what serves the interests of power, and so forth.[52]

It is no coincidence that Balthasar here ties metaphysics and anthropology together. The questions of Being and the human person must be posed together, especially as they bear on an account of truth. That which is known demands a knower. But they can be lost together as well. And when both are lost, there can no longer be truth.[53] These are the metaphysical commitments behind the loss of the saints from

---

50. *TD* 2, 417.
51. Cf. *TD* 2, 420–26 on Titanism.
52. *TL* 1, 10. It is especially interesting to note Balthasar's use of the word "pravda" to modify "truth." For Balthasar, truth in a world of the titans inevitably becomes an ideological weapon of the will to power. He sees this in the Soviet newsletter *Pravda* (1912–1991), used as a propagandist communiqué during the revolts on 1917. Scattered throughout the *Theo-Logic* are vague critiques of the Sovietism and communism, of which Balthasar was deeply suspicious. His language here ties the propogandist and idealogical weaponizing of truth to the distortions of the world that are endemic to modernity's temptation to titanism.
53. In *TD* 2, Balthasar insists that these reductions are "inconceivable apart from [the intellectual] passage through Christianity. But they all also lead to its total perversion" (420). The next chapter will spell out this claim.

theology. When knowledge trumps both love and Being, the human person is reduced to Mind at the expense of love and life.

For and Against Hegel

How Hegel fits into this largely negative assessment of modernity is a much vexed question in Balthasar scholarship. Some scholars argue that there is a great deal of continuity between the two, while others insist on something close to an unbridgeable gap.[54] We can at least say that there is no doubt of the importance of Hegel for Balthasar's thought. In Balthasar's interpretation of intellectual history, Hegel is the heir of Plotinus; and just as Plotinus is the culmination of ancient philosophy, Hegel is the conclusion of modern thought.[55] The trajectory outlined above that passes through Fichte and Schelling culminates in Hegelian absolute knowledge. This means, for Balthasar, that the trajectory of philosophical modernity that concludes in Hegel is blasphemous because it ends up substituting the personal, triune God with the god of the philosophers—an object deprived of depth, mystery, and beauty. Hegel represents a parody of Catholic truth. As someone deeply concerned with cultural dialogue and critique, Balthasar must "think eye to eye with Hegel."[56]

But Balthasar's assessment of Hegel is not exclusively negative, even if it is largely critical. It is perhaps most accurate to say that Balthasar is "for and against Hegel." He sees Hegel as an important and useful interlocutor *against* the rampant subjectivism of much of the Idealist and liberal Protestant tradition. O'Regan notes that Balthasar's appreciation for Hegel consists in the latter's conviction that religious discourse—contra someone like Schleiermacher—"aims toward absolute truth."[57] Hegel's insistence on the objectivity of truth, along

---

54. An example of the former is Ben Quash, *Theology and the Drama of History* (Cambridge: Cambridge University Press, 2005). A recent example of the latter is Cyril O'Regan, who insists that they are largely incompatible thinkers. Cf. Cyril O'Regan, *The Anatomy of Misremembering: Von Balthasar's Response to Philosophical Modernity* (New York: Herder & Herder, 2014).
55. Henrici, "The Philosophy of Hans Urs von Balthasar," 157.
56. Ibid.
57. O'Regan, *Anatomy*, 519. Hegel refuses to allow the dogma of the Trinity, for example, to be subsumed into a private, subjective "mysticism" *or* into an intellectual, dogmatic theology. One

with the confidence in the ability to know that truth, requires a crossing of disciplinary boundaries. Hegel and Balthasar both rely on art, literature, philosophy, and theology for a thorough investigation of truth.[58] Moreover, Hegel also insists that truth has a "practical dimension" because it concerns specific "forms of life" that accord with truth's demands. For Hegel, philosophy involves not only "knowing" truth, but also "making true."[59] Hegel's concern for the rational and practical claims of religious discourse are obviously attractive to Balthasar, even if he sees some significant dangers in Hegel's thought.[60]

For all of these goods that Balthasar identifies in Hegel, however, there is, nevertheless, a fundamental discontinuity between the two. O'Regan rightly claims that Balthasar's critique of Hegel centers on the gnosticism of his philosophy.[61] One sees this gnosticism at work in Hegel's failure to develop a satisfactory—or even Christian—understanding of the God–world relationship. Instead of developing what Rodney Howsare calls a "principle of unity"[62] between God and world, Hegel instead succumbs to a gnostic and Neoplatonic conflation of God and world. Hegel's is ultimately a philosophy of identity flavored by a *libido dominandi* that collapses God into the world, and, as we saw above, the world into the knowing subject.

In *Glory of the Lord*, Balthasar's mature critique of Hegel is that, though operating in a vaguely Christian register, he ends up expelling divine transcendence from Being (and revelation), and conflates the Holy Spirit with the cosmic *Geist*. This involves a severe de-personalizing and immanentizing of God.[63] This is manifest in Hegel's

---

might, however, dispute that Hegel's understanding of the Trinity is not properly Trinitarian, but rather is *triadic*.

58. Ibid.
59. Ibid.
60. The common assessment is that Balthasar derived the name of the *Theo-Logic* from Hegel himself. The *Theo-Logic* are, at every turn, an ongoing engagement with and critique of Hegelian dialectic, even when Hegel's name is absent.
61. O'Regan also sees Balthasar concerned with Hegel's Neoplatonism and apocalypticism, but it is his gnosticism that dominates Balthasar's criticism of Hegel.
62. Rodney Howsare, "Why Hegel? A Reading of Cyril O'Regan's *Anatomy of Misremembering*" (paper presented at the annual meeting of the Catholic Theological Society of America, San Diego, June 2014).

"insatiable and hateful polemic against the Old Testament."[64] Hegel's radical immanentizing of God into the world requires that he expunge Yahweh from his philosophy because a God who "acts, elects and rejects in complete freedom of will" from his lordly elevation threatens to undermine the Hegelian system. The radical otherness of Yahweh leaves us with a divine mystery and the radiance of *kabôd* in which God is both present and distinct.[65] Instead, Hegel requires a God caught up in his own process of self-knowledge, and therefore, absolutely and utterly manifest to reason. It is at this point that Hegel's thought ultimately becomes another philosophy of identity, a modernist iteration of Plotinus.

The consequence of Hegel's philosophy of identity for epistemology is significant. According to O'Regan, Balthasar sees Hegelian thought as a *Dopplegänger* of Christian metaphysics that results in "an epistemology that neither recognizes the finite limits of human knowledge nor the excess of the infinite divine."[66] Hegel's titanic epistemology abolishes mystery by silencing Being and denying the dialogical nature of knowledge. In *Theo-Drama 2*, Balthasar accuses Hegel of being an "epic" rather than a "dramatic" thinker in which knowledge of truth emerges out of the "dialogue between two personal centers of freedom (divine and human)."[67] There is no role for positive—let alone perpetual—otherness in Hegelian thought; the dialectic must ultimately dissolve in a philosophy of unity. Hegel's philosophy forces a reorientation of Christian forms of life and worship that are social and political, rather than concerned with the cultivation of holiness.[68]

---

63. According to Balthasar, Hegel replaces the transcendent, personal God (*der Andere*) with the other, de-personalizing thing (*das Andere*).
64. *GL 5*, 579.
65. Ibid., 585.
66. O'Regan, *Anatomy*, 522. What O'Regan does not note is that Hegel's is a *Dopplegänger* specifically of Johannine theology. Cf. *TD 2*, 423. The Hegelian system has room for the *Logos*, but not for the *Logos* who "took on flesh and dwelled among us" (John 1:18).
67. Ibid., 523. We will investigate the dramatic structure of knowledge in chapter 4. Cf. David C. Schindler, *Hans Urs von Balthasar and the Dramatic Structure of Truth* (Bronx, NY: Fordham University Press, 2004).
68. O'Regan, *Anatomy*, 51. This point is apropos of the current project because the saint is the distinctly Christian form of life of holiness. Metaphysics is indelibly intertwined with the practices of life in both the Hegelian and Balthasarian systems.

The Hegelian trajectory ultimately resolves itself in the confrontation between Nietzsche and Kierkegaard, the *übermensch* and Christ.[69] For Balthasar, Nietzsche represents the "titanic power-love" of philosophical modernity, whereas Kierkegaard represents a contrary descent of power and love in the person of Christ.[70] Both figures represent ways of construing and understanding the relationship between God and world, infinite and finite. For Nietzsche, finite man must be sacrificed on the altar of the *übermensch* through his erotic and titanic striving after power.[71] Such striving involves the *ascent* of man beyond man. For Kierkegaard, the human is similarly called to a self-annihilation, a kind of self-crucifixion, but only in the hope of resurrection. This man is Christ, who performs his perfect union with God (and his mastery over sin and death) in his descent from "equality with God" to the "form of a slave" (Philippians 2:6). Balthasar sees in Christ's *descent* the revelation of the God–world relationship. And so, influenced by Kierkegaard, Balthasar pits Hegelian titanism against Christic obedience. Christ

> who called himself the Way and the Truth . . . and who confirms Hegel's statement that everything that is real is reasonable . . . in a sense that goes beyond everything that can be constructed on the basis of a system and in a completely different way, namely . . . by . . . being able to unite in a single act the absolutely divine and the absolutely anti-divine, not in the insanity of a titanic superhuman gesture, but in the simplicity of his obedience.[72]

For Balthasar, the crisis of modernity is resolved not in the *übermensch* but in the God-Man; not in Prometheus bound, nor in Dionysius crucified, but in Jesus Christ, bound, crucified . . . and resurrected.

From Kierkegaard, Balthasar also gains an understanding of the human as a dialogical creature. The proper counter to the titanic *dialectic* of the Prometheans is *dialogic*. Knowledge of truth arises, Balthasar claims, not through the dialectical intercourses of reason,

---

69. See Henrici, 160.
70. Ibid.
71. Cf. *TD* 2, 423.
72. *TL* 2, quoted in Henrici, 158.

but through the living and free exchange of language and dialogue.[73] Henrici says that "the dialogical principle . . . becomes the forming principle of [Balthasar's] trilogy."[74] Later, in Balthasar's Trilogy, the dialogical principle that he learned from Kierkegaard will transform into the concrete, dialogical practice of prayer.

***

Though not typically listed among the *krisis* theologians of the twentieth century, Balthasar is immensely concerned with a European culture in crisis. Any interpretation of Balthasar must account for his cultural engagement as part of his Ignatian—and Przywaran —intellectual mission, a way of finding God present in all things and all ideas. From his earliest work, *Apocalypse*, to his last major work, the *Theo-Logic*, Balthasar endeavors to expose the Christic structure of all things, even the diabolical *Dopplegänger* of Promethean Idealism. He subjects Promethean philosophy to the rigors of a genealogical therapy, hoping to expose the toxic elements inherent in them to the transformative, healing power of a distinctively Christian and christological metaphysics. The stakes of following the Promethean trajectory are high. If Western culture continues in this trajectory, there is the very real possibility of Being falling

> under the sign of the constant dominion of "knowledge" and thus science, technology, and cybernetics [that] will overpower and suffocate the forces of love within the world. The result will be a world without women, without children, without reverence for the form of love in poverty and humility, a world in which everything is viewed solely in terms of power or profit-margin, in which everything that is disinterested and gratuitous and useless is despised, persecuted, and wiped out, and even art is forced to wear the mask and features of technique.[75]

Balthasar inherited this concern for culture from Pryzwara's interpretation of the Ignatian mission of evangelization. Balthasar's

---

73. Balthasar pits dialectic and dialogic against each other in no uncertain terms. See *TL* 2, 43–59.
74. Henrici, 161.
75. *LA*, 142.

concerns determine both his personal intellectual mission and his understanding of the church in the modern world. The danger, however, of openness to the world is that the distinctively Catholic character of the Church might be lost. This is precisely Balthasar's concern with the fallout from the Second Vatican Council. Against the prevailing relativism of the Council's *aggiornamento*, Balthasar insists on a "distinctively Catholic" form of engaging the world. His theology of the saints is part and parcel of this distinctively Catholic form.

The Church in the World

We have considered Balthasar's interpretation of his twentieth-century German intellectual culture from his standpoint as a Roman Catholic, and specifically Ignatian, theologian. It would misrepresent him, however, if we did not also consider the way he formulated the Church's cultural mission. Balthasar, despite all of his personal isolation from the church, was a thoroughly ecclesial thinker. His theology of the saints is not a paradigm for rogue, spiritual virtuosos. For Balthasar, the saint is the proper form of the Christian life, and this means that she lives an ecclesial existence. The saint's mission is to engage the world from within the church. She does this by "enlarging the chapels" of the church's mind, imagination, and love. We must consider, therefore, Balthasar's understanding of the church's place in the modern world so that we might situate his theology of the saints in its proper ecclesial context.

Post-conciliar Diminishment

By the time of the Second Vatican Council (1962–1965), Balthasar was isolated from the larger theological world. He was alienated from the Jesuits after leaving the Order in 1950. He was cut off from the intellectual circles of pre-conciliar Catholicism as a student chaplain in Munich. His work and his associations were suspect in the wake of *Humani Generis* (1950). Unlike Rahner and de Lubac, Balthasar was not invited as a *peritus* to the Council; even the Protestant Karl Barth played a bigger role at the Council than Balthasar.

In the years following the Council, Balthasar (along with de Lubac) was outspokenly critical of some of the trajectories Catholic theology took in the "spirit" of Vatican II. Though often labeled a "reactionary" and a "conservative" in response to Vatican II, Balthasar himself said that he remained in the same place he was when he wrote *Razing the Bastions* in 1952; it was the Church that had moved.

But what was it that changed at Vatican II? In his 1965 *Rechenschaft*,[76] Balthasar argued that the Council was a victim of its own success. Vatican II set out to open the Church to the world—a mission that Balthasar argued for in 1952—but its openness had become one-sided. The post-conciliar Church's emphasis on relevance to the world became "exceedingly dangerous" because the Church failed to cultivate its own "distinctive counterpoise and balance."[77] But Balthasar insists that "every program of mission to the world must at all times contain . . . 'the discernment of what is Christian'."[78] This discernment of spirits—the Christian spirit from the *Zeitgeist*—is what Balthasar identifies as lacking in the post-conciliar Church.[79] The post-conciliar Church more often "christened" worldly philosophy and culture than presented the distinctive form of Christ to the world.

Surprisingly, Balthasar ultimately lays the blame for the simplistic baptizing of secular modes of thought on a misapplication of de Lubac's breakthrough about nature and grace. Since grace does not destroy but perfects nature—that is, since "the world as a whole stands in the light of grace"[80]—then, supposedly, "the great impulses of modern times could also find a home in Christianity."[81] In this (mis-)conception, the world is *unconsciously* graced; it is therefore possible for "whoever strives" for meaning to be called an "anonymous Christian."[82] As this

---

76. Published in *MW*, 47–91.
77. Ibid., 52.
78. Ibid.
79. The discernment of spirits is also a theme of Ignatian spirituality. Cf. *TL* 3, 385–405.
80. *MW*, 53.
81. Ibid.
82. This reference is obviously to Rahner's claim that a human's *Vorgriff* can be aligned to God unconsciously, thus making them a Christian, though anonymously. While this claim allowed

theological principle was applied to the Church's *aggiornamento*, it endeavored to find the "anonymously Christian" element in any and every philosophy, politic, and psychology:

> why should a Christian truth not be hidden even in the Marxist total-labor process as the return of mankind from its self-alienation and as the transformation of the world and of man by means of technology? And if Marxism demands the self-immolation of the individual to the collective and to its ideal of the future, why can this process, this sacrifice, this anonymity and poverty of the individual not be understood much more profoundly and transfigured by the light of the salvific order in a Christian "theology of work ..."?[83]

This "supernaturalizing what is worldly" had been immensely successful in the years following the Council. It seemed the long isolation of the Church's neo-medievalism was finally being put to rest. In those heady years following the Council, it seemed that perhaps a new Catholic utopia was neigh: "Christians and Christians, Christians and Jews, Christians and non-Christians, Christians and anti-Christians: all commune at last in the great realm of God's creation, which as a whole is endowed with a dimension of grace. Grandiose."[84] The only cost demanded by this global utopian vision was the loss of anything and everything distinctly Christian. In the world of the anonymous Christian, Balthasar sees no reason why a person should adopt the name Christian at all.

One gets at the heart of Balthasar's reaction against the practiced ambiguity of the post-conciliar period by looking at his critique of Karl Rahner in his *The Moment of Christian Witness*. Here we see Balthasar situating his own mission of cultural work *as a Catholic*. While we will address Balthasar's positive statement of Catholic mission in the modern, post-conciliar world in the chapter's conclusion, here we will look at his criticism of Rahner as a reflection of his broader critique of where Vatican II went wrong.

Rahner a certain rapprochement with non-Christian theology and politics, Balthasar sees it a "christening of German Idealism" (*MW*, 53). Notice Balthasar's reference to "striving"—an etymological echo of the word "titan."
83. *MW*, 54.
84. Ibid., 56.

The Un-distinctively Catholic

We might summarize Balthasar's post-conciliar writing as focusing on the Church's obsession with "relevance" that leads it to adopt forms of mission and engagement that lack the distinctive thrust of Catholic identity. The Council's reaction against the ossified forms of neo-medieval forms of theology and philosophy had become an over-reaction. The post-conciliar Church was so open to the *Zeitgeist* that it failed to present a distinctively Christian form to the world. Instead, the Church adopted the forms, concerns, and methods of secular philosophy, communism, and the limited concerns of "modern man." In his 1975 work, simply titled *Katholisch*,[85] Balthasar highlights the tensions between the "progressive" and "conservative" responses to the Council, highlighting the limitations of each:

> There are polarizations in the wake of the Second Vatican Council ... progressive versus conservative. Some people dissolve allegedly rigid forms until nothing is left but formlessness, while others hold fast to these forms until they actually ossify. Neither is replaced by anything that promises to last, but by things cobbled together in haste, outdated even before they see the light of day. It is hard to say whether this is simply due to our period's inability to create genuine forms or a specifically Christian inability.[86]

Balthasar bemoans that the Council's emphasis on *aggiornamento* had been misconstrued to the point that the concerns and limitations of "modern man" are now taken as the standard for Catholic truth. That is, because modernity is concerned with what can be known "within the parameters of the world,"[87] theology's focus shifts away from the mystery of redemption and toward the political and social. As Balthasar argues throughout his post-conciliar writing, the movement away from the mystery of divine love as manifested in the event of redemption in Christ, involves an abstraction away from the

---

85. Translated into English as "In the Fullness of Faith: On the Centrality of the Distinctively Catholic," trans. Graham Harrison (San Francisco: Ignatius Press, 1988).
86. Ibid., 17–18.
87. Ibid., 24. Balthasar attributes this limited focus on immanence especially to the influence of Kant, Hegel, and Marx.

concreteness of the church's proclamation and the watering down
of Christian identity. Watering down the distinctiveness of Christian
identity and proclamation inevitably impair Christian mission to the
world. For an Ignatian theologian such as Balthasar, impairing
Christian mission is equivalent to cutting out the heart and soul of the
church.

The call of the Christian in the world is what Balthasar calls the
Ernstfall—the decisive moment where the Christian becomes a martyr,
a witness to the truth she professes.[88] His *Moment of Christian Witness* is a
"danger signal" that the post-conciliar church's openness to the world
had gone too far and ended up being the assimilation of the church into
the world. Assimilation to the world is the suspension of the *Ernstfall*,
the watering down of Christian identity, and the loss of mission to the
world.

Balthasar sees this very process at work in the theology of his friend
and colleague, Karl Rahner. Though both men were Jesuits, studied
with Przywara, and worked together at *Stimmen und Zeit*, Balthasar
sees Rahner's post-conciliar theological work as an attempt to realize
Vatican II's call to *aggiornamento* by tying Catholic theology to the
philosophical concerns of modernity, especially German Idealism. This,
in itself, is both admirable and good. Yet, Balthasar sees Rahner
relativizing the importance of Catholic identity through his elaborate
theory of "anonymous Christians."[89] What Rahner ends up doing, so
Balthasar avers, is escaping the Christian call to witness (*Ernstfall*,
martyreon). Rahner allows the flight *from* the cross of Christ while still
managing to "lay full claim to God."[90]

According to Balthasar, Rahner's transcendental starting point
succumbs to the Enlightenment temptation to use Christ as a symbolic
representation of humanity. Rahner anthropologizes Christology.[91]
Balthasar accuses Rahner—unfairly, some will undoubtedly say—of

---

88. We should note well that Balthasar uses the term "martyr" to mean something more than one
who dies for their faith. Drawing on Ignatius, Balthasar defines a martyr as one whose entire
existence has been given to the service of God (MCW, 140).
89. Ibid., 101.
90. Ibid.
91. Ibid., 86.

equating Christianity with a generic humanism to such an extent that the distinctiveness of Christianity—the name "Christian"—rapidly diminishes. Rahner's "anonymous Christian" could just as easily be called an "anonymous atheist" insofar as the distinctiveness of Christ is minimized—or relativized through a merely symbolic treatment—in Rahner's theology. Rahner ends up reducing religion to ethics to such an extent that he distorts the tradition so severely as to make it into a neo-Catholicism, a *Doppelgänger* of the true faith.[92] The *Doppelgänger*, this anonymous Christian, can no longer be a witness (martyr) to Christ in the world because she is no longer distinct from the world. This is the inevitable consequence, Balthasar asserts, of Rahner's decision to begin his theology with German Idealism rather than with the concrete form (*Gestalt*) of Christ.[93]

The drive behind *aggornamento*, at least in its excessive form, is to update the Church, making her relevant to the world, but on the world's terms. The consequence of this, Balthasar fears, is that the church discards her distinctive identity for the sake of earning a hearing from the world. Balthasar disputes this interpretation of the Council. He insists instead that Vatican II's call to openness to the world is in order to "direct into the secular world through the Church, the mysterious ray of trinitarian and crucified love, wholly and completely."[94] Christians who embrace the distinctive and uncompromising call to the moment of witness are the only ones who can do this.

The martyrdom Balthasar calls for does not entail a hatred of the world. Balthasar praises the Council's positive affirmation of the world's genuine goodness. Christian love, he says, should reveal God's "unequivocal affirmation of all things."[95] It is precisely this love that makes the church a martyr in the world. To be a martyr in the modern

---

92. Ibid., 148.
93. Ibid., 146. As Balthasar writes in 1965, the anonymous Christian involves a "christening of German Idealism, into whose transcendental key even the metaphysical thinking of St. Thomas can be transposed. . . . When everything goes so well with anonymity, it is hard to see why a person should still be a name-bearing Christian" (*MW*, 55, 56).
94. *MCW*, 125.
95. Ibid., 135.

world is for every moment of one's existence to be given over to the service of God.[96] The martyr is the one whose life is characterized by Ignatian indifference, an openness, receptivity, and obedience to the divine call of love.

Having considered both the intellectual and ecclesial culture of Balthasar's day, we can now make sense of Balthasar's mission to develop a correspondence between a "distinctively Catholic" form of thought and life. Here, we find echoes of both Ignatius and Przywara, especially in the emphases on the Ignatian mission of cultural engagement and Christocentrism, but developed into a form that is Balthasar's own.

The Distinctively Catholic

As we have seen, even as late as the 1980s, Balthasar claimed to stand behind the model of the contemporary church that he outlined in *Razing the Bastions*.[97] After the Council, Balthasar maintained his position on the Church's openness and mission to the world, but he insisted that this mission required a distinctively Catholic character. As his criticism of Rahner reveals, Balthasar believed that the modern church was tempted to sacrifice its identity for the sake of fleeting social approval and relevance. Such a tactic results in the watering down of the Catholic faith, Balthasar believes, and fails to do the world any good.

In 1965, Balthasar reflected on the task of post-conciliar theology:

> Indeed, it was not as though we were unaware that with an opening to the world, an *aggiornamento*, a broadening of the horizons, a translation of the Christian message into an intellectual language understandable by the modern world, only half is done. The other half—of at least equal importance—is a reflection on that specifically Christian element itself, a purification, a deepening, a centering on its idea, which alone renders us capable of representing it, radiating it, translating it believably in the world.

96. Ibid., 140.
97. Cf. *Test Everything: Hold Fast to What is Good* (San Francisco: Ignatius Press, 1989), 13.

Balthasar's response is to develop a theology of mission that emphasizes the distinctive Catholic character of the church's engagement with the world. His strategy is rooted in the person of Christ. For Balthasar, it is Christ who answers the questions that haunt modern man.[98] Theology must always begin anew with Christ through a living encounter with him.

Understanding the distinctively Catholic shape of the church's mission to the world requires a return to the sources and the spirit of the broader Tradition, re-imagining metaphysics and existence in the light of Catholic truth. From the Tradition, the modern church receives her identity; from the probing questions of metaphysics and existentialism—the situation of contemporary humanity—the church receives her mission. Let us consider each of these in turn so that we might see how Balthasar conceived of the task of Ignatian evangelization in the contemporary world.

Ressourcement

It is stereotypical to depict post-conciliar Catholicism as the conflict between two schools—*aggiornamento* and *ressourcement*. The former is construed as the progressive school, and the latter, the conservative reactionaries. But Balthasar's post-conciliar thought is simply the sounding of a "danger signal"[99] and a call to theological and ecclesial renewal along the lines of a distinctively Catholic engagement with the world. One of the chief resources for a distinctively Catholic mission is the broader Tradition. Balthasar, as we saw, accuses Rahner of breaking faith with the Tradition in his efforts at *aggiornamento*. A brief account of Balthasar's own engagement with that Tradition is therefore relevant for our understanding of the uniquely Balthasarian form of the church's mission in the modern world.

It may be pure coincidence that Balthasar's decision to enter the Jesuit Order and to adopt a "theological life" occurred alongside the

98. Balthasar wholeheartedly endorses the proclamation of *Gaudium et Spes*, that in Christ "the mystery of man takes on light" (para. 22).
99. *MCW*, 154.

completion of his dissertation on the German soul. Charles Kannengiesser believes the timeline of Balthasar's intellectual and spiritual development depicts Balthasar's own movement from the metaphysical despair of *Germanistik* to the theological training of his Jesuit formation. When he became a Jesuit, Balthasar came under the influence of Henri de Lubac who, despite not being one of Balthasar's official teachers, nevertheless introduced Balthasar to the Fathers of the Church. Kannengiesser believes that Balthasar's turn to the Fathers under the aegis of Lubacian *ressourcement* provided him with a network of resources for developing a thoroughgoing response to the eschatological crisis he identified in the German soul.[100]

Kannengiesser claims that Balthasar's own *ressourcement* was fueled by the hope that the Fathers would provide a "restorative synthesis" that issues in a profound rapprochment between the world and the church, metaphysics and faith, nature and grace. In the Fathers, Balthasar saw the potential for a renaissance of Catholic thought in the modern day. There is a significant divergence between Balthasarian *ressourcement* and that of de Lubac (or other of de Lubac's students, such an Jean Daniélou). De Lubac approached the Tradition more as a compiler and synthesizer, and Daniélou was interested in clerical formation. Balthasar's *ressourcement*, however, was driven by missional concerns. Balthasar's first extended theological project was a series of studies of the Fathers—Origen, Gregory of Nyssa, and Maximus Confessor—that brought them into conversation with the philosophical culture of the day. These Fathers provided a restorative critique of culture and a hopeful alternative to the inevitable titanism and despair of Promethean and Dionysian modernity. For example, the cosmic dimensions of Maximus Confessor's theology offer a stunning counter to the destructive titanism of Hegelian Idealism; Nyssa develops a mystical and religious philosophy that out-narrates that of Kant.

Balthasar lays out the program of his *ressourcement* project in his 1939 essay, now translated as "The Fathers, the Scholastics, and

---

100. Charles Kannengiesser, "Listening to the Fathers," in *Hans Urs von Balthasar: His Life and Work*, 59.

Ourselves" and in the foreword to his 1942 book on Gregory of Nyssa, *Presence and Thought*.[101]

In the foreword to *Presence and Thought*, Balthasar warns that the *ressourcement* of the Fathers should not be confused with a direct retrieval of their thought. He insists that the Fathers cannot be transplanted from their era to our own. History does not repeat itself, and so, the questions posed by modernity cannot be answered directly by the ancients. Balthasar is no more confident in the feasibility of a "neo-Patristic synthesis" than he is in the neo-scholasticism of his early Jesuit training at Pullach.[102] Faithfulness to the Tradition consists not in repetition, but rather, in *imitation* of the spiritual attitude of the Fathers, a retrieval of the "vital wellsprings" of their thought that emerge from their "intimate reflection" and their "audacious creation."[103] Balthasar's *ressourcement* is less a historical appropriation *of* the ancient Fathers, and more of an intentional participation in theological reflection *with* the Fathers in the communion of saints.

When the theologian turns to history in her reflection on the Fathers and the medievals, she finds that "history, far from dispensing us from creative effort, imposes it upon us."[104] Every new problem that modernity faces must be met with a new theological solution. But these new solutions will emerge *from* the Tradition, the living memory of the Church. The "intimate reflection" that Balthasar refers to is a reference to a double intimacy: that of the communion of saints and that of the saints with the Trinitarian communion of God. Theological reflection in the "spirit of the Fathers," as Balthasar's *ressourcement* project attempts, requires the contemporary theologian to share in the tradition of theological reflection—both to receive from the past and to pass on to the future (the practice of *traditio*). More specifically, this means imitating the method of the Fathers and it will, as we

---

101. "The Fathers, the Scholastics, and Ourselves," trans. Edward T. Oakes, S.J., *Communio*, vol. 24, no. 2 (1997): 347–96. PT, though published in 1942, was mostly written alongside "The Fathers, the Scholastic and Ourselves" in 1939.

102. "There is never a historical situation that is absolutely similar to any of the ones that preceded it in time. Thus there is no historical situation that can furnish us with its own solutions as a kind of master key capable of resolving all of the problems that plague us today" (PT, 10).

103. Ibid., 12.

104. Ibid., 10.

shall see, mean doing theology with an Ignatian attitude of openness, receptivity, and fidelity. It means, more concretely, doing theology as a form of prayer. Balthasar's understanding of theology mirrors that of Evagrius of Pontus: "the one who prays is a theologian, and a theologian is one who prays."

But this prayer does not denote a fideistic attitude, a retreat from engagement with the world into a spiritual parochialism. Part of contemporary theology's imitation of the spirit of the Fathers involves the creative articulation of the church's deposit of divine revelation in the language of the present moment. Only by doing so does the church truly understand its revelation as the meeting of the timeless and the temporal in the flesh of Christ; only by speaking in the language of the day does the church perform its Christic identity and articulate its truth as the good news to the world as it exists here and now.

Balthasar's emphasis on mission as it fits within his *ressourcement* project is worked out in some detail in "The Fathers, Scholastic, and Ourselves." The essay is less of a prescription for *ressourcement* as a theological method than it is an early *summa* of Balthasar's thought, bringing the cultural concerns of *Apocalypse* into conversation with his reading of the Christian Tradition and the vocation of the church. The essay attempts to identify the "central law" of each era of Christianity—the Patristic, Medieval, and Modern. These laws are then compared to what Balthasar rather presumptuously asserts as the central law of Christianity itself—namely, the mystical participation of the Christian through the church in the life of Christ. Balthasar's criticism of modernity's titanism shows up in this early essay, as does the Kierkegaardian and Johannine insistence that "[Christ] must increase and I must decrease" (John 3:30). The essay explores the way each era understands the meaning of "being in Christ"—the central meaning of Christianity—as this issue is refracted through the Christian's place in the God-world relationship. Balthasar identifies an evolution in the understanding of what it means to be "in Christ" from a "world-denying" Christian Platonism in the Fathers to a "world-affirming dying to the world" in modernity.[105] A brief consideration of the way Balthasar reads these eras will help us understand better the way he sees the relationship of the historical and contemporary forms of the church and how his theology of the saints fits within it.

The great strength that Balthasar identifies in the Patristic era is the unity of life and doctrine.[106] The Fathers theologized with the entirety of their existence. In Christ, God and world had come together; God had triumphed over the pagan world, defusing its powers and raising it to sanctified life. This is the logic behind "spoiling the Egyptians" that characterized much of Patristic theology in their absorption of Platonism. While Balthasar is no Adolf von Harnack, he does see danger in the Christian fellowship with Neoplatonism.[107] From Neoplatonism, Christianity adopts the logic of participation, which Balthasar sees as tending toward pantheism, where created Being "is understood as a de-potentializing of the divine being."[108] The Fathers, thus influenced, incline toward spiritualization. Union with God—being *in* Christ—certainly occurs, but it is achieved through an asceticism of denying materiality in favor of the greater reality of pure spirit. The Fathers nevertheless maintain a distinct ontological difference between creator and creature, shyness before the absolute otherness of God. This shyness is what nourishes the tradition of negative theology and its refusal to elevate the human to a comprehensive knowledge of God and the world. The Fathers maintain the mystery of Being; even our participation cannot overcome the ontological difference between God and the world.

What Balthasar sees in the Fathers is the great foray of Christianity into intellectual engagement with the world. Its encounter with Neoplatonism may have negatively affected Christianity with its spiritual contempt for the world, but the encounter nevertheless represents Christianity's ability to appropriate the prevailing culture

---

105. "The Fathers," 392.

106. Ibid., 371. This unity and its subsequent sundering is the focus of the following chapter.

107. Balthasar believes that Neoplatonism is a philosophy of identity, and thus, threatens the ontological distinction between Creator and creation that Balthasar sees as essential to Christian teaching and practice. For a helpful discussion of the distinction Balthasar draws between these two, cf. Junius Johnson, *Christ and Analogy: The Christocentric Metaphysics of Hans Urs von Balthasar* (Minneapolis: Fortress Press, 2013), 12–13.

108. "The Fathers," 373.

as it learned to articulate its own understanding of God's relationship with the world.

Scholasticism, as Balthasar understands it, replaces the Patristic schema of participation with that of cause and effect. Christianity is no longer tempted to interpret the world as a declension from divine Being, but rather, as *creation*, granting it positive ontic weight.[109] Relying on de Lubac's articulation of the nature/grace relationship, Balthasar asserts that High Scholasticism composed a vision of the cosmos as nature permeated by the divine. Created Being is *essentially* related to God; "the supernatural really *is* inscribed in the fundamental outline of nature."[110] According to Balthasar, High Scholasticism understands the God–world relationship as one in which nature is open to God precisely *as* nature, not only as spirit. Balthasar gives this medieval metaphysic a particularly Ignatian twist by emphasizing that "the highest nobility of the creature consists in being essentially and ontically a constantly *available* tool of the divine praise and service."[111] Created being is characterized by the *potentia oboedientialis*; the perfection of created Being is "handing oneself over" to its creator in obedience and service and praise.[112]

The temptation of Scholasticism is rationalism. Even this rationalism is rooted in an over-reliance on the Platonic tradition that sees the surest path to God requiring movement away from the material and particular toward the spiritual and universal.[113] Scholasticism is still tempted to a philosophy of identity. Balthasar claims that this is the temptation of original sin, an intellectual titanism: the attempt to overcome the ontological difference between Creator and creature. This titanic drive is the thrust of the Hellenistic influence on Christianity that, despite Christianity's diligent attempts at transformation, nevertheless haunts the church's theology.

---

109. Ibid., 381.
110. Ibid., 383.
111. Ibid. Emphasis added.
112. One might say that Balthasar sees Scholastic metaphysics as the universalizing of the opening of the *Exercises*: "Man is created to praise, reverence, and serve God our Lord, and by this means save his soul." This is not just the vocation of humanity, but it is the living entelechy of all created Being.
113. "The Fathers," 384.

The Hellenistic temptation is finally addressed, Balthasar says, by the church in modernity. The modern era of Christianity consists of two main lines. The first is the progressive appreciation of the concrete, unique, and historical.[114] Though often bemoaned by critics of modernity—including Balthasar himself—the rise of philosophical nominalism allows for a deepened understanding of the individual.[115] This leads to the second line: *personalism*. In the modern era, Christianity understands revelation as the "personal self-disclosure" of God, a free expression that comes unbidden and unanticipated. In the modern era as Balthasar understands it, the God–world relationship focuses on its meeting in the particular, historical, incarnate person of Christ.

This personalism means that God's personal and free revelation in Christ "can be accepted only in the attitude of submission, surrender, faith and service."[116] In other words, it can be accepted only through the attitude of Ignatian *indiferencia*. Balthasar sees the modern era as bequeathing the possibility of a "dramatic" Christianity taking place in a "truly worldly world" with particular and historically situated actors. This is what Balthasar means when he says that the spiritual attitude of Christianity in the modern era is one that built upon that of the previous eras and now stands in positive relationship with the world. The Christian's call to "die to the world" is now a world-affirming death: "even the factor of the Christian mortification to the world stands under the more comprehensive sign of mission."[117]

Balthasar sees the eras of Christianity building upon each other, rounding each other out, strengthening and correcting the weak spots in each other. Each era depicts in its own way the undergirding logic of the church's engagement with the world, that *gratia non destruit, sed perficit naturam*.[118] The church is characterized by mission to the

---

114. Ibid., 386.
115. There are, of course, dangers here. When nature becomes closed in on itself (rather than open to God as it was in Scholasticism), empiricism, rationalism, Deism, materialism, and historicism may follow.
116. "The Fathers," 387.
117. Ibid.
118. "Grace does not destroy but rather perfects nature."

world; the bastions of the church cannot but be razed. The church bears divine grace into the world not to condemn it, but to bring it to its perfection in God by "being in Christ." Each era has attempted this in its own way, each with its own strengths and weaknesses. The modern Christian stands in relation to the previous eras of the church, not as a stranger or corrective, but as the ongoing development of the inner structure of Christianity—namely, coming to share in the life of Christ. To share in the life of Christ is to share in Christ's mission: his incorporating descent into the world that elevates and perfects nature. Though he does not yet develop this line of thinking, this early discussion clearly reflects his later claim that it is through the obedience of love that the Christian comes to union with Christ. "Being in Christ" means sharing through the obedience of my personal freedom in Christ's mission. This is the foundation of his later theo-dramatic style of theology and a clear echo of Ignatius.

This is also where Balthasar's theology of the saints emerges. The saintly theology that he proposes plays in the intersection of Balthasar's critique of (German) modernity and his *ressourcement* project. The theology of the saints is theology on mission, the way the Christian comes to be "in Christ":

> But for modern man the rebirth that grounds love is primarily a being placed in the movement of Christ: descending from God into nature. God's "trinitarian life" expresses itself in the sending (*missio*) of the Son from the Father, in which sending the Spirit of love has his origin and *raison d'être*. For the mode of person, therefore, the statement that "God is all in all" bears the marks of an openness to the world in the manner of Ignatius' "Hollar Dios en todas las cosas" ("Finding God in all Things"). But not in the sense of a luxurious wallowing in "personal relationships," but by strictly following out Christ's mission. Thus love will certainly emphasize the "contrast" with God (*contra* the Fathers). But this "contrast" with God will be seen as the consummation of that creaturely law that decrees that we are not God and are therefore called to obey. Love and "friendship" become as it were (to use a rather oversubtle formula), the "soul" and the super-elevation of the relationship of service and obedience that is the ground of nature: *amor non tollit sed perficit et elevat oboedientiam* [love does not remove but perfects and elevates obedience]—just as the meaning of Christ's love is also perfected in his perfect obedience; that is, in the total renunciation of his selfhood as the "servant of the Lord" in Cross and

death. For it is here, in his self-disappearing and "descending" that God's love for the world manifests and perfects itself. So where the creature is most a creature, God is most God. The Christian helps to bring about this self-emptying of Christ, and does so in a "galling" service for the redemption of the world.[119]

Balthasar's construal of the task of *ressourcement* and the mission of the church come together in his theology of the saints. In the spirit of *ressourcement*, his theology *of* the saints will be a theology *with* the saints, a way of doing theology in the spirit of the Fathers and Scholastics that imitates their attitude of engagement with the world from a contemporary perspective *and* distinctly Christian—or *Christic* —heart.

The Catholicity of Truth

The purpose of these first two chapters is to introduce and orient our subsequent study of Balthasar's theology of the saints and his doctrine of truth as they are grounded in his cultural, ecclesial context and shaped by his Ignatian character. These themes are held together by Balthasar's vision of the catholicity of truth. As is well known, Balthasar believes that truth is ultimately symphonic—the harmony of difference, sounding together.

Ultimately, Balthasar's intellectual and cultural projection can perhaps best be read as an extension of Przywara's doctrine of analogy. For Balthasar, his master's distinctive take on analogy makes possible the task of Catholic integration.[120] As we have seen, Przywara opened Balthasar's eyes to the universalism of Catholic truth. Przywara showed Balthasar, "in contrast to the narrowness of scholastic theology, the *world-spanning dimensions* of what is Catholic."[121]

For Balthasar, the task of the church in the world is an evangelistic one. But the church evangelizes through the method of integration

---

119. "The Fathers," 396.
120. Cf. Peter Casarella's "Hans Urs von Balthasar, Erich Przywara's *Analogia Entis*, and the Problem of a Catholic *Denkform,*" in *The Analogy of Being: Invention of the Antichrist or the Wisdom of God?*, ed. Thomas Joseph White (Grand Rapids: Eerdmans, 2011), 192–206. Casarella helpfully shows the way that Przywara's *analogia entis* takes on a robustly christological form in Balthasar's works.
121. Balthasar, *Our Task*, trans. John Saward (San Francisco: Ignatius Press, 1994), 103. Emphasis added.

—enfolding truths scattered abroad in the world into the breadth of Christian truth. As he says at the opening of his *Epilogue*: "*Wer mehr Wahrheit siegt, hat mehr recht.*"[122] What he means by this is that less extensive truths are integrated into more comprehensive ones.

But there is a real danger with the method of integration. Those who integrate truths from a purely immanent (intra-worldly) perspective end up not with Christ, but with Hegel. The method of integration and synthesis is a Hegelian method and one that, if left unchecked, can overtake the mystery of God's loving freedom with absolute knowledge. Balthasar insists that the idealism of the method of integration must, in Christian terms, come together with the historical uniqueness of Christ.[123] Ultimately, the integration will happen through a free irradiation of grace "flowing out into the whole of history from its Christological center."[124]

One of the chief images Balthasar uses to express this point is the symphony. In a symphony, difference cannot be ignored or obliterated without signaling the end of the music. The interplay of difference, whether the difference between instrument or the chords of a single instrument, is co-extensive with the symphony itself. Yet, the successful symphony is an ordered unity—all difference is held together in the harmony of a single, overarching music. The symphony gathers in the differences around a common center: the common task of harmony. Similarly, all truth is harmoniously integrated around the common center of divine truth: the person of Christ. This in-gathering is the *Catholic* nature of the symphonic art. The symphony integrates and harmonizes difference, just as the *Catholica* strives to do with truth.

Balthasar relies on Przywara's version of the *analogia entis* to make sense of the catholicity, or symphony, of truth. The *analogia entis* evokes the dynamism of created Being's movement toward God. As a

---

122. "Whoever sees more of the truth is more profoundly right" (*Epilogue*, 15).

123. There is a critical impasse between the "ideal" and the "historical" that a Christian understanding of truth must overcome: how can immanent worldly truth come together with the transcendent? How can the universal meet the particular? Balthasar addresses this issue by way of de Lubac and the paradox "of a nature directed toward reaching God but whose natural powers render that goal unattainable" (*Epilogue*, 18).

124. Ibid., 18.

principle of Catholic metaphysical thought, analogy is the way "the all-encompassing 'yes' to revelation maintains room for every creaturely thought that can be saved and has been saved, given that the 'yes' is a way of salvation from the ever-recurrent 'no' of the sinner."[125] But as we have seen, Balthasar resists an interpretation of the *analogia entis* that refuses the task of integration—whether it be through neo-scholastic isolationism or liberal relativization of difference. The church's mission in the world is an integration that transforms.

> [The church] tries in obedience to Christ to be what he called her to be: the custodian of his graces and the evangelist of his works and words. With the task of being an evangelist come healing, preaching, and pastoral responsibilities. If she occasionally also has to take a position with respect to principles of thought, she will mainly do so where some way of thinking has circumscribed the broad compass of its proclamation and where she can knock an obstacle out of the way for the sake of achieving breadth.[126]

The method of integration ultimately requires a decision for or against the unifying form (*Gestalt*) of Christian truth—that the "final form of Being is God in Christ in the Church."[127] Just as there is no pure nature, there is also no purely natural religion. There is, for Balthasar, the either/or choice between God and idols: "truth-seeking (*catholicus*)" or "idol-worshipping (*paganus*)."[128] Catholic truth-seeking may find truth abroad, but it must return those truths to their source: the incarnate Christ, the Word of God's truth. The form of Christ becomes, for Balthasar, the key to a distinctively Catholic engagement with the world—the Ignatian calling to the church. And so, if the *analogia entis* determines every expression of Balthasar's thought, then Christ himself is the analogy. All things must be rethought in the light of the christological norm of history and Being.

According to Balthasar, Przywara's analogy is ultimately a christological doctrine. The metaphysics of Przywara's *Analogia Entis*

125. *TKB*, quoted in Casarella, 199.
126. *TKB*, 266. Quoted in Casarella, 194.
127. Casarella, 198.
128. Ibid.

gradually push toward the Christology of Przywara's later *Deus semper maior*. According to Balthasar,

> the major work *Deus semper maior* is a singular, inexorable reduction of all relations to one single relation: God in the crucified Christ in the co-crucified church, the intertwining of every direct statement about and relationship between God and man into the dialectic of the self-crossing beam of the cross (as the only concrete form of negative theology) . . . Przywara consequently takes the path of norming all logic (and thus ontology) by this Christological-historical-actualistic standard.[129]

We see traces of Balthasar's own attempt to norm history and Being to the form of Christ throughout his works. It is present in his early *Theology of History* (1959) and reaches its mature expression in his Trilogy, especially in *Theo-Drama* 3, and as the rest of this book shall show, in the *Theo-Logic* series. The latter, especially, follows Przywara's task of "norming all logic (and thus ontology)" by a historical, actualist, and the metaphysical Christology. In the catholicity of Christ's incarnate flesh, divine and worldly truth come together as symphony.

The symphonic catholicity of truth has both an objective and a subjective form. Objectively, the catholicity of truth means that all forms of expression of truth are gathered around a common center. For Balthasar, this center is the *Gestalt* of Christ. Subjectively, the symphony of truth draws on a variety of forms of knowing or apprehending truth. In the context of the current study, this distinctively Catholic of knowing—the "Catholic truth and attitude"—is done by the saints.

Catholic *Denkenform*

Hegel long believed, "that he could interpret divine life and its evolution in the world under the leading idea of love; but finally this notion disappears modestly into the interior of absolute knowledge."[130] Balthasar's project, then, is an attempt to accomplish what Hegel had rejected. Balthasar will interpret Being as love, and thus, counter

---

129. Ibid.
130. O'Regan, *Anatomy*, 206–7.

Hegel's titanic privileging of knowledge over love. The saints are Balthasar's chief defense against the sophist.

Balthasar's written work engages the philosophical—and more narrowly Hegelian—intellectual culture of his day in an Ignatian spirit, finding in the world kernels of divine truth scattered abroad—a "finding God in all things." Such a finding is possible only within a sacramental vision of the world, where the truth of Being is expressed in a myriad of forms and known primarily through love.

In the opening to *Love Alone*, Balthasar calls to mind Nicholas of Cusa's *De pace fidei*. Set before the throne of heaven, all the philosophers and teachers of the world come before the living Christ and propound their doctrine. Christ, sitting as the supreme teacher and judge of truth, gradually enfolds these truths into his own truth, showing his person to be the fulfillment of all worldly truth. All worldly knowledge ultimately gestures toward him as the central figure, the absolute form (*Gestalt*) of truth. In such a world, Balthasar's drive to "find God in all things" is possible.

But finding God in all things is not merely an intellectual or aesthetic exercise. It is, as we have seen, evangelization. As a disciple of Ignatius, Balthasar's work is characterized by its emphasis on mission. The catholicity of Christian truth is an invitation to enter into its fullness. For Balthasar, it is ultimately an invitation into the life of God, to participate in the One who is that truth (John 14:6).

Such an invitation is only possible if Catholicism can faithfully proclaim its vision of the world. This can only happen if Catholic thought manages to be open to the world while maintaining its distinctively Catholic character, not becoming a baptized form of socialism, liberalism, idealism, or any other -ism. The church can continue to "spoil the Egyptians," but all truth found abroad must be brought home and transformed by Christ. This is the church of Pentecost; it is what Balthasar sees Ignatius charging the church to be in and for the world.

Such engagement will take seriously the intellectual thought patterns of the day, understanding them and treating them critically but sympathetically. Most importantly, a distinctively Catholic engagement with the world will begin—not with the premises of the prevailing secular philosophy—but with the unique form (*Gestalt*) of Christ who, as we shall see in what follows, is the concrete universal, the norm of history and the heart of the world.

But equally important to a distinctively Catholic engagement with the world is the goal of such engagement. If the goal is cultural relevance, assimilation, or the demythologization of the peculiarities of the Gospel, Balthasar insists that this relativizes the need for a specifically *Christian* identity. Instead, the goal of a distinctively Catholic engagement with the world is the offering of one's life in service to one's neighbors as an expression of one's love for God and an image of God's love for the world through Christ.[131] The form of divine love manifested in Christ is thus the source, heart, and goal of a distinctively Catholic engagement with the world. This is what the *Ernstfall* is for Balthasar. We can interpret all of Balthasar's work in light of this central claim.

What then will model this distinctively Catholic form of engagement? Balthasar does not believe that papal decrees or institutions or even councils can serve as beacons to help the church find her bearings in this new world in which she finds herself. What the church needs are the saints.[132] It is the captivating form of saintly lives, especially the splendor of their sanctity, that will enliven, enrich, and guide the church. All of Balthasar's cultural work, both pre- and post-conciliar, is ultimately a call for a return to the saints as a wellspring of the church's life and mission.

But his is not just a call to remember the saints, but also to become them: "It is not true that we can do nothing to get saints. For example, we ought at least to try, though a bit belatedly, to become something like them ourselves. Better late than never."[133] Saintliness is the way forward for the church in the world: "whoever desires greater action needs greater contemplation; whoever wants to play a more formative

131. *MCW*, 133.
132. Ibid., 155.
133. Ibid.

role must pray and obey more profoundly; . . . lest everything in the Church become superficial and insipid, the true undiminished program for the Church today must read: the great possible radiance in the world by virtue of the closest following of Christ."[134]

And so, here the threads of this project converge: Balthasar's Ignatian emphasis on mission and service involves a distinctively Catholic form of engagement with the world. This is the vocation of the saints. And so, at the heart of Balthasar's Ignatian cultural work stand the saints, those whose lives express that divine love is the truth of all things. Balthasar's theological project is, above all, a saintly theology, one in which the truth of Being is known *as* and *by* love.

To the saints, then, our attention now turns, for it is in them that we find the distinctively Catholic *Denkenform* that addresses and fulfills the longing of the world for truth.

134. *MW*, 57–58.

3

___

Saints, Truth, and Theology

What is a Theology of the Saints?

For Balthasar, a distinctively Catholic approach to the question of truth will necessarily be theological and not solely philosophical. Unlike the philosophies of Idealism, Balthasar does not allow for a fully immanentized philosophy that sees the truth of God arising solely from inner-worldly truth. He inverts Hegel, arguing that divine truth is the source and possibility of the world's truth. For Balthasar, God is the absolute source and goal of the world's own Being and knowing.

Balthasar holds that the drama of salvation reveals that truth is Trinitarian love, as confessed in Catholic dogma. This means that the nature of truth must be conceived in a distinctively Catholic way. This re-imagining is the goal of Balthasar's *Theo-Logic*. But, going further, his account of the truth of Being also demands a distinctively Catholic form of understanding. This is his theology of the saints. For Balthasar, the saints represent the distinctively Catholic form of understanding (*Verstehen*) truth. As such, saints are an integral component to Balthasar's account of theological and metaphysical truth.

It may seem an odd pairing, the spirituality of the saints and the rigorous speculative thought of the *Theo-Logic*. What have the saints to do with Balthasar's speculative philosophy and theology of truth? But the very fact that we question the relationship between truth and the saints shows that we are operating with impoverished understanding of both.

For Balthasar, truth is the living exposition of thought in practice, the harmony of contemplation and action. The saints *are* this expositing practice, this harmony, this concrete existence that illuminates speculative thought. As such, the saints function as the paradigmatic form (*Gestalt*) of knowledge of truth. Theirs is the form of a "theological existence" that participates in and represents the truth of Christ. Through the witness of saints' lives, "the truth of Christian doctrine is grasped and becomes followable in the Church."[1] The saints help theology return again and again to the ever-new encounter with the divine mystery of triune love revealed in Jesus Christ.

The saints know and make known the truth of Christ because of their relation to the Holy Spirit, whom Balthasar names the Spirit of love and the Spirit of truth. For Balthasar, the third person of the Trinity is the Spirit of truth *as* the Spirt of love. In the Spirit, truth and love are united. It is the role of the Spirit to lead the followers of Christ "into all truth" (John 16:13–14), that is, into the fullness of the truth that is Christ himself. Because the truth in Christ is infinite (Col 2:3), "it will be impossible to come to an end in declaring this truth all down the ages, for although this truth resides in an apparently limited spatio-temporal phenomenon, it is nonetheless 'the whole fullness of deity [dwelling] bodily' (Col 2:9)."[2] The Spirit further elaborates on the infinite truth of God revealed in Christ through the free disposal of charisms, "glimpses of the very center of revelation" that "enrich the Church in the most unexpected and yet permanent way."[3] These charisms have both objective and subjective dimensions, neither of which can be neatly distinguished from the other. The objective truth of the Spirit is the institution of the Church: its offices, orders, and

---

1. Moss, "The Saints," 83.
2. *TL* 3, 21.
3. Ibid.

sacraments. The subjective truth of the Spirit is the prayers of the saints: the pneumatic disclosure of objective revelation realized in the saints' missions of personal holiness. The saints' lives are thus part of the Spirit's subjective work of preserving the truth of God present in the church. The saints serve as one dimension of the Spirit's guidance into "all truth."[4]

Characteristics of the Saints

Balthasar derives his core understanding of the saints from Ignatius, especially insofar as the latter develops an understanding of a spiritual, contemplative life characterized by receptivity, obedience, and mission.

Receptivity is the key concept for Balthasar's theology of the saints. Ignatius unsurprisingly influences Balthasar's understanding of receptivity. Receptivity is disposition, a way of being, in addition to being a concrete action. The receptivity of the saint means that she is marked by openness to God and the world. Balthasar is certainly not unique in this understanding of receptivity. The originality of Balthasar's theology comes in the way he parallels the receptivity of the saints, with the receptivity of the act of knowing, and even with the receptivity of Being itself. Receptivity is the convergence point for Balthasar's spirituality, epistemology, and metaphysics.

Moreover, Balthasar insists that the openness that characterizes created Being depends analogically on a fundamental and eternal openness in the life of the Trinity. Balthasar holds that creaturely receptivity depends on the eternal receptivity of Father, Son, and Holy Spirit in the eternal act of kenosis.[5] For Balthasar, metaphysical truth and human knowing are both analogical reflections of the divine. There is an essential symmetry between Balthasar's use of receptivity in his metaphysical, epistemological, and dogmatic thought, and its role in his theology of the saints and his Ignatian spirituality. The inter-

---

4. See Jacques Servais, "Finding God in All Things," *Communio*, vol. 30, no. 2 (2003): 209–81.
5. This topic will be further explored in chapter five.

subjectivity of the lives of the saints through the dialogue of prayer matches the receptivity, inter-subjectivity, and dialogue of truth.[6]

For Balthasar, receptivity is the key disposition of love. As such, it penetrates the heart of the God who is love. It is this mystery of eternal love that is marked by the rhythm of gift and receptivity in which the saint participates. Receptivity implies both *gift* and *giver*: something to be received and someone to do the giving. What is received is the gift of Being and the giver is God, who is also the gift. The receptivity of the saint is an image of this rhythm of gift and receptivity between God and the world. In the way she relates to God, the saint also exposits the mystery of Being itself.

Again recalling Ignatius, Balthasar combines receptivity with obedience. The principal image of saintly obedience for Balthasar is the Marian *fiat*—the "yes" wherein the saint offers herself as the handmaid of the Lord.[7] Mary's *fiat* perfectly exemplifies the receptivity and obedience that characterizes the saints.

What the saint receives, what she is obedient to, is her calling to a particular mission. The saints share in the singular mission of Christ to make the Father known, but they do so in their own particular ways.[8] "If men are to have a part in the One who is sent, they in turn must be sent out by him . . . the man who has a part in the 'Son' must be sent out from the Son's source."[9]

The saints are called to their missions in order to universalize Christ's own mission of truth. While the mission of the Son is unique, it is capable of imitation.[10] In order for Christ's mission to be universal

---

6. Balthasar's emphasis on dialogue in the *Theo-Logic* should come as little surprise. The concept of dialogue was in the midst of a renaissance while Balthasar composed his Trilogy, both in terms of the philosophical dialogicians (such as Martin Buber), but also in the language of the Second Vatican Council. According to Ratzinger, *Gaudium et Spes*, the pastoral constitution on the church in the world, is fundamentally determined by the idea of dialogue. Cf. Jospeh Ratzinger, "The Dignity of the Human Person," in Herbert Vorgrimler, ed., *Commentary On the Documents of Vatican II* (New York: The Crossroad Publishing Company, 1989), 117.

7. For Balthasar, Mary's *fiat* is a metaphysical act. Similar to how God's *fiat* in Genesis 1—*Fiat lux!*—gives rise to the world, so Mary's own *fiat* issues in the incarnation of Emmanuel, God-with-us, the agent of the re-creation of the world of sin and death.

8. Balthasar's interpretation of Christ's mission relies on John's presentation: Christ is the truth (John 14:6), who comes to make the Father known (14:7) through the Spirit of truth (16:13).

9. *TD* 3, 154.

10. The saints imitate Christ by participating in his life. Balthasar thus sets his spirituality apart from

rather than a singular historical event, the saints are the vessels that the Holy Spirit uses to interpret this truth throughout the ages. The saints are those who share in the mission of Christ, and, by so doing, they share in the ongoing dramatic realization of his divine mission.[11]

By participating in Christ's mission, the saints also come to share in the triune life of God. The mission of Christ is to reveal the Father (John 17:26), but this revelation does not happen apart from the Spirit.[12] Indeed, the sending (*missio*) of the Son springs from a primordial proceeding (*processio*) from the Father in the Spirit.[13] Though the particularities of each saint's subjective and personal realization of the mission of Christ may differ, they all contribute to the continual unfolding of the objective teaching of the church, the passing on of the truth of the triune God revealed in Jesus Christ. This is the common mission of all of the saints.

Balthasar is well aware of the tendency to relegate the saints to forms of subjective piety. But it is through the concept of mission that he breaks open the "hollow human subjectivity" that has, since the late medieval period, characterized the spirituality and the mysticism of the saints.[14] He argues that the objective mission of the saints is to

the imitation of the *devotio moderna*, best exemplified in Thomas à Kempis, *The Imitation of Christ*, in the fifteenth century.

11. Here, Sam Wells' criticism of Balthasar's dramatic theory as being too "epic" (that is, disembodied and extrinsic) rather than "improvisational" misses the point. Wells proposes improvisation as a solution to the criticism of Balthasar's project being "too much about God" (50); improvisation, so Wells claims, adds a human, existential, and ethical dimension to Balthasar's project. It gives humans a part to play in the drama of God. But Wells's account fails to see how Balthasar's *Theo-Drama* is not complete in itself, but requires his theology of the saints to bring it to completion. It is the nature of the drama that it cannot be observed in any kind of detached way, but draws the audience into active participation in it. This is the heart of Balthasar's concept of mission (not to mention his understanding of ethics). See Samuel Wells, *Improvisation: The Drama of Christian Ethics* (Grand Rapids: Baker, 2004), 50–70. See also Christopher W. Steck, *The Ethical Thought of Hans Urs von Balthasar* (New York: Crossroads, 2001). For Balthasar's account of epic versus lyrical theology, see TD 2, 57. Especially interesting to note is that Balthasar sees the *dramatic* as the union of "spirituality" and "theology."

12. Balthasar is deeply indebted to Bonaventure at this point. He goes on: "Even in the economic order, the logic of the incarnate Son cannot be restricted to the 'historical Jesus', but includes his 'from' the Father and his 'toward' the Spirit." See TL 2, 151–57. For Balthasar, it is absolutely the case that *Christus medium tenens in omnibus* [Christ hold[s] the middle in all things].

13. *TD* 3, 154.

14. Like many of his contemporaries, Balthasar is keenly interested in mysticism, both as an element of generic "religious experience," and especially as an element of the Christian tradition. But he rejects the mystalogical preoccupation he finds in so many accounts of mysticism as an undue fascination with inner states and heightened experiences. He critiques this as a reduction to subjectivist, experiential mysticism, which is, he believes, inherently individualistic, isolated from

express through their subjectivity the truth of God in Christ. As such, "mission" functions for Balthasar as the harmonious meeting place of the subjectivity of saintly lives and the objectivity of their mission from Christ for the nourishment of the church.[15]

Saints and Balthasar's Genealogy of Modernity

The saints are integral to Balthasar's understanding of truth. The tragedy, however, is that the saint as Balthasar conceives her is increasingly rare in the modern world. This absence is part of modernity's tragic severing from the past and accounts for the deep malaise of our contemporary world, both ecclesial and intellectual. More than anything else, Balthasar sees modernity as a distinctly *spiritual* problem.

The remainder of this chapter is concerned with Balthasar's spiritual genealogy of modernity.[16] Much ink has been spilled analyzing and

its proper *telos*—the communion of saints. Subjectivist mysticism is not a mysticism of love, and therefore, not a true ecstasy. Genuine mystical *ecstasis* comes only in kenotic self-giving that is an image of Triune love, participation in the christological mission.

But Balthasar takes care not to reject the subjective element of mysticism all together. He situates it rather *within* the overarching objective reality of that overwhelming *mysterion*—the original mystery "that has to do with the divine reality hidden under the forms of the human and worldly in the Bible and liturgy." This mystery is objectively given in the free act of creation (which is itself an act of divine self-disclosure), in the formation of Israel, and most fully and truly in the gift of Christ. This objective mystery always retains its primacy in Christian mysticism. But as Balthasar never tires of saying, what is objectively *given* must be subjectively *received*. There is a proper ordering for Balthasar. First comes the objective mystery (to which the "full readiness of faith" is the expected response) and "only then personal experience: which *each* believer living out his faith will let flow, each in his own way, from the mystery of the Cross and Resurrection of Christ and the outpouring of the Holy Spirit." Cf. "Understanding Christian Mysticism," in *ET* 4, 334. What we have then is the primacy of objective mystery freely given by God, and then, the subjective reception of that mystery in faith. This faith is decidedly ordinary for Balthasar—it is common to each and every believer as the necessary subjective response to the objective gift of God. But it is still mystical because it is the reception of the mystery—the mystical emerges first and foremost in the ordinary. Thus the Ignatian injunction to find God in all things.

It is only within this rhythm of objective donation/subjective response that extraordinary mystical experiences may emerge. But again, these extraordinary events are not meant to be accentuated subjective experiences. They are rather "special experiences given to individual believers for the benefit of others." Extraordinary visions and experiences are therefore possible in Christian mysticism though their importance is relativized. They are present, not for the edification of the individual, but rather, for the edification of the church, as a participation in Christ's own mission of love.

15. See *MW*, 30–37.
16. The genealogy that Balthasar sets out in *GL* 4 and 5 should not be taken primarily as a narrative of the rise and fall of Christian metaphysics. Rather than narrating a history, *GL* 4 and 5 give an aesthetic of Christian integration. Balthasar shows how Christianity enters into history and

critiquing Balthasar's genealogy. The goal here is simply to offer an interpretation of an interpretation. That is, the account represented here is a way of reading Balthasar's genealogy as a narrative of the loss of the saints or of modernity's spiritual crisis of "misremembering."[17]

The Stakes of Theological Sanctity

For Balthasar, one of the greatest threats to the integrity of the church's mission in the world has been the lack of great theologians who were also saints, and great saints who were also theologians. This is the problem that he addresses in his well-known essay, "Theology and Sanctity."[18] According to Balthasar, spirituality and theology necessarily complete each other. Their divorce is artificial because it represents a fundamental misunderstanding of the true vocation of each. A theology "at desk" insufficiently understands truth apart from a "kneeling theology" or a theology at prayer.

Balthasar sees in modernity a startling and unnatural fragmentation between the theologian and the saint, between the thinker and the lover.[19] What is at stake in this fragmentation between the theologian and the saint is not just the fragmentation of intellect and spirituality, but also the disintegration of truth and knowledge. The saint is one who holds the various dimensions of truth together in symphonic harmony. This harmony is love: intellectual and spiritual, the love of wisdom and the love of God. Saints are, above all, else lovers of God; it

---

fulfills the highest hopes of pagan myth and philosophy. He is not attempting an intellectual history per se. He is painting an image of Christianity as the integrative power of divine truth incorporating the world's truth into itself. Balthasar's genealogy of metaphysics at its heart is his way of showing Christianity's genuine *catholicity*.

17. Cf. O'Regan, *Anatomy of Misremembering*.
18. *ET* 1, 181–209. What is especially interesting about this essay is its placement in this volume of collected essays. It falls in the section titled "Word and Redemption" (the other section of essays in this volume is titled "Word and Revelation"). This placement is extremely revealing. For Balthasar, the lives of the saints spiral out from that primal Word of God, the redeeming work of Jesus Christ. The saints find themselves within the drama of redemption.
19. Balthasar is certainly not alone in identifying this division between the thinker and the lover as a problem for theology. Dante, the great poet of Christendom, juxtaposes in the realm of the Sun, the ring of the theologians and the ring of the lovers. The "reconciliation" of St. Thomas Aquinas and St. Bonaventure in *Paradiso* X–XIII represents a Dantean version of the Balthasarian task—the reunification of the speculative and the affective.

is lovers who know God most truly.[20] The saints are the ones who know truth in its most integrated reality.

For Balthasar, truth is of *all* Being. The loss of the saints has broader consequences than only for spirituality. The exile of the saints from truth has consequences for spirituality, theology, and metaphysics. Balthasar's genealogy tells the story of the divorce between the theologian and the saint that is, at the same time, a story of the crisis in metaphysics.

The Loss of the Saints

Balthasar denies the possibility of purely conceptual truth that can be known apart from engaged, subjective encounter. Truth cannot be known exclusively by detached, discursive reason (*Wissen*). Knowledge is participative and performative. As he makes clear, "there is simply no real truth which does not have to be incarnated in an act or in some action."[21] This understanding of truth undergirds Balthasar's theology of the saints. Saints know the truth by performing it. Their theology, philosophy, and metaphysics arise from the action of their lives manifested in their receptivity, obedience, and prayer. It is through prayer especially that the saints perform the truth of Being, knowing it and making it known. Balthasar claims that it is the saints more than the philosophers who make the best metaphysicians. We must now turn our attention to the way Balthasar grounds this claim in his broader discussions of metaphysics, epistemology, and Christology.

***

Balthasar sees no simplistic distinction between doctrine and spirituality. He resists modern theology's easy reification of both into isolated categories. He labors fervently for their reintegration. This integration was certainly the case with the Fathers of the church: "When Irenaeus, Basil, Gregory of Nazianzen or Augustine argue with

---

20. "Lovers are the ones who know most about God; the theologian must listen to them" (*LA*, 12).
21. "Theology and Sanctity," in *ET* 1, 181.

their adversaries, they do not operate in a forecourt of theology, but in its very center." In this early unity, we see the harmony of subjectivity and objectivity, each at play, each making room for the other: "[t]he Fathers found straightaway the appropriate dogmatic clothing for their very personal experience; everything became objective, and all subjective conditions, experiences, fears, strivings, the 'shock' in a word, were made to serve a fuller understanding of the content of revelation, to orchestrate its great themes."[22]

How, then, did the unnatural separation of theology and sanctity, and the subsequent fragmentation of truth, come to pass? Balthasar traces the disintegration of the unity of theology and sanctity to the late Middle Ages. Early medievals such as Anselm, Bede, Bernard of Clairvaux, and Peter Damian "knew no other canon of truth than the unity of knowledge and life."[23] Yet, the rediscovery of Aristotle by the West demanded certain theological concessions. Aristotle's philosophy granted to nature (and hence to philosophy) a new sense of autonomy in which a self-contained natural or philosophical truth exists. This distinctly philosophical conception of truth—*adaequatio intellectus ad rem* (the conformity of the mind to reality)—"envisaged, primarily, only the theoretical side of truth."[24] Rather than utilizing philosophical concepts as pointers to divine truth, theology granted these concepts independence that isolated them from larger theological concerns. No longer were philosophical concepts primarily "taken up as part of the

---

22. This, and the preceding quote are from "Theology and Sanctity," in *ET* 1, 190. The pattern that Balthasar identifies for the saints is grounded in Paul's own theology: "It had not yet been forgotten that Paul took all the subjective charismata and, far from rejecting them, or setting them aside, resolutely freed them from the dangers of subjectivism and reoriented them by inserting them into the factual structure of the Church." What made this harmony of subjectivity and objectivity so natural was the primacy of the church—the subjective "experiences" of the saints exist not for themselves but for the sake of the church, as a further articulation of revelation disclosed to the church. Sainthood is an ecclesial vocation.

23. "Theology and Sanctity," in *ET* 1, 184. It is interesting to note that Balthasar explicitly affirms these theologian-saints as operating "under the aegis of Augustine" opposed to those "scholastic" thinkers who operate under the "elemental force" of Aristotelianism. We should note, in light of these comments, that Balthasar makes no attempt at a "neutral" history. He clearly distances himself from the late scholastic style, identifying it as a major contributor to the sundering of theology and sanctity, at least in terms of theological style.

24. Ibid., 185. Maurice Blondel is in the background of Balthasar's concern, especially his claim that human action is the embodiment of theoretical, or metaphysical truth: "Human life is metaphysics in act." See Maurice Blondel, *The Letter on Apologetics & History and Dogma*, trans. Alexander Dru and Illtyd Trethowan (Grand Rapids: Eerdmans, 1994), 237.

assumptio humanae naturae in Christ . . . [that they might be] 'transfigured', and become, like Christ's humanity, wholly a function and expression of his divine person and truth."[25] Instead, philosophy became an independent discipline while nature became an independent and autonomous thing.[26] Both come to neglect the christic form (*Gestalt*) that is their inner logic.[27]

The effects of this shift were not immediately felt. Albert, Bonaventure and Aquinas were "peculiarly fitted for theology to irradiate and transfigure the self-subsisting science of nature [and philosophy], raising it to the plane of the sacred, and so to impart to the secular sciences a real Christian ethos, *one affecting the whole outlook of the scientific investigator.*"[28] They were fundamentally contemplative thinkers.[29]

But this equilibrium could not stand. Subsequent generations lacked the brilliance to accomplish this difficult, synthetic task. Philosophical propaedeutics to theology begin to emerge as formulations of fixed, unalterable, and religiously neutral norms and concepts that determine, without any substantial translation, the subsequent theologies. This was a threat that first emerged in Aquinas' day with the growing influence of Averroism and its philosophical isolationism. Through the influence of Averroes, philosophy and theology were each granted their own truth—philosophy addresses the truth of Being known through reason while theology addresses the truth of God known through faith. Theology loses sight of Being, surrendering it to an autonomous, isolated, and myopic philosophy.[30] Revelation ceases

---

25. Ibid. See also Peter Henrici, "The Spiritual Dimension and its Form of Reason," *Communio*, vol. 20, no. 4 (1993): 639–40 for another interpretation of this genealogy.
26. See Balthasar's claims in *TKB*, 267–80. More will be said of this in the next chapter.
27. See chapter five for an extended discussion of Christ as the archetypal of Being.
28. "Theology and Sanctity," 185. Emphasis added.
29. In other words, these great medievals understood the truth theologically and sacramentally —seeing the intelligible in the sensible, the divine in the worldly. As this study progresses, we shall increasingly use the term "contemplative" to describe this kind of understanding of worldly truth as illumined by divine.
30. This autonomous philosophy does not long maintain its association with Being. As doubts grow about the speculative powers of reason, philosophy makes the turn to nominalism and from there to epistemology. Cf. Pope John Paul II, *Fides et Ratio: On the Relationship between Faith and Reason* (Boston, Pauline Books and Media, 1998), 85. A figure such as George Berkeley (a staunch opponent of empiricists such as Locke and Hume) will even acknowledge that God can grant a subjective

to play a role in metaphysical speculation. This loss of revelation inhibits viable discourse about the God–world relationship because knowledge of the former is severed from knowledge of the latter. When the *philosophical* mystery of Being was isolated in itself, the theological mystery was forced to retreat from metaphysical discourse. Balthasar sees this as resulting in a kind of spiritualization of faith and doctrine. Christ's truth becomes parochial, designated a "religious" truth rather than a universal one.

The consequence of this disintegration is that truth was re-defined as purely intellectual concept. While truth had once been defined as the union of knowledge and holiness, the speculative and the spiritual, it came to be defined as a purely intellectual adequation between mind and object.[31] The church comes to relegate the spiritual to the science of interiority of the *devotio moderna*, a transposition of medieval mysticism into an increasingly focused study of the subjective states of extraordinary spiritual experiences.[32] The purpose of saintly existence shifts away from the active encounter of subject and object in love of truth to "one of subjective experience, individual states."[33] The more dogmatic theology becomes beholden to philosophical propaedeutic, the more exclusively it focuses on a narrowly conceptual understanding of truth. Those untrained (or disinterested) in philosophy come to be relegated to their own exclusive science of the "spiritual life" as something distinct from speculative theology. This is the beginning of "spirituality" as a reified study. In this spirituality, the

experience dissociated from the appearing of an object—"an epistemological smile on the face of an ontologically evanescent Cheshire cat" (Nichols, *The Word Has Been Abroad*, 147).

31. As a committed realist, Balthasar does not want to dispense entirely with this notion, but he does seek to enrich and extend it.

32. Readers should take care not to interpret Balthasar as suggesting that the *devotio moderna* was intrinsically negative or lacking in teachers of holiness. On the contrary, "we continue to find saints. [But] it is also true that, later, there were still teachers who were saints: John of the Cross was a doctor . . . Canisius—certainly no theologian—was an interpreter of doctrine to ordinary people; Bellarmine a controversialist; Alphonsus a moralist. None of them centered his life, I do not say on dogma, on dogmatic theology" ("Theology and Sanctity," 191–92).

33. Balthasar consistently accuses the late medieval Spanish mystics of an indulgent preoccupation with the science of the interior life ("Theology and Sanctity," in *ET* 1, 190–91, and "Understanding Christian Mysticism," in *ET* 4, 318–29). In contrast, he holds Saint Thérèse of Lisieux and Saint Elizabeth of the Trinity as supreme examples of Christian self-forgetfulness that fuels their *ecclesial* spirituality. Adrienne von Speyr is, for Balthasar, another example of this kind of ecclesial mysticism.

objective truth of revelation derives from the inner states that reveal them. An example of this tendency might be found in early modern Spanish mysticism (e.g.: St. John of the Cross), wherein an objective doctrine of the dark night of the soul emerges *from* the subjective experience of that dark night.[34] This is the ghettoization of the saints and the mystics, exiling them to the shadowy regions of subjective experientialism. Balthasar claims that the saints of the *devotio moderna* have a distinctly different focus from that of the saints of earlier periods. The focus of the new saints is their mystology—the study of their subjective, mystical experiences in its "degrees, laws, sequences, variations."[35] Theology—the explication of objective revelation—ceases to be the focus. No longer is the saint forgetful of herself, devoted to her mission to express the revelation of the truth. The connection between the two becomes more and more tenuous.[36]

Eventually, the separation of dogma from spirituality becomes a divorce, leaving dogmatic theology to the arid intellectualism of the neo-scholastic manuals that Balthasar detested. Spirituality meanwhile becomes a psychological laboratory in which the saint's personal experiences are dissected, where the saint is required to describe her experience of God.[37]

Again, what is at stake for Balthasar is the very heart of theology, and thus, the unity of Christian truth:

> Consider the doctrinal wealth drawn from the writings of the Areopagite —not without reason the most commented on of all the mystics—in comparison with that yielded by even the greatest of the moderns, John of the Cross. And then compare, if you can bring yourself to do so, the nourishment offered by a modern theological manual for a life of holiness with that contained in any patristic commentary on Scripture. The

---

34. "Theology and Sanctity," in *ET* 1, 190–91. Balthasar's criticism of the early Carmelites is bound up with a number of debates happening between the Dominican and Jesuit orders over the question of mysticism and asceticism.

35. "Theology and Sanctity," in *ET* 1, 191.

36. While the connection between this form of spirituality and dogmatic theology becomes more tenuous, it may be that the "connections, parallels and analogies with religious phenomena outside Christianity are correspondingly more frequent and prominent." The possibility opens for a "generic" spirituality or mysticism that reduces these to sociological or psychological concepts.

37. ". . . and the accent is always on experience rather than on God: for the nature of God is a subject for the [speculative] theological specialist [alone]" ("Theology and Sanctity," 191).

impoverishment brought about by the divorce between the two spheres is all too plain; it has sapped the vital force of the Church of today and the credibility of her preaching of eternal truth. This impoverishment is felt considerably more strongly by those who have to preach to the modern pagans than by professors in their seminary lecture rooms. It is the former who look round for some example of the conjunction of wisdom and holiness. They long to discover the living organism of the Church's doctrine, rather than a strange anatomical dissection: on the one hand, the bones without the flesh, "traditional theology"; on the other, the flesh without bones, mysticism, spirituality and rhetoric, a porridge that, in the end, becomes indigestible through lack of substance. Only the two together (corresponding to the prototype of revelation in scripture constitute the unique "form" capable of being "seen" in the light of faith by the believer, a unique testimony, invisible to the world, and a "scandal" to it.[38]

Modernity's Metaphysics as an "Ontologically Evanescent Cheshire Cat"[39]

According to Balthasar, the sundering of sanctity from speculation and the subsequent de-formation of spirituality plays a significant, if oft-overlooked, role in the collapse of metaphysics. When the saints are removed from speculative thought, the existential encounter with divine glory is lost from that speculative discourse resulting in the impoverishment of the thought of Being.[40] Being is no longer the object of philosophy; instead, philosophy is concerned with mental representations of the intellectual concept of Being. Things are reduced to "things for me" and rationality is less the loving, receptive reason, and more the legislating and methodological mind.

Balthasar claims that the loss of the saints from the speculative

---

38. Ibid.
39. Aidan Nichols, O.P., *The Word Has Been Abroad: A Guide Through Balthasar's Aesthetics* (Washington, DC: The Catholic University Press of America, 1998), 147
40. Or what Martin Heidegger calls the "forgetfulness of Being." Balthasar narrates it thus: "whereas during the early Middle Ages, up to about the time of Bonaventure, theology and (objective) mysticism were indivisible—something to which Augustine and Dionysius, Gregory the Great and Eriugena, the Cistercians and the Victorines, the Joachimites and the Spiritual Franciscans well attest—the 'mystic' is now identified increasingly in terms of his subjective experience of glory and is stamped as an exception, while the 'rule' is represented by the strictly logical and intellectualist metaphysics of the church. Those who are concerned to restore the lost unity (Gerson, Nicolas of Cusa, Petavius, Gerbert, etc.) remain outsiders and often pursue paths which lead to speculative Idealism" (*GL* 5, 26).

thought of the God–world relationship resulted in two forms of the devolution of Being. Being may be formalized as a concept, as was done by Scotus, Occam, and Suarez; or it might be equated with God, as in the thought of Eckhart. Both of these errors emerge from the deformation of spirituality, and result in dangerous metaphysical claims that Balthasar fears annihilate a proper account of the real distinction in the God–world relationship. These claims become some of the chief sources of the modern malaise.

The Formalization of Being

Balthasar's metaphysics are for the most part Thomistic.[41] In Aquinas' ontology, Being (*esse*) is the unlimited abundance of reality beyond comprehension, as, in its emergence from God, it attains subsistence and self-possession within finite entities. Thomas's real distinction (*distinctio realis*) between essence and existence, Being and beings, is an important concept for Balthasar because it reveals a polarity in Being that requires transcendence.

But Thomas's real distinction is not maintained by the generations after him. Eventually, Being ceases to be the principle reality *of* reality, instead, becoming a *formal concept*, the comprehensive essentiality of all things. Being can be either infinite or finite. As a concept, Being climbs above God, incorporating God within its totality. This ends up making God the object of reason *simpliciter*; the philosopher who knows Being through reason can incorporate God into this now limitless philosophical vision. This is the philosophical groundwork from which Hegelian titanism emerges.

Balthasar lays much of the blame for the formalization of Being at the feet of Duns Scotus and William of Occam. Scotus' decision to elevate Being as the univocal category of comprehensive essentiality in which both God and creature are logically contained, is the elevation of essence over existence. This bequeaths to philosophy a radical

---

41. This is not to say that Balthasarian metaphysics are a simple rehashing of Aquinas. Like Rahner, Balthasar will wed Thomism with particular forms of his contemporary German philosophical tradition, especially Heidegger. The first volume of the *Theo-Logic* is a chief example of the way Balthasar brings Thomas and Heidegger together. I examine this in the next chapter.

independence from theology, and even from revelation. According to Balthasar, it was Scotus' intention to grant to revelation its own space, free from the encumbrances of philosophical discourse.[42] The unintended consequence of this is the reduction of theology to a practical discipline that focuses on historical acts of God and the cultivation of faith and devotion. One sees here the beginning of the science of the interior life of late medieval mysticism. Theology speaks to existence; philosophy to essence. A yawning gulf opens between two very different gods—the triune God and the god of the philosophers (*tā théon*). Stripped of its access to Being, Christianity ends up losing its metaphysical dimension in favor of the practicalities of faith and devotion.

With the nominalist Occam, the undifferentiated Being theorized by Scotus defines itself according to its *haecceitas*, its "this-ness." Class and species become subjective schemes of interpretation and classification. Only specific, individual entities are real. Occam's nominalism lays the foundation for the empiricism of Locke and Hume, and of the positivism that asks no questions beyond what is merely given.[43] A thing only exists according to the freedom, rather than the love, of the sovereign will. Here, naked will rises above divine love—a strange idea for a disciple of St. Francis of Assisi for whom the world is the gift of the God who is "love beyond all limits of knowledge."

The problem that Balthasar identifies here springs from a spiritual deficiency. Balthasar asserts that Scotus' and Occam's failure to match the spiritual attitude of Francis of Assisi with their intellectual speculation is emblematic of the general thrust of theological thought

---

42. GL 5, 17. Balthasar cites *Theoremata*, though he acknowledges the possibility that this was not actually penned by Scotus himself. It should be noted that Balthasar, normally meticulous in his citations, is surprisingly weak in his references to Scotus' works. He relies almost exclusively on Siewerth and Gilson's studies of the philosophy of the medievals. Siewerth's especially is a genealogical account, very similar to Balthasar's, that attempts to defend Christian metaphysics from Heideggerian critique. Cf. Cyril O'Regan, "Von Balthasar's Valorization and Critique of Heidegger's Genealogy of Modernity," in *Christian Spirituality and the Culture of Modernity* (Grand Rapids: Eerdmans, 1998), 123–58.

43. It is in response to this that Balthasar adopts a phenomenological approach in the first volume of the *Theo-logic*. Balthasar emphasizes the theological and philosophical significance of particular, concrete existence. But it is precisely in, not apart from, these existences that their essence is revealed. As we will see, Balthasar's use of phenomenology allows him to return to a sacramental account of Thomas's doctrine of the real distinction.

in this period. By isolating Francis' saintly theology within the narrow confines of "spirituality," the speculative thought of Scotus and Occam become unmoored from the ontological and metaphysical dimensions of Christian teaching.[44] As Balthasar argues regarding Occam:

> This formidable Franciscan creates space even more radically for the sole sovereignty of God when, sweeping away the entire Platonic and Aristotelian tradition, he directly opposes to the yawning abyss of absolute freedom a world which is fragmented into irrational points of reality. With this rupture within the tradition of a mediating or natural (philosophical) theology, every contemplative dimension of the *fides quaerens intellectum* is in principle removed. Theology, which now closes itself in upon itself, must become fideistic and can ultimately be only practical.[45]

Balthasar sees a direct line connecting the formalization of Being with Scotus and Occam to the thought of the Jesuit, Francisco Suarez, the father of Baroque and neo-scholasticism. While Suarez is a spiritual descendent of Ignatius of Loyola, he is the philosophical progeny of Scotus. Balthasar sees in his thought a twisted synthesis of the Ignatian notion of "detachment" with Scotus' univocity of Being. Ignatian detachment is the spiritual form of Franciscan poverty: the emptiness of the whole self, an "ascetic transcendence of psycho-physical possession into a free receptivity to the love of God alone."[46] This self-transcendence is, for Ignatius at least, *indiferencia*, making oneself available to God. Such a spiritual, ascetic self-transcendence interrogates this new form of metaphysics that teaches the preeminence of reason for the knowledge of Being. This surrender is the passivity of a nature elevated by grace. More often than not, however, the opposite is the case: the spiritual charisms are forced into a foreign philosophical totality. This is, according to Balthasar,

---

44. The irony that Balthasar sees here is that Scotus and Occam are both trying to grant to Francis' spiritual experience a metaphysical formulation. The problem is their failure to see that such a formulation deflates Francis' deeply christological spirituality.
45. *GL* 5, 20. On the fragmentation of the idea of *cosmos* that nominalism effects, see Louis Dupré, *Passage to Modernity* (New Haven, Yale University Press, 1993), 15–40. Lydia Schumacher picks up on this same idea in her *Divine Illumination: The History and Future of Augustine's Theory of Knowledge* (Oxford: Wiley-Blackwell, 2011), 194–215.
46. *GL* 5, 21.

precisely what happens with Suarez, who bypasses the inherent intersubjectivity of the Gospel in favor of a static metaphysic of univocity.[47]

For Suarez, univocal Being is the object of all metaphysical enquiry. He trumps univocity over analogy, believing that focusing on analogy muddles metaphysical clarity because it disrupts the "unity of the concept" of Being. If either analogy or univocity had to be relinquished to achieve a comprehensive metaphysic, the former could be disposed without inhibiting the "certain" and "demonstrable" truth of the concept of Being. According to Suarez, a metaphysics that has knowledge of Being as a whole will include God in the sphere of its object. God now becomes a material object, the highest example of Being. But God is not determinative of this metaphysic, insofar as it purports to offer an *a priori* account of Being without reference to God or revelation. This flattening out of reality can only recreate the depth of reality through constructive conceptualism. Concrete reality, existence, is lost in favor of an abstract representation.

Balthasar finds in Suarez a unique conjunction of two things—the biblical vision of the opening of the heart's most inward idea of God and the Greek metaphysical speculation about God and the All. This conjunction

> in which speculation apparently gains the academic qualifications to know *about* God, his essence, his thinking and his acting within the Creation, salvation and perfection (in faith), to receive Being laid bare to its depths and to manipulate it in these depths by conceptual meanings, with the support of an immense body of tradition which is composed of what has been "worked out" partly dogmatically and partly in the schools, and has been already objectively thought (and which therefore is not to

---

47. "Thus in historical terms Christian thought is not commensurate with the forms of Christian inspiration, nor does it seek to keep pace with it, but is content rather to cut a paltry coat for it from the huge store of material of extant thought. Neoscholasticism, to which period the contribution of Ignatius belongs, was particularly burdened by the weight of prior thinking, of what was apparently already contained in the treasury of tradition, so that the original Ignatian vision of *Divina Majestas* and *Gloria* was no longer able to create any original mode of conceptual expression" (*GL* 5, 23). In other words, Balthasar bemoans the fact that Christian thought has only ever borrowed from extant philosophical traditions as its mode of conceptual expression, rather than developing (from Ignatius, perhaps) its own.

be thought through afresh): this conjunction stands behind metaphysics as it exists in the modern period both in the Church and beyond.[48]

It now becomes possible for thought alone to penetrate the essence of God, to know God as an object, to know the divine by means of conceptual thought, rather than through love. What this leads to, Balthasar fears, is the loss of the irreducible mystery of Being.[49] Because Being (and, within that, God) as a concept lies open to reason, the believer is not required to dwell on divine mystery, but is able to subject that mystery to reason, conquering it from the outside.

This metaphysics is incapable of perceiving the glory of revelation because it is limited by its conceptual rationalism. Balthasar's saints, on the contrary, can perceive this glory because it is not restricted to the narrow rationalism of the metaphysicians. This is not to say, however, that saintly perception is illogical. On the contrary, there *is* logic to the saints, but it must come in its proper place *within* the disclosure of revelation.[50] This saintly logic is chiefly a *Christo*-logic. The saints participate in the logic of Christ, that is, in the logic of divine love which faces even the contradiction of Christ's abandonment, of "being made sin." The logic of the metaphysics of the saints is faith seeking understanding from within the life of the incarnate *Logos*.

Balthasar sees a fundamental contradiction in Being in the Scotist-Suarezian picture. For Scotus and Suarez, Being is the highest concept, but also a hollow one. As a univocal concept, Being excludes all of its determinations. These determinations are existing things. They belong to and are Being (because Being can realize itself only *as* beings). The

---

48. *GL* 5, 25.
49. By articulating his genealogy thus, Balthasar reveals his reliance on Heidegger. As Cyril O'Regan rightly argues, Balthasar is in essential agreement with much of Heidegger's critique of modernity, though Balthasar will question whether or not Heidegger can actually avoid the nihilism he critiques. Nevertheless, for both, "Scotus seems to instantiate the kind of formal-logical mania that characterizes all that can go wrong in metaphysics and did in fact go wrong in Scholasticism. . . . If the tendencies of modernity hardly bode well for a theology that would be *doxological* in the strict sense, then neither the speculative grammar of Scotus, nor the Scholasticism of Suarez, nor the degenerate Thomism of the nineteenth century are calculated to preserve the irreducible moment of mystery and the emptying adorative response that defines the biblical and patristic attitude to God and the cosmos." See O'Regan, "Von Balthasar's Valorization and Critique of Heidegger's Genealogy of Modernity," 128.
50. For another Balthasarian and Ignatian interpretation of this dilemma, see Henrici, "The Spiritual Dimension," 645ff.

category of Being must therefore be contracted to the level of singularity or undifferentiated unity. There emerges here a disjunction between the *real* and the *actual*. The real is that which is realizable, not what is actual. If reality is comprehensive Being (as a concept), then existence (that is, actuality) is "being ordered to Being." God is completely cut out of the picture.

What Balthasar fears in Scotus' formalization of Being is that theology becomes inevitably profane, making philosophy absolutely autonomous. The consequence is that knowledge loses its the participative character in favor of a formalization of Being that leads to the primacy of juridical reason. This sets the stage for the cold rationalism of early modernity.

Being as God

If Scotus, Occam, and Suarez represent one side of the collapse of the Thomistic synthesis through their formalization of Being, then Meister Eckhart represents the other. Through his identification of Being with God (*Esse est Deus*), Eckhart plays a crucial role in modern intellectual and spiritual history.[51] Though his spirituality bears some striking similarities to that of Ignatius of Loyola, Eckhart expresses his in philosophical categories that do more to distort than to illumine the metaphysical and spiritual truth of Being.[52]

Eckhart's identification of Being with God is, at least initially, a devotional move. He attempts to ascribe all things, all Being, to God alone.[53] Balthasar accepts this as a genuinely Christian idea, but he thinks that Eckhart expresses it through "an extreme Neoplatonic ontology" that results in a philosophy and mysticism of identity that

51. Its arguable that Eckhart plays a more significant role in Balthasar's genealogy than Scotus. Eckhart creeps up throughout the Trilogy in a way the other figures do not. As an example, Balthasar gives an thorough critique of Eckhart in *TD* 5, 434ff.
52. O'Regan notes that Balthasar's assessment of Eckhart is largely ambivalent. On the one hand, Balthasar never doubts Eckhart's catholicity or his essentiality to the Christian tradition. On the other hand, as I shall emphasize below, Eckhart does make some theological claims that Balthasar sees as immensely problematic, even as a distortion of Christian metaphysics and spirituality. Cf. O'Regan, "Balthasar and Eckhart," 215–20.
53. See, for example, his *Sermon 6: Deus communis est: omne ens et omnium esse ipse est.* Quoted in *GL* 5, 31.

destroys the real distinction and harms the Christian understanding of the God-world relation.[54]

Eckhart bypasses the Thomistic non-subsistent *actus essendi*, opting instead for four distinct propositions: 1) God is beyond all explication. He is the *whyless* (an idea picked up later by Martin Heidegger). The divine whylessness is the whylessness of love, freedom, thought, and form. 2) This whylessness is seen in the eternal font of divine fecundity. God is born of God in the Trinity. Further, God is born spiritually in all things, especially in Christians. 3) Being a Christian is a passive attitude of letting God be born in the soul. Eckhart's picture of Christian existence is one of radical receptivity, both spiritually and ontologically; it is utter passivity. Mary is the archetypal image of the true Christian, expressing humanity's universal task and destiny: our *fiat* leads to our glorification of having God born in us. 4) Christian spirituality is becoming. It involves the dynamic movement toward divine birth, which is the same as divine Sonship. The divine birth is the central theological mystery, not just for the Christian, but for all creation. All Being moves toward the eternal generation of the Word, and thus, toward becoming God.[55] Balthasar critiques Eckhart on precisely this point, for treating the "generation of the Word" as an abstract cosmological principle that Jesus Christ only exemplifies. According to Balthasar, Eckhartian *Gelassenheit* lacks an appropriately-grounded christological foundation.

Thus, a key phrase for Eckhart's spiritual metaphysics is that "Man should grasp God in all things."[56] One need not flee from the world to attain union with God. One instead reaches for the God present in all things. But this union with God in the world is not automatic. Union can be attained only through the formation of the soul through obedience. Obedience develops the capacity for God's divine birth in

---

54. *TD* 5, 434.

55. Cf. O'Regan, "Balthasar and Eckhart," 223–24. See also *TD* 5, 435.

56. *Instructive Discourses* VI. Note how close this comes to the Ignatian injunction to "find God in all things." The difference between them is the difference between an aesthetic seeing or finding in Ignatius and a more intellectualist "grasping" and comprehension in Eckhart. For Balthasar, following Ignatius, we find God present in all things but he remains ever hidden to us, even has we find him: in every similarity, there is an ever-greater dissimilarity.

the soul. For Eckhart, obedience involves the surrender of the will in absolute passivity before the will of God. This kind of radical receptivity requires an impoverishment and abasement of the self.[57] Things are truly known only when accepted as gifts of disclosure from God, received by a surrendered self. What is received is God himself, given in all things.[58] This surrender leads to the fruitfulness of the divine birth in the Christian. This divine birth is the goal of the spiritual life.[59]

Thus far, Eckhart's spirituality accords quite well with Balthasar's desire to see a spiritual metaphysic in which the truth of Being is known and received through spiritual union with God. But all of this begins to go wrong when Eckhart adopts foreign philosophical concepts to heighten the theological mystery of the divine birth. By equating God with Being, he unintentionally blurs the frontier between God and world.[60]

Balthasar identifies the danger of Eckhartian thought in his radicalization of receptivity. Worldly Being comes *from* God to such an extent that it is identical to God. Eckhart makes no space for the *analogia entis*, but instead favors "the purely creative effulgence of Being, which *as such* endows the creature—which is itself nothing —with a being that is 'borrowed' not entrusted to it as its own."[61] The creature's "I" is in God, yes, but in such a way that it is completely assimilated. All that is needed to move from Eckhart to Idealism is the titanic shift from "I" being assimilated by *God* to God being assimilated by "*I.*"[62]

Balthasar also sees that "Being" as a concept is not adequate for

---

57. We see here an Eckhartian gloss on the ideals of Franciscan poverty and later Ignatian *indiferencia*.
58. Cf. O'Regan, "Balthasar and Eckhart," 210–11.
59. It is also, interestingly enough, the undoing of ethics. Like Luther, external works for Eckhart contribute nothing to the generation of the Word in the inner life.
60. According to O'Regan, Balthasar rejects Eckhart's move of "converting Thomas's *Deus est Esse* into *Esse est Deus* and the dismantling of analogy that this involves" ("Balthasar and Eckhart," 218).
61. TD 5, 437.
62. Eckhart equates all Being with becoming. What is Not-God is by definition, for Eckhart, Non-Being. All creatures are nothing—matter to form, pure passive receptivity. Being is nothing more than a loan of God's own divine and absolute Being. The creature is preserved in this Being solely by the perpetual event-act of God's presence. Eckhart conceives of worldly being as an ever-receptive becoming, a constant "drinking in" of God. God, therefore, can only ever be the active begetting that corresponds to the absolute passivity of being begotten.

Eckhart's God. Being is God's forecourt. His temple, so Eckhart claims, is *intellect*. For Eckhart, the *actus secundus* (knowing) is nobler than Being: God is *because* he knows; knowledge is the *fundamentum* of divine Being. But knowledge, for Eckhart, concerns *intentional* rather than *real* Being. The movement of knowledge toward real things is an act of externalization, and as such, is a fall away from interiority, the location of the spiritual divine birth. Eckhart adopts a Neoplatonic form of knowledge that involves the "reassembly" of the externalized part of the mind upon the intellect's return to its archetype in the soul. Truth, then, resides in the intellect rather than in the world. Eckhart also conceived of God as an identity of unity that comes to be in thought; he assumes that there is an absolute divine identity *beyond* the Trinity. This primordial identity *is* the intellect. In light of this, Eckhart concluded that all Being is God (*esse est Deus*).[63] Later Idealists will converge on this point by construing all Being in terms of that point of identity *in the intellect* where God and creature coincide.

Lastly, Eckhart develops a spirituality of immediacy, one which rejects the classical idea of a relationship with God mediated analogously through the cosmos. His spirituality adopts a philosophy that is "the first step towards idealistic speculation."[64] Eckhart's concern for the Christian's loving abandonment to God is ill-matched, Balthasar claims, with a philosophy that articulates the relation of finite and absolute Spirit as a kind of *knowledge*. Balthasar sees a clear divide in Eckhart between the speculative and the spiritual. He accuses Eckhart of reading his philosophy back into his spiritual theology. This is seen most clearly in the triumph of knowledge over love as the *fundamentum* of God's being, and the blurring of the distinction between the Creator and the creature.[65] "As a result, man's giving birth to the Son by grace is identified with the generation of the Son

---

63. See, for example, his *Instructive Discourses* VI, 205. Balthasar is also basing much of his critique of Eckhart on Vladimir Lossky's *Théologie négative et connaissance de Dieu chez Maître Eckhart* (Paris: Vrin Distribution, 1998).
64. *GL* 5, 48.
65. Ibid., 43.

within the Godhead: the creature thus usurps the place of the Father himself—it becomes the generating primal Ground, *causa suia*."[66]

While Eckhart's intention was to highlight the God–world relation as loving abandonment and receptivity, his philosophy ends up articulating this spirituality as a kind of gnostic understanding, a secret interior knowing that displaces the external ways of knowing God in sacrament and worldly symbols. Balthasar sees Eckhart as the progenitor of the Idealism where knowledge of the God–world relationship is reduced to the epistemological dialectic between the Infinite and finite. Here, dialectic trumps dialogue; love is subsumed into knowledge.[67] Eckhartian Being is indeed mystery, but it is not the infinite mystery of love. Being's mystery in Eckhart's thought becomes something more akin to a riddle, a problem that can and must be solved, rather than a gift to be received and enjoyed.

The philosophical systems of Idealism that Balthasar sees as emerging from the legacy of Eckhart try to solve this riddle of Being. Balthasar sees this titanic systematization of philosophy emerging with new vigor from Kant to Fichte.[68] Idealist systems negate "the sense of belonging in a world" through their obsession with "subjectivity and the self-constitution of the subject."[69]

---

66. *TD* 5, 441.

67. Thus, Balthasar's critique of Eckhart is that he is not properly *apophatic*. Cf. O'Regan, "Balthasar and Eckhart," 215.

68. Balthasar's relationship to Kant is complex. In many ways, the three parts of Balthasar's Trilogy are the direct inverse of the Kantian philosophical scheme. Yet, Balthasar does not hesitate to give Kant credit where it is due. Kant is a "frontier figure" who, though he sets the stage for later titanic Idealism, has not yet succumbed to that temptation. Balthasar holds, perhaps controversially, that Kant's philosophy still affirms a transcendent "thing-in-itself" that the subject bumps into. So receptivity remains a key element in Kantian thought. The transformation—or perhaps distortion—that the Kantian legacy effects, however, is phenomenalism: "even metaphysics 'receives' (in its receptivity) only phenomena, not Being. This is why the practical faculty, when it opens up the way to the Absolute, cannot mediate any objective ('external') knowledge, and if religion exists at all, it can do so only 'within the limits of pure reason'" (*GL* 5, 494).

69. Rowan Williams, "Balthasar and Rahner," in *Analogy of Beauty: The Theology of Hans Urs von Balthasar*, ed. John Riches (London: T&T Clark, 1986), 23. This already signals a philosophical capitulation to nominalism, as Dupré sees: "already the nominalist crisis had severed the bond between human words and the divine *Logos*. If we can no longer take for granted that God's decrees follow an intelligible pattern, then we also cease to trust that the eternal *Logos* secures the basic veracity of human speech" (Dupré, 104). Though Dupré is here referring to language, the same crisis plagues accounts of Being and truth in the wake of nominalism. In fact, the critique that Derrida will later bring against Western culture—that its logocentrism grants an undeserved discursive access to Being—misses the point. The problem, so Dupré claims (and Balthasar would

In Idealism, the Eckhartian self becomes the Absolute I, absorbing the world into its cognitive functions.[70] The world is instrumentalized. Balthasar believes that this signals the death of sacramental metaphysics. The world, rather than being the mediating stage upon which God discloses himself becomes that which is "without significance independent of the ego . . . incapable of manifesting God. Spirit swallows up nature, and the non-human world is wholly subordinated to human self-fulfillment."[71] Idealism is thus haunted, says Balthasar, by the spectre of Nietzsche's purely creative self-will of the ego. It is disembodied Mind that grants to the "I" the sponge to "wipe away the horizon."[72] Idealism is titanic, refusing to rest until it has drawn everything into the Absolute I.[73]

Despite all the talk of "absolute knowing" that circulates among the Idealists[74] (and even in Eckhart himself), Balthasar sees Idealism

agree), comes from an "impoverished interpretation of *logos* as residing exclusively in the human subject and depriving all other being of its inherent meaning" (Dupré, 24). This stripping of the world is the real problem that needs deconstructing: cosmos is replaced by nature, and so, teleological meaning is displaced and then lost altogether. This intrinsic and teleological meaningfulness of the cosmos, for ancients such as Plato and Aristotle, is based in a world that is, itself, divine. The church will later transform this "ensouled world" in terms of a sacramental ontology. Both such metaphysical views will be upended with the rise of the nominalist crisis of the late medieval period that, in many ways, returns to the Parmenadian suspicion of "appearances" or "phenomena" and searches instead for "foundations" that, ultimately, can only be found in the self.

70. There is a distinct movement in modernity that turns to introspection. This is the move that Descartes makes and, from Descartes, comes the introspection of Montaigne and others. See Dupré, 101: "When meaning is no longer given with existence, existence itself becomes a quest for meaning." It might be possible to link modern philosophy's concern with introspection back to the interiority and introspection of Augustine. Michael Hanby, however, rejects such a move, claiming that Augustinian subjectivity is grounded more in a theology of creation than in the Stoicism that deeply influenced Descartes. See Michael Hanby, *Augustine and Modernity* (New York: Routledge, 2003). Especially notable for Hanby's argument and for reinforcing Balthasar's own critique of modernity, is an excerpt from Descartes' letter *To Colvius*: "I . . . [contrary to Augustine] use the [*cogito*], to show that this I which is thinking is an immaterial substance with no bodily element. These are two very different things." As Dupré notes, Cartesian interiority and selfhood is ultimately *functional*—the self as the source of meaning and value (118).

71. Dupré, 118.

72. Friedrich Nietzsche, "The Parable of the Madman," in *The Gay Science* (New York: Vintage Press, 1974), 181–82.

73. On Fichte, see *GL* 5, 547ff. Note especially: "it is not the objective world-systems which are the focus of attention . . . , rather, the totality needs to be developed from the transcendental art-structure of the thinking and acting subject . . . the 'retreat to the man as the centre' is in no way retracted; for the first time it is 'Titanically' [*sic*] pressed home" (547).

74. Balthasar tends to speak in generalities about the "Idealists" even though there is a huge variety among Idealist thinkers on just about every topic. We should understand Balthasar's references to "the Idealists" as referring to an idealist trajectory or system, modeled especially in Fichte and Hegel, that elevates thought over Being. As Balthasar puts it, "While Kant and Schiller stop short

as the death of knowledge precisely because Idealism *absolutizes* it. Idealism's absolute knowledge destroys the mystery of Being and with it the possibility of wonder. As Balthasar makes clear: "What has been disastrously lost in the metaphysical rake's progress is the possibility of *wonder*, of *contemplative receptivity* in the face of the world's richness, the overthrowing of a contemplative (and thus potentially God-directed) mode of knowledge by a model of *Bewältigung*—thought as mastery, domination, even exploitation, Bacon's nature on the rack."[75] Balthasar claims that this is the direct result of Eckhart's spiritual *and* metaphysical error of equating Being with God, and elevating knowledge over love.

Balthasar is concerned about something far more troubling to him than the loss of knowledge. This kind of metaphysically disenchanted world—the consumption of wonder by the *technē* of the self—is the loss of prayer. "We can be sure that whoever sneers at her [beauty's] name as if she were the ornament of a bourgeois past—whether he admits it or not—can no longer pray and soon will no longer be able to love."[76] For Balthasar, the loss of Being and the loss of the saints go hand-in-hand. The result is the annihilation of the world and the loss of the ability to pray and to love. The loss of the saints from theology in the late medieval period thus creates a vicious cycle in which *all* sainthood, and all prayer, is lost.[77]

All of this helps makes sense of Balthasar's critical appropriation of Heidegger, for whom all ontological knowledge is *Dasein*, being-in-the-world. For Heidegger, "'Being' just cannot be statically comprehended as something that exists [*Seiendes*]. It is interpreted in reference to the understanding of Being, and thereby drawn into the movement of decision-making existence . . . the totality of life." Heidegger brings the

---

at the finiteness of the human spirit in a way that might be judged to be more modern, the three Titans Fichte, Schelling and Hegel want to conceive of man within the wholeness of the Absolute, as its centre" (GL 5, 547).
75. Balthasar, *Cordula*, 68–69. See also Balthasar's account of Descartes in GL 5, 455ff.
76. GL 1, 18.
77. Balthasar once again sees Eckhart and Kant in the background here. Both clung to what he calls an "ethical, aesthetic sublime" that demands "contemplation" and "adoration" [*Anbetung*]. Though Kant dismisses prayer as ethically fruitless, contemplation and adoration are powers that "lift the soul" (GL 5, 502).

knower back to the world in such a way that knowledge—"care"—of Being can only occur *as Dasein, through Dasein, as In-der-Welt-sein*. For Heidegger, we *know* because we *are*; we *know* Being *by* being. Heidegger ultimately posits the poet as the one who knows Being as *Dasein* (in which "*existentia* is made the *essential* of *esse*").[78] Balthasar will put forward something analogous to the Heideggerian poet in the saint.[79] Heidegger's poet knows by living toward death whereas Balthasar's saint knows by living, with Christ, through death toward resurrection, toward the eschatological dawn that casts a transfiguring, illuminative light on the world. In this way, Balthasar reimagines the relationship between God and world through a theological account of the truth of Being, and through his theology of the saints. If the loss of the saints is one of the causes of modernity's metaphysical sickness, then surely the rediscovery of them is part of the cure.

The Saints and the Renewing of Theology

In many ways, Balthasar's project is strikingly similar to Eckhart. Balthasar too strives to articulate the truth of the God–world relation as love, that is, as abandonment and receptivity, or *Gelassenheit*. But Balthasar does not identify Being with God, and thus rejects Eckhart's elevation of speculative knowledge over love. Instead, Balthasar develops an account of the God–world relation that finds God in all things, yet maintains a robust sense of metaphysical and theological mystery. He does this through his insistence on analogical and participative knowledge that comes in and as the dialogue of prayer. Balthasar's account resists the chains of cold rationalism and titanic idealism, returning theological metaphysics to the truth of Trinitarian love revealed in Christ and known in the Spirit.

Balthasar is skeptical that a theology where dogma and spirituality are divorced can be capable of articulating such an account of the

---

78. Ibid., 67.

79. On the metaphysics of the poets, see Dupré: "the poet not only represents the things of this world but also symbolizes those invisible forms that, according to the Platonists, constitute the true reality. He creates *idoli*, sacred images, that powerfully refer to a mysterious, invisible reality" (104).

God–world relation. The radical separation of the objective truth and its subjective performance has distorted the church's ability to articulate a truthful account of Being. What this calls for is a serious reassessment of the nature of theology itself. Balthasar tries to heal the fragmentation in the heart of theology, especially between theology's form and its content, through this theology of the saints. The saints stand with Christ at the heart of the God–world relation, the mystery of Being itself.

Balthasar insists that the content of speculative theology is the truth as revealed as Jesus Christ. Theology is not the mid-point between revelation and secular philosophy. Theology always stands at the heart of revelation, thinking and investigating the truth of Christ from *within* the truth, not outside it: the Christian cannot leave Christ in order to build a bridge between revelation and nature, philosophy and theology. Christ himself *is* that bridge, the analogy between God and world, divine truth and finite truth. The theologian's task is to make Christ known in every dimension of his truth, be it religious or metaphysical, for Christ does not exist on the periphery of the world, but at the very heart of Being.

This heart is also home to the saints. The saints live "hidden away in Christ," and they never depart from Christ. Thus, "[w]hen they philosophize, they do so as Christians, which means as believers, as theologians. . . . And this simply means that their thought is a function of their faith. . . . Their thinking is an act that is ultimately performed in the service of their faith, of Christ's revelation, which is its norm and guiding principle."[80] The content of theology—of all theologizing—is the revelation of Christ, and is "a prolongation of the message of revelation."[81]

If the content of theology is the revelation of God in Christ, then theology's form [Gestalt] must correspond to the unfolding of this revelation. Genuine theology, therefore, is characterized by obedient receptivity, dialogue, and love. Theology itself must receive and obey

---

80. "Theology and Sanctity," in ET 1, 196.
81. Ibid. See also, *Prayer*, trans. Graham Harrison (San Francisco: Ignatius Press, 1986), 170.

the Word: "True theology, the theology of the saints, with the central doctrines of revelation always in view, inquires, in a spirit of obedience and reverence."[82]

True theological knowledge will be dialogical. It will be characterized by prayer. That is how the saints theologize. Balthasar aims to develop a theological knowledge that corresponds to the nature of divine truth, which is nothing other than the person of God himself. God is the source of all theology—*theo-logos*—on whose prior Word the saints' words depend.[83] Saintly theologizing is secondary reflection spoken within the constant relationship of prayer. St. Anselm is a perfect example of this: "I cannot seek you, if you do not teach me how, nor find if you do not show yourself."[84] Notice how Anselm uses the language of knowledge—"seeking," "finding"—*within* or *as* the language of his prayer. As Anselm himself knew well, "reason too was created for the sake of faith, nature for the sake of grace, and that both form, by their interconnection, a single revelation of the incomprehensible love of the Trinity."[85] The saints thus bequeath to theology a form of receptive obedience and prayer: "Prayer is the *realistic* attitude in which the mystery must be approached: obedient faith, the 'presuppositionless,' is the attitude where theology is concerned, because it corresponds to the *tabula rasa* of love, in which the heart awaits all and anticipates nothing. This attitude, which is that of prayer, is never superseded or outdistanced by the attitude demanded by knowledge."[86]

Balthasar insists that true theology is a continuous dialogue between Christ and church, Bridegroom and Bride. "With revelation there is no such thing as an objective, uncommitted, scientific 'objectivity', but only a personal encounter of Word and faith, Christ and Church, in the

---

82. Ibid., 196.
83. We might say that the divine *theo-logos* gives rise to the saints' *theo-logoi*.
84. *Proslogion*, 1.8. See also Nicholas Lash, "Anselm Seeking," in *The Beginning and End of 'Religion'* (Cambridge: Cambridge University Press, 1996), 150–63.
85. "Theology and Sanctity," in *ET* 1, 207.
86. Ibid.

mystery of the Canticle of Canticles."[87] True theology is the dialogical interplay of subject and object, hearer and Word, in love.

Part of this theological task, this theology of the saints, is the development of an ontological account of truth that corresponds to this theological and saintly epistemology. Both Being and knowledge must be re-imagined as love.[88]

---

87. Ibid., 201.
88. The close interweaving that Balthasar attempts between truth, knowledge, love, and prayer lies at the heart of the medieval contemplative life: "Love assumed a new significance in religious life. What contemplation had been for earlier mystics, love was in the new age. Indeed, contemplation came to be identified with love. Bernard of Clairvaux declared St. Gregory's axiom, *amor ipse notitia est* (love itself is a knowledge) to be the guiding principle of contemplative life" (Dupré, 35). This emphasis on contemplation and love will, through the Franciscan emphasis on the human flesh of Christ, grant materiality an intrinsic—indeed, christological and sacramental—symbolism it had not previously enjoyed. It is precisely their "spiritual devotion" to Christ that lead the medieval contemplatives to rethink how to see, know, and understand the world: "A merely literal [even scientific or idealistic] reading of nature would have fallen far short of a full understanding. . . . Spiritual meaning resided in the cosmos itself" (36). The medieval saints were not consumed in a task of pursuing spiritual experiences but were rather embodying a new way of knowing the truth of the world in light of the truth of God, revealed in Christ: "Knowledge consisted in related one form of language to another form of language; in restoring the great, unbroken plain of words and things; in making everything speak" (Foucault, quoted in Dupré, 37).

4

———

Truth as Love

The first volume of the *Theo-Logic* is Balthasar's attempt at a constructive reinterpretation of truth that integrates scholastic concern over the nature of objective Being with the concern for the subjectivity of the knowing process, that was so prevalent in the philosophical circles of Balthasar's day.[1] Balthasar frames this integration as reconciling philosophical realism and idealism. Balthasar's *Theo-Logic* pick this up from Hegel's account of logic as an "enquiry into the real as found in knowing."[2] But Balthasar goes beyond Hegel's logic by crafting *theo*-logic, in which his philosophical investigation into the nature of Being in the first volume opens up

1. The *Theo-Logic* consist of three volumes, though it was not originally envisioned as a trilogy. The first volume, now known as *The Truth of the World*, was originally known simply as *Wahrheit* when Balthasar published it in 1947, nearly four decades before he published the second two volumes of the *Theo-Logic*. *Wahrheit* was originally intended as the first volume of a philosophical series on the nature of truth. In this series, Balthasar intended to "open up the philosophical access to the specifically Christian understanding of truth" (*MW*, 24). But the second volume of this narrowly philosophical endeavor never materialized. Instead, Balthasar republished *Wahrheit* as the first volume of his newly envisioned *Theologik*, composed and published in the mid-to late-1980s. Balthasar opted not to revise or reformulate *Wahrheit* for its inclusion in the *Theologik*. Instead, he wrote a new introduction that attempts to situate *Wahrheit*'s heavily phenomenological approach with the subsequent volumes, which are far more explicitly theological, insofar as they are dealing with truth as it is expressed in the doctrines of the events of Christian revelation: of Christology, pneumatology, and ecclesiology.
2. Aidan Nichols, O.P., *A Key to Balthasar* (Grand Rapids: Brazos Academic, 2011), 89.

to theological completion in the later two volumes. In *Theo-Logic 1*, Balthasar only begins to unify realism and idealism. Such philosophical union must await its theological accomplishment in the dramatic person of Christ.

The present chapter accomplishes three things. First, I unpack Balthasar's understanding of truth as the meeting point of metaphysics and epistemology. As a property of Being truth is a metaphysical category; but as something known, truth is also an epistemological concept. Truth belongs to both. Truth limited to epistemology results in titanic Idealism. But truth confined to metaphysics results in arid neo-scholasticism. To isolate truth to either one or the other is to mistake the nature of truth as a knowable property of Being.[3]

Second, I argue that Balthasar interprets Being and knowledge as love—as the rhythm of gratuitous, free giving and receiving between subject and object. In his *Theo-Logic*, Balthasar does not supplant the rationalism of Thomas Aquinas by replacing it with fideism or affectivism; instead, he demonstrates the mutuality of knowledge and love. Knowledge comes not solely through an act of cognition; understanding is an act of the whole self in the expressive, creative, and receptive act of the loving intellect.[4]

3. Knowledge, for Balthasar, is ontological. Knowledge is knowledge *of* something. This "something" is Being itself. Balthasar is indeed epistemologically confident. He firmly believes that it is Being that is unveiled to the knower and that it is therefore possible for a human to have genuine knowledge of Being in its objectivity. In this, Balthasar shows himself to be a fairly close adherent to Thomistic realism. But Balthasar is not keen to develop a purely passive epistemology along the lines of Eckhart. He wants, like Thomas, the subject to have an active role in knowing. And so his epistemology will involve a clear mutuality between subject and object in the full act of knowing. It is from this mutuality between subject and object that Balthasar develops what this chapter will label a participative epistemology—the participation of the subject and object in and with each other *and* the participation of worldly truth in supernatural, divine truth. Both "types" of participation correspond to Balthasar's metaphysical account of truth, but they also gesture forward to the saints. Knowledge, while certainly conceptual, is also decidedly dramatic. There is a dramatic disposition in every true knower; *knowing* means *being* a certain way. *Knowing* truly means *being* truly (Cf. *GL* 1, 99–101). If Being is love, then the knowledge of that Being is also love. Hence, the saints, as lovers of God, are the true metaphysicians because it is lovers who most fully understand the true nature of Being.

4. David C. Schindler suggests five theses for expositing Balthasar's argument for the philosophical and theological primacy of love: 1) Love is the meaning of Being; 2) Truth is simultaneously an object of intellect and will; 3) The locus of truth is the concrete *Gestalt*; 4) Mystery is convertible with truth; 5) Knowledge is essentially non-possessive. Though this chapter does not follow Schindler's taxonomy precisely, it does share with him the task of elucidating Balthasar's account of truth as a philosophy of love. Balthasar's philosophy of love is not merely a philosophy *about* love; it is, rather, a philosophy of truth *by means of love*. Such a philosophy interprets truth

Third, I end the chapter by highlighting the way Balthasar frames the truth of God as both the beginning and the end (*principium et finis*) of the truth of the world. This helps us reconcile the natural world as open to divine. Balthasar's way of parising this relationship between created and divine truth resonates with his Ignatian metaphysics outlined in chapter one. Indeed, the conclusion to *Theo-Logic* 1 lays the philosophical groundwork for finding God in all things, even in the structure of human understanding.[5]

Truth as Metaphysical and Epistemological

Father Aidan Nichols often refers to the *Theo-Logic* as the "ontological trilogy" in which Balthasar considers the question of Being in itself.[6] While it is not incorrect to identify metaphysical questions as one of the driving forces in the *Theo-Logic*, Balthasar is not only doing metaphysics. He is not asking the question of Being *qua* Being only, but also asking about how humanity can venture to speak truthfully of Being. The volumes of *Theo-Logic* are metaphysical explorations, yes, but they are also explorations of *expression*: of how Being expresses itself, how we come to know Being, and how we can express Being in finite language.

Recalling our earlier statement that the *Theo-Logic* brings together realism and idealism, we can understand the series as a direct response to (Hegelian) Idealism, as an account of reality as it is made known to us. Like Hegel's own logic, Balthasar's *Theo-Logic* takes up the challenge of truth when "thing becomes think."[7]

---

as gift, it comes to knowledge through creative receptivity, and it wills the perpetuity of the world's mystery. These are the themes that both Schindler and the current chapter explore in unfolding Balthasar's "non-possessive" epistemology. See his "Towards a Non-Possessive Concept of Knowledge: On the Relation Between Reason and Love in Aquinas and Balthasar," *Modern Theology* vol. 22, no. 4 (2006): 577–607. Cf. Pierre Rousselot, *L'intellettualismo di san Tommaso* (Milan: Vita e pensario, 2000). See also Rousselot's collection of essays entitled *Essays on Love and Knowledge*, trans. Andrew Tallon, Pol Vandevelde, and Alan Vincellete (Milwaukee, Marquette University Press, 2008). From this collection, see especially the essay "Intellectualism" (225–49).

5. One can see here Balthasar's Ignatian appropriation of Aquinas' dictum that God is known implicitly in every act of knowing. Cf. Aquinas, *De veritate* 22.2.

6. Cf. Aidan Nichols, O.P., *Say It is Pentecost* (Washington, DC: Catholic University of America Press, 2001).

7. Nichols, *A Key to Balthasar*, 90.

We must accept from the beginning that Balthasar is not skeptical about the human ability to know the truth of Being. He is optimistic that when humans know truth, they know the truth of Being itself. Such optimism is rooted in the nature of truth. But we should not confuse his optimism as a claim for the possibility of absolute knowledge. Balthasar wants to hold together knowledge and mystery. Because truth is a property of knowledge, we can really know. But knowledge is not necessarily co-extensive with comprehension. Because truth is also a property of all of Being, what is disclosed to our understanding exceeds our comprehension. Balthasar elevates truth's mystery, rather than overcoming it. What holds knowledge and mystery together, for Balthasar, is love. *Theo-Logic* 1 supplants Idealism's drive for absolute knowing with love that wills the perpetual mystery of truth.

***

Before going any further, we should offer a word of caution. Balthasar's epistemology has been criticized in some quarters for failing to be sufficiently philosophical. Victoria Harrison, for example, though she sees a great deal of potential in Balthasar's thought for developing a distinctly religious epistemology, notes that the *Theo-Logic* fails to develop a constructive, systematic rationality as a supplement to Balthasar's critique of Kantianism.[8] But developing a theory of rationality is not Balthasar's task in the *Theo-Logic*. He sets out, rather, to develop a principle for understanding the ontological reality of Being when it is interpreted as love. Whatever system of rationality that we might derive from the *Theo-Logic* is incidental. Balthasar's purpose is to inquire into the nature of truth itself.

Instead of a systematic rationality, Balthasar articulates an ontological and epistemic disposition of Being and of knowledge. This disposition is marked by receptivity. Balthasar identifies what he calls a dialogical rhythm in Being and knowledge. It is a back-and-forth

---

8. Harrison,"Putnam's Internal Realism and Von Balthasar's Religious Epistemology," 89.

rhythm of gift and receptivity, which Balthasar says is the rhythm of love. In this rhythm, Being freely gives from its objective depths. The subject receives it with fidelity and charity.

It is worth noting that Balthasar describes this epistemological disposition that corresponds to this rhythm as "adoration" [*Anbetung*]. This is clearly the language of spirituality and devotion, but Balthasar uses it to describe knowledge as an epistemic disposition of openness to Being's revelation through the subject's receptivity and creative participation. We can see even here at the outset of his philosophical study of truth that Balthasar is laying the groundwork for his portrayal of the saints as the ones who most perfectly realize the epistemic attitude of true knowledge.

Truth as a Transcendental Property of Being

Balthasar's *Theo-Logic* begins with the unequivocal assertion that truth's proper object is Being. *Theo-Logic 1* resists the narrow subject-oriented epistemology of post-Kantian Idealism. Balthasar also distances himself from the legacy of the transcendental Thomists like Joseph Maréchal and Karl Rahner, opting instead to construe truth as a transcendental property of Being rather than as *constructive* power of human mind and will.[9] Human knowing, Balthasar insists, is always *responsive*. Knowledge responds to the disclosure of the mystery of Being. The *Theo-Logic* reframes epistemological questions in such a way that truth refers first to the *making known* of Being (disclosure, revelation) and then, subsequently—responsively—knowledge of Being (trustworthy understanding). To do this, he relies on a traditional participatory understanding of truth (Aquinas' *Disputations on Truth* is never far from his mind), developed through a phenomenological method. Balthasar considers the nature of truth through the way it appears in the world.[10] Epistemology, as Balthasar conceives it, is never

9. Transcendental Thomism struck Balthasar as "unduly anthropocentric, focusing on the knowing and willing human person, rather than on the mystery of being." Cf. Fergus Kerr, "Balthasar and Metaphysics" in *The Cambridge Companion to Hans Urs von Balthasar*, eds. Edward T. Oakes, S.J. and David Moss (Cambridge: Cambridge University Press, 2004), 225.
10. One can quite fruitfully play Balthasar's *Theo-Logic 1* and Karl Rahner's *Spirit in the World* off of

simply about the structures of the human act of knowing; it is also concerned with the knowledge of Being.[11] From the very beginning, then, Balthasar insists on the connection between ontology and epistemology, Being and knowing.[12]

"Consciousness" and Being

This ontological framing of truth has significant consequences for the entirety of the *Theo-Logic* and for Balthasar's theology of the saints. As an ontological reality, truth is the *expression* (*logos*) of Being. The idea of the *expressivity* of Being (the "self-speaking of Being")[13] is important for both the intelligibility of the world *and* Balthasar's later christological interpretation of truth. There, following Bonaventure, Balthasar defines the *Logos* as the "expression" of the Father. What the saints know when they know Christ is the expression of the Father, the source and the goal of all Being. But we are getting ahead of ourselves.

Balthasar conceives truth as considering the appearance of Being in concrete forms in the world of phenomena that we inhabit. This immediately raises the issue of the relation between appearance and reality. For Balthasar, there cannot be a one-to-one correspondence between the two, but neither are the two only nominally related. He

each other. Whereas Rahner's book serves an interesting combination of Aquinas and Heidegger through a transcendental anthropology framed around the question of Being and predicative knowledge, Balthasar's is concerned more with truth as its formal object. What Balthasar shows throughout *Theo-Logic* 1 is how worldly truth always opens up to ever larger landscapes of Being. Balthasar's account is influenced far more by Blondel than it is by Kant or even Heidegger. This harkens back to our discussion of Balthasar's concerns regarding Rahner's anonymous Christianity, discussed in chapter 2.

11. Balthasar rejects epistemological skepticism in no uncertain terms. Skepticism is unsatisfactory for Balthasar because it is *phenomenologically* untenable. Skepticism flies in the face of the "naive and unreflective" concept of truth that everyone has, at least until they are taught otherwise. This intuition of truth, common to all people, is that what appears, what is seen and known, is not a mere appearance, a phantasmic mimicry, dishonestly masquerading as Being. No, Balthasar insists that what appears *is* Being, and all people are intuitively, naively, aware of that. Every person is already familiar [*bekannt*] with Being, and "this familiarity of being is the innermost essence of truth" (*TL* 1, 37). Being appears to us in concrete forms. These forms are truthful insofar as they disclose Being in a faithful, trustworthy way.

12. We must again be clear on this point. Balthasar in no way is adopting the quest of absolute knowing that so beguiles Hegelian thought. The truth for Balthasar involves knowing *what is knowable*. As we shall see, this means more than anything that true knowledge is knowledge of the mystery of a thing. It is not an unlimited, comprehensive and totalizing vision that solves the mystery of Being. It is, rather, a receptive, creative engagement or participation in that mystery.

13. *Epilogue*, 79–86.

asserts that in human consciousness (*Bewußtsein*), Being invades concrete appearances.

Balthasar's study of truth begins with a phenomenology of consciousness itself. He argues that the phenomenon of consciousness demonstrates the ontological nature of knowledge. He makes much of the word for "consciousness": *Bewußtsein.* Balthasar interprets consciousness as meaning both "being *conscious*" (act) and "*being* conscious" or "conscious being" (Being).[14] Balthasar argues that "[i]t is this Being, then, that is immediately unveiled and present to consciousness. The thinking subject is always one that exists and recognizes that it does. In this way, it knows what Being is."[15]

What appears in the determinate forms is Being itself. Balthasar takes as a given the classical notion that Being is self-diffusive, but he couples this concept with an insistence that it is also self-disclosing. Being desires being known. Appearances are the way that Being, *as* Being, is unveiled and made known in the world.[16] Balthasar develops an account of truth under two aspects that enable the trustworthy knowledge of Being: "unveiling" (*aletheia*) and "fidelity" (*emeth*).

Truth as *aletheia* is the "unveiledness, uncoveredness, disclosedness, and unconcealment" of Being in which *Being* appears and *being* appears.[17] Both emphases are critical to what Balthasar does at *Theo-*

---

14. In 1955, Balthasar describes *Theo-Logic* 1 as a meditation on the question of the relation between Being and act, or, "the "question of the event-character of the *actus* (*essendi*)" (MW, 24).

15. *TL* 1, 37. Balthasar playfully appropriates Descartes, even as he undermines him, throughout the *Theo-Logic.* "We need only recall St. Augustine's terse rejoinder to the man who doubts everything: At least the doubter is certain of his doubt, and, in being certain of his doubt, he is implicitly certain that he is thinking, and in being certain that he is thinking, he is certain that he exists" (36). Just as Augustine had to counter the skeptics in his *Contra academicos*, Balthasar counters the radical skepticism that grounds Descartes' dogmatic epistemological certainty. The drive toward epistemological (and theological) mystery at the heart of *TL* 1 is, in many ways, a response to the legacy of rationalism that aims to make humans the masters of nature.

16. All Being has the potential of being unveiled. There are not two "parts" of Being—the unveiled and the veiled. All Being is unveiled, but, paradoxically, it is unveiled as veiled. Being is always revealed and hidden at precisely the same time. A concrete example of this might be seen in a marriage. Surely a man *knows* his wife, not comprehensively, but he knows her as the one who is always *more* than what he knows. He knows her truly when he knows that she is more than what he knows. This is also related to Plato's negative thought: Socrates is the wisest man because he *knows that he does not know* (cf. Plato's *aporia* of learning, and knowledge by way of recollection in *Meno*, 81D).

17. This is why Balthasar's Trilogy begins, rather than ends, with a theological aesthetics. The appearance of Being in its self-disclosure, in its *aletheia*, necessarily communicates itself as a form, an image which must be seen and, in this, perceived. A theological aesthetics is not an

Logic 1 proceeds. According to Balthasar, it is the chief property of Being to unveil itself so that it can be known. Truth understood as *aletheia* means that the totality of Being is disclosed. The emphasis on unveiling means that the truth of a thing is not hidden in some kind of *Ding an sich* that is something other than its appearance. It also does not mean that the appearance is a mirage "floating over nothing or over an abyss of enigma."[18]

That the nature of Being consists in its unveiling, this implies that there must also be subject to whom Being is unveiled. While it may be possible to imagine *a* being that is potentially, but not actually, known, this is not possible for Being itself. Were Being unveiled only for itself, it would remain locked up in itself, and not truly be unveiled. Truth requires both known and knower. Truth understood as *aletheia* thus reveals that Being is essentially relational because it is always related to some self-consciousness.[19]

Balthasar's account of *aletheia* is what underpins his optimism that what is unveiled to the knower is, in fact, Being itself: "If Being is really disclosed in its appearance, and if, in being disclosed, it can bear witness to itself, then all suspicion of mere seeming, illusion, or deception vanishes to make room for a certainty that reflects in consciousness the firmness, validity, and reliability of Being. *The knowledge is genuine because the thing known is itself genuine.*"[20] Balthasar adds the attribute *emeth*, fidelity, to his previous definition of truth as unveiling. As *emeth*, truth ends what Balthasar calls "a bad infinity" of

---

aesthetic embellishment of theological truth, but the very possibility of this truth coming to be known. This is why Balthasar insists that the truth of God takes on a concrete form in Jesus Christ. Contrary to Rahner's transcendental starting point for theological reflection, Balthasar emphasizes an aesthetic starting point in the flesh of Christ, the *Verbum caro*. Balthasar sees this as the distinctively Catholic starting point that theology needs to reclaim in the post-conciliar Church.

18. *TL* 1, 37.

19. As we will see below, these claims about truth as unveiling eventually lead Balthasar to assert the necessity of God for all creaturely knowledge. Truth requires not only the *potential* unveiling of Being, but that Being is already unveiled to a subject *in actuality*. For Balthasar, this absolute Subject is God. God's knowledge of created Being is the condition of the possibility of human knowledge: "Truth is the unconcealment of Being, while the full notion of this unconcealment requires someone to whom it is unconcealed. This someone is God and can only be God, because not all worldly being can be revealed to every worldly subject. Because it is unveiled to God, it can be unveiled to other subjects, without needing to be actually unveiled to them" (*TL* 1, 269).

20. *TL* 1, 38. Emphasis added.

epistemological uncertainty, suspicion, and conjecture. One can trust the validity (the fidelity) of what is unveiled. Truth is the *faithful* unveiling of Being.

We must take care not to misunderstand Balthasar on this point. Truth is unveiling so that Being can be known, but, contrary to titanic Idealism, this does not mean that truth can be *absolutely* known.[21] Truth as *emeth* opens up a "good infinity" of the limitless depth of Being's mystery.[22] Being is always *more* but never *other* than its appearance. There is a "unity of disclosure and concealment in every worldly truth."[23] This is why truth, even when known, retains its mysterious character. Again, truth is known *as* mystery.

These two dimensions of truth highlight the ecstatic nature of Being and knowledge. Truth is the ecstatic offering of Being itself to the subject's knowledge. However, it does not open itself only as single, particular object, but as the whole of Being. At the same time, truth as *emeth* opens up the subject to the "invitation to entrust oneself to this promised manifestness, to follow the certitude that truth imparts, and to give oneself over to this movement, which is already underway."[24] The ecstasy of truth thus indicates how it can be rationally *apprehensible* without being *comprehensible*: "the singular being becomes the place where we apprehend and penetrate the meaning and essence of a sample of 'world'. But this specimen of the world is only a tiny excerpt of Being as a whole, which, while unveiled in principle in this bit of Being, nonetheless remains transcendent and

21. "This closure of uncertainty and its bad infinity is the un-closing and unsealing of a true infinity of fruitful possibilities and situations. . . . Once Being has become evident, this evidence immediately harbors the promise of further truth; it is a door, an entrance, a key" to an ongoing journey into further truth. Balthasar insists that "[t]ruth never imprisons or constricts the knower. No, truth is always an opening, not just to itself and in itself, but to further truth. . . . It opens up the prospect of hitherto unknown territory" (*TL* 1, 39). It is the role of the Holy Spirit to lead the way into this unknown territory, as I will show in chapter 6.

22. Balthasar's insistence on the mystery present in truth's unveiling signals his resistance to Heidegger's famous claim that Christianity cannot ask the question of Being. The *Theo-Logic* thus battles on two fronts: it resists the totalizing vision of Hegel by insisting on truth's perpetual mystery and resists Heidegger by situating Being within the eternal mystery of God. God does not solve the riddle of Being, but heightens and deepens it. Cf. Kerr, 230–31.

23. *MW*, 24.

24. *TL* 1, 39.

veiled in its totality. . . . For this very reason, it awakens in the knower a[n erotic] yearning for *more*."[25]

The act of knowing therefore consists in harmonizing two seemingly contrary experiences. Knowledge involves *possessing* the object of knowledge in such a way that one has "the experience of being flooded by something that overflows knowledge in the heart of knowledge itself, or, to put it another way, the awareness of participating in something that is infinitely greater in itself than what comes to light in its disclosure."[26] This sense of being flooded opens the subject up in receptivity to the ever-greater disclosure of Being's truth.[27] That Balthasar adopts the language of receptivity here should alert us to the Ignatian flavor of Balthasarian knowledge. Knowledge requires receptivity, and so knowledge also requires love.

Knowing and Loving

Parsing the relationship between truth and knowledge leads Balthasar to develop a clear correspondence between ontology and epistemology. Balthasar frames the correspondence between them as love. His ontology is such that he identifies Being with love. Insofar as love is Being's truth, knowledge too must be love because "the inner reality of love can be known only by love."[28] Being-as-love requires knowledge-as-love, or what we might call participation.

Throughout the remainder of *Theo-Logic* 1, Balthasar develops a participative account of the subject/object relationship in order to show the way that love lies at heart of knowledge. Such an account frames knowledge as an act of love that involves the free, ecstatic participation of subject and object in each other. Balthasar "approaches the question of the intellect . . . from a rather different point of departure, which recasts the terms of the problem in a

---

25. Ibid., 40.
26. Ibid.
27. One can perhaps hear in Balthasar's thought an echo of the Ignatian *magis*, the "ever-greater" glory of God that structures Jesuit action and worship.
28. *LA*, 75.

fundamental way, and which in the end allows a view that integrates"[29] Being and knowledge, truth and love, into a seamless tapestry.

One cannot approach truth with a pre-determined, rationalistic framework that delimits its meaning. Such an approach inevitably results in the constriction of truth, the annihilation of its mystery. If one's epistemology can solve the mystery of truth, one can also solve—by eliminating—the mystery of Being altogether. Balthasar sees this as the tendency of the Prometheans, but he sees it also as the temptation of the neo-scholastic philosophy in which he was educated at Pullach. Any approach to truth that reduces the latter to mere theory, and denies the participative dimension of knowledge loses that truth. In response to these twin dangers, Balthasar focuses on the mutual participation of subject and object in each other as the source of truth and knowledge. Moreover, it is his focus on participation that allows him to thematize both Being and knowledge as love.

Participation and Love

Balthasar's participative epistemology addresses the relation between subject and object, mediating between a strict objectivism (his concern about neo-scholasticism) and a titanic subjectivism (his concern about Idealism). There is an ecstatic, and therefore participatory, character to the relationship between object and subject in Balthasar's thought. He argues that both the subject and the object reach their full potential only in the ecstatic extension of their boundaries and their standing outside themselves *in* and *for* the other.[30] This subjective–objective polarity forms the inner structure of human reason.[31]

---

29. Schindler, "Toward a Non-Possessive Concept of Knowledge," 579.
30. For Balthasar, "the very act of appropriation is an act of expropriation: the mind, one might say, leaves it own home, its mother and father, in order to cleave to its object and become one with it. . . . In a word, it is not only the will that represents the soul's movement beyond itself, but reason, too, is *essentially ecstatic*" (Schindler, "Toward a Non-Possessive Concept of Knowledge," 596). For a parallel of this kind of idea in Aquinas, see *Summa Theologiae* I-II, 28, 3. Henceforth abbreviated as *ST*.
31. "Rationality, taken in the narrower sense of the (in one way or another) conclusive disclosure of Being in knowledge, requires, as its condition of possibility, the disclosure of being as a whole, which is anything but conclusive. The foreground, namely, the individual Being susceptible of definition, becomes visible only against the background of Being as such, which, though present to awareness, is infinite and, therefore, cannot be defined. Rationality, taken in its comprehensive

Balthasar visualizes knowledge as the intellect's embrace of Being, a kind of taking possession. In the act of possessing Being in knowledge, the object is enclosed by the subject. But at precisely this moment of possession, the subject finds herself "initiated" [*inittiert*] into the limitless realm of disclosed Being. The knower who awakens to *particular* being (through, for example, the sight of her mother's smile) is initiated into a perpetual unfolding of *all* Being.

This initiation involves the subject's act of measurement. Intelligence measures objects and this is how they are known. Knowledge is possible only when an object is measured by the measuring subject. An object can be an object of knowledge only when it presents itself *as* an object, that is, as something that has already been measured, and not just potentially so. Measurement is what determines an object as "this" or "that." No object exists as a *pure* thing-in-itself, but always must be measured by a subject in order to be known.[32] Balthasar's definition of knowledge necessitates the mutual interplay of subject and object. Balthasar builds on this mutuality by explicating it as a kind of dialogue. This lays the ground for our later account of Balthasar's metaphysics of prayer and contemplation.

What this means in regard to truth is that humans know in two ways. First, humans know through the *adaequatio intellectus et rei*: "when knowledge, by virtue of an 'adequation' to the thing as it really is, lets

---

sense, thus entails two things at once: certainty of [subjectively] possessing some being as it in fact is—within a[n objective] totality of Being that, while disclosed in principle, *in concreto* always remains" (*TL* 1, 40–41).

32. In making this claim, Balthasar gestures toward a necessary transcendent third beyond the polarity of subject and object: "For an object to be knowable, it must not only be measured in principle but also already measured in fact. Now, since the object is not measured by itself insofar as it *is* an object, and since the finite subject already presupposes that the object is in fact measured, it follows that the object's measure must lie in the hands of the infinite subject, God. A being that was not known by God could not be known by a finite subject, for the simple reason that it would not exist in the first place. But it would not exist because, being unknown by God, it would have no measure for its being and thus no truth. All things, therefore, stand completely unveiled before the divine knowledge, and by that same knowledge they are measured. Their truth lies with God, and whoever wants to know them must know them in their adequation to the mind of God. This does not mean that the finite subject has no immediate relation to the object, as if, in order to know the object, it had to make a detour via God. It does mean, however, that the knowability of the object stems from its being actually known by God and that he alone knows its full truth" (*TL* 1, 56).

itself be determined and measured by the thing."[33] The object provides the decisive shape of the subject's knowledge of itself.

If Balthasar stopped here, however, the subject's knowledge would be purely passive receptivity. But Balthasar wants to maintain the passive *and* the active intellect. Though the object always remains the measure of its own truth, it is the subject's creative freedom that is the active agent of that measuring. In other words, the object offers itself as a *possible* object of knowledge that becomes an *actual* object through the creative agency of the subject.

Further, because an object's disclosure is meaningful only when it is disclosed to a subject, that subject's "freedom and spontaneity include the ability, not only to apprehend truth, but also positively to bring it into being [*setzen*]."[34] Subject and object thus participate in each other, but Balthasar describes this participation in *dramatic* terms: the subject receives and creatively *performs* objective truth.

Receptive Objectivity

Since the subject/object relation is one of mutual participation, both must be characterized by receptivity. An epistemology such as Balthasar's must consider the *nature* of the object, rather than focusing exclusively on the *conditions* of the object's knowability. For Balthasar, the order of knowing always corresponds to, and follows, the order of Being.[35] The type of ontology needed for a participatory epistemology involves more than the projection of the structure of knowing upon the object. And so, Balthasar interprets objective Being in terms of Being's receptivity.

We must here return to the idea of measurement. It is only when Being is unveiled in actuality, that is, in determinate *forms*, that it is inwardly illumined and measured. Only thus does it become an object

---

33. *TL* 1, 41.
34. Ibid.
35. This will be crucial for our conclusion. If the truth of Being is the divine love as revealed in Christ, then the corresponding form of knowing will be a participation and performance of that divine love in Christ. Hence I will argue that the saints at prayer is Balthasar's image of a genuine theo-logic as a performance of truth.

that can offer itself as an object of knowledge. Balthasar makes a sly theological move here: if Being is ever to be knowable to a finite subject, it must have been measured already. This means that the knowability of all created things indicates that they have already been known by an eternal Subject: God.

God's measurement, or God's idea of the object, is that object's *eidos*. Knowledge of any object, then, must know it in God. "Their truth lies with God, and whoever wants to know them must know them in their adequation to the mind of God."[36] Human knowledge participates in God's own knowledge. We should take care not to misunderstand Balthasar at this point. He is not suggesting some sort of Idealist "absolute knowing" where the finite subject knows all things with some sort of divine, objective knowledge. Balthasar knows that truth is always situated in subjectivity and can only be known thereby. Instead, he stresses that God's knowledge of Being, as its absolute source, serves as the *exemplar* of knowledge that determines every object and all of its relations.

Further, the divine eidetic plan for each object means that each object is a "living entelechy" that has meaning [*Sinn*] beyond itself. Because the *eidos* of the object lies hidden in God, Balthasar claims that the truth of the object always transcends its determinative form. Created things thereby become significant by pointing beyond—or *through*—themselves to the infinite source of their measured Being.

This raises the important but complicated relation between the object's *appearance* (its showing itself forth in its existence) and its *essence* (what it is "in itself"—insofar as any object can be "in itself"). The truth of the object always is more, though not other than, its appearance.[37] By nature of its grounding in God, truth transcends its

36. *TL* 1, 56. This is the rationale for subsuming *Wahrheit* into the *Theologik*. Even a philosophical work like *Wahrheit* is ultimately part of a *Theo-Logic* insofar as it explores the concrete world where God has encountered us through Christ. We can find an interesting precursor to Balthasar's thought throughout Dante's *Paradiso*, where Beatrice knows all of the pilgrim's thoughts—and indeed, nearly everything else in creation—because she sees things "in the mind of God."

37. "And so we see before us a progressive, seamless transcendence of the truth of the object. On the first level, truth dwells within the object and holds the measure of its existence. Truth on this level expresses only what the object in fact is at any given moment. But, as a living entelechy, truth rises above the factual level to achieve the unity of a plan. Finally, this entelechy is itself

determinative object, even if we can only encounter this transcendence in the particular, finite form.

There are two points we must note here. The first is that no object is strictly identical to its factual existence. The object's eidetic transcendence is what grounds Balthasar's account of the mysteriousness of the object, and, from that, of all Being. Because the fullness of the object lies solely in God's infinity, and not in the object itself, all things have a fundamentally mysterious transcendence to them.

The second point follows from this. Because the object is naturally mysterious, *all* knowledge of that object is, at least implicitly, an act of revelation, not just from the object, but also from its absolute, divine source. God reveals the object's reality (*eidos*) to that object. The revelatory quality of knowledge means that every object is constituted by receptivity. Its openness to its absolute measure is what constitutes it as an object. The object is not static, but rather characterized by ongoing receptivity before God. This allows Balthasar to conclude, perhaps surprisingly, that the object is *being* that, at its core, is *becoming* in the mind of God, because it always receives itself anew from God.

Knowledge, then, consists in the subject's endeavor to know the relation of the object's immanent form (*Gestalt, morphē*), its appearance, to its transcendent *eidos*. But this is possible only if the subject endeavors to behold the object in, before, and with, God. In other words, true knowledge occurs only in a double participation: that of the subject and the object in each other and of both in God.

Subjective Knowing

Let us now turn to Balthasar's account of how the subject knows. Balthasar, playing off of Aquinas, says that subjectivity has two poles: the creative and the receptive. The intellect receives truth (*intellectus*

transcended in an overarching plan knowable only to the providence that orders creatures in relation to one another. The mysterious center and summit of this providence is the total idea that God in his sovereign freedom has of an entity, by which he measures it and which he reveals to no other thing in its totality" (*TL* 1, 58).

possibilis) and produces it (*intellectus agens*). Reason's functions are twofold: a "receptive, consenting self-abandonment [*Hingabe*] . . . and judgement."[38] Knowledge moves as the balanced arbitration of these two functions, receptivity and creativity. Knowing is therefore contemplative as *theoria* and creative as *poesis*, or, in Balthasarian language, as "measured" and "measuring."[39]

Knowledge begins, according to Balthasar, in self-consciousness. Self-consciousness is self-measurement. A being that measures itself is called a "subject." This subject is full of light and becomes transparent to itself. This is the coincidence of being and consciousness. This self-consciousness grants the subject access to the *inner* dimension of itself and to the *outer* dimension of Being. These two disclosures are identical:

> If the disclosure of the subject's inner dimension were primary, while the disclosure of the outer dimension of objects were merely posterior, the original measure with which the subject measured and judged things would be exclusively subjective. Because it would always be applying *itself* to things, it would never attain objective knowledge. If, conversely, the dimension of the world were disclosed before the subject's own inner dimension, the subject would have no measuring stick to apply to objects, because this measuring stick has to be the full measurement of Being. But the full measure of Being entails self-consciousness. The coincidence of the two disclosures—that of the self and that of the world—guarantees the true objectivity both of the knowledge of the self and of the knowledge of the world.[40]

It is a being's self-consciousness that allows its openness and receptivity to what is other. Self-consciousness is the key to receptivity and vice versa. But Balthasar does not interpret receptivity as a kind of bland passivity. Receptivity is an act of the will, a form of genuine hospitality, a willed openness, an invitation to participation.

There are a few significant consequences for Balthasar's claim here.

---

38. *TL* 1, 58.
39. The disposition of *Hingabe* plays an important role throughout Balthasar's work. *Hingabe* is a characteristic of subjective knowledge in his epistemology, but it is also one of the chief characteristics of the saints. Both forms of *Hingabe*, the epistemological and the saintly, are, we shall see, possible because they share in the *Hingabe* or kenosis of the divine *Logos*.
40. *TL* 1, 44.

The first is that there is a clear correspondence between *a* being's self-consciousness and its ability to host that which is other than itself. Balthasar here adopts the language of interiority. It is this self-consciousness that allows one to recognize and receive the other as other. Plants and animals, though receptive to external things, have no subjectivity, and therefore, no ability to accept them as other. The external world is not an object to them because they themselves are not subjects: "The world is unlocked in its objectivity only to man, because his self-consciousness gives him the measure of being."[41]

The second thing of note is that this subjective receptivity involves reciprocity with the object. It is not the case that the subject stands complete in itself and hosts the object as a stranger. The subject's knowing is not monological, but dialogical. The subject's knowledge requires a willed openness to the other. The subject may have the measure of Being, but it does not have an all-encompassing, all-penetrating vision of Being in its totality.

Third, the subject must adopt a certain intellectual poverty and humility before the object, a surrender (*Hingabe*, or *Gelassenheit*). The poverty of the subject is what enables her receptivity. This poverty indicates that truth cannot exist without the exchange between subject and object: "self-knowledge and the disclosure of the world are not just simultaneous but intrinsically inseparable."[42] The self-consciousness that gives rise to subjectivity should not be misunderstood as primordial self-preoccupation that only ventures outside itself *after* comprehending its own ego. The subject comes to herself, and hence, to knowledge, only by being addressed in the dialogue with the object. More specifically, the subject comes to herself in the surrender in which the mutuality with the object occurs. This surrender and mutuality is the subject's ecstasy.

It is at this point in his account of subjectivity that Balthasar most clearly articulates his thesis that love is the nature of Being and knowledge. His emphasis on subjective receptivity allows Balthasar to

41. Ibid., 45.
42. Ibid., 46.

113

make the gradual reduction from self-consciousness to love. For him, subjective receptivity is only possible if it is motivated by love.

Balthasar conceives of subjectivity and objectivity coming to fullness only through the ecstasy of their mutual indwelling and participation.[43] Each has a mission to and for the other; if either remains enclosed in itself, knowledge does not occur. Balthasar articulates the meeting place of subject and object as "form," *Gestalt*. This is how Balthasar begins to bridge the gap between realism and idealism—between thing and think—in his logic.

Objects of knowledge are never self-enclosed. The object is dramatic and the *sensorium* of the subject is the stage of its drama: "Without the subject's sensory space, [the object] would not be what it is; it would be incapable of fulfilling its *raison d'être*, the idea that it is supposed to embody,"[44] that is, to be known.

But why is the divine knowledge (its *eidos*) of the object not sufficient for the object's coming to be? Why does the object need also a *finite* space in order to come into being? Balthasar distinguishes here between the object's "ontological truth" and the "truth of knowledge." The object's ontological truth is hidden in the divine *eidos*, but the truth of knowledge "consists solely in the subject's conformity to this already established [ontological] fact."[45] This raises once again the issue of "appearance" and "reality." The object presents itself through an appearance which is its self-offering to the subject. Once the appearance of the object has made its home in subjectivity, so to speak, that appearance conveys its "full ontological weight."[46]

---

43. "The revelation of the object can occur only in the space provided by the subject. This space alone, in fact, has already the creative light to draw from the object possibilities that it can no more unfold by itself than a seed can develop without sunlight. On the other hand, the revelation of the subject can occur only in an encounter with the object. Without the resistance of the object, it could never transform its possible light into actuality, just as sunlight becomes a brightness only when it enters into the medium of air. The subject's self-knowledge can reach its actuality only by taking a detour by way of the knowledge of another; only in going out of itself, in creatively serving the world, does the subject become aware of its purpose and, therefore, of its essence" (TL 1, 62).

44. Ibid., 63.

45. Ibid.

46. "For it now comes to light that this appearance within the subject is the expressive field of the soul. A smiling face is not simply a dull reflection of inner joy but rather its embodiment, its communication, its formation, its liberation. In the same way, the appearance of the object is

The object realizes itself by means of the subject. Understanding (*Verstehen*) is neither the object's impression on a passively receptive mind (a kind of empiricism) nor a unilateral act of the mind upon a passive object (as in Idealism), but rather the mutual participation of subject and object in each other.

This is where Balthasar's concept of *Gestalt* plays a mediating role. It is the "intelligible manifestation" that is neither purely subjective nor purely objective.[47] *Gestalt* is the knowable "third thing" between subject and object, the "fruit" of their mutual, ecstatic encounter. The subject rises up out of itself in a creative inhabitation of its object. The knower's ecstatic indwelling (*conformitas*) with the object realizes the object's own nature.

But *Gestalt* is something more than the "fact" of the object known. *Gestalt* is what David C. Schindler calls the object's "being-for" the knower. It is Being's manifestation of itself in a particular, concrete form of appearance. But, just as in all appearances, what appears always points through itself to some unseen, unknowable depth. The possibility of knowledge arises in the *Gestalt* because it is home to both the manifestation *and* the mystery of the object's truth.[48]

Balthasar describes the subject's participation in the object as an *active receptivity*. Knowledge is an act of service—the subject's

---

not a pale duplicate of its self-quiescent essence but the necessary unfolding in which its inner plentitude becomes manifest for the first time" (*TL* 1, 65).

47. Schindler, "Toward a Non-Possessive Concept of Knowledge," 593.

48. Operative in the background here is the scholastic understanding that knowledge involves the abstraction from particulars toward the *quidditas* or universal "what-ness" of a thing. Aquinas, for example, says that "the soul *first* apprehends its object intellectually, by abstracting the intelligible species—the essence—of the thing, becoming 'intentionally' identical with it through the act of understanding . . . and thus quite literally 'internalizing' its intelligible form . . . insofar as 'the proper object of the human intellect, which is united to a body, is a quiddity or nature existing in corporeal matter', some immaterial 'aspect' of it must be abstracted from it for such an adequation to be possible: this is the form, which is distinct from the object's matter and thus can be distinguished by the active power of the mind (active intellect) as an intelligible species. . . . 'For it is quite true that the mode of understanding, in one who understands, is not the same as the mode of a thing in existing: since the thing understood is immaterially in the one who understands, according to the mode of the intellect, and not materially, according to the mode of a material thing" (Schindler, "Toward a Non-Possessive Concept of Knowledge," 581). Aquinas here insists that what dwells immaterially in the intellect is the thing-in-itself, an idea that Kant will reject in favor of our "concept" of the thing-in-itself. Balthasar is attempting to mediate between the two approaches though he leans a bit more, though not uncritically, toward realism. See his emphasis on the situated-ness of truth in *TL* 1, 179ff.

obedience and willed conformity to the object. Knowledge begins with "the unannounced invasion of a motley jumble of objects that get thrown into the subject's unoccupied space"[49] rather than with ordering judgment. The subject is expropriated by the world, laboriously bent with the task of sifting, until it "grasps that the world is just as truly in itself."[50] The subject's obedience gradually allows it to penetrate the appearance of the object, to discover the truth of the object *in* (not apart from) that appearance.[51] The task of the subject is to become "cosmoform," to be *in-formed* by the truth of the world.[52] In the mutuality of this participation, the intellect changes by conforming more closely with the sea of objects that it carries within itself.

Knowledge is not a type of domination, or will-to-power. Knowledge rises from the creative intellect of the subject (*intellectus agens*) as moderated by the receptive intellect (*intellectus possibilis*). For Balthasar, receptivity governs the process of knowing. The subject's self-forgetfulness and self-abandonment (*Hingabe, Gelassenheit*) allows her to abandon herself willfully for the sake of receiving the object. Notice how closely Balthasar's language here parallels the language of Ignatian spirituality. The surrender, the *indiferencia*, the receptivity—in short, love—funds all knowledge.[53]

---

49. *TL* 1, 63.
50. Interestingly, the idea of expropriation runs through Balthasar's account of the mystics and the saints as well. The mystic, he says, will always find herself "expropriated" from the church—and this is precisely her mission *for* the church. The mystic, like the subject, is expropriated by love so that she can know and make known the truth more fully. See *GL* 1, 410ff.
51. "The subject learns to understand sensible words as an expression of an intelligible content, to read them as a signification and revelation of a sense that is immanent in the sign itself" (*TL* 1, 63).
52. Balthasar is influenced at this point by Maurice Blondel's idea of *conformitas*. For Blondel, truth comes, not through conformity to some kind of "objective reality" that is cold and impersonal. It comes, rather, through conformity with the *givenness* of the object, with the "will-willing" and "will-willed." Blondel's is a philosophy that is very much in accord with the movement toward a personalist, agapeic interpretation of truth. Truth comes, not solely through the factuality of the object, but also attends and corresponds with the object's act of giving itself. For Blondel, this also means the *conformitas* between mind and life. See Oliva Blanchette, *Maurice Blondel: A Philosophical Life* (Grand Rapids: Eerdmans, 2010), 149ff, and 311–12. One knows, according to Blondel, through the unfolding of action in one's human life, rather than through a mere act of intellection.
53. "Accordingly, the knowing subject's fundamental attitude must be the posture that is required by the phenomenology itself: total, *indifferent* readiness to receive, which presupposes the exclusive desire to receive and reproduce the phenomenon as purely as possible." In this way, knowledge is "objective"—that is, it is *justice*: "inasmuch as with incorruptible honesty it acknowledges, and metes out to the object, what in fact is its due" (*TL* 1, 76).

Freedom and Interiority

Balthasar's account of participation, especially as he interprets it as a kind of love, would crumble if the indwelling of subject and object were forced or automatic. Love requires freedom. Participation, if it is to be understood as love, cannot occur by means of force, coercion, or exploitation. And so Balthasar must supplement his account of participation with a renewed emphasis on the freedom and interiority of both subject and object. These two factors will safeguard Being's irreducible mystery and help Balthasar's account of truth resist the charges of absolute knowledge.

Balthasar distinguishes between a being's external appearance (*Erscheinungen*) in the realm of the subject's *sensorium*, and that which produces this appearance. He broaches the problem common in the wake of Kant, namely, the relationship between the appearance of a thing and the thing-in-itself.

The interiority of beings is precisely what safeguards their mystery. It is their *magis*, their transcendental "more," that shines within and through appearance, without being reduced to that appearance. This is their interiority, and without it, every thing that exists could be subjected to the penetrating, comprehensive gaze of the titanic knowledge. As it stands, however, studying a thing's *phenomenal* appearance only yields hints, suggestions, and intimations of the essence that is not directly available to sense perception. There is therefore no dogmatic certainty, no encompassing vision, that comprehends the full reality of a thing. Ever-fuller, richer conceptions that make better sense of the mystery of the thing-in-itself can supersede these provisional hypotheses. Exact science "is no more and no less than a never-ending attempt to woo the core of the material world, which is not directly available to sense perception."[54]

The knower is always aware that she has not penetrated the very heart of a thing through the outward manifestations of its particular life. She *perceives* that the possibilities of life are abundantly *greater*

---

54. Ibid., 85.

than what she has seen, even if these possibilities are not *other* than what she has beheld. She recognizes that there is not a one-to-one correspondence between the outward manifestation of the thing and its inner essence. The being of a thing is always more than what is on display, just as the truth of a painting is not exhausted when one beholds the collection of brushstrokes on canvas. The depth of the thing radiates in and through the surface.

The meaning of an object "so utterly eludes exhaustive investigation that it can continue to engage inquirers until the end of time yet never ends up as a heap of unmysterious, completely surveyable facts."[55] And yet, the knower recognizes that she beholds nothing more than "the primitive movement from an inexhaustible inside into an always determinately formed outside. Things thereby show that they live their own life and that the point of their experience is not simply limited to being an object of some knowledge."[56] They are, rather, "silent words" that rely on a subject to interpret and articulate their silent life to the world. The subject penetrates the intimacy of their interiority to whatever extent is possible, and brings that interiority to expression in the world.

What lies between interiority and expression is freedom. Humanity has the ability to administer its own reality self-consciously. Because of this, humanity is the first creature that can speak both truth *and* untruth.[57] In the human person, it is the subject who possesses the measure between itself and its expression. In a human, Being reveals itself *to* itself in an illuminated self-consciousness. This revelation thus enables a sharing of that revelation to others. But the crucial change here is that this revelation is now an act of freedom. The human is predisposed to communication, but not impelled by nature to communicate itself. Silence and hiddenness are possible in freedom.

This freedom results in an "entirely new attitude" in knowledge. The object may freely unveil itself *genuinely* without *completely* giving itself.

55. *TL* 1, 85.
56. Ibid., 88.
57. This will be an important concept for Balthasar's theological exposition of soteriology. What Christ heals is "the lie" that created Being embraces through Adam.

Free objects unveil and veil themselves in the same act of disclosure in exterior manifestation, being-for-itself and being-for-another at one and the same time. The self-communication of the object is not therefore a merely passive emanation of its internal world. It is rather a *testimony* [*Zeugnis*], and its truth is *fidelity* (*emeth*). The interior word of the object is not forced outward in determinative forms. It emerges creatively, as disclosure and trust and, most importantly, as *free* surrender. It is freedom that is the condition of the possibility of *Gelassenheit* that surrenders itself as an object of knowledge.[58]

Mystery and Form

That creatures have freedom and interiority means that mystery is an essential characteristic of Being and knowledge. Balthasar refuses to reduce mystery to a product of finitude. This would mean that mystery is only temporary. Knowledge and mystery would then be stuck in a zero-sum game where an increase in knowledge causes a decrease in mystery, and vice versa. Rather than opposing knowledge and mystery, Balthasar sees knowledge as operating *within* and *for the sake of* mystery. As we will see, this is a further extension of Balthasar's reimaging of truth as love.

In fact, Balthasar sees an analogy between the knower and the lover. The lover is neither rationalistic nor fideistic about his beloved, but his love *is* supra-rational. So too the thinker. Just as the lover's first awakening to love draws him into a new life of loving—for the lover "must live every day anew at the very origin of love and therein continue to probe and question it"—so too the thinker's search for truth perpetually renews itself, never content to rest on its laurels.[59] Just as the lover never comprehends his beloved, no rationality can

---

58. "Receptivity is thus like a deep, unclose-able breach opened up in the closed circle of being-for-itself. Only by welcoming things from the outside and remaining open to them, only by being given over to the service of what is other than itself, can man's spirit lay claim to being of its own" (*TL* 1, 98).

59. *TL* 1, 24–25.

ever fully comprehend an object, not even the essence of a fly.[60] Nor should knowledge ever desire to comprehend its object fully.

Balthasar believes that knowledge desires its object by desiring its object's mystery. The lover desires to receive his beloved anew every day. The same applies to the knower. Knowledge is perpetually nourished by the freshness of wonder and rapture. Knowledge as a form of love is neither fideistic, insofar as it desires truly to *know*, nor rationalistic, insofar as refuses to comprehend its object. Love opts instead for the bedazzlement of the object in her mystery. Love resists titanic, discursive comprehension through the delight (*dilectus*) of receptivity and mutual indwelling.

Claiming that knowledge should desire an object's mystery might strike us as a strange claim at first. But Balthasar insists on it. As we have seen, he holds that the nature of knowledge must correspond with the nature of what it knows. If the object is fundamentally mysterious, then a proper knowledge of that object must know and love it in its mystery. Let us begin with the former point, that all objects are irreducibly mysterious.

It is in the form or image that subject and object first meet. But Balthasar insists that images are insubstantial in themselves, and therefore, awaken the yearning for more. Thus, the image is always understood as a sign through which the interiority of the subject looks and penetrates the interiority of the object.

Balthasar identifies two potential dangers in determining the relation between image and truth. One danger is the assertion that truth occurs totally apart from the image and lies solely in the essential that lies beyond the image. According to this view, truth is nothing other than interiority; appearances evoke not truth, but only opinion. Balthasar identifies this mentality with rationalism and what he labels "idealist mysticism." The goal is to penetrate the essence of the object by bypassing the image entirely.[61] This negative mysticism tries to

---

60. Aquinas, *In Symbolum Apostolorum* proemium. For more on this theme in Aquinas, cf. Frederick Christian Bauerschmidt, *Thomas Aquinas: Faith, Reason, and Following Christ* (Oxford, Oxford University Press, 2013), 112–14.
61. *TL* 1, 136–37.

"clarify the images by dissolving them into a concept or immediate intellectual intuition, as if the appearances were merely a mist that dissipates in the rising sun."[62] In the end, this tendency renders appearance completely superfluous to knowledge and to truth.

One might also err in the opposite direction by trapping truth within the image. This is the tendency of empiricism and what Balthasar calls mysticisms of immediacy. This tendency "foregoes any truth behind the appearances, in order to seek it immediately in the abundance and flow of the appearances themselves."[63] The consequence of this, of course, is that truth is never substantial, and therefore, never realized. Truth is always in flux, always becoming.

These mysticisms are attempts to derive meaning and significance without a signifier. They attempt to comprehend truth apart from any mediation. They both deny the world its vocation as mediator and signifier. Both end up losing the world because they fail to see the world as signifying truth *through* itself that is *other* than itself. But as Balthasar's phenomenology of Being has shown, every appearance discloses something beyond itself, yet this something more can manifest itself in no other way than through the mediation of that appearance. Idealist mysticism attempts to attain an immediate relation to the thing-in-itself solely through the machinations of thought. Empiricist mysticism strives after an immediacy of the image itself, forsaking any sort of meaning beyond that image. In one way or another, both lose the concrete reality of the world.

Expression

For Balthasar, the object's appearance is the very form of that object's ecstatic self-expression. The appearance communicates the meaning and significance of the thing-in-itself (*Bedeutung*). It is when the image [*Bild*] of a thing and its sense [*Sinn*] come together that a symbol

---

62. Ibid.
63. Ibid.

[*Sinnbild*] emerges.[64] This symbol "from now on transcends the sum of its parts."[65]

No aspect of the [thing's] sense has remained behind the expression; everything that was meant to be expressed has found its form. The upshot is that precisely the perfection of the expression is a perfect mystery. Indeed, it is an essential mystery, which no interpretation can progressively approach or gradually clear up. Every time we encounter, it is whole and intact and resists all analysis. Here we begin to sense that mystery is an abiding property of truth itself. In the empty dialectic between being and appearance, the mystery was present only in the form of incomprehensibility, of opacity. Now it appears as a quality of transparent revelation.[66]

For Balthasar, truth is the opening of Being in willful self-disclosure for the sake of another. This other is both subject and object, both I and Thou. This disclosure for another requires a threefold movement: 1) that which discloses itself; 2) the appearance as that which is actually disclosed; 3) the movement itself of the ground into the appearance.

---

64. But there is perhaps something more going on here than even Balthasar's critique of epistemological immediacy. Michel de Certeau suggests that modernist epistemology arises from modernity's inability to know *orantically*: "In this multifarious history of a 'sacramental body' in search of its 'Church body, or of a visible 'head' in search of its 'mystical' members, one trait is of special interest in the question of the apparition of mystical science: the progressive concentration of the debates around *seeing*. Without this new focus, it would be impossible to understand how much was being instituted during that period [16th and 17th centuries] in the visual mode: the revolution in painting in the fifteenth century . . . and the invention of perspective; the cartographic encyclopedism of knowledge; the role of optics in modern scientificity; the theories of language as 'painting'; the dialectics of the look and of representation; and so on. It was a real modification of man's experience: vision slowly invaded the previous domain of touch or of hearing. It transformed the very practice of knowledge and signs" (Michel de Certeau, *The Mystic Fable*, trans. Michael B. Smith [Chicago: Chicago University Press, 1992], 89). Surely, de Certeau's emphasis here on the visible is correct. The connection between visibility of empiricism is clear enough. But it is common even among the rationalists, especially Descartes, that champion of the science of optics. Yet what it most interesting is that Descartes' rationalism begin with a suspicion of the visible (how could he trust his senses?), but ended up with the visibility of reason, where the rational part of a man penetrates and beyond the thing in itself. These philosophies turn on the same theological problem of the mystical—that hard and fast dichotomy between the visible and the invisible. Because these philosophies simply assume this dichotomy, an unavoidable implication emerges: that there must a fundamental re-structuring of the relations between fact and meaning, between appearance and the thing-in-itself. The natural, signifying relation between appearance and thing is severed here, just as was the natural relation between subject and object. This philosophical dichotomy is the result of a corruption in the Christian mystical tradition, or as de Certeau says, an inability to hold together a "structural homology between the mystical knowledge of the *oratikos* and the [visible] ecclesiastical hierarchy" (90).
65. *TL* 1, 141.
66. Ibid.

This movement is an act, an expression, and a bestowal of participation of the appearance in the reality of its ontological ground. This means that the appearance is not a second being alongside the ground, but is, in fact, the appearance *of the ground*. This is truth as *emeth*.

But there is not an absolute stasis between ground and appearance. The movement between the two is the dynamic third that makes possible this polarity in Being. It is also this movement, which has no absolute beginning,[67] in which Being measures itself, and thus, becomes light to itself; this movement distinguishes dynamic Being-for-another from a static Being-in-itself. Being therefore *is* communication. For Balthasar, there is no deeper ontological ground than this communication; there is no silent un-word that undergirds Being's self-expression. Being *is* expression, albeit free and mysterious.

Balthasar insists that there is nothing *beyond* Being's self-communication. "Here the ground becomes bottomless. The ground of the communication is, in fact, nothing other than the communication itself, which is therefore groundless."[68] Because one cannot penetrate to any mechanism behind this communication, it is no longer possible to answer, or even *ask*, the question why anything should will to disclose itself to us in its Being. Truth has no why. There simply is the truth of Being as the inexplicable will-to-give. It is Being's groundless communication and self-giving that characterizes it as love. Thus, truth is nothing other than the mystery of Being interpreted as love:

> Insofar as we consider the mystery of love as lying "behind" the truth, we have to say that all truth is reducible to it, that truth derives its meaning as truth from it, and that, far from mastering and explaining it as mystery, truth must fall silent in humility before it. But insofar as the mystery indwells the truth itself, insofar as truth is a moment in the self-disclosure of Being, the mystery is not something alien to truth. From this point of view, the mystery is not some irrational background from which

---

67. ". . . we must not imagine that Being begins with a self-contained, not-yet-disclosed depth, which then, as a kind of afterthought, opens itself to the outside and, if it is so minded, goes out of itself into an appearing surface. No: Being does not get its depth until it becomes inwardly illumined, until it obtains an interior space, an intimate zone, until it passes over (or better: has always already passed over) from the superficiality of mere being-in-itself into the depth and interiority of being-for-itself" (*TL* 1, 218).

68. *TL* 1, 223.

truth emerges. Rather, truth itself irradiates mystery, and it is of the very essence of truth to manifest this radiant mystery through itself.[69]

Truth, when structured by love, wills the perpetual mystery of the object rather than attempting to overcome that mystery.

What kind of mind can understand truth as Balthasar has framed it? For Balthasar, the knowing mind is aesthetic before it is conceptual. "Though we might try to circumscribe, even to describe, the content these things express, we would never succeed in rendering it adequately. This expressive language is addressed primarily, not to conceptual thought, but to the kind of intelligence that perceptively reads the *Gestalt* of things."[70] Knowledge becomes a kind of *form-reading*. The knower *sees*, yes, but seeing truly is the perception of Being's form as it is revealed in the appearance of beings, in the fruit of the meeting of subject and object in the *Gestalt*.[71] If Being's manifestation of itself in an image is the movement from interiority to exteriority, then knowledge is a movement from the external to the internal by means of self-remembrance or re-collection (*sich erinnert*).[72] The images themselves invite knowledge to this "searching

---

69. *TL* 1, 223.

70. Ibid., 140.

71. "This, then, is how the aesthete lives and views the world. He correctly apprehends that there is such a thing as significance. Yet he falls into another, albeit more subtle, form of detaching the phenomenal image from the core of Being as if it were a thing in its own right. Because the image world really shows on its surface the whole self-expressing depth, the aesthete believes that he can dispense with the depth itself. He does not see that the signifier stops being significant as soon as there is no longer anything here for it to signify. Yet again the world of images is isolated in itself. As a result, it is once more haunted by unreality. As soon as we cut off the living world of signification from the ontological root that sustains it, it withers and dies. The aesthetic life is therefore just as solitary as the sensory image that has not yet ben elevated into spirit. By isolating the experience of beauty, the unreality and solitude of pure aesthetics eventually cause even its beautifying character to fade. When one tries to cultivate beauty in an abstract purity, it produces only surfeit and bitter *Weltschmerz*. And it does this, not only because it happens to be temporally fleeting, but because of its own essential, intrinsic properties" (*TL* 1, 144). With this in mind, it is not surprise that Balthasar begins his Trilogy with aesthetics, but that *TL* 1 was first volume written.

72. Walker's translation of *sich erinnert* as "recollection" needs qualification. This recollection should by no means be limited to a purely Platonic sense. Operative here is a theological understanding of the world of images as vestiges of God. Knowledge is not a recollection of a primal but forgotten unity. It is rather a re-*collection*, a drawing together of those scattered expressions of the primordial Word and seeing in them their absolute source. It can only be, as we shall see below, christological and pneumatological. Balthasar's term is at least as Pentecostal as it is Platonic. This divine Source is not something the mind has access to in and of itself by recollection. It is, rather, something that is gradually disclosed in and through the images themselves. It understands images as images *of something*, or as *vestiges*. Knowledge as recollection is a gathering of all images

movement," of an increasing penetration into the heart of the appearance wherein lies its truth.

Truth is thus conceived as an act of love, a *donatum* and an invitation, which is creatively received and known *by* love. We turn now to make explicit an assumption that has been operative in all the preceding: that knowledge is itself a metaphysical act of love.

Knowledge as Love

The mystery of Being requires an epistemology that unites the knower through love with the mystery of Being's truth as love. To make sense of this, we must consider the ontological vision that Balthasar has presented. The image of Being that has emerged thus far is that Being is co-extensive with love. If Schindler is correct that Balthasar is attempting to overcome the dichotomy between will and intellect, then by equating Being with love, he draws the acts of knowing and loving together into a single metaphysical act of truth.

> It is possible, of course, even for a non-lover to perceive certain states of affairs accurately. But his intelligence resembles the vision of the nearsighted man: acute, even excessively so, in seeing details, it is incapable of surveying the broad prospects of truth [its *Gestalt*]. It is no accident that the devil is said to be smart and stupid at the same time. Because the full truth can be attained only in love, only the lover can have the real eye for it. He alone is ready to disclose himself truly and thus to bring to completion the movement in which the truth of being comes into existence. Moreover, he alone is able to respond selflessly when another confides in and opens up to him, perhaps seeks his help, questions him, or calls to him. In this way, the lover brings to completion the movement in which the truth, this time of knowledge, comes into existence. We therefore have good reason for saying that truth originates from love, that love is more original and more comprehensive than truth. Love is the ground that accounts for truth and enables it to be. And yet, we cannot say that love was on the scene before truth and that love can be conceived without truth. For the self-disclosure of Being and knowing, whose primordial name is love, also directly and immediately bears the name of truth.[73]

through Christ and the Holy Spirit, into a higher, more unified *Weltenshaunung*, a mosaic of worldly truth that intimates the divine.

73. *TL* 1, 112.

Unveiling, Mystery, Love

We have seen that the nature of truth is trustworthy unveiledness, *aletheia* and *emeth*. When an object unveils itself to a subject, it is an act of ontological confession: "this is what I am." This confession in the appearance is faithful to its hidden reality; truth's unveiling is therefore an act of faith and fidelity. An object's disclosure of itself in its external appearance is also an act of vulnerability. The object's disclosure must be met by the outstretched love of the subject who receives the vulnerable object with benevolence and mercy. The object's unveiling is not absolute. The interiority of Being forms the boundary of each act of disclosure. Things are not totally unveiled. There is a limit to their unveiling which emerges naturally within the *real distinction* of essence and existence. Attendant with every unveiling is a subsequent, and even greater, veiling.[74]

We are left then with a seeming paradox: truth is unveiled veiling [*als verhüllte enthüllt*]. This paradox is not an antinomy, but rather, the natural conclusion of the appearance of Being. Balthasar's optimism that Being itself appears is coupled to an intuition that there is something *more* than the appearance of the thing. Thought grasps at appearances, finds them lacking, and so, sets off on its quest for the "more" intimated through those appearances. In every act of knowledge, we are confronted with the infinite horizon of truth. This confrontation with infinity begets wonder.

When thought stands before the inexhaustible wealth of Being, the proper attitude is *thaumazein*, wonder, at Being's truth "hidden in plain sight." Wonder is an immanent characteristic of knowledge *per se*. The sense of mystery permeates all knowledge. If mystery were something eradicated by the acquisition of knowledge, then wonder would be satiated and knowledge would cease. Being's mystery and knowledge's wonder are two sides of Balthasar's concept of truth. Only something

---

74. We have here another of Balthasar's deliberate echoes of Lateran IV: *in tanta similitudine maior dissimilitudo* ["in every similarity [between God and world], there is an ever greater dissimilarity"

fundamentally and irreducibly endowed with mystery can stimulate wonder, and only mystery is worthy of the love that is the way of truth.

The subject's wonder can be neither pure act nor pure potency. Were it pure act, the subject would *anticipate* the actual reception of truth.[75] This is precisely what it cannot do, because then truth would be nothing more than an innate idea, and knowledge would be the monologue of modernist representation. But neither can knowledge be pure potency because the subject is already equipped with all of the active capacities that engage the forthcoming cognition.

Significantly, Balthasar adopts the language of spirituality to navigate the relationship between active and passive wonder in the subject's knowledge. He uses the language of the French spiritualist of the Grand Siècle, Jean Pierre de Caussade, to describe the subject's knowledge as "active potency" or "active passivity." He also turns to Ignatian *indiferencia*. This language ends up arbitrating the philosophical *impasse* Balthasar has reached: "The truth of another has to be received in the readiness [disponibility] of total indifference, which as such is pure potency. On the other hand, because this potency entails a capability for every cognition, it is a thoroughly active potency."[76] Crucially, and very much in line with Ignatian spirituality, Balthasar conceives of this active passivity as "a readiness to spring into action wherever the object's self-display might send or employ it."[77] Indifference is the mediating disposition between potency and act and is thus a ready obedience to receive the object and creatively perform its truth.

This disposition of indifference, this active passivity, is situated in the subject alongside its self-determination and freedom. The seeming tension between passive receptivity on the one hand and self-determination on the other is resolved only in the indifference of love. It is the love of the subject that opens the subject up to receive and to be determined by another; her *ekstasis* arises from her love. The

---

75. Anticipation is also the root of Balthasar's understanding of sin, as we shall see in the next chapter.

76. *TL* 1, 49.

77. Ibid.

epistemic poverty of the subject does not resolve itself automatically by driving the subject out of itself toward another. Her poverty is a willful act of kenosis, an emptying and an opening up in indifference, in readiness, and in receptive openness to another's truth. The subject's *indiferencia* denies the possibility of a monological knowledge of "innate ideas," and instead, opts for the way of love. Indeed, a non-receptive, monological knowledge "would prevent any true dialogue, wound courtesy, and make love impossible."[78]

It is this love that safeguards the mystery of Being, and the mysterious quality of knowledge. This metaphysical love wills the mystery of its object so that it might receive that object ever afresh: "Love would gladly give up a great deal of what it knows if it could thereby receive it anew from the beloved; indeed, it would happily perform the miracle of unknowing the things that it knows in order to receive them anew as the gift of the beloved."[79] This wish of love is answered by the very nature of truth as mystery. The epistemological disposition of the subject corresponds to the nature of the object known. The love of the subjective knower thus wills for Being to be the mystery that it is. And indeed, for Being, its disclosure *is* its mystery, its transcendental excess.[80]

But because the mystery of Being increases when it is known through receptivity, through love, one comes to a seeming paradox. Knowledge as love does make "authentic progress" in knowing a thing. But *in* every certainty looms an *ever greater* mystery, a perpetual "enlargement" of the field of truth. We see here the influence of Erich Przywara on Balthasar's early thought: "The more of the truth the

---

78. Ibid.
79. Ibid.
80. Balthasar's transcendental interpretation of Being at this point safeguards truth from becoming finitized. Balthasar recognizes that finitized truth is fatally nihilistic. "If truth could be like this, then it would have already ceased being truth. It would have become finite, and this would suggest the possibility of attaining a standpoint that comprehended truth from above, a standpoint, then, that was beyond truth. But if it were beyond truth, then it would also obviously be outside of being, which is to say, in the middle of nothing. For this reason, the only view of Being and of truth to be had from such a standpoint would be nihilistic, self-destructive, and self-contradictory. In particular, truth, which always presents itself as just a sample or a taste of a still transcendent truth, toward which it spurs and opens, would have deceived the knower with an appearance of infinity and, in so doing, proved itself to be untruth" (*TL* 1, 50).

subject manages to master, the more the truth overmasters it."[81] The subjective *indiferencia* before the disclosure of Being is not something that is eventually transcended, but rather, a perpetual disposition before the mystery of Being. Subjective receptivity, then, is the receptivity of love. This love corresponds to the mystery of its object that is unveiled to the loving subject precisely as veiled.[82]

What then might be said of the creative, spontaneous intellect? For Balthasar, the *intellectus agens* is always at the service of the receptive intellect by receiving, but creatively determining, the object known. It is the spontaneous intellect that measures the object:

> The process by which the subject first stands under the measure of things and subsequently measures both its own measure and the measure of things is the context in which the world and the self are formed simultaneously. Informed by the measures of things, the I consciously forms and measures them in relation to itself, thereby regaining its own measure and receiving inner structure and proportion. The subject, then, is like a statue under the external pressure of hammer strokes and, at the same time, like a formless mass that inwardly crystallizes and structures itself . . . in other words, the *raison d'etre* of knowledge has nothing to do with the will to power. *The subject's task becomes creative only if it remains an emanation of the primary attitude imposed on the knowing subject on account of its receptive nature: readiness to serve the truth.* Not dominion, but service is primary for knowledge.[83]

Knowledge is an act of love precisely because it knows Being, and Being is love. Because Being is wondrous and mysterious, knowledge of that truth will be characterized by wonder and the love of mystery. Being's truth requires a certain intellectual disposition; love is captivated by wonder and wills the perpetual mystery of its object, not so that it

---

81. *TL* 1, 50.
82. This means that we must characterize Balthasar's "love" in two ways. Because it is love that opens the subject up to another, that spurs the subject to give of itself as well as to host another within itself, we may see this love as *agapeic*. But because of the hiddenness, the ever more, that is revealed in the object's disclosure, we may character the subject's love as *erotic*.
83. *TL* 1, 69–70. Emphasis added. Balthasar continues: "Nor is striving for the satisfaction of the urge to know the first thing, because this urge awakens only after the disinterested exposition of the other's truth has already begun. The first lesson that existence teaches the subject is the lesson of self-abandonment [*Hingabe*], not domination in the pursuit of interest. And the second follows the first: Self-abandonment opens up more of the world and reaps a richer harvest of truth than self-interest, because the self-interested hear only what they want to hear, not what in fact is and is true."

will remain in ignorance, but that it can receive its gift ever anew.[84] Knowledge interpreted as love is, therefore, a kind of attunement to Being, a process of "being in-formed by the primal form or archetype (*Urbild*)."[85] One knows through the ecstatic receptivity and the transformative participation of love.

Love as Vision

As we have seen, one of the distinctive characteristics of Balthasar's epistemology is the natural relationship and correspondence between subject and object:

> In the object, the truth consisted in an increasing self-revelation, in which the revealer was always more, and always remained richer, than its revelation. But this movement is none other than the interior illumination of Being, in which the object becomes a subject. Therefore, looking at things from the point of view of the subject, we can make a complementary observation: Behind the subject's factual state of openness, there is a movement of self-opening; hence, behind the intellectual luminosity characterizing the subject as intelligence, there is an abiding will to the act of self-disclosure and to the state of being displayed. . . . A being has meaning only if it has being-for-itself, but this being-for-itself is meaningful only if it possesses the movement of communication. What is more, being-for-oneself and communication are one and the same thing; together they constitute the one, indivisible illumination of being. But this implies that the meaning of Being consists in love and that, in consequence, knowledge can be explained only by and for love.[86]

The object's disclosure and the knowing subject's willful receptivity are two forms of a single event of love; it is an ecstatic self-gift, a willful donation and acceptance.[87]

---

84. As Schindler notes, for Balthasar, "mystery and manifestation are in reality interdependent aspects of a single thing. Mystery thus acquires here a decidedly *positive* character: it is not the *withdrawal* of Being from the illumination of reason, or simply that which, as exceeding the intellect, is not given to it. Rather, it is for Balthasar precisely the *givenness* of Being that is mysterious, insofar as the generosity at the heart of the act of manifestation is the reason for the mystery. *Because* Being does not hold itself back, but *appears*, it reveals itself as gloriously transcendent of the appearance—in the appearance" ("Toward of a Non-Possessive Concept of Knowledge," 596).

85. See *GL* 1, 99ff.

86. Ibid., 111.

87. The subject's act of receptive love is caused by, not apart from, its creative spontaneity. "It

There is thus a natural relationship between truth and love. Love is not incidental to knowledge or truth, but rather, the living heart of each. Love is the ground that accounts for truth and enables it to be. But this does not mean that love exists apart from truth. Balthasar conceives of love as vision; it is the way of seeing truth. It is the lover who can see the truth of Being most clearly.[88] Balthasar says the task of philosophy is the willed desire to know *in* and *with* love: "The will to understand [the decision *for* the object] is love, and this is why no true and fruitful thinking is possible outside of love. But true love never makes blind; rather it gives the power to see."[89] True knowledge is available to the one who "sees the form" of the whole. One thinks of Balthasar's famous jigsaw story: only by seeing the whole (i.e., Being as love) does one understand its parts.[90] This is why Balthasar says the saint is one who knows truly, because she is the one who has surrendered herself to the divine, and can see the form of the whole as she looks upon God's face.[91]

Faith plays an important role here. Faith is the "self-abandoning

requires no small exertion of the subject's spontaneity to bring it to the point of deciding once and for all to be nothing but receptivity. The subject gives up its own word in order to hear only the word of the thing in all its objectivity" (*TL* I, 113). This requires of the subject an attitude of disponibility before the object as well as a kenotic self-opening that can rise only from its *Hingabe*, its self-surrender to the object. The subject, in the act of knowledge, listens and surrenders its own truth for the sake of the object's truth.

88. Cf. Josef Pieper, *Nur der Liebende singt* (Ostfildern bei Stuttgart: Schwabenverlag AG, 1988). Part of Pieper's concern in this book is to associate aesthetics with a particular way of seeing. But Pieper insists that the contemplative vision cannot be separated from the contemplative (and artistic) life. Balthasar would be sympathetic with such a claim.

89. *TL* 1, 209.

90. See Jacques Servais, "Balthasar as Interpreter of the Catholic Tradition," in *Love Alone is Credible: Hans Urs von Balthasar as Interpreter of the Catholic Tradition*, ed. David L. Schindler (Grand Rapids: Eerdmans, 2008), 191: "Balthasar had a chalet in the village of Rigi, perched high in the Swiss Alps where he would spend vacations working, often with de Lubac. One evening, I and another—then young—Jesuit where there with them and, knowing Balthasar to be an aficionado of handmade puzzles, we set out to complete a particularly difficult one, with plenty of blue sky and no two pieces quite the same. As the evening drew on, so did our perplexity: we were puzzled by the heavens, divided out as they were into many tiny pieces on the table before us. Balthasar watched from a distance, tempted to help but holding back, while de Lubac began pacing beside us: perhaps a bit agitated because we were delaying the daily evening get-together. Finally, Balthasar walked up and joined us, picking up a piece, and putting it into place, then the next, and the next, until the whole puzzle is finished, and in less than 10 minutes. We, quite frankly, would have been there for 10 hours."

91. This is not to suggest, of course, that true knowledge is available only to the saint. A non-lover certainly may perceive things accurately. But her vision is limited when it is apart from love. "But his intelligence resembles the vision of the nearsighted man: acute, even excessively so, in seeing details, it is incapable of surveying the broad prospects of truth" (*TL* 1, 112).

confidence" that receives the object in its mystery.[92] "Faith attunes man to Being (*fides ex auditu*); it confers on man the ability to react precisely to this divine experiment, preparing him to be a violin that receives just this touch of the bow, to serve as material for just this house to be built, to provide the rhythm for just this verse being composed."[93] The subject attunes herself to the object of knowledge in an act of obedience that is at the same time receptivity and *poesis*: "In faith . . . man is at one and the same time artist and artifact."[94]

Faith and love hold together the veiling and unveiling of *aletheia*. The relation between lover and beloved again depicts this dynamic: "Suppose a lover thinks that he has known and surveyed as much of his beloved as there is to know; this conviction would be the infallible sign that his love had reached an end. Love would no longer be in movement; it would no longer be able to court the beloved; it would no longer need surrender or help; it would no longer be capable of encounter."[95] The analogy is apt. The love for the beloved leads to an increase in knowledge of her without ever *exhausting* the fullness of the beloved herself in her essence. The beloved is always both *known* and *unknown*.

The consequence of this is that the unveiling of knowledge is always penultimate.[96] There is a circle here: love wills mystery and mystery increases love. "The lovers must again and again lose their privileged view of the whole; they must enter into a sort of darkness, into a discouragement over the ever-greater mystery of the beloved, over their incapacity ever to resolve it."[97] Of course, the "sort of darkness" that Balthasar references is not the absence but the excess of light. "In a loving being, there can be much mystery, but this mystery is light. In love, there is infinite depth, but no darkness."[98]

Knowledge as love involves the reception of Being as it offers itself

92. *TL* 1, 25.
93. *GL* 1, 220.
94. Ibid., 221.
95. Ibid.
96. Ibid., 210.
97. Ibid.
98. Ibid., 211.

132

as mystery, as the excess within and beyond appearance, as mystery. Balthasar's language shifts at this point from that of the Idealists to that of the mystics. It is the excessiveness of Being's light that overwhelms the knower's vision, yielding a "dazzling darkness" that radiates, not secrecy, but the super-abundance of disclosure.

This "luminous darkness" that the knower encounters in and as love must be properly understood as sheer positivity. Balthasar is not here making recourse to radically negative philosophies. Those are the descendants of the empty mysteries of rationalism and empiricism. His understanding of mystery is not one of absence or emptiness. Balthasar's epistemology is the path of the aesthetic *and* the ascetic—the embrace of images and the transcendence of them. His epistemology is the entering into the mystery by receiving Being *as* love *through* love.[99]

Finding God in All Things

For Balthasar, worldly truth arises from the mutual indwelling of subject and object in each other through an ecstatic expression of love. But what has this to do with divine truth, with *theological* knowing, and, above all, the saints? In a rather abrupt transition at the end of *Theo-Logic I*, Balthasar considers explicitly what has run implicitly through his entire account thus far: that worldly truth and knowledge presuppose a divine grounding as their condition of possibility.[100] It is God alone who guarantees Being's mystery and its knowability; therefore, God can be known implicitly in every act of knowing. This is where *Theo-Logic 1* takes a distinctively Ignatian turn: Balthasar explains how it is that God can be found in and through all things. Here we see Balthasar beginning to shift from the general concept

99. On the necessity, as well as the limitation, of the apophatic in Christian thought, see *TL 2*, 90ff. Karen Kilby criticizes Balthasar for not being properly apophatic. But Kilby's failure to engage the *Theo-Logic* is most glaring. She misses Balthasar's most elaborate account of the apophatic. Most tellingly, his account of the apophatic occurs in the context of his *Theo-Logic*, indicating that a theologic is necessarily couched in mystery. Cf. Karen Kilby, *Balthasar: A (Very) Critical Introduction* (Grand Rapids: Eerdmans, 2012), 81.

100. This is not to say that Balthasar is engaged in a Kantian epistemological project that treats God as a conceptual placeholder—the condition for the possibility of there being truth. Indeed, worldly truth only *is* because it participates in God *in truth* and not just *in concept*.

of knowledge to the more specifically theological concept of contemplation.

In the conclusion of *Theo-Logic* 1, Balthasar's account of Being becomes theophanic, and his epistemology becomes contemplative. Finite truth reveals God in two ways. First, it reveals God as a mystery through self-consciousness, that is, through the act of knowing. Second, finite truth reveals God as *magis*, the ever-greater reality of every finite thing. Finite truth reveals God through its *Geborgenheit*—its security—within the divine embrace. The first is participation; the second is revelation.

In this final section, we will follow Balthasar's gradual unveiling of the divine depths of created truth and conclude by arguing that the decisive attitude of finite knowing in its encounter with the truth of Being is contemplation. As we shall see, the way Balthasar characterizes the proper attitude of finite knowledge is nearly identical to the character of the saint.

The Divine Hinterland[101]

The preceding has brought us to a critical juncture. Balthasar's phenomenology of truth as we have followed it has led us to a point where what is unveiled in truth is the full measure of Being. But Being's truth is always veiled in mystery and is therefore best understood or apprehended through the disposition of love: the mutual indwelling of subject and object, receptive spontaneity, and trust or faith. His phenomenology has taken us to the groundlessness of creaturely Being, and thus to the plentitude of truth's mystery.

Theo-Logic 1 concludes with a decidedly theological turn by showing how God and divine truth are known within the structures of creaturely Being and creaturely knowledge. The abruptness of this transition may be jolting to readers, but Balthasar insists that the theological turn is not only necessary, but that its necessity is obvious if we attend to the structures of knowledge. Up to this point, Balthasar

---

101. Nichols, *Say it is Pentecost*, 59.

has shied away from offering specific epistemological formula. But at the conclusion of *Theo-Logic* 1, he finally turns to a consideration of the way the structure of human knowing naturally opens up to the divine. The finitude of human knowledge is torn between the poles of two empty infinities that can only be reconciled by the true infinity of divine truth. Human reason is not locked up in its own finitude, but rather, by knowing itself, it demonstrates that there is a God.[102]

Let us back up a bit. As we have seen, Balthasar understands truth as the measure of Being; just as created Being is finite, so too is truth. The way creaturely truth expresses its finitude is through delimitation and definition, or what Balthasar calls "analysis." Analytic knowledge parcels up Being by "narrowing of the universal through increasingly more particular definition" that delimits what is known from other potentially known objects.[103] Analysis leads to a false infinity, or what Balthasar calls an "immanent finitude." Our knowledge of a single thing or domain of knowledge can come only at the expense of our knowledge of *other* things. We know "more and more about less and less."[104] We might gain a pseudo-absolute knowledge of a particular thing as a kind of hyper-specialization, but even this is not truly absolute. One can only dissect a frog to understand its parts by losing the whole. The same goes for Being; to know a part "absolutely" is to lose the whole. The consequence of this empty infinity is that "rather than progressing toward a maximum of truth, [knowledge] would end up with an absolute minimum."[105]

Knowledge also consists in synthesis. In synthesis, the mind situates the object of cognition in increasingly larger but more general contexts. The sentence "The tree is green" presents a good picture of this. The particular object, the tree, is understood within the more generalized, synthetic category of "green." This synthesis is not a simple comparison between two things; it is a creative act; synthesis requires an act of judgment.[106] Yet, synthesis too results in an empty

---

102. *TL* 1, 253.
103. Ibid., 245.
104. Nichols, 59.
105. *TL* 1, 246.

infinity because it loses the determinate shape of knowledge by focusing on broader and broader generalizations. A synthesis can become so universal that it is no longer personal. Balthasar explains:

> Taken by themselves alone, both directions are deadly; only insofar as they temper one another do they generate the life of the spirit. Although knowledge strives by its very essence to attain unity, it can seek unity only in two contrary directions. On the one hand, it seeks unity in the direction of the subject of judgment. Proceeding analytically, knowledge breaks down and sifts in the attempt to fathom the original, indivisible unity of the existent subject, the *individuum ineffabile*. On the other hand, knowledge seeks the same unity, with equal immediacy, in the direction of the predicate of judgment. Operating synthetically, it attempts to categorize the atomic individuals under more and more encompassing unities and thereby to achieve a unity of being and meaning for the whole in its universality.[107]

Human knowledge is unable to approximate God's absolute knowledge. "The intellectual laws of finite thought are from beginning to end dictated by formal logic, which with its sub- and superordinations of concepts, its never-ceasing delimitations, unmistakably express the inner limitation of this thought and of the truth that lies within its grasp."[108] Creaturely truth and creaturely knowledge are finite by nature and are therefore pulled apart by these poles of knowledge. Only in God are the two poles reconciled.

We can see that this is so, Balthasar avers, when we recognize the finitude of human knowing and accept it as an aspect of our creatureliness. To recognize ourselves as finite creatures is to know implicitly that God exists, or at least that there is an infinite Subject. In this way, we can attain to a partial knowledge of God by means of reason's self-transcendence. Reason is not locked up in finitude, but by "performing its finite work of knowing finite things [finds itself] already in contact with the infinite."[109]

As should be readily apparent at this point, Balthasar's emphasis on

---

106. "At first, a thing announces itself to the knowing subject in a sensory intuition, while remaining totally unknown insofar as it is a subject in itself, hence, in its particular existence. Synthesis then converts this thing into something known or, at least, no longer wholly indeterminate" (*TL* 1, 247).
107. *TL* 1, 248.
108. Ibid.

truth's finitude is his way of countering Idealism's drive for absolute knowledge and the kind of anthropological reduction that we have previously outlined. Balthasar is building a theological response to Kant's transcendental synthetic *a priori*. For Balthasar, the condition for the possibility of subjectivity—of all knowledge *tout court*—can only be God. The Balthasarian response to the philosophical Idealism of his day is to ground Idealism in God, thus neutering the drive for absolute knowing and supplanting its aim of intellectual control with the receptivity and the service of love.

Finite truth, as we have seen, turns on the paradoxical claim that an object is "unveiled as veiled." An object of truth is unveiled and its revelation is faithful and true, but it also unveils itself as something "ever greater" than what can be known. This *magis*, this ever-greater, is what safeguards mystery. And yet, finite truth relies on measuring. In order for something to be knowable, it has to have already been measured. From this claim, Balthasar makes an "explicit and necessary inference to an infinite consciousness, which functions as the condition of the possibility of even finite subjects."[110] Finite knowledge relies on the absolute measuring of God that Balthasar calls the identity of thinking and being in God. Finite subjectivity is possible only as an offshoot of this divine measurement.

In a sense, then, Hegel was correct that thought thinks being *reciprocally.* But Hegel's mistake was twofold. First, he erred by elevating thought above Being. More significantly, though, he triumphed thought over love (as we have also seen with Eckhart), failing to grasp both that love is the condition of the possibility of thought, and that Being itself is most truthfully understood *as* love.

That a human being can become an agent of truth is solely a gift of divine grace; it is an invitation to participate analogously in God's own knowledge. From God's perspective, Balthasar claims, such a gift is divine manifestation; from the human perspective, it is an intrinsic, natural, and necessary participation in God's own knowledge.[111]

---

109. Ibid., 253. We hear echoes on Maurice Blondel's method of immanence throughout *TL* 1, but here most especially.

110. *TL* 1, 228.

Accordingly, Balthasar can conclude that God is implicitly known as this absolute measure in every act of consciousness and in every object. Here, we see Balthasar's interpretation of Aquinas' "*omnia cognoscentia cognoscunt implicite Deum in quodlibet cognito.*"[112] This is Balthasar's theological Idealism at work. God is not an object of knowledge, but knowledge's transcendental presupposition.

Balthasar insists that our human participation in divine knowledge is analogical. Insofar as the subject participates in the measure of infinite truth, it analogously shares in divine truth itself. But because the subject is not herself the infinitely measuring measure, there is an even greater dissimilarity from divine truth, which remains ever more veiled in its transcendence.[113] The subject's self-knowledge (*cogito ergo sum*) is possible only because the subject always finds itself within the act already being known (*cogitor ergo sum*—I am thought, therefore I am).[114]

Theophany

If the preceding section outlined Balthasar's theological idealism, this one focuses on his theological realism: his account of the way God makes himself known in the created world. The preceding section focused on knowledge of God through human subjective participation in divine truth. This section turns to revelation as God's free disclosure of himself through created, sensible forms. This is where the Ignatian injunction to "find God in all things" becomes vital force in Balthasar's *Theo-Logic*. Balthasar sees the world as theophanic. The world is the theater of divine glory because it bears the weight of God's free self-

---

111. Ibid., 232.

112. *De Veritate* 22.2.1. "God is implicitly known in all things." See *TL* 1, 230: "God is necessarily affirmed concomitantly, whether explicitly or not, in every cognition of truth."

113. "The subject's act, then, necessarily displays an analogy to the divine subject, although this analogy can never become an identity. The more the knowing subject understands of the world and the truth it contains, the more it also understands that it is not God. Its knowledge of the truth can never transgress the limits of its starting point, namely, the subject's active-indifferent potency to any and every truth" (*TL* 1, 53).

114. Balthasar derives this idea, though without credit, from Franz von Baader. See Ramon Betanoz, *Franz von Baader's Philosophy of Love* (Detroit: Wayne State University Press, 1999) for an account of von Baader's philosophy that arises from this idea.

revelation. This should not come as a surprise to those familiar with Balthasar's theological aesthetics; indeed, *Theo-Logic 1* is the philo-theological groundwork for his entire aesthetic endeavor.

Balthasar renders the world symbolic, that is, as the location—or dramatic stage—where God and world come together. As the created theater of the divine Creator, the world is awash with theological significance. God manifests himself in the world; the creator uses creation as his "expressive field."[115] Balthasar insists that knowledge of God always comes mediated through sensible forms. There is no immediate apprehension of God apart from the "interpretation of worldly signs, if for no other reason than that all of man's knowledge of intelligible reality outside the I is restricted to the expressive field constituted by the senses."[116] Balthasar insists that God's essence becomes transparent in creation, rendering creation symbolic:

> The image, then is filled to the brim with the whole significance of the ground—so that the vessel appears almost to overflow, better, that what the vessel contains seems greater than the vessel itself. By the same token, worldly truth, *by God's gift*, often appears to contain an instrinsic infinity, an inexhaustible truth, beauty, and goodness, an immediate gleam of God's eternity and infinity, an irradiation of something more than it could contain simply on account of its creaturely truth. This mysterious "more" . . . is the utter-most filling of the vessel of the worldly symbol with the divine content. This explains how a kind of plentitude can invade a moment of time, making it seem to be an immediate appearance of eternity, or how a work of art can be so perfect that it seems to have the quality, no longer of an earthly, but of an immediately divine idea.[117]

The perfection of this trait of creation will be the incarnation, where the "fullness of God dwells bodily" (Col 2:9). But the logic of the incarnation carries forward into Balthasar's entire sacramental vision. The incarnation is the perfected truth of the entire created cosmos: that it can be and has been used as the theater of God's free manifestation.

Seeing the world in this way requires a transformed vision for seeing

---

115. *TL* 1, 233. In what follows, we hear clear echoes to the Ignatian examen.
116. Ibid., 234.
117. Ibid., 236–37. Emphasis added.

the universal form revealed in the particular. Here, Balthasar makes the critical move of his phenomenological study. His theophanic interpretation of the world is a philosophical working out of Ignatius' "finding God in all things." It requires seeing the world contemplatively, that is, with the eyes of love:

> But if we view creation with the eyes of love, then we will understand it, despite all the evidence that seems to point to the absence of love in the world. We will understand the ultimate purpose of creation: not only the purpose of its essence, which we seem to make some sense of through the various intelligible relationships among individual natures, but the purpose of existence in general, for which no philosophy can otherwise find a sufficient reason. Why in fact *is* there something rather than nothing? . . . Only a philosophy of freedom and love can account for our existence, though not unless it also interprets the essence of finite Being in terms of love. In terms of love—and not, in the final analysis, in terms of consciousness, or spirit, or knowledge, or power, or desire, or usefulness. Rather, all of these must be seen as ways toward and presuppositions for the single fulfilling act that comes to light in a superabundant way in the sign of God.[118]

This aesthetic *seeing* is also an epistemic *knowing*. Seeing the world as a symbolic manifestation of God requires expression in the "language of similitudes," or the language of analogy.[119] Only by seeing, knowing, and expressing the world as a bearer of God can one give a faithful testimony to the actual truth of the world. Any description of the world that denies its theological and sacramental character—whether philosophical materialism, on the one hand, or pantheistic philosophies of identity, on the other—fundamentally misunderstands and misrepresents the world's truth.

It is precisely the sacramental character of the world that safeguards created Being's mystery. Balthasar insists that the doctrine of creation is the necessary backdrop to the philosophical claims about the "groundlessness" of finite Being. Because the world participates in the mystery of God, it shares in that divine mystery. Created Being can make no absolute claim to self-sufficiency; its truth and its reality are

118. *LA*, 143.
119. *TL* 1, 233.

groundless because they are grounded in God.[120] But even God's truth is groundless because it rests only on its own infinity. Thus is the truth of the world given its proper theological dimension, which is what safeguards its dignity, its fidelity, and its mystery.

The Character of Knowing

By way of conclusion, let us turn at last to the character of the subject, the one who knows. According to Balthasar, at the heart of any epistemology is a particular anthropological form (*Gestalt*).[121] Balthasar's theocentric epistemology requires the form of the saint. That such a claim strikes us as bizarre only goes to show how far we have fallen into a kind of titanic Idealism that privileges technological mastery over the receptivity of love.

The temptation toward titanic absolute knowing has been a temptation since the Garden. Humanity was created with a natural desire for knowledge, but truth was meant to be received directly from the hand of God as a gift. Knowing is an act of faith. The great temptation of the serpent in Genesis 3 is to draw humanity away from the receptivity of the Tree of Life toward an autonomous, self-serving knowledge by eating from the Tree of Knowledge of Good and Evil.[122] The serpent reifies truth, presenting it as "something thing-like, something generally accessible and at hand, which is withheld from a certain man only for some unnatural reason."[123] The serpent is the first to instrumentalize knowledge by shifting the locus of truth from God's gift of himself to human striving.

It is significant that the very first sin involves the question of truth. The serpent's fraudulence is crafty indeed because it takes what is good and proper to the human being—her desire to know—and subtly twists it into something diabolical, something that tears apart the receptive

---

120. "All created truth is groundless to the extent that it does not have its ground in itself, to the extent, in other words, that is breaks through its own ultimate ground into the depths of God's ultimately inexhaustible mystery" (*TL* 1, 231).
121. *TL* 1, 258.
122. Ibid., 262.
123. Ibid.

unity of infinite Being and created Being, divine knowing, and finite knowing. The serpent is a proto-Cartesian, the first to conceive of knowledge as the way to become a master and possessor of nature: "It seems perfectly legitimate to infer from the disclosure of Being in itself, which is always given in the evidence of which we are speaking, that Being as a whole may and should also be disclosed *for me*. . . . The error we thereby commit, which is the primal and archetypal sin, is that man makes himself the criterion" of truth.[124] Adam settles for "mere knowing" that is discursive, effective, technological knowledge, rather than receptive faith.

To draw out the social consequences of this technological dominance, let us consider again this quote from *Love Alone*, and reevaluate Balthasar's point in light of our argument thus far:

> But wherever the relationship between nature and grace is torn asunder in the sense of the aforementioned dialectical opposition between "knowledge" and "faith", worldly Being will necessarily fall under the sign of the constant dominion of "knowledge" and thus science, technology, and cybernetics will overpower and suffocate the forces of love within the world. The result will be a world without women, without children, without reverence for the form of love in poverty and humility, a world in which everything is viewed solely in terms of power or profit-margin, in which everything that is disinterested and gratuitous and useless is despised, persecuted, and wiped out, and even art is forced to wear the mask and features of technique.[125]

What counters this technological conquest for Balthasar is the theocentric theory of knowledge that he lays out in *Theo-Logic* 1. Such theocentrism gives an ontology of love and a corresponding *agapeic* epistemology. Here, the saint emerges, as yet unnamed, as the one who embodies the proper anthropological form of true knowledge. Here, Balthasar articulates his epistemology in explicitly Ignatian terms.

Balthasar is clear that the desire for truth is not in itself problematic. Such yearning is part of humanity's created nature; the desire for knowledge is a gift from the God of truth. The problem—the loss of the

---

124. Ibid., 263.
125. *LA*, 142.

good of the intellect—comes in the manner in which truth is sought. Balthasar's thinly veiled critique of the Idealist legacy of Eckhart continues. Objective knowledge is only possible, he avers, via the *receptive* rather than the *appetitive* intellect. Balthasar sees the Idealist tradition as an untamed, titanic appetite for knowledge for a self-aggrandizing end: "If this spontaneity were fundamentally about striving, this striving would inevitably be grounded in the subject's dissatisfaction, so that the object striven for would be sought insofar as it could fulfill a need. The movement of striving would have its primary ground in the subject itself, and the object would be a means by which the subject pursued its own ends."[126] A titanic epistemology, rooted in human subjectivity alone, would certainly end up using even God as a means to an end located in the self alone.

We have returned then to the anthropological reduction of modernity. A knowledge that emerges from the appetitive intellect would be a knowledge of titanic striving, a self-serving exploitation of the world of objects. It would indeed be the "Absolute I" of Idealism that Balthasar so feared: the "I" that consumes the world.

Against this, Balthasar posits spontaneity as a receptive act.[127] This is true within finite knowing, and it is true theologically as well: "It is not the knowledge-hungry subject that first prowls about in search of prey and then pounces upon the object; rather, it is the object that first displays itself as gift in the subject's space, and, by so doing, enables it to do what it otherwise could not, namely, perform an act of knowing."[128] Receptive faith is the inner form (*Gestalt*) of true knowledge: love is the proper form of the intellect.[129]

---

126. *TL* 1, 263.
127. "The spontaneity manifested and grounded in finite self-consciousness includes a deeper receptivity toward God's infinite spontaneity." It is interesting to note that Balthasar makes specific use of Ignatian language when he describes this receptivity as an "active indifference of spontaneous receptivity." See *TL* 1, 255–56.
128. Ibid., 258.
129. This is not to say that Balthasar is a fideist. Christians do not hold the corner of the market on knowledge. What Balthasar means here by epistemological faith is *analogous*, not identical, to religious faith. As we have seen, the subject and the object must entrust themselves in receptivity to the other in order to know and be known. This epistemological faith, however, *opens up* to its archetype in the religious faith that sees *more* (not *other*) than a secularized knowledge because it sees God. As we have mentioned previously, Balthasar believes that the saint is the one who sees and integrates more truth, and so she is the one who is most profoundly correct about the world.

The language Balthasar uses to describe the proper disposition of the knower is decidedly Ignatian. The knower must present herself with an "indifferent readiness" and with an openness of obedience and service. The knowing subject serves the object, as we have seen, but she also serves God. If knowledge is an act of participation, it is also an act of service and obedience. This was already intimated in the subject's service on behalf of the object—completing it by making it known. But now all worldly truth is shown to be in service to the divine: "What appeared primarily as creatures' service of and under one another . . . we now ground in a deeper service of God, which is the prior condition on which the intrinsic meaning of worldly truth rests."[130]

This service of obedience is the service of love. The entire argument of *Theo-Logic* 1 climaxes in Balthasar's claim that "truth is the measure of Being, but love is the measure of truth."[131] The manifold tasks of this opening volume of the *Theo-Logic*—the reconciliation of Idealism and Realism, the dialogical interplay between subject and object, the participatory metaphysics that ground epistemology—are held together by this claim. Love is what unites ontology and epistemology because Being is coextensive with Love.

The temptation of the serpent, the temptations of Idealism, and the anthropological reduction of modernity are all forms of the same thing: placing the measure of truth above the measure of love.[132] This is sin. This is titanism. This is technocracy. This is the legacy of a bad spirituality, a distorted Eckhartian mysticism that privileges knowledge over love.

Knowledge of truth is the mutual exchange of love. Because all finite knowledge implicitly reveals God, all understanding is rooted in love and propelled by love. Here, the dialogical exchange between subject and object in the act of knowing is raised to its theological fulfillment in the mutual surrender of love between finite subjectivity and its divine possibility:

130. *TL* 1, 256.
131. Ibid., 264.
132. Ibid.

For it is not simply knowledge alone that gives joy to God and glorifies him, but the creature's free self-surrender, its bringing him, together with its being and its unconcealment, its love. In this way, the love that God has lavished on the world in freely turning to the creature is returned to him in the form of reciprocated love. God shares his truth with creatures inasmuch as he makes his ever deeper mystery visible *as mystery*; and the creature shares its truth with God insofar as it acknowledges this mystery and gives it back to God.[133]

Love does not strive to possess or control truth, but rather, delights to receive its free disclosure, whether it be from the object of knowledge or from God himself. Moreover, love wills the ongoing mystery of its object; it is patiently receptive: "the lover wants to know only as much of the beloved as the beloved wants to communicate to him. He would find it loveless and shameful to spy out secrets that the beloved had good reasons, which are always reasons for love, for keeping silent. An urge to know that inconsiderately tears aside every veil would very quickly kill love."[134] Love unveils and veils at same time; love is where the desire to know and the will to mystery meet.

Eventually, creaturely knowledge finds its way into its source in the abyss of divine mystery. It is in the God of love alone that the various streams that we have followed through this chapter—knowledge, mystery, and truth—converge:

If truth were ultimate in God, we could look into its abysses with open eyes. Our eyes might be blinded by so much light, but our yearning for truth would have free reign. But because love is ultimate, the seraphim cover their faces with their wings, for the mystery of eternal love is one whose superluminous night may be glorified only through adoration.[135]

133. Ibid., 270.
134. Ibid., 264.
135. Ibid., 272. Note Balthasar's use of "adoration" [*Anbetung*] here at the end of *TL* 1. We saw earlier this chapter that the subject's attitude must be one of adoration. We now see the theological form of that adoration.

5

"I am the Truth"

Christ and Truth

We might interpret the account of Being that Balthasar develops in *Theo-Logic* 1 as a philosophy of insufficiency. All creaturely truth has a mysterious *magis* that points to the divine infinite. We might be tempted to think that we can, therefore, reason our way to divine truth. But there is no philosophical scheme or technique that can prepare us for Christ's shocking proclamation, "I am the truth" (John 14:6). The consequences of Christ's startling identification reverberate through the entire realm of metaphysics and epistemology. In the light of Christ's claim, we cannot speak of Being, truth, or knowledge apart from the mystery of his incarnate flesh.

Balthasar's *Theo-Logic* makes an abrupt transition from a phenomenology of worldly truth in volume 1 to an explicitly theological account of truth in volume 2. It effects this transition by turning to Christ as the interpreter and expositor (*Ausleger*) of truth under three aspects: God, world, and the relationship between them. Many of the concerns of the previous chapter will be recapitulated here under a new light as Balthasar draws ontology and epistemology into orbit around the identity and mission of Christ. For him, the mystery of Christ is the twofold revelation of the triune God, and of all things in relation to God.[1] As such, Christ *is* theology, that is, the truth of God, world, and the God–world relation.

This chapter explores Christ's identity as the truth under these three aspects. Our exploration is divided into two main parts. The first examines these three aspects through the lens of Christ's *nature* as the truth. This section unpacks the relationship between creation and God through Balthasar's Trinitarian theology and his christological metaphysics. The second section examines the three aspects of Christ's identity, but this time, through the lens of Christ's life as the performance of his identity. I show in this section how Balthasar's account of Christological truth requires that he actualize his metaphysical truth as the incarnate *Logos* in history. It is in Jesus's historical existence that eternal, metaphysical truth is revealed as the depths of divine love.

Why does Balthasar's turn specifically to Christology? The previous chapter indicated that worldly truth is possible only in its relation to God as the eternally measuring Subject. Why push his *Theo-Logic* beyond the philosophical-religious concept of God in the direction of a seemingly mythical account of the incarnate God?[2]

The answer is that Balthasar is not interested in positing God as simply a "theoretical placeholder," or the condition of the possibility of knowledge. He sees this as a strategy of some forms of idealism. He insists instead that eternal, infinite, and absolute truth expresses itself in concrete and historical forms. Christ is the archetype of those forms,

---

1. See Aquinas' account of *sacra doctrina* as the explication of just this reality. ST I.1.7: *Omnia autem pertractantur in sacra doctrina sub ratione Dei, vel quia sunt ipse Deus; vel quia habent ordinem ad Deum, ut ad principium et finem* [In sacred doctrine, all things are considered under the aspect of God, because they are God himself, or because they have God as their source and goal].
2. Junius Johnson offers a helpful typology to clarify Balthasar's theological metaphysics. The truth of Being that exists as the *eidos* of the triune God, he called the "Ideal Metaphysic." This metaphysic turns on the expression and exemplarity of the Logos. The incarnate Christ, however, ushers in the historical realization of the Ideal metaphysic in a way that the structures of Being are fundamentally altered. Johnson's typology has Christ as the Alpha of the Ideal Metaphysic and as the Omega of the Historical Metaphysic. See Johnson, *Christ and Analogy*, 114–15. While this typology might be overdrawn, it is nevertheless a helpful framework for parsing the relationship between the *logos asarkos* and the incarnate Word.

the eternal *Gestalt* in which all other forms reach their fulfillment. As the archetype of truth historically present among all worldly forms, Christ reveals worldly truth to itself. The incarnation, Balthasar avers, "accomplishes a cosmic transformation whose implications are still barely graspable, and that among the most important of these is the revelation of the radically relational structure of Being itself."[3]

Although Balthasar's Christology is developed in different ways in other places throughout his Trilogy,[4] in the *Theo-Logic* he interprets Christ chiefly as the *expression* and the *expositer* of truth. These correspond to Christ's theological identity and mission. For Balthasar, Christ's identity and mission are co-extensive; Christ *is* what he *does* and vice versa.[5] This chapter explores Balthasar's Christology under the two aspects of his identity and his mission by explicating the way Christ expresses his identity as truth in his life, death, resurrection, and ascension. In the first part of this chapter, we examine what it means to say that Christ is the truth. In the second, we turn to see how Christ definitively reveals that the truth is love, and thus, that the form of Christ's existence *as* the truth is existence as dispossessing, kenotic, love. As both truth and love, Christ reveals the inner heart of God and exposits the truth of the world.

Truth

The previous chapter ended at an impasse that attends all human knowledge. Humanity desires to know the truth in full. Yet this fullness of truth always exceeds the ability to grasp it. Does this mean that humanity is driven by an ultimately hopeless quest for truth? Balthasar insists that humanity's desire for truth need not result in frustration and despair.

> There was only one way out of this impasse, namely, that infinite eternal Being should utter its own self in the form of a relative being. That in this epiphany and *parousia* it should become actually present and give

---

3. Mark McIntosh, "Christology," in *The Cambridge Companion to Hans Urs von Balthasar* (Cambridge, Cambridge University Press, 2004), 24.
4. See *GL* 7, and *TD* 3, especially.
5. See *TD* 3, 153ff.

an authoritative interpretation of itself. Then we could hear the infinite Word in the finite, and see the eternal, imageless archetype in the finite form.[6]

Christ is ultimately the hope and possibility of truth and knowledge. He figures in the *Theo-Logic* as the full expression of truth that condescends to humanity in order to make the truth known. Christ's identity as the truth has three dimensions. First, there is the truth of divine aseity: how does Christ reveal the truth of God? Second, there is the truth of the world *in se*: how does Christ reveal the world's truth? Third, there is the truth of the analogical relationship between the truth of God and the world.[7] Balthasar places the divine Son at the heart of each of these dimensions. As the truth of both God and world, the divine Son acts as the expression and exposition of each. It is in the incarnate Christ, in whom the fullness of God was pleased to dwell (Col 1:19), that these twin dimensions of truth meet in harmonious, analogical exchange.

The Truth of God: *Expressio dei*

The truth of God, as Balthasar understands it, is straightforward: "God is love." This claim is decisive for Balthasar's *Theo-Logic*. The way that Balthasar works out the implications of this claim through his Christology draws all existence, all of creation, into this fundamental truth that God subsists as love. This is the divine truth that Christ exposits and expresses.

For Balthasar, truth is the self-speaking of Being.[8] Insofar as Balthasar conceives of God as Absolute Being, we should not be surprised to find him interpreting the eternal *Logos* linguistically, as the self-speaking of divine Being. Balthasar appropriates the phrase

---

6. Ibid. Significantly, what Christ reveals about Being is that it is not Being-for-itself (as we demonstrated in the previous chapter), but neither is it solely Being-for-another. It is now a Being-together.

7. Although we will parse out the "truth of God" as something set alongside of an autonomous "truth of the world," it should be clear that Balthasar does not hold to any sort of univocity of Being (nor of truth). The truth of God is the fundamental and absolute reality in which creaturely truth participates by grace.

8. See Balthasar's *Epilogue*, 77–86.

expressio dei from St. Bonaventure, who Balthasar believed signaled a revolution in Trinitarian theology.

From Bonaventure, Balthasar derives three forms of divine expressivity: "word, image, and Son."[9] It is as the "Word" that the Second Person of the Trinity is most thoroughly expressive of God. The *Logos* "is God as he is in being expressed."[10] As such, the *Logos* is the "unsurpassable 'resemblance', 'assimilation', 'correspondence' and so 'truth'."[11]

According to Balthasar, the Word's expressivity is twofold. It is, on the one hand, *expressivus (ausdrücklich)*: an exact reproduction of that which it expresses. In the case of the Father and the Son, the relationship is one of perfect representation. *Expressius (ausdrückend)*, on the other hand, is a far more active term, drawing attention to the act of expression. It is the genius of Bonaventure's use of *expressio*, that the content of the expression is "always understood and explained (so to speak) in the shadow" of the act of expressing. Divine truth, Balthasar avers, is always performed by—or *as*—the Son. It is this performance that is the content (*expressivus*) truth.

Balthasar interprets the Son's expression through the concept of, once again, receptivity. The expressive receptivity of the Son is seen in his eternal generation from the Father. Perfectly receptive to the Father's eternal act of generation, the Son is the *expressio expressa* of all that the Father is. This means, as Johnson points out, that the Son is archetype of every *eidos* in the Father. While this will have important implications for the metaphysics of the incarnation discussed below, in the divine life this means that the Son as *expressio dei* is also the measure of the Father. This is what it means to say that the Son is the truth of God. This also means that the Son, as measure, is what makes the Father known.

9. *GL* 2, 286. "However, these twelve forms of expression may be reduced in number. The first four deal with the elements, at a stage before organic life. Among the second four, the concept and the picture have a pre-eminence: the concept, as an inner word which is amplified in the outward word, and the picture, to which the type of knowledge that comes from the object may be related back. In the last four, which deal with organic reproduction, everything can be reduced to the perfect natural begetting, fatherhood."
10. Ibid., 289.
11. Ibid.

Balthasar makes recourse here to the explanatory principles of participation that are so important to his ontology and epistemology. In *Theo-Logic* 1, Balthasar showed how knowledge involves the mutual participation of subject and object. He now frames this participation as dialogue.[12] The eternal Son is both the recipient of the Father's word and the content of that word. Jesus's High Priestly Prayer in John 17 is illustrative of the eternal I–Thou relationship between the Son and the Father, "a relation in which the Son turns to the Father in knowledge, love, adoration, and readiness for the Father's very wish."[13] The Son's perfect receptivity of the Father's address corresponds to the Father's self-giving. The Father's address is also a substantial begetting. This allows the Son fully and truly to image and express the Father.[14]

In the Father, love and truth are co-extensive, and so we can assume that the Son is the expression of divine truth precisely *as* the expression of the Father's love. Love is the determining characteristic of God, the content of the *Logos'* expression as well as the act of his expressing. Balthasar calls divine love *Selbstübergabe*: the giving over of oneself, or what I have called *Gelassenheit* and receptivity.[15] The Son's expression is grounded in his "whence" from the Father, the ground and source of the Godhead, and Absolute Being.[16] But the Son is not a

---

12. The difference between subject and object dialogue and divine dialogue is that the latter is the archetypal dialogue which creaturely dialogicality can only mirror. Balthasar insists that what we find in the Trinity is not just a transcendent example of natural metaphysics, but rather their very source, archetype, and foundation. It is the Trinity that is the truth in which all other truths participate.

13. *TL* 2, 126. Note Balthasar's use of the term "adoration" [*Anbetung*], a clear echo of the epistemic disposition of the subject toward the object as we noted in the previous chapter.

14. Balthasar spends a considerable amount of time on the problem of "subsistent relations." How can the processions of the divine mind of the Father be substantial? In his discussion, he highlights the solutions of Augustine and Anselm before ultimately settling with a decidedly Thomistic distinction between the processions and the relations. The relations between the divine hypostases are determined by their means of process, begetting, and spiration. In this, Balthasar is saying nothing new. But his way of appropriating this tradition is twofold. First, he ties the processions to divine missions. It is the mission of the Son to proceed as the image and expressive truth of the Father. This mission will carry the Son into his earthly mission as Jesus Christ. It is the mission of the Spirit to exposit and carry on the truth that the Son expresses, illuminating it from within through the formation of the Church. As such the Spirit is truth and love.

15. This is an especially Ignatian idea, though it also has a legacy in Eckhartian thought.

16. That is to say, the Son is not generated by an abstract, "general" divine essence, but by the Person of the Father. This emphasis on the personality of the Son's generation wards off a potentially Hegelian interpretation of hypostatic generation. The divine processions are not subsequent "clarifications" of the one generic divinity, brought forth by some abstract, impersonal process, but rather, by an intentional and personal act of love and freedom. See *TL* 2, 129–34. Balthasar's

passive recipient of the expressive will of his Father because passive receptivity is neither truth nor love.

Insofar as the Son proceeds eternally from the Father, his Trinitarian mission is to co-represent the self-giving of the Father by, together with the Father, giving rise to the Spirit. "This means that the *Logos* has a 'toward' together with his 'from': the groundlessly loving production of the . . . Holy Spirit."[17] The Trinitarian truth as expressed by the eternal Son is that divine love is perfect being-for-another. To say that "God is love" is to claim that God *is* the rhythm of creative giving, receptivity, and exchange—all characteristics of Being and knowledge. The Son receives from the Father and gives what he has received toward the Spirit. This is the way that Balthasar develops the idea of the Son as the mediator of the Godhead.[18] The Son's mediation is his expression, and this is his divine nature. The Son's nature is to be the ecstatic expression of divine love.

The Son's "toward" movement actually moves in two directions. On the one hand, it moves ecstatically toward the Spirit. But at the same time, because the Son pours himself out in love, that is, as the "absolute love *per se*" that *is* the Father, the Son's "toward" movement to the Spirit is also toward the Father as an act of obedience. "This movement constitutes the *Logos*' entire being, inasmuch as his subsistence coincides entirely with what he owes objectively to the Father and, therefore also does subjectively."[19] In other words, because the Son has received all that he is objectively from the Father, his subjective response in co-generating the Spirit is an act of loving obedience and self-offering back to the Father.

language of *Unvordenklichkeit* is significant here. He insists on *"die unvordenklichkeit der Liebe"*—"love cannot be pre-thought." The Father's generation of the Son and the Spirit is the result, neither of his reflexive thought, nor of his knowledge of himself (as would be the case in an Hegelian dialectic) but is, rather, nothing other than an act of his love. No thought, no reflection, no intra-divine process, can get behind the Father's loving act of generation. The Father simply acts what he is: love.

17. *TL* 2, 152. Balthasar is a thoroughgoing filioquist, though he is clear that it does not particularly matter whether the Son's role in the generation of the Spirit is that of source or instrument, "from" or "through." Balthasar's point is that the Son plays an active role in the Spirit's generation as part of his divine vocation as the expression of the Father.

18. According to Bonaventure: *Christus medium tenes in omnibus* [Christ holding the middle in all things]. *TL* 2, 156.

19. *TL* 2, 153.

This "from" and "toward" movement is constitutive of the Son's divine being. Within the Trinity, the Son *is* what he *does*, namely, imaging and expressing the absolute love of the Father through his relationship with the Father and the Spirit.[20] The truth of the *Logos* rests, theologically, on the Father's generative act and the Spirit's ongoing exposition and perfection. The truth of the Son is Trinitarian truth, and that truth is love. Balthasar's insistence of the expressivity of the Son therefore wards against an Idealist privileging of knowledge over love.[21]

Conceiving the *Logos* as expression also allows Balthasar to ground the dynamic of truth and the possibility of knowledge in eternity by grounding communicability in the person of the divine Son. The Son as *expressio dei* makes the rhythm of donation-receptivity the very life of God. Divine expressivity funds the interchange of truth and knowledge and enables the possibility of participation.[22] It is for this reason that Balthasar is drawn more to Bonaventure's account of the Son as *expressio* than to Aquinas' *Verbum mentis*. For Aquinas, the *Verbum mentis* is "primarily the internal conception of the mind" of the Father.[23] The consequence of this is that it renders the external

20. This same Trinitarian structure can be seen in the economy of salvation. Salvation, Balthasar asserts, cannot be conceived of in Joachimite terms as a linear progression through the mutually exclusive ages of Father, Son, and Spirit. Rather, drawing on Gregory of Nyssa's tripartite unity of divine action, Balthasar insists that there is no historical Jesus that is not the Trinitarian Jesus. Every action that Jesus does in his earthly ministry is "from" the Father and "toward" the Spirit. An example of this is Christ's *tetelestai* on the cross (John 19:30). This cry is a completion of his mission from the Father as well as movement toward the Spirit: "into your hands I commit my Spirit."

21. The privileging of thought or mind over love is, Balthasar fears, the first step of the road to the titanic Idealism of Hegel. Balthasar sees this trend in certain medieval figures, especially Eckhart, but also in Aquinas: "We had earlier spoken of the treatises that interested Aquinas the most. Among these would not be the three central theological tractates: *De Deo Trino*, which gave Thomas an excellent formal training but which had no further role to play in shaping the course of his *Summa*; *De Christo*, which Thomas wrote with extraordinary care but introduced only after he had treated the whole of natural-supernatural ontology, epistemology and ethics in the *Tertia Pars*; and *De Ecclesia*, which never did have much of an impact, either on Thomas himself or on any other theologian of his time. But it is precisely these three subjects that are the central theme of theology! And in this sense, they are theology's *propria principia*, which formally and materially structures and dominates everything in it and upon which theology must continually reflect if it is to develop according to its own most intimate identity" (*TKB*, 263).

22. Cf. Johnson, 49.

23. For Aquinas, the *Verbum mentis* is the highest of all of the Son's names. It sums up all the others: Son, radiance, image, etc. See *ST* I.34.2: "[I]n the term *verbum* the same property is designated as in the term Son, for which reason Augustine says 'he is called Son in the sense that he is called Word'. . . . As a matter of fact, the Son's generation—his personal property—is designated with various

utterance of the divine word (*vox*) "dubious." Aquinas' *Verbum mentis* may be *de facto* expression, but it is not logically necessary that it actually expresses.[24]

But if the truth of God is the expression of love, then naturally this truth will not remain bound up in itself, but will pour outward in the act of creation. "[W]hat the *Logos* manifests visibly of the Father is, once again, love in all its divine dimensions and, therefore, in all of the consequences for a possible free creation that follow from this love."[25] To think truly of the world, then, is to think of it in relation to the eternal expression of God. Creation is intelligible, we have seen, only against the background of transcendence. Balthasar has developed this idea to the point where he grounds worldly intelligibility in the love of God as expressed by the *Logos*. Creation images and expresses God because it *is* the image and expression of God the Son. The Son is the truth of the world *as* the expression of the Father.[26]

names that are attributed to him in order to express his perfection in a differentiated manner. Insofar as he is consubstantial with the Father, he is called 'Son', insofar as he is coeternal, 'radiance' (Hebrews 1:3), insofar as he is like him in all things, 'Image', insofar as he is generated in a purely intellectual manner, 'Word'. For it was impossible to find a single name whereby all these things would be expressed simultaneously."

24. In fact, Balthasar acknowledges precisely this in a footnote by indicating that for Aquinas, the Word is expressive of both the Father and creatures: *unicum Verbum eius est expressivum non solum Patris sed etiam creaturarum.* See TL 2, 166.

25. TL 2, 152.

26. Again, Balthasar sees this somewhat lacking in Aquinas: "In accordance with the Aristotelian way of thinking, Thomism emphasizes thinking from below up: it moves from the world of concrete experience and sensation, through abstraction, to universal concepts and a demonstration of the principles contained in them. Here again we have a methodology that is predominantly philosophical, whose use in theology is quite limited. For theology deals primarily with God, the *concretissimum*, from whom nothing can be abstracted. And insofar as theology deals with the revelation of this one, only and unique God in the world, its object is historical: 'Sacred doctrine deals with singulars, such as the deeds of Abraham, Isaac and Jacob, and the like' (ST I, q 1, a 2 ad 2). The trouble is, of course, that this sentence stands as one of the initial objects to which Aquinas must later respond, and his answer shows little inclination to let these *singularia* be the main focus of theology: 'Particulars do not affect the perfecting of what is intelligible.' In short, in Thomas' *Summa* the particulars—that is, concrete events—were not allowed to stand as the chief object of theology. In his thought, they rather represent examples of God's eternal, supratemporal wisdom vouchsafed by God only because of our temporality. And sacred doctrine has for its primary focus this wisdom. That is why Aquinas was so interested in the general, suprahistorical essence (*quidditas*) of things, while the historical and actualist dimensions must step back. And so he focused on the lasting structure of the universe, in contrast to which the temporal nature of salvation history as standard-setting *singularia* recede into the background" (TKB, 264). But as we saw at the end of the previous chapter, for Balthasar, thought cannot anticipate love. It can only respond to love, being caught up into its supra-logic. Love expressed eternally but dramatic, not thought or ahistorical abstraction, is the depth of all Being. Here again, we see the root of Balthasar's critique of Idealism.

The Archetypal Truth of the World

As the expressive truth of God, the Son is also the expressive truth of creation. For Balthasar, the Johannine claim that "through him [the *Logos*] all things were made" (John 1:4), is central to understanding the truth of both God and the world. Because the Father has expressed himself fully in the Son, he has given to the Son the fullness of his power and capacity: *dixit similitudinem suam, et per consequens expressit omnia quae potuit* (he has spoken his own likeness and consequentially has given expression to all that he could). The Son is the *ars suprema* [the highest art] of creation because he is the *ars Patris* (the art of the Father).

Balthasar construes the Son's expression of the Father in creation through a retrieval of Bonaventurean exemplarism. As the exemplar of creation, the Son stands as the mediating link between God and world as the one who bears the truth of God into the world as the agent of creation *and* reflects the truth of the world back to the Father as the supreme idea (*eidos*) intended for creation.[27]

Balthasar advances two forms of the Son's exemplarism: divine and cosmic. First, as the expression of the Father, the Word is receptive to the Father in every respect. Crucial for Balthasar, the receptivity of the *Logos* serves as "the mediating link between the supreme God and creation."[28] Balthasar echoes the Pre-Nicene idea of the *Logos endiathetos* and the *Logos prophorikos*, the internal and the external. The mission of the *Logos* is to express the Father to the world, and of the world to God.[29] He is the "one mediator between God and man" (1 Tim 2:5) by being externalized in the act of creating.

We must note a subtle but critical distinction that Balthasar makes at this point. The Word's exemplarity is the result, not of containing

---

27. *GL* 2, 300. This takes up the previous chapter's discussion of the object's *eidos* being God's knowledge of it.
28. *TL* 2, 168.
29. As a consequence of this, the incarnate Christ is not conceived primarily as the "solution" to the problem of sin. Rather, the eternal Son was always intended to become incarnate precisely as the fulfillment of his divine mission to express the Father's love. See Balthasar's account of Irenaeus for more on this theme in *GL* 2, 70ff.

all possible ideas of creation, though he does. Rather, the Word's exemplarity is based on his nature as divine expression.[30] This means that the Son is not a kind of cosmic cypher. He is rather the truth of Being through the form and character of his divine existence: his receptivity, obedience, and love. It is because the Son is the true expression of the Father *as* the agent of the Father's creative love that he acts as the "archetypal originality [*ratio examplandi*]" of all creation: "the Son, by being the expression of the Father, is at the same time *the* expression universally, *i.e.*, the expression of everything: 'The Word expresses the Father as the primal cause which essentially underlies all things.'"[31]

But how there can be a creation at all if the triune God is Being itself? Balthasar's doctrine of exemplarity is fused to a very particular understanding of the kenotic dynamic in the God–world relationship. Balthasar, following Sergius Bulgakov, develops a threefold account of kenosis that undergirds his more traditional focus on exemplarity.

We have seen that Balthasar's theological interpretation of truth depends on re-imagining love as a metaphysical and theological reality. The form of love—being-for-another—manifests itself most truthfully in the event of kenosis. Balthasar sees kenosis as "a law of the divine being which is imaged in the world here below."[32] There are three distinctive "events" of kenosis in Balthasar's theological metaphysics: 1) Trinitarian kenosis; 2) the act of creation; 3) Christ's flesh-taking and passion. These three "events" reveal that the inner dynamic of Being: the donation and the unitive receptivity that the divine Son and the incarnate Christ perform. This dynamic of love is not an incidental theological *addendum* to Balthasar's ontological and epistemological thought, but is instead its inner form.

Balthasar holds to an intra-Trinitarian dynamic of love as the *Ur*-kenosis, the first kenotic "event." The Trinitarian processions are

---

30. *GL* 2, 293. See also Johnson, 51. Johnson points out that framing exemplarity in terms of the Son's expression means that the Son is the head of creation on accord of nothing other than his divine identity.
31. *GL* 2, 290.
32. Johnson, 176. The following analysis of kenosis relies on Johnson's discussion from 171–87.

the eternal form of this kenotic love. In generating the Son, the Father pours himself out absolutely, with no remainder. The Son's eternal existence is determined and characterized by his absolute receptivity; his divine personhood arises only by receiving in himself the love of the Father. But in his timeless and perfect receptivity, the Son offers his entire existence back up to the Father. The Son's eternal receptivity is also his perfect surrender (*Gelassenheit*) and self-giving.[33]

Balthasar's insistence on this Trinitarian kenosis is his way of guarding against Eckhart's dangerous elevation of knowledge over love in God. For Balthasar, the Father's outpouring of himself in begetting the Son is an act of love that is one with the Father's self-knowledge. If the Father's generation of the Son were primarily an act of knowledge rather than of love, two errors are possible. The first error is to assume that the Father has generated the Son in order to gain knowledge of himself. This would lead into a sort of Hegelian dialectic, where the original Concept must come to self-knowledge by positing an Other against itself. The second possible error is that the Father generates the Son as a result *of* his self-knowledge. This is Eckhart's error, and leads to a kind of Arianism that reduces the Son to an exalted, but strictly passive recipient of the Father's fullness.

Neither of these alternatives are viable options for a theology of love of the sort that Balthasar proposes. Nor do they truly allow the Son to be the expressive image of the Father because they deprive the Son of the co-eternality necessary for a Christian doctrine of the Image. What the Son expresses and makes possible is knowledge of God. The truth that the Son expresses is that God is love. The Son *reveals* this truth by *being* this truth. He is the eternally generated fruit of the Father's love. The Son is the Father's eternal kenosis, his self-abandonment (*Hingabe, Gelassenheit*) in begetting the Son.

In light of the Trinitarian processions, Balthasar concludes that love is the willingness to pour oneself out for another.[34] Moreover, the

---

33. On Balthasar's reliance on Sergius Bulgakov for his concept of the *Ur-kenosis* of the Trinity, see Jennifer Newsome Martin, *Hans Urs von Balthasar and the Critical Appropriation of Russian Religious Thought* (Notre Dame: University of Notre Dame Press, 2015), 185–97.

34. At this point, Balthasar is open to criticism for defaulting to circular reasoning. He adopts a

Trinitarian processions also reveal the true meaning of personhood. The person is not primarily the one who exists as "being-for-self," but rather the one who images the Trinity's "being-for-another." Divine relationality is written into the constitution of all creaturely being. Trinitarian kenosis reveals, in Balthasar's Ignatian language, that divine love is *indiferencia*, self-abandonment, and a willed surrender to the point of absolute poverty.[35]

The Son's kenotic poverty is his perfect fullness expressed as perfect surrender. What the Son has received from the Father's gift he offers back in love: "Father, into thy hands I commit my spirit" (Luke 23:46). Christ's comment to the Rich Young Ruler that whoever loses their life will save it (Matt 16:25) is a truth grounded in the eternity of divine life. Kenosis is the fundamental principle that undergirds Being insofar as it characterizes the divine life.

Going one step further, Balthasar posits that divine fullness expresses itself in willed kenotic poverty that also makes space for the created world. Balthasar's logic of kenotic love has significant implications for his understanding of the God–world relation. As we saw at the end of the previous chapter, the logic of creaturely truth pushes against its boundaries of finitude, and gestures, however hesitantly, toward the necessity of its participation in divine infinity. But how precisely is this participation possible if God is, as Balthasar will relentlessly insist, absolute wealth and fullness—the "all in all" (1 Cor 15:28)?

He addresses this problem by claiming that the God who is "all in all" willfully chooses to limit himself in order to create a space of participation for created Being. God wills to surrender his "all" for

certain definition of love for interpreting the Trinitarian processions and then claims that the Trinitarian processions determine what the nature of love is. Balthasar might respond to such a critique by gesturing to the example of Christ himself: "Greater love hath no man than this: that he lay down his life for his friends" (John 15:13). We should pause to clarify. While our discussion of Balthasar's trifold kenosis has proceeded according to a logical ordering (Trinity, creation, incarnation), Balthasar would insist that this is decidedly not the proper ordering of theological knowledge. Theological knowledge of these kenotic moments begins, not with speculation into the inner life of the Trinity but rather in the concrete revelation of the life of Christ.

35. Johnson describes this well: "Thus, all divine actions, *ad intra* as well as *ad extra*, insofar as they demonstrate the character of love, will demonstrate the character of abandonment, of emptiness" (158).

the sake of the "other." God willfully chooses to be a *latent* presence in all reality: "But they [created beings] only attain freedom when the freedom-granting [*freilassende*] God recedes into a kind of latency; when he who can be absent from no place, assumes a certain incognito. . . ."[36] Creation is thus in God, and through his willful kenosis, God is in creation.

The kenosis within the life of the Trinity allows the Son to be the archetype and expression, not just of God, but of creation. The Son is "the grounding of the act of creation in the act of generation within the Godhead."[37] For Balthasar, this means that creation is an aspect of the Son's expression of truth. Balthasar makes much use of the doctrine of analogy at this point. The transcendental properties of created Being—oneness, truth, beauty, and goodness—analogically image the Trinitarian *taxis* of Father, Son, and Holy Spirit. All created Being emerges from the Trinitarian event of love. Each existent being has a unity that finds its source *ex alio* (its operative cause, the Father), a truth and knowability that finds its source in its *secundum aliud* (its model, the *Logos*), and its participative goodness according to its *propter aliud* (its final end, the Holy Spirit). Every created thing is this harmonious interplay of the qualities of being *ex alio*, *secundum aliud*, and *propter aliud*, and as such, reflects the triune God who himself exists as *ex se*, *secundum se*, and *propter se*.

The truth of the created world is thus grounded and made possible within the framework of this Trinitarian kenosis. Creation emerges out of the kenotic self-giving of the Trinity which is archetypal for that creation: "Its openness for the world portrays in it the fundamental behaviors [of creaturely existence]: reception and giving, service and creation, justice and love, which are all just different forms of self-

---

36. *Theodramatik* II, 248: "Raum für Freiheit aber erhalten sie nur, wenn dur freilassende Gott in eine gewisse Latenz zurucktritt, wenn er, der von keinem Ort abwesend sein kann, ein gewisses Inkognito annimmt . . ." This idea of the divine incognito will be especially important for the Holy Spirit.

37. *GL* 2, 291. Balthasar continues: "To base the creation in the Trinity in this way avoids both the danger of subordinationalism which is found in the early Greek Fathers, because every appearance of locating the purpose of the generation of the Son in creation is avoided, and likewise, the danger of an absorption of the natural order in the supernatural, because the natural order and the reason are unreservedly granted their relative independence."

giving."[38] Creation is possible through the kenotic openness of divine fullness but in such a way that creation itself is fundamentally marked by, because it participates in, this selfsame logic of kenotic love.

The Metaphysical Consequences of the Son's Exemplarism

The foregoing results in two significant consequences for metaphysics. The first consequence is that the *Logos* is understood as the ontological grounding of all created truth. This is what Balthasar calls the "cosmification of the *Logos*"—the immanent presence of God in the world. The divine Word is abroad, underlying and expressing itself in and through the things it has made. There can be no such thing as an absolute *natura pura*.

Christ's exemplarism also establishes a symbolically rich world in which all the creaturely forms are, as the Areopagite once put it, "sacred veils" of the divine wisdom that is their foundation.[39] To see the world this way is to see it theologically, as a theophany. It is here that we see the theological fulfillment of worldly truth's necessary participation in God, as indicated in the previous chapter. The cosmification of the *Logos* not only makes worldly truth possible, but also reveals the world as the bearer of divine truth. This allows Balthasar to claim for his own theology what he claims for that of Dionysius: what he offers is not "an immanent ontology of creatureliness (a doctrine of the cosmos), but—because it is a matter of theology—a doctrine of the structure of the world conceived as having God completely and utterly as its goal, and indeed even as its *formal object*."[40]

Such a world should be understood in relation to the *Logos*, as characterized by a necessary esotericism. The *Logos* is present but hidden, both under the signs of those things that are symbolically

---

38. Ibid.
39. *The Celestial Hierarchy*, 121C. Balthasar's account of this theme, especially as it works out at the end of the medieval period with Cusa in *GL* 5, 205ff. For a Protestant attempt at reclaiming this tradition, see Hans Boersma, *Heavenly Participation: Weaving a Sacramental Tapestry* (Grand Rapids: Eerdmans, 2011).
40. *GL* 2, 163. Emphasis added. God as the formal object of creation will be especially important in our characterization of the saint as the true philosopher in chapter seven.

fitting for him and under that which is his opposite. All the world, then, becomes useful for coming to understand the one to whom it points. The exemplarism of the *Logos* fundamentally transforms the way the world is to be seen and understood.

Because creation cannot be reduced to God or absorbed into God (either of these options would mean that the act of creation was not an act of love because if either were true, God would only be loving himself), it takes on a concrete reality of its own. But this reality is something it receives fully as a gift of love. Creation's givenness and receptivity is an image of the Son, who is himself the first and true Image of God. Creation is a freely generated image of the truth that God is love because it has been made according to the image of the Son. But because it is divine love that makes space for creation, God's presence is never absent from it. Creation participates in the eternal dialogue of the Trinity.

For Balthasar, God's truth is *parrhesia*: openness and non-concealment, a "sincere self-communication and manifestation."[41] This *parrhesia* is the eternal expression of the Father in the Son, which overflows out of the "native invisibility and unapproachability"[42] of his divinity and "shines forth" (Ps 79:2) into creation through the Son. Balthasar claims that every procession from the Father is either a begetting—the Son—or a consequence of this begetting. *In* the Son, the Father communicates and manifests himself. *Through* the Son, all finite Being is caught up in God's "will to expression."[43] What it expresses, in expressing itself in and through the Son, is the truth of God.[44]

The Son

is therefore not only the archetype, of which images are made in the

---

41. *Prayer*, 45.

42. Ibid.

43. It is caught up in a double way: "first, in as much as the archetype in God is itself an expression, and second in so far as the individual being is the goal of a particular intention of expression on God's part, expressissime and distinctissime chosen to be as it is, and addressed by God with this intention. Thereby it is the destination of a particular act of God's condescension, of a particular form of speech of the eternal Word" (GL 2, 296).

44. The works of Bonaventure from which Balthasar is drawing are especially *Collationes in Hexaëmeron* I and *Breviloquium* 8 (324a). See also Joseph Ratzinger, *The Theology of History in St. Bonaventure*, trans. Zachary Hayes (Chicago: Franciscan Herald Press, 1971), 145ff.

world: *he is God as expression, that is, as truth,* and therefore he is the principle of the fact that the things in creation have been expressed and of the fact that they express themselves as created essences: *"ratio exprimendi est ipsius exemplaris"*: the fact of being an expression (which belongs to the creature) comes from the original. . . . All things are true and have the capacity to express themselves by virtue of the power of expression of that highest light, *i.e.,* of the Word.[45]

The implication of this is that created beings are most truly themselves when they are found in the *arte aeterna* [the eternal art] which, for Balthasar, is the expressive *Logos* himself. The latent, immanent presence of God in all created Being is the divine Son, the *Logos*, through whom and to whom creation is ordered.

The Son is not just the archetypal truth of creation; he is also the agent of divine love that brings it into existence and undergirds it in both its distance from and nearness to the Father. Created beings receive their truth and their own expressivity from that "likeness which is the truth itself in its expressive power."[46] The eternally expressive Word knows better and says better what every created thing wishes to say. We have seen how the subject and object meet each other in the *Gestalt* of worldly knowledge. Christ's exemplarity fundamentally transforms the concept. If Christ is the true form of creation, then every form finds itself in relation to the Son as its source and archetype. Knowledge of anything, then, is necessarily *christological* in light of the Word's role as the exemplar of all things. Metaphysics, therefore, must be theological because created Being is referential. It "points beyond itself to the archetype both by pointing outside of itself and by pointing within itself."[47]

The Concrete *Analogia Entis*

Let us reconsider a few of the major themes of the God–world relationship as we have explored it in previous chapters, but now under the rubric of Christology. Balthasar holds that all philosophical

---

45. *GL* 2, 290. Emphasis added.
46. Ibid.
47. Johnson, 53.

and religious history has been an attempt to address this mystery of Being, but "[n]o philosophy could give a satisfactory response to that question."[48] This is the same impasse that Balthasar himself reaches at the end of *Theo-Logic 1*: the finite is not the infinite. Balthasar's later volume on metaphysics in *Herrlichkeit* analyzes the history of philosophy as wrestling with this mystery. The philosophical and religious solutions to the mystery of Being have typically emphasized either the absolute difference or the absolute identity between the finite and infinite.[49] Idealism, we have seen, is often the descendent of these philosophies of identity.

Neither of these options are viable for Balthasar. He sees Thomas Aquinas' doctrine of the "real distinction" between *esse* and essence as one of the great accomplishments of Christian thought, "the source of all the religious and philosophical thought of humanity."[50] There is an ontological gulf between God and world that can never be overcome. To refer to the world as "creation" is to name this ontological relationship between God and world, and to identify it as a free and willed action of God.[51] Creation is always *other* than God. There is no place in Balthasar's construal for metaphysics of identity.

But in creation, all things share in the *esse* as the source of their perfections. The key difference between creation and God lies in the fact that the former's *esse* is non-subsistent, while the latter's is perfectly subsistent. There is, then, not an *absolute* difference between God and world. The relationship between them is analogical.[52] Balthasar derives his definition of the doctrine of analogy from Lateran IV: *in tanta similitudine maior dissimilitudo* ("in every similarity [between God and world], there is an ever greater dissimilarity").[53]

---

48. *MW*, 113.
49. Ibid., 112–15. Cf. Johnson, 31–89.
50. *MW*, 112.
51. Cf. Johnson, 93. For Balthasar, to speak of "creation" is to speak of it being *ex nihilo*, thus guaranteeing God's freedom in the act of creating.
52. On the relationship between Thomas and Balthasar on the question of analogy, see Nicholas Healy, *The Eschatology of Hans Urs von Balthasar*, 26–53.
53. *TD* 3, 223. The dynamic that powers this analogical relationship is love: "Love which is the highest level of union only takes root in the growing independence of the lovers: the union between God and the world reveals, in the very nearness it creates between the two poles of being, the ever-greater difference between created being and the essentially incomprehensible God" (*CL*, 64).

Balthasar learned his emphasis on the dissimilarity between God and world from Przywara, though he rightly criticizes his mentor's over-exaggeration of the difference as eventually annihilating the possibility of union between God and world in the person of Christ.[54] All of Balthasar's teaching on analogy is grounded in the ontological dissimilarity between God and world because it is *difference* that makes love possible. Indeed, as we have seen, Balthasar does not see difference as fundamentally antagonistic in the way that Hegel does. Balthasar's metaphysics do not rely on the dialectical overcoming of difference. The world's positive metaphysical otherness is rooted in the Trinitarian difference that constitutes divine Being.[55] The difference of Father, Son, and Holy Spirit is a positive otherness that fuels the divine love that is co-extensive with who and what God is.[56]

For Balthasar, Trinitarian difference grounds the dissimilarity and the similarity between God and world. Even "being different from God is a way of imitating God."[57] We have seen that the Son is the Father's *will to expression* and that creation is the fruitful extension of this loving will. God has expressed himself in creation in such a way that creation, even *in* its otherness, is a mode of divine expression. The Son as the mediator of the Trinity, the expression of the truth of God, can thus also be the eternal analogy, the exemplar, of creation.[58]

One might think this Trinitarian framing of analogy would be enough, but Balthasar's doctrine moves from the realm of eternity to historical particularity in the person of Christ.[59] He turns to Christology

---

54. Healy, *The Eschatology of Hans Urs von Balthasar*, 94.
55. Cf. *TL* 2, 129–30.
56. "For how could worldly difference in its *maior dissimilitudo* with respect to the divine identity not ultimately be deemed a degradation, rather than something 'very good', if this difference did not have a root in God himself that was compatible with his identity—especially since worldly difference (in every existent!) must essentially spring both from the perfect but non-subsistent and, in consequence, ungraspable being that God has given away in his *liberalitas* and from God's will and archetypal being? A world marked by difference that springs from a God utterly devoid of it can only be the degraded result of a fall, as every religion that has attempted a speculative penetration of the God-world relation as inevitably concluded" (*TL* 2, 184).
57. Johnson, 143–44.
58. "Furthermore, the *Logos*' disponibility for every creative resolution of God and his archetypal expressive form, whereby, as was shown, he not only expresses in himself the entire Trinity but is also the prototypical image of every possible creative self-expression" (*TL* 2, 169). As such, only the *Logos* can become incarnate.
59. I have opted to discuss the *analogia entis* in this chapter on Christology rather than elsewhere

because he wants to grant creation real, if not absolute, autonomy. Balthasar relies on the Aristotelian notion that universals are only known in and through particulars.[60] Balthasar builds on Aristotle's claim with reference to Christ by insisting that the universality of Being's truth emerges from within, not apart from, particularity.[61] The divine presence in the world is not limited to eternal, latent archetypality, but has become historical in the incarnation. This is one of the crucial structuring elements of the entirety of Balthasar's thought: through his Christology, he writes history into metaphysics at a fundamental level.[62] "In Jesus Christ, the *Logos* is no longer the realm of ideas, values and laws which governs and gives meaning to history, but is himself history."[63] *Verbum caro factum est.*

Balthasar's move to embed metaphysics in history safeguards his understanding of the *analogia entis* from a kind of Idealist takeover. Were Balthasar to stay with the Trinitarian grounding of analogy, he could be misunderstood as positing a kind of Hegelian modalism wherein history is construed as the mode of God's own coming to self-knowledge and self-realization.[64] Were this the case, history would not have any meaning in itself and there could be no genuine *drama* in the God–world relation. More crucially, creation would only be an instrumental extension of God's own self-realization, and thus, would lack an integrity of its own. All apparent interchange between God and world would be a divine pantomime, and God's love for creation would be a narcissistic love for self.

No, for Balthasar, analogy only functions properly in terms of Emmanuel, God with us. It is the God-Man, Jesus Christ, that is the concrete *analogia entis*. His christological interpretation of the doctrine of analogy allows Balthasar to address the ontological difference, the

based on Balthasar's insistence, that Barth "is absolutely right that the problem of analogy in theology must finally be a problem of Christology" (*TKB*, 55).

60. Balthasar's *A Theology of History* (TH) is an outworking of this Aristotelian notion. TL 2 relies quite a bit on this earlier work and so our analysis of the theme of Christic historicity will conflate the arguments of both volumes to draw out a fuller picture of Christological metaphysics.

61. Cf. *TL* 3, 196–205.

62. Johnson, 115.

63. *TH*, 24.

64. Cf. Johnson, 109.

"total abyss" between God and world. It is Christ, the God-Man, who alone bridges this abyss. He does not destroy the ontological difference, but holds God and world together "undivided" but "unconfused" in his own person. This means that Christ is "concrete *analogia entis* itself."[65] To call Christ the concrete *analogia entis* is to indicate that he is the apocalypse, the disclosure, of triune and creaturely Being.[66] Christ is both a theological and metaphysical figure.

We can interpret this claim on the level of Christ's nature and on the level of his dramatic, mission-shaped life. Balthasar's Christology is Chalcadonian, focusing on the hypostatic union of divine and human in the person of Christ. Mark McIntosh has identified two chief voices at play in Balthasar's Christology: Maximus Confessor and, unsurprisingly, Ignatius of Loyola.[67] What Balthasar does, and what the second section of this chapter exposits, is reinterpret the Christological question—how are the two natures related?—from ontological terms to more dramatic or obediential terms.[68] McIntosh explains Balthasar's unique construal of Christology by stressing that Christ's humanity "while remaining perfectly human in its essence, is lived out according to that particular pattern of life or mode of existence which is the perfect enactment in human terms of the Son's eternal mode of existence."[69]

If the mode of the Son's eternal existence is as the expression of the Father's truth and love, then what we find in Christ's incarnate life is the performative expression of the selfsame truth and love in human terms. The Son eternally hands himself over to the Father's will in an perpetual act of perfect dispossession, surrender, and obedience. Christ's historical life dramatizes this truth. In the incarnation, and especially in his death, Christ reveals himself as the truth of the Triune God's self-giving love and mutual surrender, and as the summation of all things that exist. Christ's humanity is perfectly "transparent" to the

---

65. *TD* 3, 222.

66. Cf. Nicholas Healy, *The Eschatology of Hans Urs von Balthasar*, 96.

67. Mark McIntosh, *Christology from Within: Spirituality and Incarnation in Hans Urs von Balthasar* (Notre Dame: University of Notre Dame Press, 2000), 4.

68. Ibid., 5.

69. Ibid.

Son's eternal obedience of love; thus does Christ perform in history the truth of divine and created Being.

We would misrepresent Balthasar's Christology and metaphysics if we were to posit a Christic *analogia entis* strictly along the lines of an essentialist rather than actualist reading. We cannot get to the truth of Being apart from the way that truth is expressed in action. We recall Balthasar's definition of truth from "Theology and Sanctity" as the living synthesis of theory carried into action. Christ's dramatic action as the concrete *analogia entis* is the concern of the second part of the chapter. But as a preamble, we can say one or two things about Balthasar's Christic *analogia entis* on the level of natures, even if artificially separated from the dramatic performance of his life.

Balthasar describes Christ as a kind of metaphysical hourglass "where the two contiguous vessels [God and creature] meet only at the narrow passage through the center: where they both encounter each other in Jesus Christ."[70] Balthasar develops this idea more concretely in his study of Maximus where he posits Christ as the "synthesis" between God and world. For Balthasar, "in that synthesis of Christ's concrete person is not only God's final thought for the world but also his original plan."[71] The incarnation is not, therefore, a secondary response to the problem of sin, but rather the theological fulfillment of all analogical relationships or proportions between God and world.[72] Indeed, there is an analogy between the mystery of Christ's two natures and the mystery of Being, the God–world relationship.[73] Balthasar believes that Maximus gestures toward the "real distinction" in his Christology, underlining once again the need for a dramatic construal of the natures.

The union of God and the world in Christ could not be adequately

---

70. *TKB*, 197. Balthasar continues: "The purpose of the [hourglass] image is to show that there is no other point of contact between the two chambers of the glass. And just as the sand flows only from top to bottom, so too God's revelation is one-sided, flowing from his gracious decision alone. But of course the sad flows down into the other chamber so that the sand there can really increase. In other words, there is a countermovement in the other chamber, but only because of the first movement, the initiative of the first chamber."
71. *CL*, 207.
72. Healy, *The Eschatology of Hans Urs von Balthasar*, 21.
73. *CL*, 209.

expressed simply in terms of an essentialist philosophy. If its "natural" and "ontological" aspects were emphasized (as "union of essences") or "union of natures", the consequence was the mixture of the two poles in a new "essence". But if one hoped to avoid this kind of mixture, the only alternative seemed to be the accidental, extrinsic, "moral" union of an "intellectual relationship" between the two natures. Certainly, both the Eutychian and the Nestorian position saw part of the truth. But the level on which they came into conflict cannot itself be the context of a real solution—it can only be the scene of an empty dialectic of thesis and antithesis.[74]

Balthasar saw Maximus' major accomplishment as moving away from conceiving the Christological synthesis on the level of natures which could only result in either Monophysitism or Nestorianism. Both formulations are problematic: the relationship between God and world collapses into either identity or the difference of a kind of *tertium quid*. Neither can sustain analogy, dialogue, or love.

Again, Balthasar conceives of the hypostatic union in dramatic and obediential terms. The *analogia entis* cannot be reduced to a univocal concept of shared Being or the transference of God's being to the world. Christ as the concrete *analogia entis* does not fuse creation to God, but rather, *enacts* the truth of Being as openness and transparency before God.[75]

Excursus: Christic, Metaphysical Anthropology

Balthasar's claims about the incarnational shape of truth bears significantly on his theological anthropology. That Christ took on human rather than nonhuman flesh tells us something significant about both Christ's cosmic exemplarism and the spiritual vocation of humanity.

Balthasar develops a meta-anthropology that plays a critical role in his interpretation of the cosmic significance of Christ.[76] According to this scheme, humanity has a twofold purpose. It is meant to be the

---

74. Ibid., 212.
75. *TD* 3, 223.
76. See Martin Bieler, "Meta-anthropology and Christ: On the Philosophy of Hans Urs von Balthasar," *Communio*, vol. 20, no. 1 (1993): 129–46.

summation of the cosmos and to represent, vicariously, the cosmos to God. It accomplishes this by virtue of being the microcosm of creation. Balthasar claims that humanity "unites in itself all the elements of the universe in contracted form."[77] He argues that all created things are recapitulated in the dignity of the human. Man is the "knot" (copulatio) between the upper spiritual world and the lower physical world. The human is tertius mundus . . . ratione medietatis.[78]

Humanity's mediatory role in the cosmos is a function of his unique constitution as a hylomorphic being. One central aspect of humanity's representation of the cosmos is the fragility of the flesh, seen most clearly in the unavoidable reality of death, that represents the entire rhythm of cosmic self-surrender. According to Balthasar, nature itself is a "sacrificial process" that gives itself materially to humanity. A human is by nature one who receives being, not only from God's breath, but also from the material world from which he is formed. Lower organisms "surrender" themselves to the higher, and thus become "the successive formations of matter [that] constitute the substratum of the delicate, naked, defenseless being who is thrust into the exposed middle of the world" as the adam. Nature is, for Balthasar, a "self-oblation for the sake of the end that was intended from the very beginning."[79] It is the special vocation of humanity to sum up the material cosmos and to hand it over (tradere) to the Father. But it is only in Jesus that humanity's mission is fulfilled in fact and in deed. This transforms the nature of the created cosmos: "It is only in this sacrificial shape that man would be both the embodiment of the universe as well as its dispositive opening to the 'loving sacrificial death' that occurs once for all when the Word of God becomes incarnate—the death that eucharistically fills up the cosmos with triune life."[80]

---

77. TL 2, 226.
78. Balthasar sees this notion as a helpful ally in overcoming the strict separation of nature and grace so prevalent in mid-twentieth-century neo-scholasticism.
79. TL 2, 229.
80. Ibid. The second part of this chapter will address this significant claim that Christ's surrender unto death fills up the universe with the life of God. The implications of such a claim will be significant for our next chapter: if the world has been fundamentally transformed, filled with the life of God in a way that it was not prior to Christ's death and resurrection, then our way of

This language of metaphysical anthropology is important for Balthasar, though he is far more concerned to see humanity's cosmic mediation as emerging from its being the dialogue partner of God. Balthasar insists that "[t]his dialogue unfolds steadily and gradually through the ages, so that man, who by himself is weak and 'in need of the glory of God', may partake of it and, as a 'living man', be 'to God's glory'. But 'God's life-communicating power is brought to perfection in weakness, that is, in the flesh.' For only as flesh is man really man."[81] It is as a *dialogical* creature that humanity is the center of the cosmos.

Further, as a dialogical creature humanity is *missional*. The human, by virtue of being ensouled flesh, holds together in his person the entire material and intelligible cosmos. As such, humanity is called to bear in itself the fullness of creaturely truth. Through his dialogical relation with God, the human bears divine truth, disclosed freely through the graced relationship with the Father. This mission of truth-bearing only comes in and when humanity is addressed by God, and thus, becomes a uniquely dialogical creature.

Through this meta-anthropology, Balthasar reflects back on the ontological claims we developed previously to demonstrate how the human—and ultimately Christ—can express Being itself. He develops this connection in three ways. First, he returns to the idea that Being does not subsist in itself, but surrenders itself in finite essences. Being divests itself in order to enable creaturely beings to come into existence. Being has a decidedly "chalice character" insofar as it surrenders itself, making itself poor as an expression of its fullness.

Second, this divestiture of Being in beings implies an unsurpassable unity among all things, connected to each other by means of a common enabling ground: "every being that becomes actual is rooted and communicates with all the others."[82] Together, these two points are not competing first principles of Being, but gesture toward the truth

---

inhabiting and knowing that new world too must be remade. Epistemology must once again be seen an extension of ontology; knowing and Being must be united.

81. *TL* 2, 228.
82. Ibid., 229.

that all things come forth in the same creative act of divestiture, and are thus united by acts of kenosis, surrender, and love.

If Christ is to express the truth of created Being, then his human existence must be one of radical finitude that embraces the depth of creaturely fragility, even death. This emphasis on the contingency of Christ's existence leads Balthasar to appropriate the early church's *Logos-Sarx* Christology. His emphasis on the fragility and temporality of *sarx* is at the heart of his theology of Christ's death. In his death, Christ shows himself to be the one who perfectly expresses the truth of created Being and, by so doing, heals it. Balthasar therefore holds with many of the early Fathers that "the flesh is the hinge of salvation."[83]

Third, the implications of this metaphysical summary highlight two decisive principles for Balthasar's theological anthropology. If humanity is the product of the sacrificial process of both Being and nature, that is, if humanity is constituted by receptivity on the natural level, then theologically, humanity is also "dispositively open to . . . the self-surrender of the Son in the will of the Father through the Holy Spirit."[84] The true disposition of humanity is *potentia oboedientialis*: "Needless to say, what man sees nature living out unconsciously is something that he himself must freely and knowingly understand and appropriate."[85] The consequence of this constitution and vocation, however, is that humanity also has a "terrible capacity" for titanic striving to be gods through their own strength and power. This striving is the root of sin and the root of the titanisms of German Idealism.

The immediate consequence of this for Christology is that, by becoming human, that is, by taking on not just human nature but human *flesh*, the incarnate Christ takes on humanity's vocation. Christ realizes in himself the full truth of created Being through the drama of his existence: "And because the whole of the cosmos is indivisible from man, and because man himself emerged and developed from that same cosmos and is meant to rule over it as if it were but his own body

---

83. *Epilogue*, 99.
84. *TL* 2, 230.
85. Ibid.

writ large, the lordship of the enfleshed Son necessary becomes the lordship over the universe."[86]

How exactly does this lordship become reality? For Balthasar, the lordship of truth comes from *within* as creation's own offering up of itself, and not through an extrinsic imposition on creation. This occurs through the archetypal and paradigmatic existence of Christ who, as the truth, reveals himself as the love that carries all truth within itself, accepting even the contradictions of the world, bearing them and transforming them. Creation offers itself up to God when God becomes creation, and surrenders itself as he surrenders himself. Here, Christ's truth is performed in the drama of his life and shows itself to be co-extensive with love.

Love

Balthasar is not content to end his christological discussion at the level of the two natures of Christ. Instead, he plunges into the depths of Christ's dramatic existence and discovers there how the form of Christ's life expresses the truth of his nature. Balthasar points to the deeds of Christ's life as the demonstration of his truth: "Jesus' whole human existence becomes God's self-expression and self-surrender."[87] This section explores this performative dimension of Christ's truth, especially as it reveals the unity of truth and love.

God's truth—God's eternal measuring of Being—does not occur solely in some heavenly sphere. Such would lead in the direction of some sort of gnostic spiritualism. Rather, this measuring, the condition of the possibility of all human knowing, comes through the particular human existence of the incarnate Son. In this way, Balthasar holds that Christ is not just the goal of human knowing but also the way. As we

---

86. *Epilogue*, 102. It is important to distinguish between Balthasar's point here and Decartes' claim that humanity can be masters and possessors of nature. See Descartes, *Discourse on Method*, VI.62. The lordship that Balthasar describes is one characterized, as we saw above, by service, and of course, by love. His is not an exploitative lordship, but a proper governing, cultivating, and protecting. Humanity is charged to be the "shepherd" of created Being.

87. Ibid., 90. Emphasis added.

shall see, the dramatic performance of Christ's existence that funds Balthasar's theology of the saints.

Kenosis

Kenosis provides the structural key for Balthasar's dramatic Christology. We can unpack Balthasar's account of Christ's kenotic existence under three main modes: Christ's receptivity, his poverty, as well as his self-abandonment and self-surrender (*Hingabe*). All three of these modes show that Christ's truth is the outworking of his eternal obedience. Together, these modes are all expressions of his mission and his identity: the eternal source of all truth is divine love. He alone is the way into the truth and life. This is Christ's mission, grounded in the logic of his kenosis:

> . . . if the kingship of the God who reveals himself as love comes to light precisely in the Son's humble obedience to the Father, then it is clear that this obedience is essentially love. It is certainly the paradigmatic attitude of love the creature must have before God's majesty, but far more than that, it is the radiant paradigm of divine love itself: precisely in—and *only* in—the kenosis of Christ, the *inner* mystery of God's love comes to light, the mystery of the God who "is love" (1 John 4:8) in himself and therefore is "triune."[88]

Kenosis is the overarching form of love and the inner structure of all truth. It is the form of the divine truth that walks the dusty roads of Galilee.

For Balthasar, Christ's kenotic existence accomplishes two things. First, it existentially expresses truth. In so doing, Christ's existence is the true *analogia entis*—the space where divine and creaturely truth meet. Second, Christ's kenotic existence creates space for the ongoing dramatic understanding of his truth; the Christic form of love is the condition of the possibility of Balthasar's subsequent, saintly epistemology of love.

In this way, Christ becomes the meeting place of truth. This will lead us to our conclusion that the epistemological way into truth that Christ

88. *LA*, 87.

opens through his existence, the way that knowledge corresponds to the form of his truth, is love performed as the dialogue of prayer.

Receptivity

Christ is the archetypal expression of receptivity. The receptivity of Being finds its fulfillment in the human life of the God-Man. Receptivity lies at the heart of Christ's mission of expression. "No one can give himself as mission . . . where a person is entrusted with a substantial mission that summons him to put his very existence at its disposal, the person thus sent (*der Gesendete*) can, as a result, become (to a degree) identified with the mission (*Sendung*)."[89] For Balthasar, Christ *is* what he *does*. That this is so is due to his perfect receptivity.

> It is of his essence as Son to receive life insight, spirit, word, will, deed, doctrine, work, and glorification from another, from the Father. He receives it, indeed, in such a way that he has it all *in himself* and disposes of all that he receives as of his own; yet never with any denial of that receiving, but affirming it always, eternally, as the ground of his very being.[90]

Christ's life is lived with perfect openness before God, perfect receptivity of his mission and person, and perfect obedience to the word spoken to him. Christ recapitulates in his existence the metaphysical rhythm of truth by receiving in himself the truth of the Father and creatively appropriating it in his life. Christ's person is *receptio* and *agens*.

For Christ, this rhythm of reception and appropriation is a cyclical act. His "having" is never separated from his "receiving." The receptivity that we examined in the previous chapter is thus shown to be but a reflection of the true human: "The Son's form of existence, which makes him the Son from all eternity, is the uninterrupted reception of everything that he is, of his very self, from the Father. It is indeed this receiving of himself which gives him his 'I,' his own inner

---

89. *TD* 3, 154.
90. *TH*, 30.

dimension, his spontaneity, that sonship with which he can answer the Father in a reciprocal giving."[91]

Christ's human receptivity is an expression of his Trinitarian identity.[92] The receptivity that characterizes Jesus is the double expression of his hylomorphic nature. The historical drama of Jesus's receptivity corresponds perfectly to his eternal reception of the Father as the divine Son. It is here that the historical temporality of Christ takes on a cosmic significance as the location of his performance of divine receptivity.

Christ's receptivity comes to expression, first of all, in his temporality. Christ does not stand outside of time and survey his history extrinsically, as if his life were a chess game laid out before his all-seeing eye. If his existence was simply the enactment of an eternally pre-determined plan, then it would not be a truly dramatic event. There can be no obedient receptivity unless his drama plays out in history. Christ does not anticipate his history. Indeed, sin, as Balthasar conceives it, is anticipation, the attempt to step outside of the rhythm of historical receptivity. Sin is the attempt to *possess* what one can only ever *receive*. The Christian claim that Christ "knew no sin" is not, for Balthasar, an abstract bit of arid theorizing, but is rather the form of Christ's perfect identification as truth in the world.

An extrinsically realized, ahistorical, non-dramatic performance would destroy the possibility of Christ's receptivity, his faith and hope, and, ultimately, his love:

> In its perfection, hope is simply the readiness of love to say yes to everything, to be available for everything, always open to the infinite, in the knowledge that God is always its greater good; faith is simply that disposition in the creature by which it makes an offering and a surrender of itself, and thus of all its own truth, all its own evidence, in a love which prefers God's invariably greater truth to its own. . . . But when hope and faith are open at this infinite angle, then both are, at heart, true modes

---

91. Ibid.
92. "For the man Jesus, his hypostatic union with the *Logos* is not a religious entity, a theme in its own right; rather, the form of his human self-awareness is the expression, in terms of this world, of his eternal consciousness as Son" (*TH*, 32).

of love, which death cannot destroy, nor even the supreme face-to-face vision can supersede.[93]

The preceding implies that the incarnate existence of Christ cannot be other than an entirely original, historical event: "[t]he Incarnation is not the *n*th performance of a tragedy already lying in the archives of eternity."[94] Nor is the incarnation simply a symbolic retelling of a generic myth of Being. Balthasar insists that the incarnation is the true event of history. Christ is the true center of history. His receptivity and obedience are not mere examples. They are archetypes of truth. Here, Balthasar casts off any possible vestiges of a Hegelian logic that relativizes the particularities of Christ's history. Instead, Balthasar maintains that the fullest manifestation and expression of truth comes in the historically contingent particularity of Christ's human life. Christ is the whole in the fragment.

Christ's perfect receptivity is expressed in his form of life, both in his spiritual disposition to the Father's will and in the activities of his life. We will consider two specific forms of Christ's receptive existence: his poverty as manifested in his radical surrender (*Gelassenheit*) and his obedience.

Poverty

Love undergoes kenosis, willing to become poor through reckless prodigality, so that it can receive anew.[95] The willful poverty that Christ adopts is a further expression of his kenotic existence and his radical receptivity. His poverty is seen not only in his kenotic act of becoming flesh, but also in every renunciation of power, authority, and will throughout the course of his earthly existence. Because Christ resolves to be nothing in himself, his earthly poverty is a further disclosure of his perfect receptivity. Rather than striving after power, Jesus opts instead to be perfectly disposed to the Father's will. "Jesus

---

93. *TH*, 45. This is why there was not "some other way" to save the world apart from the cross.
94. Ibid., 39.
95. At this point, we can hear an echo of the previous chapter's emphasis on mystery.

is the bringer of salvation, equipped only to pass on what he has to others; for himself, he has nothing."[96]

Christ's ontological poverty is performed through the poverty of his earthly life. The homelessness of Christ is significant for Balthasar. That "there was no room in the inn" (Luke 2:7), and that "the Son of Man has no place to rest his head" (Matt 8:20), show that Jesus rejected all forms of social stability and self-sufficiency. Christ's existence is, at every moment and in every respect, in absolute dependence on the Father (Matt 6:25).[97]

Christ's poverty is seen especially in the way he prays. His Lord's prayer is "a beggar's prayer from start to finish."[98] It is significant that Christ teaches a petitionary prayer rather than, say, a contemplative one.[99] The relationship with the Father that Christ models through his prayer is not one of striving for mystical union. It is, rather, a prayer of desperate dependence on the Father. Christ resists the twin temptations of self-sufficiency and the will-to-power—"turn these stones into bread" and "I will give you all the power and glory"—by accepting his poverty and absolute dependence in his petition to the Father to "give us this day our daily bread."

Christ's radical poverty, ontological in the kenosis of the incarnation, and existential in Christ's state of life, leads to his perfect solidarity with the poor of every form.[100] The tragic logic of this

---

96. GL 7, 131. In this way, Christ's existence is proleptically foretold by the prophets of the Old Testament: "if the word that the prophet possesses and the attitude of poverty of the now can become identical in their orientation toward the same 'soon' of God's action, then we would possess a model (the content of which could not be filled out) for what the Incarnation of the Word is."

97. By virtue of his particular mission of expressivity and his identity as the God-Man, the mediator between God and created being, Christ's poverty is both representative and inclusive of all things. Christ represents the poverty of all created Being by drawing that poverty into his own. Thus drawn, Being's own poverty is transformed; it becomes, not absence or lack, but the fullness of love.

98. GL 7, 134. This line of interpretation has been more recently confirmed by Pope Emeritus Benedict XVI in his Jesus of Nazareth, trans. Adrian J. Walker (New York: Doubleday, 2007), 128ff.

99. And yet, Balthasar insists that it does fall to the Christian to pray contemplatively. But this style of prayer is couched within a more fundamental child-like prayer of petition. Petitionary prayer is the fundamental acknowledgment of our impoverishment, contingency, and need. Contemplative prayer cannot act as a sanctified tower of Babel; all prayer begins and ends from the desperate need of creatureliness.

100. Balthasar notes the way Christ acts in solidarity with all of the forms of the poor of ancient Palestine. Christ takes the side of the tax collectors and sinners (Luke 15:1ff); children (Luke

solidarity leads to Christ's deadly confrontation with the "powers and principalities" of un-truth and un-love that dominate the realm of the poor. The logic of Christ's perfect receptivity leads to its tragic fulfillment in the crucifixion. It is on the cross that Christ's perfect solidarity with the poor most properly belongs to him: "because he now must really 'be reckoned among those who have broken the law' (Luke 22:37)."[101] Christ suffers and dies in perfect solidarity with the poorest of the poor, those who lived and died under the curse. He exists in absolute solidarity with created Being in the incarnation and, in his poverty, with the poor of every form. The consequence of this solidarity is the cross, and, beyond that, the poverty of God-forsakenness in death.

Christ thus draws together and sums up in himself the radical contingency of all created Being, enfolding its contingency into the free expression of his perfect receptivity. We see that Christ's radical receptivity is also an expression of his perfect obedience to the Father. His obedience, his receptivity and solidarity with the poor, are all expressions of his love that, at the apex of its expressivity, is *Hingabe, Gelassenheit*: the surrender that directly embraces its own contradiction on the cross and the descent into hell. Here, in its abandonment and surrender to the deformed mendacity of the world's sin, Christ's life perfectly expresses truth: "the transparence of the one sent, who does not his own will, but the will only of the one who sent him (John 6:38), who does not speak from himself, and accordingly does not seek his own glory, [is] precisely for this reason 'true' (John 7:18)."[102]

Surrender and Obedience

What Christ has received, he has received from the Father, though not claiming himself as the sole possessor of the gifts given. Instead, he surrenders all that he has received, all that he *is*, back up to the Father

---

18:15ff); the persecuted (Luke 6:22). The scandal of Christ's solidarity expresses the Father's perfect love for "those who have lost their way." The "weakness" of the Father's heart for the poor is made visible in the life of Christ. See *GL* 7, 137–38.
101. *GL* 7, 138.
102. Ibid., 142.

in an act of abandonment. Christ's self-surrender expresses itself in his humiliation, revealing that the heart of his person, and hence the heart of divine Being, is absolute, self-giving love:

> It is too good to be true: the mystery of Being, revealed as absolute love, condescending to wash his creatures' feet, and even their souls, taking upon himself all the confusion and guilt, all the God-directed hatred, all the accusations showered upon him with cudgels, all the disbelief that arrogantly covers up what he had revealed, all the mocking hostility that once and for all nailed down his inconceivable movement of self-abasement—in order to pardon his creature, before himself and the world.[103]

Obedience to his mission to testify to the truth of the Father is part of the Son's vocation as the expressive *Logos*. But this obedient expression in the world is bookended by two profound silences: that of the womb and that of the grave. It is in his quiet that the Word made flesh disposes himself to be the agent of the Father's will. As the Synoptic gospels make clear, the Word only breaks his theological silence after being addressed by his Fatherly Thou and commissioned in his baptism in the Jordan. Only then does he begin to speak, as an obedient response to his Father's will.[104] Christ's words are receptive and to the prior word of the Father.

According to Balthasar, Christ's obedience is *traditio*, a handing over of himself to the Father's will in an act of trust, faith, and love. That is, Christ's obedience involves perfect surrender, absolute abandonment (*Gelassenheit*) of himself, and the utter impoverishment of his being. He wills to be poor and receive not the fullness of the Father but the cup of his Father's rejection. In abandoning himself, the Son is abandoned by the Father. We have seen the centrality of abandonment for Balthasar's Ignatian spirituality and his metaphysics. Now we see that *Gelassenheit* is grounded in the passion of Christ. In the drama

103. *LA*, 102.
104. On the theme of Christ's silence as his receptivity and self-abandonment see *GL* 7, 143ff. On Christ's silence before Pilate as a signal of his obedience and surrender, see *TL* 2, 87ff. Interestingly, Balthasar's negative theology is grounded precisely in this christic silence. Negative theology for him is less an epistemological "unknowing" than it is a disposition of obedience and surrender before God.

of Christ's passion, we see the archetypal act of surrender, and the possibility of all subsequent spiritual and metaphysical abandonment.

In the passion, the *Verbum caro* "abandons itself and dissolves itself." His truthful Word becomes un-word. Through his sacrificial act, we encounter the paradox that lies at the heart of Christian truth: that love is cursed, that which is holy has become sin, life has died, word has become un-word, form has become formlessness, truth has become lie. For Balthasar, this is the heart of Christian truth precisely because it is here, in his suffering, in his act of self-abandonment that results in his forsakenness by the Father, in his embrace of every contradiction, that Christ perfectly discloses his love.

Contradiction

It is Christ crucified, dead, and buried, that is the full expression of truth. When Christ undergoes suffering and death in the face of every logical and moral contradiction, truth shows itself as absolute self-giving love. Christ's truth does not annihilate or synthesize its contradiction along the lines of Hegelian dialectic. Instead, Christ's truth demonstrates its perfect receptivity, not only of life and of love, but also, of death and curse.

The abandonment that Christ undergoes on the cross results in the breaking apart of the unity of logic and love that the Son is in his nature. "Because every love is withheld from him, all he has left is pure 'reasoning', this 'dreadful faculty', pure logic, which (because love is lacking) is precisely 'absurd': 'Thought can no longer keep up; nothing is logically conclusive.' . . . One is deprived, not only of thinking, but of speech itself. . . ."[105] The unity of truth and love that is constitutive of Christ's nature and existence has led him to this point of dereliction. His dereliction is both the full expression of his truth and the un-making of his expressive form. The *Gestalt* of Christ becomes *formlessness*: "The Son's obedience even in death, even in hell, is his perfect identity in all contradiction."[106]

---

105. *TL* 2, 358.
106. Ibid., 354. He continues: "At no point in his life can one draw a boundary between love and

This is another example of Balthasar's subtle dismantling of Hegelian dialectic. "And because, being the Word pure and simple, he is also the truth pure and simple, the contradiction of him is also the untruth, the lie pure and simple. Etymologically *dia* means 'apart', 'asunder', so that contradiction, *dia-legein*, dialectic means the yawning abyss of sheer irreconcilability and enmity."[107] A Christo-logic cannot be a Hegelian dialectic and synthesis for the simple reason that the contradiction Christ undergoes by "becoming sin" is well beyond the possibility of synthesis and reconciliation. The contradiction of the lie cannot be sublated into a higher synthesis; it can only be healed from within.

Christ's passion consists of a series of contradictions that destroy his expressive form. The joyful irony of Christian logic, though, is that it is precisely through this destruction of Truth himself that we see the fullest image of truth. Christ's truth is revealed as love when Christ is "made sin," when his truth becomes the lie.[108] Only thus can every other contradiction that reverberates through Being be taken on and healed from within. This is the heart of Balthasar's theology of Holy Saturday, and in many ways, the heart of all of Balthasar's thought.[109]

The first contradiction that Christ takes on in his descent to the dead is the very possibility of hell itself. For Balthasar, hell is the "latrine" of sin. Hell's essence is nothing substantial. Hell exists only as the contradiction of the truth of Christ. Hell can only "be" insofar as it is the repository of everything that willfully counters the truth of Christ. It is lie, silence, hate. In a way, hell is a diabolical impossible possibility: "Hell is and at the same time is not."[110]

But Christ's descent into hell is not just a descent into the dregs of

---

mission, task and everyday existence, obedience and voluntariness, obedience and personal sphere, obedience and the assumption of the task. He made all this a unity, so that out of the unity of love [speaking trinitarianly] he must now endure the unity of abandonment. It was his own rule that condemned him to death."

107. *TL* 2, 317.
108. Ibid., 317ff.
109. Even Balthasar's critics note the centrality of his theology of Holy Saturday. See, for example, Alyssa Pitstick, *Light in the Darkness: Hans Urs von Balthasar and the Catholic Doctrine of Christ's Descent into Hell* (Grand Rapids: Eerdmans, 2007).
110. *TL* 2., 351.

sin, but also, into death itself. The contradiction, the sin of hell, is the "sting" of death. In his descent, Christ demonstrates perfect solidarity even with the accursed dead. This is the depth of his kenotic poverty. Christ's harrowing is not an active, triumphant charge into the depths of Hades, but rather, the passive becoming like one of the dead.[111] His descent is a sinking into the "essence of the second death: that which is cursed by God in his definitive judgment sinks down to the place where it belongs. In this state, there is no time."[112] The abyss of the second death is absolute hiatus, the annihilation of time and Being. The abyss of the second death is what Balthasar calls the second chaos that is outside of the Father's creation. It is sheer god-forsakenness. The truth and the contradiction of Holy Saturday is that God is forsaken by God.

The irony of Holy Saturday is that Christ's perfect solidarity with the poor occurs in the context of utter and absolute abandonment, in the context of hell in which, according to Balthasar, there is no community.[113] Hell is solitude. Here is the second dimension of hell's contradiction: its ontological mendacity. The utter solitude of hell is the destruction of the love, of being-for-another, and of being-together. Since love and Being are convertible, hell is the utter annihilation of Being. Again, we see how Balthasar can say that hell both is and is not—the impossible possibility.

If hell is indeed the annihilation of Being and love, it is also absolute atemporality. In hell, every past and future completely disappears; its gate is always closed. Hell is "definitive and affords no prospect of escape on any side."[114] Its timelessness is the nihilistic counter to the

---

111. *TL 2*, 347: "Holy Saturday is not Easter Sunday." For Balthasar, Hans Holbein's is the most accurate depiction of Holy Saturday. In Holbein's haunting vision, Christ's corpse lies bare and exposed to our vision. His body is bruised and broken; his fingers are frozen in rigor mortis; his eyes stare sightlessly into the Void that has become his only reality, even as it is a non-reality. Christ in his death is human, all too human—abandoned, forsaken, contradicted. And it is precisely this Christ that Balthasar sees as the crowning revelation of divine truth, beauty, and goodness.
112. Balthasar, *Mysterium Paschale: The Mystery of Easter*, trans. Aidan Nichols, O.P. (San Francisco, Ignatius Press, 1990), 50.
113. *TL 2*, 349ff.
114. Here, Balthasar's thought is significantly influenced by the mystical theology of Adrienne von Speyr. Speyr's almost yearly participation in the Triduum yielded a number of theologically rich meditations on the "nature" of hell and of Christ's descent. According to Balthasar, Speyr would, on every Easter for many years, spiritually descend with Christ into death, and there, existentially know the utter Godforsakenness of Christ. In Balthasar's mind, her share in the

fullness of triune life, and a parody of Trinitarian kenosis. The latter is the eternally reciprocal movement of love, but the other is the frigid *stasis* of nothing.

The atemporality of hell results in what we might call the "existential contradiction" of the dead Christ. The one who is the Word, the very expressivity of truth, becomes mute in the atemporality of hell. The dialogicality between Father and Son ceases for the dead and abandoned Christ. Stripped of his Father's word, that is, stripped of himself, Christ becomes de-formed to the point of utter formlessness. Apart from his Father's "Thou," Christ ceases to be an "I"—his personhood is surrendered and he becomes "a pure impersonal 'one.'"[115] The person that is the meaning of all creation suffers as the one who is now absolute meaninglessness. As a dead man, Christ has "lost his Word-character."[116] The one whose perfect obedience resulted in the kenotic silence of the womb now embraces the consummate silence of the grave.

But Christ has not just lost his Word-character. He has become accursed, the *un-word*, untruth. By handing himself over to sin, Christ does not only *confront* the contradiction of hell. He *becomes* that contradiction. He becomes sin (2 Cor 5:21). But therein lies the beauty and the goodness of Christ's truth.

Healing the Lie

By becoming the lie, Christ takes on the lie of estranged creation, its failure to bear faithfully the divine truth. He becomes the formlessness of the lie. Truth and life become lie and death. He does this not in order

---

visio mortis gave her a profound, almost "insider's view," into the nature of Holy Saturday. In fact, Balthasar's entire constructive argument about the anti-logic of Holy Saturday in *TL 2* is an adoption and exposition of Speyr. For many commentators, this fact makes Balthasar's thought here immediately suspect. More often Balthasar's relationship with Speyr has been dismissed as irrelevant to understanding his thought. See, for example, Kevin Mongrain, op.cit., and Edward T. Oakes, *Pattern of Redemption: The Theology of Hans Urs von Balthasar* (New York: Bloomsbury Academic, 1997). We do not have the space here to support or critique Balthasar's appropriation of Speyrian mystical insight. We can only note that Balthasar himself said that his theology was inseparable from that of Speyr. His theology of Holy Saturday is a perfect example of this dependence.

115. *TL 2*, 350.
116. Ibid., 352.

to sublate the lie extrinsically into a higher truth, but to heal the lie from within.

The healing of creation's lie is possible because of Christ's exemplarism. His exemplarity of creation becomes vicarious representation. Christ represents creation vicariously in his descent into utter forsakenness. Christ's vicarious representation is an act of love, a literal "being-for-another" that explodes the ugly solitude of hell. He enters into the abyss of forsaken solitude, bearing all of creation in the exemplary community of his flesh. The illogic of hell is confronted by the supremacy of the logic of self-giving love. Hell withers in the confrontation. Christ's death was the Father's "no" to everything in creation that stands opposed to him. But because that "no" is represented vicariously in Christ's exemplary "yes," the contradiction is resolved.[117] Through the presence of the one who is perfect truth, perfect obedience, and perfect love, the negativity and contradiction of the grave are overwhelmed, forgiven, graced, and healed.

What Christ's *descendus ad inferna* effects according to Balthasar is Christ's taking on of "everything that is contrary to God, of the entire object of divine eschatological judgment which here is grasped in that event in which it is cast down."[118] Christ's unadulterated forsakenness is his "existential measure" of the depths of the pit. It is not accidental that Balthasar uses the epistemological language of "measurement" to describe Christ's sounding of the depths of hell. Through his measuring the second chaos of hell, there is now truly nothing that has not been comprehended by God. God's measurement, his divine truth, encompasses all things, even its contradiction, having healed it from within. Through his existential presence in the *visio mortis* Christ is able, as Aquinas says, to "take possession" of death, Hades and hell.[119] This ownership of hell means, therefore, that when he is raised by the Father (another passive act to parallel his passive, powerless descent),

---

117. *Prayer*, 55.
118. Balthasar, *Mysterium Paschale*, 174.
119. Thomas Aquinas, in *Symbolum Apostolorum Expositio*, a.5, (Rome: Marietti, 1954, vol. 2, pp. 204–5), a. 5.

he brings all of hell with him. Christ's mortal kenosis circumscribes death itself.[120] At the resurrection, Christ takes full possession of death and breaks its boundaries.

Christ's obedience to the point of utter abandonment effects the healing of corrupted nature: the "descent to the tragic point in man, where sin, as opposition to God, has come into its own."[121] In his assumption of the fullness of creation, even to the point of identifying himself with its contradiction and mendacity in Hell, Christ "exposed [himself] to contradiction for our sakes, in order to destroy the contradiction within his very self. 'Not as I will, but as you will' . . . he does violence to his own will in order to subject it fully to the Father."[122] Through Christ's perfect archetypal obedience, his truth overwhelms creation's mendacity. The Lie is not synthesized; it is healed. Such a healing demanded that Christ take on hell itself, for "whatever is not assumed is not healed." By assuming in himself the lie of creation, Christ healed it utterly and absolutely:

> And if the Lord brings the marks of his wounds into his victory and eternally remains the "Lamb as slain", it is surely not in order to integrate the contradiction of sin and hell into his heaven. He does have the keys of death and the underworld in his power, but only as the victor over both. The Lamb is at the same time "the Lion of Judah", whose victory gives him alone the power to open the book of the history of the cosmos.[123]

For Balthasar, Christ's resurrection from the depths of contradiction and abandonment opens up a way from that diabolic abyss, opening the isolation of hell.[124] From the depth, the pathway out of death has been opened. According to Gregory the Great, "Christ went down into the deepest abysses of the sea, when he went into the lowest hell, to

---

120. Such a notion hinges on Christ being the "concrete-universal" and the sacrament of humanity. According to Gregory of Nyssa, by becoming a member of humanity, all of humanity became members of Christ's body. As Balthasar explains it, "But insofar as Christ's fulfillment was given the form of kenosis 'in the fashion of our guilty nature, to make amends for our guilt', the Son experienced not only the human situation as such but all those situations which lie between complete fulfillment and complete non-fulfillment" (TH, 67).
121. CL, 263.
122. Ibid., 268.
123. TL 2, 359.
124. Balthasar also sees the resurrection as opening up the possibility of Purgatory. Cf. TL 2, 355.

fetch forth the souls of his elect. Before the redemption, the depth of the sea was a prison, not a way. . . . But God made of this abyss a road."[125]

Christ's resurrection is the breaking of the eschatological dawn. It effects the transfiguration of the entire world. The road that Christ cuts out of the Pit opens the possibility of entering into the full truth of the Trinity. Christ as the truth bears creation's mendacity into the grave and back out of it, bearing it upwards, in the full rush of his resurrection glory, to the Father. The resurrection of the Truth transfigures all worldly truth. This is more than a mere restoration of Eden. The grace that Christ effects over all nature is its elevation and perfection.[126]

Truth and the *Ascensio Christi*

But, of course, Christ's resurrection is not the end of the story. By way of conclusion, let us turn to Christ's ascension, the final, critical piece of Christ's work of truth in the world. In his ascension, Christ brings the truth of the God–world relationship into new light that is significant for both metaphysics and epistemology. If the incarnation was the in-breaking of eternity into history, the ascension draws created time and Being into the eschaton, transfiguring both in the process. Christ overcame the mendacity of the world in his passion. That he healed the world allows us to interpret the ascension in a positive rather than a negative light. Rather than fleeing the broken world, discarding it in favor of a flight of the alone to the Alone, Christ bears the entire created order up into the very life of God in his ascent. Creation participates through Christ in the life of God in a new, eschatological way.

When it comes to his doctrine of the ascension, Balthasar adopts the ancient Alexandrian model of *procession* and *regression*, or *exitus/reditus*. Just as the world proceeded from the Father, through the redemptive

---

125. Quoted in *PT*, 145. One need no longer abandon all hope.
126. Balthasar agrees with Aquinas that grace does not destroy nature (as if Christ's resurrection opens the possibility of a non-natural, quasi-gnostic spiritualist existence in heaven), but rather, perfects it.

work of the Son, it returns to the Father. The eternal truth of God descends, uniting in himself the fullness of divine and creaturely truth. He then descends to the depths of contradiction. But he also rises from that contradiction, both in the resurrection and, in its fulfilling movement, in the ascension. Christ unites worldly and divine truth in his person, ontologically, and restores their union existentially through his death, resurrection, and ascension. All created truth is thus summed up in Christ's flesh and drawn into the very life of God. Christ's death, resurrection, and ascension are intended to achieve the redemption of all creation by drawing it step by step toward God.[127]

Through Christ, we have the "reentry of the creature into God."[128] The re-entry of creation into the divine life is made possible because "the cosmic struggle between the nature [truth] of God and the nature [truth] of the world took place within a single soul."[129] Christ reconciles God and world in the union of his flesh and through the dramatic confrontation with death and sin in his passion. Christ's exemplarism and his vicarious representation effect a metaphysical shift in Being, reestablishing "the continuity between heaven and earth and '[proving] that heavenly and earthly beings join in a single festive dance, as they receive the gifts that come from God."[130]

This marks a fundamental transfiguration of creation and its truth. No longer does created truth derive its autonomy from its estrangement from God. In light of Christ, creation bears a porous integrity, an ontological density that is nonetheless open to its fulfillment in transcendence. This is exactly the obedience Christ accomplished in his own human nature, now writ large for all of creation. Christ's *kairos* gives theological value to all times and all places.

As Balthasar describes it, creation has the Trinity as its formal truth

---

127. As Maximus will insist, "Christ brought his historic work of salvation to completion for our sakes and ascended along with the body he had assumed, he united heaven and earth through himself, corrected sensible creation with the intellectual, and so revealed the unity of creation in the very polarity of its elements" (*Ad Thalassium* 48: PG 90, 436A).
128. *CL*, 271.
129. Ibid.
130. Ibid., 273.

because it has been borne by the resurrected and ascended Christ into that divine reality. We hear echoes of John Scotus Eriugena in the background: "For what he brings to completion in himself, he will do in all those who are made perfect. I do not say merely in all men, but in all physical creation too; for when God's Word took human nature to himself, he excluded no created substance that he would not have taken up with him in that nature."[131] The redeemed creation exists under an open heaven whose light shines not only upon, but also, within the world.[132]

The ascension transforms creaturely truth, lifting it into the realm of heaven. Participating in the life of God fulfills created truth. This leads us to Balthasar's final role for Christ. Christ is the *raptus* that carries the world back to the Father. In a way, just as Christ is the *analogia entis*, so too, as "expression" and "*raptus*," he is creation's procession and return to the Father.[133]

The elevation of creation into the life of God through the ascension is the fulfillment of Christ's mission as the truth. The ascension "causes the whole of creation to radiate with inner meaning."[134] This inner meaning is Christ: "It is only 'in Christ' that things can attain their ultimate goal and meaning . . . even with mundane truth, it is the [divine] man who imparts meaning to things, helping them, through his whole existence, to achieve this intra-mundane truth."[135]

It is important to note that it is the incarnate Christ, not the *Logos asarkos* that is creation's inner meaning. Balthasar is again resisting the reduction of truth to an abstract concept or idea. For Balthasar, Christ's ascension gives the world a truly *sacramental* character. The eucharistic reality of the ascended Christ opens up new vistas of truth in the transfigured world. The world is again drenched with divine—*Christic*—meaning and significance.

131. Quoted in *TD* 5, 379.
132. Ibid., 119.
133. The dual tasks of Christ to be "the concrete expression of God and the *raptus* which carries this entire cosmos back to God, are both fulfilled in the Person of the Son. And this Person is the Father's Word from all eternity, just as he is the original Idea in which the whole cosmos was conceived, founded and brought into being" (Ibid., 56).
134. Ibid., 64.
135. Ibid., 65.

This metaphysical transfiguration of creation in the ascension of Christ demands a renewed epistemology. Christ "united the heavenly spheres with the earth, thus proving 'that all sensible creation is a unity in the intelligible order."[136] Christ reassembles and reorients all truth within the logic of his incarnate person, drawing it to the Father in the *raptus* of his ascension. Creation then becomes once again a trustworthy pathway to God.[137] For Balthasar, this new eschatological epistemology takes the form of contemplation—a form of knowledge that understands the world through its relation to God. This is *theo-logic*: a knowledge of God and all things in relation to God. "Our temporal life [and knowledge and truth] only has meaning within our eternal life [and knowledge and truth]."[138] Christ's ascension creates the religious significance and sacramental meaning of worldly truth. He opens "the real path of contemplation" that stands in stark contrast to natural mysticisms and philosophies of identity that "are always in danger of losing both the world and God."[139] A true christo-logic of the sort that Balthasar develops in his Trilogy, on the contrary, is conceived as the divinization of the cosmos.[140] Christ reveals the relationship between Word and world not as abstract Archetype to Type, or as Ground to Existent, but rather as a personal one in which created spirit comes to knowledge of truth through personal acts of knowing, through faith, contemplation, and prayer. These mark the fundamental character of thinking and Being that is worthy of the eschaton.[141]

Conclusion

Christ's *regressio* to the Father is the heart of both philosophical and theological truth. Truth and knowledge exist in the eschaton as a

---

136. Ibid.
137. The term "trustworthy" is essential here. It echoes the fidelity of truth outlined in the previous chapter: truth as *emeth*. It was the reliability of truth that was fundamentally marred by sin (especially idolatry), significantly hindering the possibility of knowledge of God, and therefore, true metaphysic knowledge.
138. *TD* 5, 113.
139. *Prayer*, 54.
140. *CL*, 274.
141. See *GL* 2, 304ff.

"eucharistic permeability" of all subjects to one another. But the critical point here is that this permeability occurs within the person of Christ and the eschatology that his incarnation, passion, and ascension inaugurate. For Balthasar, eschatology quite simply *is* the inclusion of all things in Christ, accomplished through the ministry of the Holy Spirit.[142] Balthasar's christological eschatology opens a horizon for a distinctively Catholic renewal of metaphysics. The truth of Christ sheds light on the nature of reality from within the divine engagement and offers surprising resources for the Church's missionary opening to the world.[143]

The distinctive form that Balthasar's christological metaphysics presents is one that discloses truth and knowledge as co-extensive with love. As we have seen, if truth is love, then it can only be known through love. The truth of Christ that the saints know through the Holy Spirit, and make known to the world, is that Christ is the truth that pulses in the heart of Being. It is the saint who beholds Christ's life, participates in it and says, with Bonaventure, *hic notitia est.* The saint is the one who, through the Holy Spirit, shares in Christ's kenosis, his abandonment and his resurrection, and thus walks along the contemplative path to truth that is Christ himself.[144] The saint is the one who proclaims that Christ is the truth, the way, and, as such, the life of the world.

---

142. Healy, *The Eschatology of Hans Urs von Balthasar*, 92.
143. Ibid., 6.
144. See *TD* 5, 111–12: "[A]t the same time he is visibly on his way back to heaven, taking his earthly body and his entire earthly fate with him. Yet, nullifying the distance between heaven and earth, he remains on earth, invisibly, to the end of time, thus in a more concrete manner than ever before (cf. Isa 55:10–11), in order to promote the exchange between heaven and earth; indeed, he is this exchange."

6

Spirit of Truth, Spirit of Love

In this chapter, I turn to Balthasar's pneumatology. The Holy Spirit is the agent that Christ promises to his disciples as the one "who will guide them into all truth" (John 16:13). For Balthasar, Christology always extends into pneumatology. We have seen that Balthasar's account of truth has both an objective and a subjective dimension. In the previous chapter, I focused on Balthasar's "objective" truth of the nature of the God–world relationship as revealed and transformed by Christ. In this chapter, I turn to the subjective dimension of truth by turning to the Holy Spirit, who is divine subjectivity. It is the vocation of the Spirit to take believers and form them into knowers and lovers of God. It is the Spirit who makes saints. The task of this chapter is to situate Balthasar's pneumatology as the agent of the ever-contemporary, subjective understanding of the historical, objective truth of Christ.

The Spirit and Logic

We must begin by considering the possibility of the Spirit's place in a theo-logic. We might be willing to give Balthasar's Christology a pass;

after all, as the incarnate *Logos*, Christ is at least etymologically related to *logic*. But what about the Spirit? Is not talk about the "spiritual" antithetical to talk of rationality? What role can the Spirit possibly play in the knowledge and exposition of metaphysical truth?

Balthasar has two chief reasons for including a pneumatology in his *Theo-Logic*. The first reason is his commitment to orthodox Trinitarianism. He refuses to speak of Father and Son without also speaking of the Spirit. The second factor motivating Balthasar's pneumatological logic is Hegelian *Geist*. *Theo-Logic 3* is a further undoing of Hegel's philosophy insofar as Balthasar supplants the Hegelian *Doppelgänger* with the true *Heilige Geist* of Catholicism.[1] Our previous discussions of Hegel will therefore have to be kept in mind as we work through the pneumatology as Balthasar develops it in the final volume of the *Theo-Logic* and the conclusion of his Trilogy.

Both Balthasar's Trinitarianism and the counter-Hegelian character of his *Theo-Logic* arise from St. Paul's claim that in Christ "are hid all the treasures of wisdom and knowledge" (Col 2:3). The infinity of Christ's truth gives the Spirit his eternal vocation as the "expositor" of the Son. The truth that Being is coextensive with divine love is revealed in the incarnate flesh of Christ. Even though the Spirit is given to the disciples after Christ's ascension at Pentecost, Balthasar insists that everything Christ does is done "in the Spirit." The Spirit attends Christ from conception and ascension. Christ's performance of truth is always pneumatological.

The Spirit's task is to make Christ's infinite truth known. Truth has a Trinitarian structure. The Son is the performative exemplar of the Father's love, and the Spirit is the one that illumines and makes Christ known. The manner in which the Spirit makes truth known is not absolute knowledge. The Spirit makes the truth known by drawing the knower into participation in God through love. We thus return to our theme of participation from chapter four. In *Theo-Logic 3*, the mutual participation of subject and object is raised to its theological

---

1. This is seen most explicitly in section 5 of *TL* 3. Balthasar's categories for discussing the Spirit's work—objective and subjective—are Hegelian categories transposed and transmuted into a Balthasarian key.

fulfillment. The chief task of the Spirit in a theo-logic is incorporation of the knower into the life of God. The Spirit is not satisfied to interpret Christ's truth extrinsically or as a teaching accessible to reason alone. Rather, the Spirit leads into all truth by guiding into the vital depths of truth itself, into the union of God and world in the hypostatic flesh of Christ.[2] The Spirit illuminates and incorporates the knower into that truth. This is his subjective work of deification.[3]

But the Spirit also has the objective mission of universalizing Christ's particular truth by revealing the eschatological reality of creation in the wake of Christ's ascension. This is an extension of the Spirit's incorporation of humanity into the life of God, but is focused on the world as the object of knowledge, rather than the human as the knowing subject. The Spirit concretizes creation as a theophany.

Though Balthasar holds that the world is always theophanic by nature because it bears the vestiges of the *Logos* that created it, he nevertheless insists that the *Logos spermatikos* of creation must have a corresponding *pneuma spermatikos* of redemption that gathers creation around the person of Christ, causing the divine light to shine through all things. Part of the Spirit's mission, therefore, is to render the world sacramental and, by so doing, perfect the transfiguring *raptus* of Christ's ascension. This is the task of what I will call in this chapter the Spirit of Pentecost.

All of this has, admittedly, some Hegelian overtones. Balthasar and Hegel do overlap in some significant ways, both in form and in content. But for an Ignatian theologian such as Balthasar, the discernment of spirits is part of the task. What distinguishes Hegelian *Geist* from the Spirit of Catholicism is the priority of love over knowledge. Hegel's *Geist* is the self-realization of God through cosmic dialectic, but Balthasar's Spirit is the dialogue of love between Father and Son. Hegelian *Geist* realizes itself, whereas the Holy Spirit is the subject of divine love, "the space between Father and Son, into which the Spirit introduces us, is in a certain respect the Spirit himself."[4] As we shall

2. *TL* 3, 18.
3. Ibid., 19.
4. Ibid., 18.

195

see, the Spirit of truth that "searches the deep things of God" (1 Cor 2:10) and makes them known is not intellect or reason, but the Spirit of love. In other words, the Spirit's mission of illumination expresses his identity as the love of the ecstatic Trinity. Balthasar's pneumatology distinguishes itself from Hegelian *Geist* at precisely this point. Rather than the titanic conquest of Being through absolute knowledge, Balthasar's Spirit conforms the knower to the heart of Being itself. For Hegel, the philosopher attains the height of Being, but for Balthasar, it is the saint. It is the task of this chapter and the next to demonstrate this point.

Who Is the Spirit?

The question of the Spirit's identity may seem prosaic and obvious to anyone familiar with the creeds of Christianity. But for Balthasar, the answer to this question is far less obvious than we might first expect. The Spirit is not exactly an object of theology. Balthasar doubts the possibility of a theology *of* the Spirit because never does the Spirit appear in the divine drama as an object to be known. He appears, rather, as the one who reveals, mediates, and illuminates divine truth. Balthasar draws on St. Basil's famous discourse *On the Holy Spirit* to reinforce this idea: the Spirit "wishes only to breathe through us, not to present himself to us as an object; he does not wish to be seen but to be the seeing eye of grace in us."[5]

Balthasar insists that the Spirit is the subject of theology. As such, the Spirit remains "anonymous," tasked with the mission of making the truth of God known rather than offering himself up as an object to be known. The Spirit's anonymity is an expression of the Spirit's mission as the agent of truth and love. His mission is co-extensive with his nature. The Spirit is always "being-for-another" because his nature is completely one with his mission of revealing and expositing the truth of Christ. To speak of the Spirit is to speak of Christ in the same

---

5. Basil of Caesarea, *On the Holy Spirit* VIII.40, quoted in *TL* 3, 26.

breath. For a Christocentric theologian like Balthasar, the mystery of the *Logos ensarkos* is the heart of "all truth" that the Spirit reveals.[6]

In this section, we will work out the structure and implications of Balthasar's Christic interpretation of the Spirit in terms of his Spirit-Christology, and then turn our attention more specifically to the subjective work of the Spirit. The former leads us to contrast Balthasarian and Hegelian thought as it relates to the Spirit, while the latter sets the stage for Balthasar's constructive undoing of Hegel, laying the final theological groundwork for his theology of the saints.

The Spirit of Love

Balthasar's pneumatology, focused as it is on Christ, is thoroughly Trinitarian. The Spirit deepens, enriches, and, in many ways, makes possible the identity of God as love. The foundational understanding of the Spirit in Balthasar's pneumatology is that of the *donum*, the Spirit as the gift of love in the life of God.

We have shown the way that Balthasar conceives of the eternal relation of the Father and the Son as one of gift and receptivity. But Balthasar insists that the Son's receptivity is active rather than passive. The Son is the Beloved and the Lover who returns the Father's love. In a way that echoes biological fertility, Balthasar understands the Spirit as the fruitfulness of Father–Son reciprocity. The Spirit is the "excess" of divine love, its sheer gratuity. He is the "proof and the fruit" of the love of Father and Son.[7]

For Balthasar, Spirit is not just the *dilectus*, the loving interchange between Father and Son, but also the object of the shared love of Father and Son.[8] Balthasar quotes Richard of St. Victor's arrangement of the Spirit as both the object of the Father and Son's love and subjective agent of Trinitarian love:

---

6. Balthasar quotes Jean Yves Lacoste to this effect: "no Christology can ever be developed without an *indirect* Pneumatology, and conversely no Pneumatology can be developed except as a way into Christology; Christology must be the measure of Pneumatology" (*TL* 3, 27). That Christology measures the Spirit is yet another way Balthasar distances himself from Hegel.
7. *TL* 3, 159.
8. Ibid., 164.

When two love each other, exchanging the gift of their heart in intense longing, and love flows from the one to the other and from the other to the one and thus in each case tends in an opposite direction toward a diverse object, there is indeed love on both sides, but the partners do not yet love with each other [condilectio]. We cannot say that they love with each other until the two love a third in harmonious unity, lovingly embracing him in common [socialiter], and the affection of the two surges forth as one in the flame of love for the third.[9]

We should take care, though, not to reduce the Spirit to the principle of the Father's and Son's love.[10] Such a reduction limits the Spirit to a divine object, lacking personhood and mission. The Spirit is the fruit of love that also bears witness to that love by interpreting and revealing it. To call him the Spirit of Love is to highlight both the objective and subjective dimensions of his identity.

The Spirit subsists as the dynamic of charity between the Father and the Son, and as such, denies the possibility of a Hegelian or dialectical interpretation of that relationship.[11] This means that it is the Spirit who, as love, knows the deep truth that God is love. The Spirit knows this from within the divine life of the Father's loving begetting of the Son, the overflow of which "results" in the eternal spiration of the Spirit. The Spirit's knowledge is the eternal grounding of all love, truth, and knowledge. The Spirit is both the objective and subjective love of God. As such, he "searches out the deep things of God" (1 Cor 2:10). And so, it is the Spirit as Love that understands the truth of God, the Logos made incarnate in Christ.[12] The Spirit is, therefore, inseparable from the person of Jesus.

---

9. Richard of St. Victor, *De trinitate*, 3.19, quoted in *TL* 2, 41. Emphasis added.

10. *TL* 3, 162.

11. "The Spirit is simultaneously the (objective) attesting of this love between Father and Son (as the third Person, dogma would say) *and* the inner fruit of this reciprocal (subjective) love; thus he can be called the Spirit of love of the Father and of the Son (Rom 8:9)" (*TL* 3, 74).

12. There is another way of getting at Balthasar's point. It is the eternal Son, incarnate as Jesus Christ, who *is* the truth of God. But, for Balthasar, this identity (that is, *mission*) is one that the Son eternally *receives* from the Father, perhaps even *through* the Spirit. We here meet a possible difficulty: how can Father and Spirit give rise to the Son *and* yet the Spirit is the love *between* Father and Son? Balthasar refuses to unravel this mystery, opting instead to return to the idea of perichoresis—that in the eternal dynamic of Trinitarian love, especially the mutual *kenosis* among the divine Persons, love is the willingness both to *give* and to *receive* divine existence *at the exact same moment*. See *TD* 3, 25ff.

Spirit Christology

The Spirit is always the Spirit of Christ in Balthasar's theology. As he set about parsing the relationship of Christ and Spirit, he turned to the ancient tradition of Spirit Christology. Even a traditionalist like Balthasar sees something in that tradition worth reclaiming, despite Protestant and Catholic liberalism's attraction to it. More significantly, though, is the pressing need Balthasar sees for a renewal of Spirit Christology in the wake of Hegel. The "speculative Pentecost" that is Hegelian philosophy leaves "no doubt that Hegel produced the most comprehensive outline of a Spirit-Christology, that is, a theological philosophy in which the Spirit is that which is the all-embracing, the Alpha and Omega, yet in such a way that it is centered in a Christology that alone renders it intelligible as Spirit."[13]

Why a Spirit Christology?

Of all of the possible ways to parse the relationship between the missions of Son and Spirit, why does Balthasar opt for Spirit Christology, especially considering the ways such early Christologies were later deemed inadequate?[14] Balthasar is well-aware of the dangers of a simplistic Spirit Christology—such as some of the ancient Antiochenes—that often result in Nestorianism. Despite this danger, Balthasar thinks that a robustly Catholic Spirit Christology is necessary for: 1) a Trinitarian—but still Christocentric—soteriology that results in deification as the Spirit-led conformity to Christ, and 2) a theological metaphysics and epistemology in which Christ is presented and known as the truth of all things.

In the dramatic soteriology that Balthasar has elsewhere constructed,[15] he frames the incarnation as an act of the Spirit. There is a "trinitarian inversion" at work in Balthasar's soteriology: the chronological or objective structure of salvation (the Father sends the

---

13. *TL* 3, 40.
14. We should note that Balthasar disavows the claim of theologies that set Spirit Christology against *Logos* Christology as if the two were antagonistic and irreconcilable. Cf. *TL* 3, 36.
15. Mainly in *TD* 3.

Son who sends the Spirit) is inverted in the subjective order of *being saved* (the Spirit reveals Christ who reconciles us to the Father). The incarnation occurs *within* the work of the Spirit, prepared for in the Old Testament and carried on into the contemporary moment.

One example of this will suffice. Balthasar's Spirit Christology begins with the event of the incarnation in the Spirit's overshadowing of the virgin. The event of the incarnation highlights the relationship between Christ and the Spirit. The incarnate Son never exists from himself; he does not "take on" his humanity, but rather, hands himself over (*tradere*) to the Spirit, entrusting himself to receive his humanity.[16] In the economy of salvation, both Christ's nature and his mission are always from the Spirit. The event of the incarnation is, therefore, a performance of the "*a priori* obedience of Jesus" and a manifestation of the perfect receptivity that constitutes his incarnate life.[17]

This shows that what is at stake in Balthasar's use of Spirit Christology is an emphasis on Christ's perfect, obedient receptivity of the Spirit.[18] We have seen in the previous chapter how important receptivity and obedience are for Balthasar's interpretation of Christ's identity as truth and love. Spirit Christology funds his schematization of Christ's receptive identity. Christ never lives from himself, but only from the Spirit. This is true at his incarnation in the womb of Mary, at his baptism in the Jordan, and at his crucifixion when Christ surrenders his spirit and breathes his last. It is true, too at the resurrection where Christ does not raise himself, but is raised by the power and love of the Father through the Spirit.

Balthasar's Spirit Christology also funds his theology of the saints. In the Son's perfect receptivity in the incarnation, he vicariously renders all of humanity open to the Spirit. Christ, who is the life of believers (Col 3:4), lives only from the Spirit; the Christian too, through the

---

16. *TL* 3, 48.
17. "This means that the Incarnation event is Trinitarian: the Spirit bears the 'seed of God' (1 John 3:9), the seed of the Father, that is, the Son, into the womb of the Virgin; the Son, in is 'a priori' obedience, allows himself to be carried, and so begins his mission" (*TL* 3, 51).
18. Ibid.

transitive property of grace, also lives from the Spirit. The one who animates Christ animates those who are in Christ. We might say that Christ's absolute openness to the Spirit creates an "acting space" that the saint inhabits through the incorporative power of the Spirit. Christ's *a priori* obedience to the Spirit allows the saints not only to imitate Christ's life, but, through the same Spirit, to participate in it. Balthasar's saints do not only imitate Christ. They participate in him.

Hegelian Spirit Christology

The other major factor in Balthasar's retrieval of Spirit Christology has to do with, unsurprisingly, the influence of Hegel. We have discussed already the danger Balthasar sees in the Hegelian system, namely, that it is a *Doppleganger* of Christianity that results in the titanic subversion of the love and receptivity that constitute truth. But one cannot ignore Hegel on this point simply because his influence is so pervasive.[19]

O'Regan notes that Balthasar's critique of Hegel turns on the latter's distorted Trinitarianism. While Hegel should be congratulated for his "theological philosophy in which the Spirit is that which is the all-embracing, the Alpha and Omega, yet in such a way that it is centered in a Christology that alone renders it intelligible as Spirit,"[20] he nevertheless antagonizes the Christian doctrine of the Trinity through his necessitarianism and his ahistoricism.[21]

The roots of the Hegelian *Doppleganger* are found in his portrayal of the immanent Trinity as that which sublates [*aufheben*] the economic Trinity into itself. The history of salvation becomes the history of God's self-realization, the coming-to-be of Spirit [*Geist*]. Hegel's Trinitarian

---

19. Balthasar gives a long list of modern theologians who are "unthinkable" apart from Hegel, precisely on this point: Barth, Jüngel, Pannenberg, Moltmann, Rahner, Küng, Bruaire, Chapelle, Brito, Léonard, Fessard (*TL* 3, 40).

20. Ibid.

21. O'Regan, *Anatomy*, 205: "Nevertheless, for Balthasar, it is with respect to the Trinity that all of Hegel's problems, including those of the nature and limit of knowledge, epic figuration, and Christology, come home to roost. It is precisely Hegel's trinitarian articulation that justifies the charge of gnosis, accusations of monism, eroticism, necessitarianism, and the operation in Hegelian discourses of an ironic and iterative form of kenosis, and that gives credence to the criticism of his monophysite christological commitment, and of the related tendency to blur incarnation with creation on the one hand, and with the eschaton, on the other."

realization turns on a dialectic based on *lack*: lack of particularity, finitude, reconciliation, and so on. The Trinitarian relations become necessary for the divine self-realization that overcomes this lack, rather than being the eternal expressions of the plentitude of divine love.[22] The relationship between finitude and divine infinity are antagonized.

How does Hegel's Trinitarianism bear on his Spirit Christology? Hegel's religious philosophy surveys the history of God as the movement in which "[t]he Idea gives itself existence in nature and, thereby coming to itself, makes itself Spirit, that is, knowledge of itself."[23] History is the realization of God as *Geist* through the unfolding of history. Hegel's God (or Idea) posits an "other" in itself. This other is both creation and Son. The incarnate Son stands as the summit of the world process, the apex of finitude. For Hegel, the cross represents the pinnacle of the alienation of the Other, the antithesis to the divine Idea. But at Christ's crucifixion—the sublation of his life into death—he releases the Spirit from the broken finitude of his historical flesh. Christ's death is the "negation of the negation" that reaffirms the Infinite, allowing it to know itself and thus be known as *Geist*.

In Hegel, too, Christ's finite existence is tied to the Spirit. The critical difference between Hegel and Balthasar at this point is that the finite flesh of Christ is sublated and left behind as it is universalized within the infinitude of the Spirit. Christ lives from the Spirit only as the negation within the Spirit's self-affirmation.[24] Hegel's reading of the Trinity within the arc of history parodies Christian thought, substituting the drama of divine love with the drama of divine self-knowledge. Hegelian Spirit Christology, Balthasar concludes, is only such in a "very general (philosophical) sense."[25]

Hegel's *Geist* functions not as the living Spirit of Christ who exposits his infinite truth, but as God's means of knowing Godself. Hegel deprives the Spirit of his own divine personhood and otherness,

---

22. Ibid., 42.
23. Hegel, *Philosophie der Religion*, ed. Lasson, II/2, 230 quoted in *TL* 3, 41n20.
24. *TL* 3, 43.
25. Ibid., 46.

reducing him to a kind of divine self-consciousness. Hegelian *Geist* makes possible a knowledge of God that is virtually monistic by raising the knower to identity with the divine. In an interesting move, Balthasar equates Hegel's moves here with the Idealist legacy of Eckhart that we outlined in chapter 3. For Balthasar, Hegel's *Geist* allows "the believer's knowledge of God . . . to be understood 'only as a knowledge of God within him'. . . . Or as Meister Eckhart says, 'the eye with which God sees me is the eye with which I see him; my eye and his eye are one.'"[26] Hegel completes the trajectory that Eckhart began by constructing a *Dopplegänger* of both the Spirit and the Trinity, positing both as philosophical symbols. Hegel ultimately constructs a Trinity in which the divine relations are structured, not just by lack, but also by contradiction, even if this contradiction is constantly sublated. The Christian proclamation that God is love is here subtly but definitively undermined, replaced by a modalistic God of universal dialectic, a God of titanic self-knowing.[27]

All of this has important consequences for the "form of life" necessary for living in accord with the truth of Being, as Hegel conceives it. First, as O'Regan notes, by collapsing history and the economy of salvation into the history of God, Hegel recognized neither the contingency nor the openness of history to God: "Considered thus, human beings are instruments in the self-referential narrative of the divine in which the divine becomes the same through the hiatus of difference." This deprives humanity—and ultimately God—of the agency of freedom and love.[28]

With agency diminished, one's form of life cannot be characterized as mission. Hegel ultimately does away with the receptivity and the obedience that constitute human existence, especially the christic anthropology of the saint, which Balthasar says best accords with

---

26. Ibid., 42–43n23.
27. "For Hegel, Being is necessarily self-presentation: Spirit, conceived as thought, is always both what thinks and what is thought. Thomas would call it the 'inner word.' Hegel, however, holds the identity of these two (Father and Son, in Christian terms) to be the Spirit. This makes Three: the One, the Other, and the Unity of Both. This concrete Idea is known to us . . . as the Trinity-in-Unity" (*TL* 3, 46).
28. O'Regan, *Anatomy*, 211.

Being itself.[29] Within the Hegelian horizon, identity arises from one's "self-making" or "*liberum arbitrium*" manifested in the titanic ascent of absolute knowledge that conflates "self" and "God." This directly counters Balthasar's own Spirit Christology in which Christ, and all of those who find themselves "in Christ," refuses titanic self-making, and instead surrenders through perfect, obedient receptivity.

One can see quite readily how Hegel gives us a spirit of truth, but this Hegelian *Geist* remains an insufficient and dangerous parody of biblical pneumatology where he is only the Spirit of truth insofar as he is the Spirit of Love. The remainder of the chapter unfolds Balthasar's constructive pneumatology as the intersection of these two titles for the Spirit.

The Spirit of Truth

We saw in the previous chapter how Christ's identity is coextensive with his mission. The same is true for the Spirit to such an extent that the Spirit acts not as an object of knowledge in himself, but as from and for the Father and the Son. For Balthasar, the Spirit is entirely *dative*, and this is what it means for him to be the Spirit of love. But as love, the Spirit also lives ecstatically, giving and revealing the truth of the Trinity to the world. This is the given mission of the Spirit in the Gospel of John: "But when he, the Spirit of truth comes, he will lead you into all truth" (16:13). By virtue of his identity as love, the Spirit is also the Spirit of truth.

Searching the Depths of God

We have seen several times now that Balthasar's account of truth and knowledge turns on his claim in *Love Alone is Credible* that "the inner reality of love can be known only by love."[30] What we now begin to see

---

29. "In defining human being in terms of 'mission' Balthasar ensures at once that his anthropology is christologically grounded and that it admits, even demands, a trinitarian horizon for its full and adequate articulation. For in Christ and through the Spirit [that is, through a Spirit Christology] each human being participates in the mystery of the Trinity, which is a mystery of love and donation" (ibid., 212–13).

30. *LA*, 75.

is that this phrase is first and foremost a reference to the Spirit. This phrase implies two things of the Spirit's knowledge of the Godhead. First, the Spirit's knowledge arises from his own activity of loving. Second, the Spirit himself is love.[31]

As we saw in our discussion of *Theo-Logic* 1, love's knowledge does not consist in a totalizing absolute knowledge that solves the mystery of Being. Love continually wills the mystery of Being in order to receive it ever anew with wonder and delight. Similarly, the dynamic of love that is the Trinity is not "solved" by the Spirit's knowing. Never does his searching the depths of God reach the ground of divine Being. The God who is love has no ground but the fathomless depths of love: "for if love, as such, is genuine, it has no other ground but itself; this love that has its source in the Father is, initially, the Father himself (since, as Father, he is nothing other than the pure surrender of himself; the Father does not 'have' love, he 'is' love); this being so, it is impossible to discover the ground of this groundless love."[32]

Because God is this dynamic of love, he makes himself available to knowledge. Love, as Balthasar conceives it, is being-for-another and involves a certain self-surrender and handing over. This is precisely what divine love does: it hands itself over (*tradere*) to the searching of the Spirit and, through the Spirit, to "all the saints" (Eph 3:18–19).

The saints are drawn into the Spirit's own subjective knowing, and thus, know with the Spirit.[33] This is the heart of the Spirit's operation and, according to Balthasar, the essence of the Spirit's role in a theo-logic. As Balthasar puts it, "If the truth that has appeared in Christ

---

31. "In searching these depths, the Spirit acts as the witness and fruit of this reciprocal love; but he is not an observer here: he himself *is* this love. No wonder, then, that this unimaginable mystery occupies him for a whole eternity" (*TL* 3, 441).

32. Ibid.

33. Balthasar is playing here with the traditional formula of Christian prayer that prays "to" the Father, "through" the Son, "with" the Holy Spirit. In knowledge and in prayer, the Spirit is the subjective agent with whom Christians join, caught up as they are in the rhythm of divine life. Also at play here is the participatory theology of Jesus' high priestly prayer in John 17: "May they also be in us so that the world may believe that you have sent me. I have given them the glory that you gave me, that they may be one as we are one—I in them and you in me—so that they may be brought to complete unity. Then the world will know that you sent me and have loved them even as you have loved me" (20–23). Believers are to share in the perichoretic love of Father and Son which is, for a filioquist like Balthasar, the Spirit. In all of these things, the Spirit is "anonymous," appearing not as an object to be studied but as the knowing, loving, binding, unitive subject.

is infinite, since 'in [him] are hid all the treasures of wisdom and knowledge' (Col 2:3), it will be impossible to come to an end in declaring this truth all down the ages." The Spirit is the one who perpetually opens up the infinite depths of the form (*Gestalt*) of Christ.[34]

Truth, then, in the light of the Spirit, involves a "making known" (John 1:18). He is thus the Spirit of Truth at various levels: "[He] utters the truth and can 'witness' to it because he knows it; and he knows it because he is internal to it, that is, internal to the relationship between the Father (who allows himself to be made known) and the Son (who makes him known)."[35] The Son has exposited the truth fully and completely through his life and most especially his death. But his truth is infinite, and therefore must be continually exposited by the Spirit who comes, as promised, to lead into "all truth."

The Exposition of Christ

But how can a discussion of truth move beyond Christ, the one who is that truth? Of course, in a way, our discussion has never occurred outside of Christ, who is both Beginning and End (Rev 22:13), both the protological and the eschatological human. But according to Balthasar, the fullness of Christ is not a divine monologue, truth speaking itself for itself. It is, instead, an ongoing dialogue. This dialogue is rooted in the Trinitarian relation itself because the Son is the truth of God as he receives, and thus, *is* the Father's Word. And this dialogue spirals out from the divine freedom as the dialogicality of love and gift in the relationship between Creator and creature. And this double-dialogicality, both intra- and inter-divine, leads directly into the drama of Emmanuel, God-with-us.

The fullness of Christ revealed in the historical drama of his life and death is such that it creates space in itself for its own ongoing

---

34. This is why, for Balthasar, Christian truth is irreducibly trinitarian: "Christian truth is trinitarian because Jesus Christ, the Father's Son made man, incarnate through the Spirit and accompanied by the same Spirit through his life and work, and suffering, is revealed Word and hence 'the truth' (Jn 14:6) in that—unto death—he gives an adequate [*adäquat*] portrayal of the Father's love" (*TL* 3, 23).

35. *TL* 3, 70.

interpretation and dramatic realization. The responsibility for this interpretation and realization falls to the saints. Christ's action is both drama and improvisation.[36] It is not a purely objective *datum* that can be studied by a neutral observer, as in a laboratory.[37] It is through the Spirit that the saints are drawn into this dramatic participation in Christ's life and mission. It is the Spirit who "opens up" Christ's life and draws the Christian into it, to share it, indeed even to "complete" it.[38]

And yet, the claim that Christ's drama is "incomplete" may seem odd, perhaps even unbiblical. What else, after all, could Christ's *tetelestai* mean except that Christ's drama had indeed accomplished everything and needs no further actualization. While Balthasar does insist that Christ accomplished the full will of the Father, he also insists quite adamantly on the Ignatian concept of mission, according to which, the missions of the saints are extensions and continuations of the fundamental mission of Christ. Considered under the rubric of truth, the missions of the saints are to express and exposit the eternal Word of truth and love spoken by the Son.[39]

In fact, the truth of Christ is such that it actually demands subsequent articulation through the saints as a kind of extension of Christ's own historical life. Though Christ's existence was a limited spatio-temporal phenomenon, "the whole fullness of deity" dwelled

---

36. For more on this theme, see Francis Young, *The Art of Performance: Towards a Theology of Holy Scripture* (London: Dartman, Longman and Todd, 1990); and Nicholas Lash, "Performing the Scriptures: Interpretation through Living," *The Furrow*, vol. 33, no. 8 (1982): 467–74. See also Ben Quash, *Theology and the Drama of History* (Cambridge: Cambridge University Press, 2005) and Tina Beattie, *New Catholic Feminism: Theology and Theory* (London and New York: Routledge, 2006), 19–26, for criticisms of Balthasar's treatment of drama and improvisation. We might draw a musical parallel here to illumine this idea. As a young pianist, Balthasar would practice musical "invention"—the creative building upon and expansion of a continuous musical foundation, the *cantus firmus*. The improvisation of the saints functions similarly. The saints elaborate and develop *in continuity with* the foundational truth of Christ.

37. See Balthasar's critique of "scientific" and "critical" biblical scholarship in *GL* 1, 20ff. Balthasar is not rejecting critical scholarship as such. He is criticizing a non-dramatic reading of Scripture that fails to engage and involve the reader existentially. Such is his critique of all forms of theology and spirituality that restrict the possibility of the Christian's dramatic participation. As Balthasar will routinely insist: what is objectively given must be subjectively received.

38. Cf. *TL* 3, 21 and St. Paul's claim to complete whatever is lacking in Christ's sufferings (Col 1:24).

39. This idea is also grounded in Balthasar's Johannine theology. See John 21:25: "Jesus did many other things as well. If every one of them were written down, I suppose that even the whole world would not have room for the books that would be written." The saintly performance of Christ's truth is our contribution to the writing of those books.

bodily in him (Col 2:9). The concrete individual who identifies himself as truth is the one in whose particular individual existence "is hid all the treasures of wisdom and knowledge" (Col 2:3). Christ's truth cannot be exhausted because it is co-extensive with his person and work. "There is much more truth in Christ than in the Church's faith and much more truth in the Church's faith than in the formulated dogmas."[40] The boundless fullness of christological truth could not be summed up in his one finite life. It requires the ongoing exposition by the Holy Spirit. It is the Spirit, breathed by Christ upon his disciplines (John 20:22), who will guide Christ's followers into "all truth" (John 16:13). The Spirit does not teach a truth *beyond* or *other than* the truth of Christ, but instead, interprets the boundless fullness of the truth that Christ himself is. Infinite truth can and must be articulated in an infinite number of ways.[41]

Balthasar rather neatly divides the Spirit's interpretation of Christ into "subjective" and "objective" forms, the former being the experiential and existential, and the latter being the ecclesial and the dogmatic.[42] But crucially, the main instrument of both of these forms is the saint through whom the Spirit effects its ongoing interpretation of the truth of Christ. It is the saint whose own theological existence dramatically inhabits that of Christ, and in so doing, interprets his truth through the Spirit.

The Spirit accomplishes this dramatic openness in Christ's existence. The truth of Christ cannot be known exclusively through historical study, nor by a "scientific" theology. Such would be a theology of the "dead letter." Christ is a form (*Gestalt*) that is graspable only through the Spirit: "[Christ] can never be understood as a mere brute fact: only the faith that is likewise permeated by the Spirit can grasp him as the

---

40. Ibid.

41. There is an important parallel here with *TL* 1. There, Balthasar developed the idea that the known object is completed by being known by a subject. This does not mean that the object was deficient but rather that part of its essence, its *mot juste* is to be known. Analogously, it is constitutive of Christ's mission that it be shared and only thus does it realize to its proper *telos*.

42. Of course, as we may presume given the argument of our fourth chapter, the subjective and objective dimensions of the Spirit's interpretation participate in each other. The Spirit is subjective and objective together, all at the same time. The "objective" is never not also "subjective" and vice versa.

'objective' reality he is."[43] Consequently, for Balthasar, all truth and all knowledge—whether metaphysical, philosophical, or theological—depends upon the Holy Spirit.

Illumination and Contemplation

The Spirit affects this kind of knowledge through his work of illumination. As both objective and subjective, the Spirit illuminates and *is* the illumination. He is the one who is visible as the lighting up of objects *and* the one who lights up the understanding of the knower.

As the objective Spirit, he lights up the object, making it knowable. This objective illuminating occurs most especially through the institutional forms of the church in which the Spirit works: liturgy, sacraments, canon law, and dogmatic theology.[44] The Spirit's subjective work is to be the one in and through whom we come to see, to contemplate, and to know divine truth. He accomplishes this by illuminating the eyes and the mind, not with information, but with love: "He who does not love does not know God; for God is love" (I John 4:8). As Balthasar explains,

> if "all the truth" is nothing other than the love that is made manifest in God and his revelation, this love that is lived out in act and being ("God is love", 1 John 4:8, 16) must be implemented by those who inhabit the realm of truth, and implemented in both directions exemplified by the Son, namely, toward the Father and, coming from the Father, toward the world.[45]

---

43. *TD* 3, 27.

44. These are what Balthasar calls aspects of the Petrine character of the Church: the institutional structure and form. But the Petrine is not the full character of the Church. It also has a Johannine character—the loving and contemplative aspect—and the Marian—the bleeding heart of obedience and surrender. Only together do these three make up the Church. But Balthasar does prioritize the Johannine and the Marian for it was John and Mary who witnessed the glory of God in the dying Jesus. It is Peter who comes later, who safeguards and protects the fragile heart of Christian truth. Thus, we have in Balthasar an admittedly existential heart to the Church that, though not apart from the institution, does carry a certain theological priority. See, *Razing the Bastions*, trans. Brian McNeil (San Francisco: Ignatius Press, 1993), 40–41. For commentary on Balthasar's reading, see Antonio Sicari, "Mary, Peter and John: Figures of the Church," *Communio*, vol. 19, no. 2 (1999): 189–207.

45. *TL* 3, 76. Here, we can see Balthasar's use of what could be called a "mystagogical" model of knowing. We are drawn from the world into the inner sanctum of divine mystery with the Spirit, through Christ, to the Father and then commissioned *in the same way* to the world.

Subjectively speaking, the Spirit is the form (*Gestalt*) of true knowing. The anonymity of the Spirit with which this chapter began, is his spiritual "facelessness." The Spirit is "faceless," not in the sense of lacking personal identity, but by being "disinterested." As we have seen, this anonymity is the grounding disposition of knowledge; even the Spirit bears the Ignatian character of *indiferencia* and *Gelassenheit*. The Spirit's *indiferencia* is the condition of the possibility of the receptivity and obedience of all knowledge and, not coincidentally, of saintliness. The charisms of the Spirit grant the possibility of theology, or a *theo-logic*.

The Spirit's illumination allows us to see the divine radiance *by means of* that very radiance: "in your light do we see light" (Psalm 36:9). The revelatory work of the Spirit is to illuminate both the object of knowledge and the one doing the knowing. What the Spirit reveals as the deep truth of Being is the groundless Trinitarian love that grounds all things, that creates the world from its inner logic (*Logos*). This logic is interchangeable with love.

The Spirit's illumination lights up this divine truth, which is known subjectively, Balthasar insists, through "attunement."[46] The Spirit labors to attune the knower through an intellectual adequation. But this adequation is not exclusively intellectual. It also involves an ontological, existential, and spiritual attunement orchestrated by the Spirit.

The mystery of divine love that the Spirit illuminates by attuning the knower to it is the invisible light that renders Being intelligible.[47] The ability to read this divine light off of the intelligible things of the world is the charism of wisdom (*gnōsis*). The wisdom accomplished by the Spirit funds theological and Ignatian metaphysics: the art of finding God in all things and thereby uncovering the supreme truth and the inner logic of all things.

Wisdom, in this sense, depends on the illumination of the Spirit: "[n]othing on earth or in heaven could be known if God had not 'given

---

46. Cf. *GL* 1, 241–57.
47. Ibid.

wisdom and sent [his] holy Spirit from on high'" (Wisdom 9:16–17). Knowledge, Balthasar insists, is based on wisdom; wisdom, in turn, is based on love. The illumination of the Spirit of truth who is love allows Balthasar to claim, alongside Gregory the Great: "It is through love that we attain knowledge . . . and 'love itself is knowledge.' Love's ultimate evidence is within it, and all reasoning knowledge is dependent on it."[48]

As Balthasar develops the illuminative work of the Spirit, he turns to contemplation, which he defines as the gift of spiritual perception. The invisible Son suffered to be made visible, and thus to be perceived by humanity. But this perception of the form and meaning of the visible Son is not automatic; "seeing" is not necessarily "perceiving." Balthasar's aesthetics require the eyes of faith. It is faith that allows humanity to perceive the Absolute Beauty shining through the lesser beauties of creation. Faith itself is a charism of the Spirit.

The gift of perception is a gift that descends through the revelation of the Christ-form, yet the utilization and enactment of this gift is a fully human activity; that is, it is an activity that utilizes the fullness of the human person. Perception is an activity of the five bodily senses, but Balthasar also emphasizes the role of the Holy Spirit in the five *spiritual* senses. It is through these spiritual senses and the imagination that the Holy Spirit enables the faculty to apprehend God's revelation. This is the root of contemplation for Balthasar.

The Spirit-created faculty within the believer that allows that believer to perceive the form of revelation is the same faculty that allows contemplation and prayer. For Balthasar, contemplation means looking towards God. This involves looking toward God through His manifestation in earthly forms. Contemplation is a looking toward God by way of analogy, seeing the form of God shining through the sacramental tapestry that is restored through Christ. Contemplation by analogy is made possible only by and through the revelation of Christ in the incarnation. Many of the themes of previous chapters converge in the way that Balthasar expands this point about the contemplative character of knowledge:

48. Ibid., 442.

The first dimension in which the one, unchangeable love moves and is delineated before our eyes is that of human life. Here contemplation is easiest. The contemplative only needs to let himself be led from image to image, and to see the human aspect of each as a revelation of the eternal love of the Trinity. In the first place, all that is simply human: the child with his natural characteristics, the boy, the youth with his, the grown man; each stage of life, each condition; waking and sleeping, alertness and fatigue, solitude and human intercourse, the events of morning, midday and evening, work and rest, eating and fasting, enjoyment and abstinence, human affections and absence of all feeling, days of festivity and of grey routine—each of these human conditions was conceived and formed by God the Creator, and now, in the fullness of time, he has sent his Son to share in them, in order to try them himself and to make of them "experiences" of God in human nature, assume them on his own account, to crown them as work fulfilled, to carry over their truth, their quintessence, into eternity. Henceforth, the relation between the human life and the divine life is no longer a vague "similarity in a still greater dissimilarity"; there is communion, and the transitory becomes the vessel of the eternal, filled to the brim and overflowing with signs manifesting the divine love.[49]

Balthasar goes on to say that "[e]verything human is sacramental, a transparent symbol, containing and manifesting God's love effectively." Caught up in the *regresso* of Christ's ascension, all things human have been "taken up into Christ" and now become vessels of the Christ-form. Contemplation of the Christic form of revelation is found in Scripture and liturgy, but also in the movements, moments and activities of "secular" life. All of creation bears a *potentia obedientiae* that manifests God's love and Being to the believer through the believer's act of contemplation.

We see that Balthasar's aesthetics serve as the theological foundation for the spiritual act of contemplation. That contemplation plays a vital role in Balthasar's theology may clearly be seen in the fact that scattered throughout *The Glory of the Lord* are studies of several Christian contemplatives: Eckhart, Tauler, Ruusbroec, Juliana of Norwich, John of the Cross, Catherine of Siena and Catherine of Genoa. It is significant that Balthasar calls these contemplatives "saints." In fact, as we shall see in the next chapter, contemplation is one of the

49. *Prayer*, 201–2.

chief characteristics of the saints. Through the act of contemplation the Spirit's illumination effects a saintly form of knowledge. Contemplatives probe the mystery of Being in its fullness. They are not satisfied with articulating the content of Christian revelation with the theologians or elaborating the conditions of knowledge with the philosophers. Balthasar praises the contemplatives because they participate in the reality of truth by means of their contemplation. To put it another way, contemplatives participate in truth through their performance of that truth.

Illumination consists, then, in attunement to the form of truth, and thus to the *Gestalt* of Christ. The believer must therefore undergo a form of kenosis, the *indiferencia* that funds their receptivity. Spiritual illumination is the fruit of ascetic discipline, the self-surrender and self-emptying in order to be filled up with the form of Christ. According to Balthasar, "there is no Christian experience of God that is not the fruit of the conquest of self-will, or at least of the decision to conquer it."[50] What this means for Balthasar is that illumination occurs through Spirit-enabled participation in the experience of Christ. Attunement to Being, to truth, to love: all of this is possible only through the adequation of one's entire life to the entire life of Christ. This adequation, Balthasar claims, is the Christian doctrine of participation, the true form of humanity's desire to know the truth of Being, raised now to its religious fulfillment in the life of God.

Participation

The Spirit's illumination consists, as we have seen, in the subjective attunement to objective reality. This means that knowledge must be both *noetically* and *existentially* realized. The Spirit perpetually exposits the truth of Christ, having plumbed the depths of incarnate divine mystery and knowing it for himself. He makes that truth known to the world by illuminating and attuning the knower to this reality. Illumination is the result of participation.[51]

---

50. Balthasar, "Experience God?" in *New Elucidations*, trans. Sr. Mary Theresilde Skerry (San Francisco: Ignatius Press, 1986), 28.

Knowledge consists of something more than gaining information. It becomes "a disclosure and surrender of what is one's own *to* someone, which, if it is accepted, becomes a *movement into* someone. 'Truth' is simultaneously 'grace'."[52] The Spirit of truth "leads us from inner participation into inner participation."[53] In his well-known statement on aesthetic attunement, Balthasar highlights the participative element of the Spirit's illumination:

> Along with the ontic order that orients man and the form of revelation to one another, the grace of the Holy Spirit creates the faculty that can apprehend this form, the faculty that can relish it and find its joy in it, that can understand it and sense its interior truth and rightness. Supported in this manner, however, man can and must consciously take his stance before the form of revelation and its storehouse of mysteries: he must accustom himself to live within it, and he must attune his whole person to it. Both things, the ontic and the experiential dimensions, go together, and . . . this unity henceforth deepens the "in-formation" of the whole person. . . . Before the beautiful—no, not really *before* but *within* the beautiful—the whole person quivers. He not only "finds" the beautiful moving; rather, he experiences himself as being moved and possessed by it.[54]

While this participation is the work of the Spirit, the knower is not passive. Echoing again the spiritual categories of Ignatius, Balthasar stresses the necessary "openness"—the *indiferencia*—of the human subject. This openness is coextensive with obedience and with faith.[55] Faith is the surrender and the opening of the self to the Spirit's grace of participation.

Participation consists in the Spirit's incorporation of the Christian into the inner reality of life of God. This incorporation involves *theosis*, but Balthasar insists that divinization comes solely by means of incorporation into *Christ* and not into an atemporal or abstract religious concept.[56] Balthasar points back to Irenaeus as the progenitor

---

51. For a very different account of illumination that emphasizes the role of the Spirit without adopting the category of participation, cf. John Webster, "Illumination," *Journal for Reformed Theology*, vol. 5 (2011): 324–39.
52. *TL* 3, 74.
53. Ibid.
54. *GL* 1, 247.
55. Ibid., 220.

of the idea of divinization. Irenaeus developed this idea, Balthasar says, to counter the claims of the Valentinian Gnostics that humanity has a "natural divinity." Against this idea, Irenaeus emphasized the corruptibility of humanity and its absolute reliance on God's grace for divinization. The grace of *theosis* must be received.

Balthasar's use of Irenaeus at this point is telling. Irenaeus functions in Balthasar's Trilogy as the anti-Idealist, especially as the foil of Hegel. If O'Regan's assessment of Hegel as a modern Valentinian gnostic is correct, then Balthasar's Irenaean analysis of divinization is a veiled critique of the titanic divinization of Hegelian dialectic. For Irenaeus, knowledge of God is eternal life.[57] But the crucial distinction between Irenaeus and Hegel that Balthasar exposes is that Irenaean knowledge—and therefore, *theosis*—is a gift that comes not through dialectic, but through the Spirit's act of conforming the Christian to Christ. *Theosis* occurs when the soul becomes deiform, *christic*. This Christ-form is, as Balthasar never tires of showing, nothing other than the abandonment, receptivity, and obedience of love. Participation in the Christ-form requires sanctification. Attunement and conformity to Christ can only come through holiness.

The possibility of the Spirit's unifying comes from his dwelling *in* and *as* the loving inner-dynamic of the Father–Son relationship. It is this dynamic in which the Spirit allows believers to participate.[58] Initiation into truth is thus, for Balthasar, an actualized, spiritual union with the triune God. The Spirit leads back to the eternal truth made flesh in the Incarnation. The Spirit, then, "does not replace an *absent* Jesus, but on the contrary renders him present in a new way."[59]

The Spirit's guidance into all truth goes beyond theory and into the existential participation, in the truth of Christ. Knowledge arises from discipleship. Through the Spirit's incorporation and illumination, knowledge arises within a christological mode of existence. This,

---

56. *TL3*, 187.
57. Ibid.
58. Balthasar's claim here is radically Johannine. See Jesus's high priestly prayer in John 17. Cf. David Crump, "Re-examining the Johannine Trinity: perichoresis or deification?," *Scottish Journal of Theology*, vol. 59, no. 4 (2006): 395–412.
59. *TL* 3, 80.

Balthasar insists, is the heart of Christ's High Priestly Prayer: "that they may all be one; even as thou, Father, art in me, and I in thee, that they also may be *in us*, so that the world may believe that thou hast sent me" (John 17:21).

Pentecost

In the previous chapter, we saw the way that Christ as the concrete *analogia entis* effects an eschatological transformation in the nature of Being through the drama of his life, death, resurrection, and ascension. Jesus re-establishes the sacramental meaning of the world since Christ is a "metaphysical Janus" in whom the divine face looks to the world and the human looks to God.[60] The Spirit exposits both dimensions of the God-Man—the divine and the human—and therefore, shines his light on the fullness of metaphysical truth. The conclusion of this chapter must show how, as the Spirit of truth, he also operates as the pentecostal Spirit who gathers all created truth into a single confession of God. By so doing, the Spirit effects the redeeming return of all things to the Father, that God can be "all in all" (1 Cor 15: 28).

This is an important dimension of truth for Balthasar because he stresses that, with few exceptions, the truth of Being is mediated to us through created forms. Knowledge of truth, and thus union with God, comes not through a kind of gnostic mysticism, but through the Spirit's re-establishment, in Christ, of a sacramental ontology. It comes by attaining to God in the created world as it is created *through* Christ.[61]

Eschatological Metaphysics and Theological Knowledge

Because there is nothing that remains untouched by the splendor of Christ and the illumination of the Spirit, creation, time, and history

---

60. Cf. *Prayer*, 255.
61. This is Balthasar's interpretation of 1 John 5:21 and the admonition to "keep yourselves from idols." Balthasar sees the "idols" as the attempt to move away from the world of history in favor of a gnostic spiritualization of truth. Most especially, Balthasar insists that a genuinely Christian account of truth cannot "move so much as a step away from the Incarnation" (*TL* 3, 78). See also Cyril O'Regan, *Gnostic Return in Modernity* (Albany, State University of New York Press, 2001), 110–17.

must be re-imagined in the Taboric light of the resurrection dawn.[62] To effect this reimagining, Balthasar relies quite a bit on St. Bonaventure's theology of history. In Bonaventure's scheme, history is divided into seven ages, the sixth of which is the "fullness of time" in which Christ is born. The seventh age is the eschatological "secret time" of the sabbath life of the Trinity. In his interpretation of Bonaventure's theology of history, Balthasar writes:

> The axiom "the seventh age runs alongside the sixth" . . . is characteristic: alongside the sixth age of the world, in which Christ is born and goes to heaven, the seventh age has already run its course. The sabbath of the world has already begun with the Ascension, and will last until the general resurrection; then is the dawn of the eighth day. Because through Christ heaven is now in principle open, mystical-eschatological contemplation and existence are already possible.[63]

Just as the incarnation bursts open the limits of human nature so that it can bear the weight of the divine, so too does history open up to what transcends it. Both creation and time become thin places where the eternal age draws close, breaking through, drawing creation's history into the eternal divine life. For Balthasar, there is in Christ and the Spirit no such thing as a *historia pura*. All creation has tasted its redemption and now groans for its fulfillment (Rom 8:22). Created truth actively participates in divine truth. Christ has re-established the possibility of metaphysics by restoring to fallen, mendacious Being its vocation as a bearer of the presence of God.[64] As we have seen, the infiltration of Christ into history re-establishes the unity of God and world. Christ and the Spirit restore theological metaphysics.

What then is this theological metaphysics according to Balthasar? It is the fundamental re-imagining of what developed in the wake of

---

62. See *GL* 5, 119: "The Son overcame, and annihilated in himself, the whole of the distance [sinful contradiction] between heaven and earth: as true man, he is at the same time the likeness of the Father in God. . . . Through him the redeemed live under an open heaven, since God has created heaven in the new earth, or the new earth in heaven. The risen Son is earth in heaven; his Eucharist is heaven on earth." Christ himself is the *theandric* one who does human things divinely, and divine things humanly (cf. Pseudo-Dionysius, *Letter* IV, 1072C); the eschatological creation images a similar kind of relationship.
63. *GL* 2, 273.
64. Cf. Hans Boersma, *Nouvelle Théologie and Sacramental Ontology: A Return to Mystery* (Oxford: Oxford University Press, 2010).

Eckhart, especially as it is expressed in German Idealism. Balthasar thinks that the change that Eckhart sundered the cosmic dimension of the God-world relation. Eckhart no longer holds to a relationship with God mediated through the cosmos. He instead privileges the immediacy of knowledge. The truth of the world can no longer bear the weight of the divine under a christological or sacramental form. Nature is either identical with and absorbed into, or separated and lost to the divine. Either way, when Eckhart comes to his logical fulfillment in Hegel, grace and nature collapse into each other. The task of the human being, then, is to achieve an "immediate contact" with God through an abstract and absolute knowledge—an idealist speculation—achieved apart from the mutuality of subject and object. The forgetfulness of divine Being results in the titanic anthropology where knowledge becomes power, and power alone runs the world. Hegel and Nietzsche haunt Eckhartian thought.

One of Balthasar's chief tasks is to return to the cosmos its proper mediating role in truth by developing a cosmic aesthetic emphasizing the *Gestalt* of Christ that grounds all metaphysical knowledge.[65] This involves an aesthetic vision of creation and its history as forming a tapestry of sacred veils through which we encounter the truth of God. Worldly truth participates in divine truth, receiving its intelligibility from it. Going further, divine truth actively penetrates worldly truth through Christ and the Spirit. By so doing, divine truth reveals worldly truth to itself.[66] Christ has borne up the truth of God in his ascension,

---

65. It is just this kind of Christological tension between worldly and divine truth that plays out in the drama of contemplative prayer of the saints: "the apostles and saints are not daydreamers in flight from the world, living in a fairyland divorced from reality. The Acts of the Apostles is sober, serious reality in the midst of history, but the breath of the Holy Spirit breathes through it, blowing believers where he will; they must take him seriously as the principal actor as they make their calculations and decisions. That contemplation is realistic which seeks the reality of heaven, yet not by dissolving or allegorizing away the reality of earth. It endures and holds the tension between the two, which is ultimately a Christological tension. Ultimately the only thing strong enough to hold it is the bond between the two natures in Christ, i.e., only Jesus Christ can hold this tension; it is impossible for man per se and totally impossible for contemplation per se. Only a Christian contemplation can endure the tension and see heaven, concretely, in what is most concrete of earth" (*Prayer*, 291).

66. Cf. *Gaudium et Spes*, 22. See also the relevant sections of Joseph Ratzinger's "The Dignity of the Human Person," in *Commentary On the Documents of Vatican II*, vol. 5, *Pastoral Constitution on the Church in the Modern World*, edited by Herbert Vorgrimler, translated by W. J. O'Hara. New York: The Crossroad Publishing Company, 1989), 159–63. Ratzinger notes that this pastoral constitution

situating all truth in and with himself. This is but one aspect of Christ's inauguration of the new creation. Nature itself is "charged with the grandeur of God."[67] The language of creation again hymns God through its created *theo-logoi*.

There are several complicating factors to this statement. In one way, Balthasar is simply adopting a patristic chronology of redemption: paradise created, paradise lost, paradise regained. But Balthasar is also operating with a thick eschatology. His eschatology is not simply a "restoration" of what has been lost. Christ is not a solution to the problem of sin, nor is heaven a solution to earth. Balthasar's vision is far more complex. The eschaton is the healing and the elevation, the perfection and fulfillment of creation. The "new" creation is the "true" creation just as Christ is not technically the "new" Adam but the "true" Adam, the archetype of genuine humanity. The paradisiacal state of Eden is an image, a metaphor, a sign, of what is to come. Balthasar's eschatology is one in which "paradise" is the Christian eschatological hope projected backward in history.

Pentecost and Analogy

The "all truth" into which the Spirit leads encompasses the truth of the entire cosmos, because he exposits the incarnate divine Son. The Spirit is scattered abroad throughout created Being as the "wisdom in the whole of creation (Prov 8:22ff., Wis 7:22)." It can be traced "right back to the creation of the world, in which God's 'spirit', brooding over the chaos (together with God's 'word'), began to bring order to the world (Gen 1:1)." Indeed, "the whole of nature, in its life and constitution, remains dependent on the 'spirit' (the 'expiration') of God."[68] The Spirit is breathed out (ex-spirated) by the Father and the Son, over all of creation, accompanying the *Logos* in his grounding and ordering of all

teaches that "On the basis of Christ this dares to present theology as anthropology and only becomes radically theological by including man [and, thus, creaturely truth] in discourse about God by way of Christ, thus manifesting the deepest unity of theology" (159).

67. Note especially how Balthasar intentionally plays off of Hopkins' great poem, "God's Grandeur": "Because the Holy Ghost over the bent/World broods with warm breast and ah! bright wings." See, *GL* 3, 390, for Balthasar's take on Hopkins' sacramental, poetic vision.

68. *TL* 3, 64.

worldly truth.[69] As with Christ, so too with the Spirit: there is no purely profane space, no absolutely profane truth. All truth belongs to the Spirit.

We might best articulate the eschatological transfiguration of the cosmos as a re-establishment of the possibility of analogical knowledge. This is possible because Christ has, as we have seen, re-established the *analogia entis* in himself.[70] This transfiguration of the world in light of Christ demands a transfigured epistemology, one that knows and articulates the world as a gift of love, as a sacred veil, as an image of divine truth. This epistemology must be *contemplative:* one that receives and knows the world as mystery and beholds the truth in and through the sacred veils. It must also be *mystical:* one that receives and knows the world in and through union with God. It must ultimately be *love:* an epistemology in which the sterile dichotomy of "object" and "subject" is drawn into a relation of mutual participation and delight (*condilectio*).

The Spirit of Pentecost can lead into all truth because he gathers the world's every expression of truth together into a harmonious, revelatory word. This Pentecostal Spirit brings the words of Being into a harmonious—not *synthetic*—expression of that primordial Word, that primordial truth, the proclamation that Being and love are co-extensive.[71] The Spirit of Pentecost gathers every expression of worldly truth into a common "language" that bears and testifies to the truth of God. In other words, the Spirit is the agent for bringing all worldly

69. On the *filioque*, see *TL* 3, 207ff. Balthasar is an unabashed filioqueist. Indeed, the filioque is determinative for the Spirit-Christology he develops in *TL* 3. The *filioque* allows him to avoid difficulties to which ancient spirit christologies succumbed.

70. Cf. D. L. Schindler, "Sanctity and the Intellectual Life," *Communio* vol. 20, no. 4 (1993): 657–58: "[I]n Jesus Christ, God has assumed human nature—and indeed, in and through human nature, in some sense *all* of nature. Nature from the beginning finds its integrity and freedom (it's "legitimate autonomy") in obedience: in a relation of service to the Father, and thus in love. The consequence is twofold: nature maintains a wholeness or integrity proper to nature; and yet this wholeness is actualized always and everywhere (*de facto*) within a inner orientation to the order given in grace: and inner orientation, that is, to the Trinitarian God as revealed in Jesus Christ in and through Mary and the church by the Holy Spirit. Thus every created being in its depths exhibits an orientation toward and movement from God, and in this way vestiges or images of God" (657–58).

71. "Thus 'all the truth' does not mean a synthesis of a given number of individual truths but the one truth of the Son's interpretation of God in the inexhaustible fullness of its concrete universality" (*TL* 3, 74).

truth into conformity with Christ.[72] The Spirit is the one who draws the *logoi* of creation to the *Logos,* and therein, allows them to speak of God, to hymn their *theo-logoi.*[73] The disparate words of creation are gathered together *by* the Spirit, *in* the Spirit, into a genuinely catholic truth.[74]

We return to our earlier notion of the catholicity of truth. We must consider this catholicity as a harmonization rather than synthesis. Catholicity does not mean particular truths are surrendered to an abstracted totality. Truth in the Spirit is *symphonic.*[75] The Spirit does not absorb all worldly truths into a single homogenous word, but rather, draws all truths around a common center—namely, the eternal Word that has spoken all other words into existence from the limitless depths of his divine truth. The words of the creation, transformed by the Spirit, confess that their truth is also the truth of God: even the stones cry out (Luke 19:40).

Reditus

Balthasar's Trilogy concludes by considering a particularly theological interpretation of history as the Spirit-guided movement toward reunion with the Father.[76] This eschatological unity is the "embrace of our origin," and thus the longing of every heart and the fulfillment of

72. The entire Patristic practice of "spoiling the Egyptians" turns on this Pentecostal Spirit. Paul's sermon on the Acropolis in Acts 17, drawing as it does on the Greek poets and philosophers, is a specific example of this Pentecostal language.

73. One thinks of Psalm 19:1: "The heaven declare the glory of God." See Stratford Caldecott, *Beauty for Truth's Sake: On the Re-enchantment of Education* (Grand Rapids: Brazos Press, 2009), 53–70 for a way of seeing the beauty and ratios of the world as a hymn to divine order. Caldecott's book, though not a direct commentary on Balthasar, draws heavily on Balthasar's understanding of truth, especially for developing what he calls the "poetic imagination" (37ff).

74. Balthasar's use of "catholic" throughout the *Theo-Logic* parallels that of his mentor, Henri de Lubac. Genuine catholicity consists, for both de Lubac and Balthasar, not in uniformity, but rather, in the "gathering in around a common center." Cf. Henri de Lubac, *Drama of Atheist Humanism,* trans. Edith M. Riley and Anne Englund Nash (San Francisco: Ignatius Press, 1995), 14.

75. See Balthasar's *Truth is Symphonic: Aspects of Christian Pluralism,* trans. Graham Harrison (San Francisco: Ignatius Press, 1987): "A bass trumpet is not the same as a piccolo; a cello is not a bassoon . . . [before Christ and the Spirit] each player plays to himself, while the audience take their seats and the conductor has not yet arrived. . . . Before the Word of God became man, the world orchestra was 'fiddling' about without any plan: worldviews, religions, different concepts of the state, each one playing to itself" (7-8). After Christ, in the Spirit, such fiddling about is ordered in and around the cosmic plan, the exemplar, of truth now revealed in flesh.

76. Balthasar relies on *exitus-reditus* model that he sees structuring the majority of religious and philosophical metaphysics, including Parmenides, Heraclitus, Plato, Plotinus, and even non-Western religions such as Buddhism.

human desire to know the truth of things.[77] Balthasar quotes Ignatius to this effect: "There is a living stream murmuring within me and saying 'Upward and onward to the Father.'"[78] If it is in the en-spirited, particular *Gestalt* of Christ that the *diastasis* between heaven and earth is overcome, then it will be in the en-spirited church that this healing performed.

The Spirit is abroad throughout the world as a kind of *pneumata spermatika*, but the Spirit's truth is especially concentrated in the Church. The ecclesial Spirit is both pentecostal and catholic. He brings all of the scattered words of truth and concentrates them within the Church's vision and practice. Though this project is not primarily concerned with Balthasar's ecclesiology, it is worth considering briefly the way he conceives of the Pentecostal Spirit at work in the Church.

Using language that echoes both Hegel and Adrienne von Speyr,[79] Balthasar says that the Spirit works in the Church both objectively and subjectively. This double work of the Spirit gives the Church a twofold structure, what Balthasar calls the "Petrine" and the "Marian" character. The Petrine is the Church's objective holiness, consisting in the priesthood, the liturgy and sacraments, canon law, dogmatic theology, and the canonical (or representative) saints. The Marian principle, in many ways, transcends that of the Petrine; it is the subjective holiness that is the burning heart of the Church. The Marian principle is the dynamic of love that expresses itself in openness and surrender to God. Balthasar will call it the bridal spirit that funds the Church's prayer, forgiveness, witness, and, offering an Ignatian element, the discernment of Spirits. We can see this Marian principle in "customary" sainthood, which Balthasar thinks is the vocation of all Christians.

It is important for Balthasar that the "entire Church is priestly; the

---

77. *TL* 3, 433.
78. Ibid.
79. Adrienne von Speyr, *Das Wort und die Mystik: Objective Mystik*, vol 6 of *Die Machlasswerke* (Einsiedeln: Johannes Verlag, 1970); and *Das Wort und die Mystik: Subjektive Mystik*, vol 5 of *Die Machlasswerke* (Einsiedeln: Johannes Verlag, 1970). For a helpful summary and analysis in English, see Matthew Lewis Sutton, *Heaven Opens: The Trinitarian Mysticism of Adrienne von Speyr* (Minneapolis: Fortress Press, 2013), 37–60.

entire Church is Marian."[80] The Holy Spirit does not obliterate himself in his quest for objectivity, as in the Hegelian dialectic, but rather holds together the objective and subjective together. Again countering Hegel, Balthasar holds that what is objectively given in the Church must be subjectively received by the faithful. Peter and Mary make up the Church, and in so doing, truth and love are held inextricably together. The Marian principle participates in the subjectivity of the Spirit, and it illuminates and conforms us to the Petrine principle—the objective truth revealed in Christ. One knows the truth through the dynamic of love. This is the heart of the Church; it is the work of the ecclesial Spirit, as Balthasar defines the Spirit of Truth and the Spirit of Love.

The goal of the ecclesial Spirit is to carry the Church in two directions: outward in the mission of truth and charity to the nations (Matt 28:19–20), and inwards with the in-gathering embrace of all truth within her "pleromatic unity."[81] The Church, therefore, has a twofold responsibility of translation: first, to express Christian truth to the world in such a way that its distinctive character is unabridged; second, to translate the broken, fragmented truths of the world into the language of the Church. Balthasar is careful to show that the Church is not the Church if it keeps only to the first task without also performing the second: "the Church exists only when she is ready to transcend herself by going into the world in missionary mode."[82]

This second translation is not meant to distort or colonize the various truths of the world, but rather enfold them into greater truth so that they might be more truthful to themselves. If grace does not destroy, but perfects nature, then *mutatis mutandis*, divine truth does not destroy, but rather perfects creaturely truth, wherever it is found.[83]

In this twofold mission, the Spirit of truth, at once pentecostal and catholic, renders the Church the historical location of the cosmic

80. *TL* 3, 312.
81. Ibid., 259.
82. Ibid., 416.
83. Balthasar plays with this Thomistic idea in *TL* 3, 261ff. The subtitle of that section quite nicely summarizes Balthasar's point: "the Church becomes the world, and the world becomes the Church."

movement of return to the Father. The Church is *catholic* insofar as it is the space for the in-gathering of the nations. She then becomes the space in which the cosmic, metaphysical drama of the return to unity with the Father is performed.

This performance universalizes Christ's ascension. It is the dramatization of the Truth who has gone out from the Father and returns to the Father, carrying all things back to the Father with him. As Balthasar says, "If the world is to return to its origin, the trail must be blazed by him who has already completed, emphatically and archetypically, the circle of coming forth and return."[84] The Spirit takes all things and binds them into the archetype of Christ in the Church, and bears them to the Father.

Metaphysically, this return to the Father is articulated as the return of the Many to the One. It is common among the great religious and philosophical traditions, but Balthasar resists interpreting this movement as an identical conflation that destroys difference. Instead of a unity that results in the sublation of difference, the Spirit's return of the cosmos to the Father is the unity-in-difference of the Trinity, of love. To return to the source of Being is to inhabit through the Spirit the inner reality of divine love. This inner reality of Love is truly known only by those conformed to the Spirit of love, the saints.

---

84. *TL* 3, 436–37.

7

Love Itself is Understanding

Christ is the truth. His life, death, resurrection, and ascension unveil the truth of God and world. Balthasar's account of truth is undeniably christocentric, in terms of Christ being the performative locus of truth and that truth's content. The Spirit universalizes Christ's truth, enabling its eschatological imitation and participation in the *Gestalt* of Christ.[1] Balthasar's theology of the saints emerges at precisely this point. The saint lives her theological existence through surrender, receptivity, and obedience that inhabit this reality of Christ. The saint performs a living exegesis of truth through the structure, habits, and actions of her life. What the saint provides, then, is a distinctively Catholic form of knowing truth *and* making it known. The form of both

---

1. See Ratzinger, "On the Dignity of the Human Person": "Thus Christ no longer appears as a merely general form to which human existences are conformed. His exemplarity means the concrete summons to follow him, and this gives meaning to man's cross; it calls him to share in the *pro me*"of Jesus Christ in a Christian *pro invicem* based on the *cum Christo*. . . . Just as, from the point of view of the theology of the cross, the ontological idea takes concrete form in Christ, so also the ontological affirmation that by the incarnation all human reality, must now be understood as a statement concerning personal life. Its concrete meaning is the claim made on me and the consent to its being made on me by the '*pro me*' of Jesus Christ, and this expresses the concrete spiritual reality of the doctrine of the two natures" (161).

of these things is love. In Balthasar's theology of the saints, then, love itself is understanding because love alone is credible.[2]

This chapter serves as the culmination of our presentation of Balthasar's theology of the saints. The previous chapters have drawn out the metaphysical, christological, and pneumatological dimensions of Balthasar's account of truth, but our attention in this chapter is how the previous dimensions of truth come together in the saints. The saints are, therefore, the necessary culmination of Balthasar's *theologic*.[3]

According to Balthasar, neither the philosopher nor the dogmatician can successfully hold together divine and creaturely truth. It falls to the saint to understand the inner nature of the world eschatologically transfigured by Christ and the Spirit. As we have seen, love is the deepest mode of knowledge. The lover knows as a receptive rather than self-seeking subject.[4] If the mystery of Being is that it is self-giving gift, *donum*, and if gift-receptivity is the central rhythm of both metaphysics and epistemology, then it follows that love *as* that rhythm must be the truest way of knowing God and the world. The saints are therefore a distinctively Catholic form of eschatological knowing.

The previous chapter argued that the entire mission of the Spirit is to guide Christians into all truth. This guidance involves conforming the Christian to the *Gestalt* of Christ, or what Balthasar calls "holiness." Sanctification, then, is a central component of knowledge. One knows through adequation *of the entire person* to truth. Balthasar's version of *adaequatio ad rem* is dramatic, and requires the attunement of one's entire self to the object known. This, we shall see, is what occurs in prayer. In the case of Balthasar's theological metaphysics, this means that the Spirit conforms the knower to the inner life of God, and thus, makes known by making holy. For Balthasar, truth is hidden in the

---

2. In chapter 2, we saw how Balthasar's post-conciliar claim was that the church needed to maintain its distinctively Catholic identity so that it could continue as a witness to Christ's truth. The form of that witness, as we saw, was the saints.

3. The lack of capitalization is intentional here. I do not mean that Balthasar's *Theo-Logic* series ends with the saints (though arguably they should). What I mean is that the saints are the form of Balthasar's entire approach to the nature and task of theological knowledge.

4. *TL* 1, 239.

holy realm of God. This realm can be entered and inhabited only by those who are themselves holy: "Be holy, for I am holy" (Lev 20:26; 1 Peter 1:16). The saints, made holy by their performative participation in the love of God, are permitted to enter and inhabit the realm of truth through the Holy Spirit.

> It is only because we are thus the Father's children that God gives us a participation in things the mere servant cannot know, for the servant serves in the house only for a time, whereas the son "continues for ever" (Jn 8:35). This "continuing" is also an "indwelling" and can also be applied to the Spirit himself. . . . Again, by this same indwelling of the Spirit we are initiated into that indwelling whereby the Father and Son indwell the believer (Jn 14:23).[5]

This is the "all truth" into which the Spirit leads. In a crucial inversion of Eckhart and Hegel, the saints are drawn to truth not through knowledge, but through love. The saints are the ones most attuned to truth because their lives conform to the fundamental character of Being. One cannot really understand the truth of Being outside of participation, faith, and prayer. This is not fideism, though. Real knowledge is possible outside of the religious and theological categories Balthasar uses. But he insists that this "secular" knowledge is not as full as it might be. Purely secular knowledge is genuine, but it has settled for an impoverished form by not developing into—or converting to—love. This renders its knowledge fundamentally incomplete, not only in the sense that all knowledge is inadequate to the plentitude of Being's mystery, but also in the sense that this secular knowledge has failed to fulfill its proper vocation by becoming faith and love. The prying eyes of the philosopher may indeed see, but the *heart* of Being is hidden from all but the eyes of love.

The crucial thing to note here is that Balthasar's theology of the saints utilizes the same language as his metaphysics, Christology, and Ignatian spirituality. Balthasar portrays the saints as those whose theological existences are constituted by love construed as receptivity,

---

5. *TL* 3, 76.

surrender, and obedience. Being is co-extensive with love; those who dwell in love dwell in truth. Such is the existence of the saint.

***

I develop the following analysis of Balthasar's theology of the saints in two ways. First, I look at the structure of the saint's life, especially her prayer, as her participation in the *Gestalt* of Christ. By focusing on contemplative prayer, I highlight both the manner in which the saints understand the mystery of Being *from within*, and the way Balthasar reclaims the metaphysical scope of contemplation. Rather than restricting prayer to pious devotionalism, Balthasar establishes it as the source and the form of theological and metaphysical knowledge.

Second, having grounded Balthasar's theology of the saints in contemplation, I turn to two of the ways that Balthasar's saints know the truth of Being. This section will conclude the argument of this chapter by expositing what it means to say with Balthasar that the saint is the proper guardian of metaphysics today.

The Saintly Form of Knowledge

How does one properly know the truth of Being that has been revealed in Christ through the Spirit? Balthasar's answer is clear: one knows as a saint knows. We have repeatedly asserted that saintly knowledge arises from love. But how can love actually generate knowledge? Love can easily be described as an intellectual disposition, but can it be accurately described as an epistemology?

In many ways, the ancient construal of knowledge as an erotic drive serves as the background here. Both the ancient and Balthasarian forms of the erotics of knowledge turn on the ecstatic union of subject and object, but Balthasar transfigures the ancient tradition through his Ignatian reimagining of love's desire as the will to surrender and receptivity.

Theo-Logic 1's epistemology of love is ultimately grounded in the theological disclosure of the Trinitarian God as the transcendent source of the subject and the object, and thus, the eternal possibility of knowing created truth as participating in divine truth. By knowing God, one knows, in principle, the "inner truth" of all things. As Maximus Confessor put it, "Just as straight lines which proceed from the center are seen as entirely undivided in that position, so the one who has been made worthy to be in God will recognize in himself with a certain simple and undivided knowledge all the preexisting principles of things."[6] Or as Gregory the Great rhetorically asked, "What do they not see that see Him who sees all things?"[7]

Love is knowledge for Balthasar because it is through love alone that one receives and participates in the truth of all things by dwelling in their eternal source.[8] The epistemology of love that the saints represent emerges from the mystery of their union, through the Spirit, with the triune God. Knowledge must be a love that wills its own ignorance, that wills to receive truth in its mystery. Paradoxical though it may sound, knowledge is a learned ignorance, a willful humility before truth that receives that truth as gift.[9] This is an intellectual disposition that stands in stark contrast with those titanic Idealisms that dominated the intellectual landscape in the wake of Hegel. Insisting on the necessity of the humility and furtiveness of love for all forms of knowledge, Balthasar writes:

[i]t is not that reason is incapable of knowing anything: rather, it is

6. Maximus Confessor, *Centuries on Knowledge* 2.4. See Balthasar's reference to this in *CL*, 95, 121, 346.
7. Quoted by Aquinas in *ST* I.92.3.
8. See, David L. Schindler, "God and the End of Intelligence: Knowledge as Relationship," *Communio*, vol. 26 (1999): 510–40. Schindler gives a thoroughly Balthasarian reading of the implications of an epistemology that arises from a "relational anthropology" grounded in Christ. Schindler relies, as does Balthasar, on a thoroughly Chalcedonian Christology, articulating the "anterior unity between faith and reason in the God of Jesus Christ, as the origin and end of both" (516). This is significantly different from the "mechanical relation" between the two in Descartes where "x and y [that is, faith and reason] each retain their integrity only from outside each other" (516). In the relation of love, Schindler insists with Balthasar, "we find a relation wherein the unity of the partners and the rightful distinctiveness of partners grow directly-intrinsically and not inversely-extrinsically in relation to each other. Each finds his or her integrity from inside and not outside their relationship. Married partners (in a genuine relationship!), for example, do not grow less but more free and autonomous as they deepen their unity" (516–17). Cf. Pope John Paul II, "The Sacramentality of Marriage," in *The Theology of the Body: Human Love in the Divine Plan* (Boston: Pauline Books and Media, 1997), 330–32.
9. See David. L. Schindler, "Is Truth Ugly? Moralism and the Convertibility of Being and Love," *Communio*, vol. 27, no. 4 (2000): 701–28. See also, Adrian J. Walker, "'Original Wholeness': (Living) Nature Between God and Technê," *Communio*, vol. 38, no. 4 (2011): 643–56.

precisely the beauty of Wisdom that seduces it to pride in knowing much, to satisfaction with the things of this world, and finally to a Faustian drive to experience: *cult homo cognoscere et cognate experiri et per consequent eis uniri* [man wishes to know, and to experience what he knows, and consequently to be united to what he knows], and therefore the nuptial mystery is perverted into an intellectual harlotry: It is a very great abomination, that the most beautiful daughter of the king (i.e.: wisdom) is offered to us as a bride, and we prefer to fornicate with a base servant-maid and resort to a prostitute.[10]

The erotics of knowledge are operations of the Spirit meant to draw the knower toward that union with that which she longs to know. It is love that spurs on knowledge, as we saw in the first volume of the *Theo-Logic*. But it is also love that disciplines knowledge, trains it to pause, to receive truth as something that transcends the capacity to be known. Love alone can receive the truth in its ontological fullness since Being itself is love. But love, Balthasar insists, requires a distinct form of life, a way of being in the world. This form is the saint and her way of being is the contemplative life.

The Life of Contemplation

That the saint is the true metaphysician is not a claim unique to Balthasar. He believes that he is simply appropriating an established tradition of the ancient and medieval church.[11] His theology of the saints is simply Balthasar's *ressourcement* of the logic and practice of the ancient monastic tradition, in which philosophical speculation is enfolded into the existential theology of the saints. Balthasar develops his most sustained interpretation of this tradition in his essay, "Philosophy, Christianity, Monasticism."[12] This essay works out how it was possible for ancient and medieval Christianity to view monasticism, and *mutatis mutandis* the saintly life, as "the Christian philosophy."[13]

According to Balthasar, the ancients held that philosophy reaches

---

10. *GL* 2, 279.
11. Cf. Balthasar's discussion of this point in relation to Bonaventure in *GL* 2, 278ff.
12. In "Philosophy, Christianity, Monasticism," in *ET* 2, 333–72.
13. Ibid., 333.

its summit in the religious ideal. This leads Balthasar to interpret the philosophical life as "a life for the divine truth that was hidden in the world." The ancient tradition held together religious *theôria* and philosophical *speculatio*. For the Fathers, the perfected form of philosophy requires intellectual and practical attunement with the truth of Being. For a figure like Clement of Alexandria, true philosophy consists in "wisdom of the soul, correct judgment, and purity of life."[14] To translate that into Balthasarian idiom, true philosophy arises from the collusion of knowledge (*gnosis*) and holiness. Holiness, the conformity of love and receptivity, prevents knowledge from becoming titanic, an "intellectual harlotry."[15] Philosophy in the ancient sense is "transmitted to us by the Son."[16] How can this be? It is because Christ is the truth, the living *analogia entis*, the proper exegesis of Being.

True philosophy, according to the Fathers, is something more than (not necessarily other than) pagan dialectic and rhetoric. Balthasar insists that pagan *dialectic* must become Christian *dialogic*. Origen argued that philosophy is practical as well as theoretical and requires the imitation of—Balthasar might say the spiritual participation in—the *Logos*. Balthasar sees the Fathers interpreting the Christian life as a "pneumatic philosophy" that "makes the soul and the spirit ready for the *theôria* through the utter engagement of the 'praxis'."[17] Philosophy, in this sense, cannot be done apart from a "form of life" in which one's existence—*praktikē*—is completely offered up toward the highest "theoretical" goal of union with God.[18]

Balthasar's narration of the tradition is unsurprisingly colored by his appropriation of Ignatian spirituality. We saw in chapter 1 that Dominicans such as Garrigou-Lagrange criticized the Jesuits as an insufficiently "contemplative" order, devoted more to the active life. The Christian life, for Balthasar and his sources, is the union of the

---

14. Ibid., 334. Cf: *Stromata* 6.7.55.
15. *GL* 2, 279.
16. "Philosophy, Christianity, Monasticism" in *ET* 2, 334.
17. Ibid., 335.
18. Ibid., 336.

contemplative and the active in the receptive obedience of the monastic and the saint.[19] A contemplative life apart from action falters because it would be insufficiently christological. The *Logos* was not content to rest in the eternal silence of contemplation, but took on flesh, enacting and performing eternal truth. Whoever would understand that truth cannot know it apart from imitation and participation.

It is worth noting that Balthasar turns to the ancients not as an escape from the pressures of modern philosophy, but rather, *because of* modern philosophy. Neither Hegel nor Heidegger ignored the ancients, writing them off as obsolete. Both thinkers appropriate the ancient tradition. Those who would engage contemporary philosophical culture cannot, therefore, neglect the ancients either. Indeed, ancient, medieval, *and* contemporary philosophy are driven by the mystery of the relation between the eternal and the temporal, God and world. These questions are perennial. Christianity does not solve these questions, but rather reveals their full profundity. Just as there is no *natura pura*, there is no ontology, no metaphysics without theology.[20]

The form of life that Balthasar sees in the monastic and the saint is contemplative, by which he does not mean a retreat from action and service, but rather, an Ignatian life in which understanding and obedience are united in love. In such a contemplative life, one sees God's presence in all things through the contemplation of the mystery of Being. Such contemplation is possible through illumination by the inner reality of God's wisdom and love through the Spirit who gives the Christian the capacity to see.[21] This is true understanding of Being. But contemplation, illumination, and understanding are most efficacious

---

19. "Is there any reason, therefore, why it should be impossible to seek God in all things in the world and find him, and to be *in contemplatione activus* on the basis of an enduring settled presence of the spirit to God that accompanies all that one does, instead of fleeing from the world (although one will not be rid of the world even in a monastery) in order to bury oneself in an inactive contemplation?" (ibid., 340).

20. "[God] cannot be Being *tout court*, without this implying that each being, when it looks into the ground of its own being, looks up to him, whether it knows this or not. There cannot exist any ontology without theology, no matter how formal the manner in which one would develop the ontology. The path to being, which is the path of reason in general, is the path to God" (ibid., 352).

21. Ibid., 363.

only within a life that is handed over to God, dedicated to truth, and open to the coming of Christ. This is a dispossessive, self-surrendering life. It is the life of love, the life of the saint. Balthasar thus unifies the philosophical and contemplative life, describing the way the latter fulfills the former.

What are the characteristics of this philosophical and contemplative life? Balthasar insists, first, that we cannot think of philosophy, even secular philosophy, as anything less than an act of love. Philosophical love has as its object, not the act of knowing, but rather, the mystery of Being.[22] Christian contemplation, however, goes beyond this. Contemplation builds on philosophical wonder and ecstasy at the miracle of Being by becoming *prayer*. In Balthasar's sense, prayer is not only the dialogical relation of I-Thou, but the existentially realized handing over (*traditio*) of one's I to the divine Thou. It is the performance of Christ's receptivity to the will of the Father. This handing over is the fulfillment of philosophy, the beginning of theology, and the fulfillment of both by prayer. This is Balthasar's interpretation of Evagrius's oft-quoted dictum: "If you have knowledge of God (*theologos*), then you truly pray, and if you truly pray, you have knowledge of God." True prayer involves the conformity or adequation of the entire self to God.

The saintly philosopher, then, is the one whose love propels her contemplation of the world into the deep, abiding mystery of truth that lies at the heart of the world: the "fire of love" of the Father and Son, in which all created Being participates. To understand Being from *within* this dynamic of divine love is the "science of Christ." Balthasar makes recourse to Maximus Confessor's *Gnostic Centuries* to solidify this point: "The science of Christ needs not a dialectical soul but a dioratic soul"—a soul that "sees through" material things to the theophany carried within them.[23] The saintly philosopher is the one who finds God in all things. This dioratic soul is an extension of the orantic life of the saint.

22. Ibid., 365.
23. Ibid., 367.

Orantic Anthropology

Prayer is the theological form (*Gestalt*) of the life of the saint. "The saint is one who tries to hand his entire being to God, and this surrender is essentially prayer."[24] Saintly prayer is the theological fulfillment of the chief characteristics of humanity—as a dialogical creature.

Throughout his work, though especially in *Theo-Logic* 2, Balthasar leans quite heavily on dialogicians such as Martin Buber and Ferdinand Ebner.[25] Buber's construal of the I-Thou relation is especially prominent in Balthasar's *Theo-Logic* as the principle of inter-subjectivity that allows for knowledge and ultimately faith.[26] Through Buber and Ebner, Balthasar construes relationality as foundational for anthropology. For Balthasar, to be a person is to be in relationship with the Other and to receive oneself *in* that relation. Metaphysically considered, this means the human person is being-as-relation in miniature (or, as Balthasar puts it, as a microcosm of the cosmos): human relationality here approximates "being as self-giving relation."[27]

Balthasar insists that the dialogue written into the heart of Being and into the heart of the human person must be specified as prayer.[28]

---

24. Adrienne von Speyr, *The World of Prayer*, trans. Graham Harrison (San Francisco: Ignatius Press, 1985), 223.
25. *TL* 2, 54ff.
26. Balthasar's appropriation of Buber both explicates the human being and offers a surprising (and unintentional) analogy of Trinitarian personhood (which, as we shall see, Balthasar depends on for his anthropology). Buber's turn to the inter-personality of the human being situates the human subject in an unescapable network of relationship. The human subject, Buber claims, is never an "I" in itself, but exists in one of two possible relationships: the "I-Thou" or the "I-It." This "inter" [*Zwischen*] is, for Buber, "being as relation." Relationality is the source of all things—it is certainly the source of the I. Though, like Balthasar, Buber will insist on the necessary polarity in Being (though he stresses more than Balthasar the absolute incommunicability between the poles), a certain reciprocity between I and Thou is possible: there is an "innate Thou in the I."1 The subject becomes an I within a metaphysical matrix of being-as-relation: I am myself by means of the "inter" that draws me into relationship with the Thou. "Buber tends to call this realistically conceived 'inter' 'spirit', which comes to fulfillment as exchange and speech" (*TL* 2, 54).
27. *TL* 2, 55. It is also significant that for Buber, God is revealed in this human relationship as the "eternal Thou" that grounds every human Thou. And so, Buber will conclude that the language or dialogue that "invokes" both the I and the Thou is prayer.
28. Cf. "Who is Man?" in *ET* 4, 20. "These times have witnessed an important trend that appropriately honors the dialogical principle, which in fact has only today been really recognized and appreciated. But we must nonetheless absolutely transcend it. Not only are most dialogues between people hopelessly superficial and full of misunderstandings, they can also silt up, break

Augustine, for example, "understands [his] act of addressing God essentially as an answer [*Antwort*]—as the word [*Wort*] that has been implanted in the praying subject by the gift of the primordial Word [*Urwort*]."[29] It is the word from God that addresses (that is, creates) the human subject who, in response, offers up herself, her "I," to the eternal Thou. This dialogue between the I and the Thou itself depends on the primordial Word that calls us forth as dramatic persons, that is, as agents in the theological drama of human existence.

To be a person—a *dramatis persona*—is to be constituted by dialogical receptivity. This receptivity is operative on three distinct but inseparable levels: metaphysically, the person, as a particular, concrete being, receives her existence from Being, appropriating it through her obedient sheltering of Being in that particular existence: "the finite, since it is subject, already constitutes itself as such through the letting-be of Being by virtue of an *ekstasis* out of its own closed self, and therefore through dispossession and poverty becomes capable of salvaging in recognition and affirmation the infinite poverty of the fullness of Being."[30] Anthropologically, the person is always engaged in dialogue with a Thou. In this dialogue, the person receives the Thou as an Other, and by so doing, knows herself as I. This too involves a certain ecstasy of the self insofar as the dialogical word is an "ex-pression" of the self—a donation (*donatum*) to the Other that anticipates receiving the expression from the Other as well. Theologically, the person receives that which enables both the metaphysical and anthropological receptivity, namely, the initiatory act of God's love, that groundless glory, that is the creative ground of Being, the harmonization of the Ontological Difference, and the primal Word that initiates every subsequent word of Being and of humanity. The human person is the one who receives herself as she receives this personal Other, the gift

off, bog down. And in the very place where a person unfolds himself in a lifelong exchange of love, he must draw on the power of keeping his promise from the provisions of a silent and lonely fidelity that can be found only in the inner core of his self and not in the dialogical principle per se."

29. *TL* 2, 58.
30. *GL* 5, 627.

of Being, and the very life of God that comes freely to call one from nothing into Being, into relationship, and into mission.

Thus, Balthasar's orantic anthropology is grounded in the Trinity. Drawing on Ferdinand Ebner, he insists that the inter-personality of the I-Thou relation is the "sole truth of man's being."[31] Further, the truth of Being solely is "experienced in the speech exchange [between the I and the Thou] as gift, a gift that can be answered only with the basic stance of 'gratitude'."[32] From Ebner, Balthasar interprets the primal word of Being as an ex-pression, a speaking out from the mystery of Being's spiritual interiority. The human "I" goes out of herself in ecstasy toward the Other who receives her in gratitude: "this fundamental attitude . . . is identical with a primary giving of self into the word of the other."[33] In the I-Thou relation, each ex-presses herself by the gift of herself which the Other receives in faith: a loving, trusting openness to that which is other than the self.

But, of course, all of this presupposes both an I and Thou, established in themselves, that can freely will just this expression and gift. Beyond the polarity of the I-Thou, Ebner thus posits a relationality between God and humanity that enables every other worldly I-Thou relation. For Ebner, divine Being is the Word (*Logos*), the divine expression, through whom all things were made (Col 1:6). It is this divine *Logos* "who makes possible every worldly I-Thou, who enables all speaking as 'inter-change,' and who releases both the I and the Thou into the freedom of self-initiation."[34] Worldly I-Thou dialogue is subsequent to and contingent upon a more fundamental dialogue between God and world, articulated through the *Logos*.

But we must go a step further. Balthasar grounds his orantic anthropology, just like his metaphysics, in Christology. We must, therefore, return to Christ, and show how Balthasar interprets Christ's existence as prayer. We have already seen how the "all truth" that the Spirit leads into is the love between Father and Son. The form this

31. *TL* 2, 56.
32. Ibid.
33. Ibid.
34. Ibid.

love takes in the world is Christ's perfect receptivity, surrender, and obedience. It is his prayer, especially that of Gesthemane that fully reveals *his* truth, which is also the truth of all things. To understand Balthasar's use of contemplative prayer, we must briefly re-consider his Christology under the rubric of prayer.

Christ's Truth as Prayer

In his confrontation with the powers of sin, the Son, through his incarnate suffering and death, heals the mendacity of the world that stands in rebellion against God. Such healing effects a fundamental, eschatological change in the truth of the world and our access to it. Christ restores the integrity of worldly truth through his resurrection. Through his ascension he opens a path of contemplation—knowledge of the truth—that is his own truth writ large throughout the cosmos. In this way, Christ acts not only as the source and the content of truth, but also, as the path of knowledge.[35] Christ is the truth *and* the way.

Balthasar conceives Christ's life as a triune life of prayer, as a perpetual dialogue with his Father through the Spirit. Interpreting Christ's life as prayer involves identifying three orantic characteristics of Christ's life: 1) the dialogicality of his existence; 2) the contemplative orientation of his life; 3) the absoluteness of his surrender in his prayer during his passion.[36]

At the heart of prayer lies the dialogicality of the I-Thou relation. Christ lives within this relation, receiving his "I" from the Father's "Thou" at his baptism, and thus realizes in history his eternal receptivity. Christ lives from the Father through the dialgue of his prayer. This is the heart of his lived faith: "And just as, in prayer, he returns to the truth of his existence—which is not his own truth, but God's—so he lives in faith by this truth."[37] The truth of his existence

---

35. See, Hugh of St. Victor, *De laude caritatis* IV: "We run to God on the path of God."
36. Cf. *TD* 5, 122–23: "What is not difficult is the idea that the Son, as man, continues the eternal dialogue of prayer of the Divine Persons in heaven; it is not difficult to think of the eternal Word clothing himself in human words. And since Christ gives us a share in his own prayer, every word of the Lord is a prayer to the Father and a gift and a task for the Church."
37. *Prayer*, 61.

is his perfect dialogue with the Father. Christ's sonship is a matter of his nature being dramatically realized through his perpetual, prayerful communion with the Father in the Spirit.

Further, the incarnate *expressio Dei* realizes in himself the dialogue between God and world.[38] He is the Father's Word to the world that creates that world. Through this divine and incarnate Word, the world too can hear and understand the language of heaven, now translated into earthly language. But, more than this, through the incarnation, the world can now *respond* to the Word through the Spirit. "We cannot bypass that aspect of the incarnation which sees it as a concession on God's part to our hardness of hearing. God's language *has* become unmistakable for us in the life of Jesus."[39]

Through the receptive dialogue of his existence, Christ lives in unbroken awareness of the Father. Christ is the perfect contemplative. His contemplation is the basis of his obedient action: "the Son only *does* what he *sees* the Father doing" (John 5:19). His contemplative, prayerful life is the basis for his transformative obedience.[40] The dialogicality and contemplative orientation of Christ's existence are articulate, expressive forms of Christ's truth. They are, in Balthasar's language, *parrhesia*, the "shining forth" of Christ's truth in his prayer. In fact, Christ's *parrhesia* is identical to prayer.[41] His life is the analogical openness of creation and heaven to each other. In Christ, heaven speaks to the creation, which in response offers up its own obedient *Yes* to the Father in Christ's cry of dereliction on the cross: "He is grace ascending just as much as grace descending; he is just as much creation's highest response to the Father as he is the Father's Word to creation."[42]

---

38. "There was only one way out of this impasse, namely, that infinite eternal Being should utter its own self in the form of a relative being. That in this epiphany and *parousia* it should become actually present and give an authoritative interpretation of itself" (*Prayer*, 157).

39. *Prayer*, 269. Cf. Hans Urs von Balthasar, *Christian Meditation*, trans. Sister Mary Theresilde Skerry (San Francisco: Ignatius Press, 1989), henceforth *CM*. Balthasar says that the "openinig of the finite to God was always present in Jesus Christ, seeing that as a man he directs his every Word to the world and simultaneously to the Father as a Word of prayer" (*CM*, 16). Again, Christ is the mediator; he holds the middle of all things.

40. "Beyond Contemplation and Action?" in *ET* 4, 299ff.

41. *Prayer*, 46ff.

42. *Prayer*, 170. "He is the twofold channel—of God to us and of us to God" (*CM*, 13).

The perfect *Gelassenheit* of Christ's existence radiates outward as the articulate offering of his prayer. Therefore, Christ's entire existence is summed up by his prayer in Gethsemane: "Yet not what I will but what you will" (Matt 26:39). Christ's radical disposal to the Father's will is summarized by handing over (*tradere*) his life through his prayer.

Even more radical than Gethsemane, perhaps, are Christ's final words from the cross. His "Father, into your hands, I commit my spirit" (Luke 23:46) and his Johannine "*tetelestai*" (John 19:30), are the chief expressions of his self-abandonment. Following his "*Eloi, Eloi, lama sabachthani*" after his abandonment by the Father, these prayers perfectly express his obedience, surrender, and self-abandonment. Insofar as Christ's life is constituted by openness, receptivity, surrender, and obedience, his entire existence is best described as an act of prayer.

How does the saint hear the word (*Wort*) of the Word (*Ur-wort*), especially as it echoes out into the void of death as un-word? How does one come to know the truth that Christ expresses in his life, through his prayer? For Balthasar, it is precisely *in* Christ's existence, in his prayer, that humanity is revealed to itself. We hear the Word, we know the Word's truth, because through the full existential flesh-taking in his incarnation, suffering, and death, we exist *within* the Word. "[T]he Word who became flesh takes us into himself, giving his own self as our mode of existence. Grace has not imparted some general, vague, 'supernatural elevation' to us, but as participation in the personal existence of the eternal Word of God, who became 'flesh' like us so that we should become 'spirit' in him."[43]

Insofar as the human person comes to exist *in* Christ, Christ exists in him. Christ becomes the inner teacher: "the truth of God which illuminates me interiorly . . . fundamentally different from my 'psychic depths,' my archetypes, the categories, classifications and ideals which

---

43. *Prayer*, 58. Balthasar interprets the mystical body of Christ (eucharistic and ecclesial) as a literal participation in Christ's existence. But he goes further by suggesting that the general mission of every human is to enter into this christological participation. In other words, what the human is properly ordered to is not "grace" in an abstract sense, but rather, Christ himself. We participate in his death to share in his glory (Rom 8:17). When we do this, we are saints.

are most intimate to me."[44] Christ's prayer, in which he both expresses and exists *as* truth, becomes the mode of humanity's own being and hence the mode of our knowing truth: "The Son's contemplation is and remains the ontological framework within which all other valid Christian contemplation takes place."[45] The way we exist and the way we know cannot be neatly distinguished for Balthasar. And so, he will insist that, in the light of Christ, "prayer and worship [*Anbetung*] are indispensable to the inner act of reason."[46] Prayer and reason are not identical, but they are integral to each other.

For Balthasar, the Son is expositor of—which is to say, the *way to*—the Father, in whom is the ultimate source, meaning, and end of truth.[47] Christ is "the Father's fragrance in the world. He is both ultimate and not ultimate. As God he is absolute; and yet, as absolute, relative: as the Son who is a relationship proceeding from the Father and returning to him."[48] This relationship is prayer—the "I" eternally receiving and expressing the "Thou"—nowhere more perfectly expressed than in his incarnate existence handed over in obedient surrender and abandonment. And it is within this prayer, both eternal and historical, cosmic and existential, that all persons find themselves, drawn ever on by truth toward truth, drawn by love toward love:

> For the incarnation of the Word has brought about a reality which includes and sustains the individual, enabling him to perform the act of contemplation as worship, as obedience, and as understanding in faith. This arises, ultimately, from the very fact that the Absolute has appeared in the midst of human history, bound to humanity through conception, birth, life and death, linked to all generations—who are in turn profoundly affected a priori by this link, by God's having appeared among them.[49]

And it is only now, in the wake of this christological grounding,

44. *Prayer*, 63.
45. Ibid., 275.
46. Ibid.
47. "Here is pure motion from the Father and back to the Father, in such a way that he leaves the Father every opportunity to speak to us, ultimately through the surrender of his Son and Word," *TD* 5, 122. See also Victoria S. Harrison, "Homo Orans: Von Balthasar's Christocentric Philosophical Anthropology," *The Hethrop Journal*, vol. 40, no. 3 (1999): 288–89.
48. *Prayer*, 69.
49. Ibid., 166.

expressing, and transforming of truth, that we can return to the saints and charge laid upon the church to continue the expressive mission of Christ, to know and testify that truth is love:

> In this way the person who prays within the Church is already sharing, at the level of being, in the mysteries of the act of divine revelation. Not only may he behold these things from outside: he is privileged to experience them from within. He is privileged to understand that the Father's self-revelation in the Son, through the Son's descent into flesh, takes the form of a sacrifice of love in which the Son makes himself poor (2 Cor 8:9); through his total abandonment of himself the Son becomes an unmistakable sign of the origin and nature of divine love, which thus glorifies itself.[50]

Kneeling Theology

Balthasar follows Aquinas in understanding theology as the study of "God and all things in relation to God." It therefore encompasses the full range of objective themes that fall under the rubric of created Being as it exists within the drama of the God–world relationship. Theology, insofar as it shares through the Spirit in the *theologoumena* of the eternal Son and the chorus of creation, is a "meditative clarification of [the] confession of faith in order to understand it and make it intelligible to others."[51]

This means that theology is always a rational discipline. It is, after all, a *logic*. Balthasar does not overlook the value of careful, systematic theological thinking. He does, however, view such rational theology as inherently limited, as a fragment of a *theo-logic* concerned with unfolding the mystery of truth. The rational theologian—the theologian as we have come to think of her—is but a preparation for the saint. It is in the saint that the theologian comes to herself, for the saint theologizes not only as knower, but as lover. The saint is the one who is caught up into the eternal dialogue of divine expression and love as it is revealed in the incarnation. The holiness of the saint arises, Balthasar insists, from taking Christ's humanity seriously.[52]

---

50. Ibid., 170.
51. *TL* 3, 367.

Contemplating the humanity of Christ, in which the fullness of God (and thus, his truth) is pleased to dwell, the saint comes to know, that is, is *united* to that which she knows. She becomes holy by being bound to that which is holy; she knows the truth by inhabiting that truth. She is the one who shares in the divine dialogue of Christ by means of her own dialogue in Christ. She beholds and knows the truth because she prays. This is why Balthasar insists that the way to overcome the estrangement between dogmatics and spirituality, is to reclaim prayer as the "continuous dialogue between Bridegroom and bride."[53] We must re-imagine the nature of theology itself in light of the nature of truth as we have discussed it in this book. Thus, for Balthasar,

> the "rational" theology, which did not begin with Thomas but always had to be put forward by the Fathers incidentally, so to speak, in order to defend the faith against heresy and which consists in illuminating and ordering faith's inner textual unity (*sapientis est ordinare*), can be nothing other than an indispensable preliminary to a praying and confessing theology; "this abstract discourse cannot, however, be elevated into a paradigm or norm" for theology.[54]

Balthasar goes on:

> Intimacy with the Holy Spirit of truth thus cancels out the spectator's uninvolved objectivity, with its external, critical attitude to the truth, and replaces it with an attitude which one can only describe as prayer. This prayer is total; it encompasses our beholding and our readiness to be beheld, our receiving and self-giving, our contemplating and our self-communication, in a single, undivided whole. In fact, *no other attitude but prayer is appropriate and (in a true sense) objective in the presence of eternal truth.* There *is* a speculative, theoretical approach in faith, in theology and in Christian life as a whole, and it is very necessary, but it can only be a constituent part of prayer's totality and it *retains the essence of the whole from which it comes.* And while it is true that the believer, in "thinking" about divine truth, is inspired to further prayer, and that acts of the will (of surrender, of love, of trust) normally follow upon the acts of rational insight, it is also true that the reason would never be concerned with divine truth at all if it were not somehow aware, in a rudimentary and inchoate "experience," of truth's divine quality, of a kind of implicit

---

52. *Prayer*, 172.
53. "Theology and Sanctity," in *ET* 1, 201.
54. *TL* 3, 365.

attitude of prayer. This underlying prayer provides the only effective motivation for our own preoccupation with divine truth and with making it known to others.[55]

The human person has a natural, restless longing for God.[56] This erotic drive is intellectual, spiritual, and bodily. We desire God with our whole selves; our entire person yearns for its fulfillment in union with God. And so, the rational desire of the human for rational truth cannot be excluded from the theological endeavor. But this rational theology is but one dimension of Balthasar's far broader re-conceptualization of theology. Rational, systematic theology is situated within the larger context of an *orantic* theology—a theology at prayer. Discursive—or perhaps academic—theology is the narthex of the sanctuary, but *kneeling* theology bears us toward the altar-rail where we encounter Christ. This is the way the saints theologize; this is how the truth is known by and expressed through them. In saintly prayer, dogmatics and life, the intellectual and existential apprehension of truth, come together:

> Contemplation is the acceptance of revealed truth by the believing, loving person (with all his faculties of intellect, will and sense); therefore the particular form this truth takes must shape and determine the way it is received. A knowledge of theology's fundamental principles will promote such contemplation by shedding a clearer light on what the person is experiencing existentially; it will save him entering on circuitous and erroneous paths in prayer. Conversely, the person who is accustomed to pray will gratefully accept all the central insights that come to him from theology as an enrichment of his prayer.[57]

A theology at prayer emerges from that first "call" of God to us, and our *inspired* "Abba, Father" reply.[58] This is the beginning of the dialogue

---

55. *Prayer*, 79–80. Emphasis added.
56. Augustine, *Confessions* I.1.1. Harrison also develops this idea in *"Homo Orans,"* 293ff.
57. *Prayer*, 307.
58. Cf. Harrison, *"Homo Orans"*: "God created human beings such that, to be truly themselves, they must contemplate Christ in prayer . . . von Balthasar interprets this in the light of the fulfillment of an individual's nature . . . for von Balthasar, this 'seeing and hearing God' is, in fact, contemplative prayer. It follows that, on his view, this prayer is not something that human beings can just as well do without. Rather, it is precisely what they have been created for. Thus, without contemplative prayer a human being remains less than herself. [Balthasar] compares such an unfulfilled individual to a mere torso, a shadow of what she should be" (283–84).

by which we find ourselves participating in the fiery inner dynamic of truth that Balthasar identifies as the love between Father and Son. Theology is practiced from within the life, and the prayer, of God. It is this life that the Spirit makes known to believers by drawing them, through prayer, into the inner filial dynamic of God:

> The person who prays not only stands before truth and contemplates it objectively; as John is fond of saying, he lives "in the truth" itself, he "abides in the truth", he is "of the truth." Hence the direct connection between "spirit and truth", and "The Spirit of truth." Praying within the truth means that we must not start with a kind of aloofness, as if first of all we had to convince ourselves that the word of God which we are about to contemplate is the truth, in order to affirm it on the basis of our own insight. Rather, we start from this affirmation as something pre-existing from time immemorial; it is as if we had long since given up and abandoned everything which could mitigate against it. It means living by the knowledge that the truth (*which is the Spirit within us*) is more interior to us than we are to ourselves; that we have been predestined and chosen in God, in God's authentic truth, prior to the foundation of the world, prior to our own existence, to be his holy, unspotted children.[59]

Balthasar concludes that "theology is the kind of thing that does not work without prayer."[60] The consequence of this for Balthasar is quite radical: "nothing is worthy of theological reflection unless it can [also] be the subject of prayer."[61] There can be no theology, and therefore, no *Theo-Logic*, without prayer, nor without those whose lives are constituted by prayer, the saints. The saint at prayer is the proper form (*Gestalt*) of theological knowledge.

We must return one final time to the theme of dialogicality. Balthasar's ontology is grounded in the inner-Trinitarian dialogicality of the relation of love between Father and Son in the Spirit. This dialogicality is the divine prayer from which all created words and dialogue emerge.[62]

---

59. *Prayer*, 77–78.
60. *TL* 3, 358.
61. Ibid.
62. It is Christ who, through the Spirit, transforms all inner-worldly words and dialogue into prayer. It is Christ who overcomes the oppositional dialectic between "I" and "Thou," "subject" and "object": "Only in Jesus Christ is it possible for the earthly dualism of language between a free 'I' and 'thou' to coincide with a prelinguistic or supra-linguistic horizon encompassing both of

The dialogue of prayer is the theological fulfillment of the dialogue of knowledge. It is epistemic dialogue lifted to the level of everlasting love. The aspects of dialogue that we have previously examined, the trust and receptivity that make all dialogue possible, are here raised to the *nth* degree. Trust becomes faith and receptivity becomes surrender and obedience. Prayer is not only mutuality of speech, but also the surrender, the handing over (*tradere*) of the self in an act of faith. Prayer participates in christological reality and is, therefore, true theological action. This is Balthasar's existential theology.[63] Theology participates in the *theologic* of Christ's own life, and it does so through prayer.

Prayer is the language of the saints, and thus the highest form of language. "Just as in Plato the most sublime and arcane things are uttered in the form of myth, in Christian theology they are uttered in the hymn of adoration."[64] Note once again Balthasar's use of "adoration" that has cropped up since chapter four. His theology of the saints, his metaphysical epistemology, and his Christology converge on this orantic disposition of adoration.

Theological language speaks most faithfully as prayer. Prayer is the language of the Spirit. As Bernard of Clairvaux expresses it, "the illumination of this revelation that is carried out by the Holy Spirit is not only to give us knowledge but also to ignite our love. . . . The Spirit's doctrine does not provoke our curiosity but fans our love into flame."[65]

---

them: namely, in a God who is simultaneously himself and his 'Word'." Jesus' hypostatic identity as "utterance and horizon" is the objective focus of theology; it is the truth, the first Word, which all created words strain to articulate. But it is the Spirit who "puts [this] objective light into man's subjective core in the form of conversion, faith, and the imitation of God." The Spirit makes known the *pro nobis* of the divine mystery, that through Christ, the all the world has been transfigured, all worldly speech is filled with the divine, that inner dynamic of the dialogicality of understanding is prayer.

63. Cf. *GL* 2, 278.

64. *TL* 3, 366. "*Wie bei Platon das erhabenste und Geheimste in Gestalt des Mythus ausgesagt wird, so in der christlichen Theologie im anbetenden Hymnus* (Theologik III, 338).

65. Bernard of Clairvaux, *Sermones in Cantica* 8, 5–6, quoted in *TL* 3, 366. Balthasar goes on quoting Bernard as saying that theology is a *doctrina spiritus* (cf. chapter six). This means that there is "no theology without prayer."

Prayer as Metaphysics in Act[66]

Christ is the true Theologian who reveals the truth by *being* the truth. All subsequent theology is done in the shadow of Christ through the Spirit. Theology as a discipline, then, is best understood as a *doctrina spiritus*. Theology contemplates truth as the Spirit makes it known. But as we have seen, the Spirit's mission is not simply to bring knowledge but to inflame love.

Knowledge and love go together, but without confusion. Not all knowledge is love. Love is the fulfillment of knowledge because reason is necessarily insufficient for true understanding of the limitless depth of Being.[67] Only when knowledge participates in orantic love do we arrive at a genuine model of how prayer is "metaphysics in act." It is the act of love that *performs* the truth of Being by *inhabiting* the truth of Being, that is, Christ incarnate. The gift of the Spirit does not just allow the saint to speak *to* God or *about* God, but allows the entrance "into God's personal dialogue"—through the Spirit into the eternal Speech, the eternal Word.[68] Prayer is the dialogue between God and the person, which is, at the same time, the dialogue of understanding between absolute truth and its knower.[69]

Prayer is metaphysics in act because it is the living participation in the fundamental metaphysical truth of the dialogue of love between Father and Son in the Spirit. Prayers enters into this reality by praying as Christ taught us to pray in the Lord's Prayer.[70] The saint also enters

---

66. I am grateful to Dr. Anne M. Carpenter for her feedback and suggestions on the material in this section.

67. One thinks of Dante's journey through Paradise. His capacity for understanding increases as he is adequated to the love that moves the sun and the other stars. His love transcends but fulfills his knowledge: "*d'ammirazione omai, poi dietro ai sensi vedi che la ragione ha corte l'ali*": reason has short wings (*Paradiso* II.56–57).

68. *TL* 3, 371.

69. In prayer, "the very same personal encounter is meant to take place as in the Lord's earthly life. In holy scripture or some other grace filled medium . . . we have genuine mediation, just as, in the days of his flesh, the very air was the medium of communication between the mouth of the Son of Man and the ear of the person addressed" (*Prayer*, 83; quoted in Harrison, "Homo Orans," 291).

70. See Pope Benedict XVI, *Jesus of Nazareth*, vol. 1, trans. Adrian J. Walker (New York: Doubleday, 2007), 138. On the Our Father: "[Calling God, "Father"] gives the concept of being God's children a dynamic quality: We are not ready-made children of God from the start, but we are meant to become so increasingly by growing more and more deeply in communion with Jesus. Our sonship turns out to be identical with following Christ. To name God as Father thus becomes a summons to

by praying *with* Christ, by participating in his prayerful expression of love and truth through his receptivity, obedience, and surrender. This is the Ignatian character of prayer. Through the series of contemplations of the *Exercises*, one comes to know the truth of Being from within through the performance of that truth in the action of prayer:

> The final meditation of the *Spiritual Exercises* opens the contemplations of Jesus' life out onto a meditation on the cosmic dimensions of the divine plan for the world and places itself anew at God's disposal for carrying out this plan. Besides the offering *Suscipe, Domini*—"Take, O Lord, and receive . . ."—there is that other word, *sume*—despoil and consume even what I perhaps do not dare to offer. . . . In becoming aware of the extent of the divine self-giving, the individual who meditates is catapulted out of his would-be closed personal being, not into a destruction of his personhood but into its fulfillment: the creature's attainable approximation to the unalloyed being-for-others within the divine, trinitarian mystery.[71]

True understanding of the God–world relation happens *in* the truth of that relation: in Christ. This "true theology" is theology at prayer. The true practice of theology is prayer because it is participation in the eternal theological act—the *expressio Dei*. Indeed, "theology and exegesis may border on prayer, but their pursuit is not necessarily prayer; or, at any rate, not explicitly. They can and should be accompanied with a disposition to worship in the depths of the soul. . . . Indeed, the reader and student of Scripture may well—like St. Anselm and many other theologians who were also saints—enshrine and penetrate his reading and reflection with habitual adoration, and, in this way, bring a liturgical attitude to bear on the work of the mind."[72]

The one at prayer is the "true metaphysician," who knows Being *as* the infinite mystery of love. Prayer is dialogical contemplation; it involves beholding the form of truth in its sacramental reality through

---

us: to live as a 'child,' as a son or daughter. 'All that is mine is thine,' Jesus says in his high-priestly prayer to the Father, and the father says the same thing to the elder brother of the Prodigal Son (Lk 15:31). The word *father* is an invitation to live from our awareness of this reality."
71. *CM*, 84.
72. *Prayer*, 94.

the dialogical rhythm of gift and receptivity, that is, through hearing the Word of the Father echo in the words of the world by means of the Spirit of Pentecost.

Prayer is also a kind of metaphysical confession, that *this act*—praying—is the truth of God and of the world. But prayer makes this confession, not primarily through a series of logical postulates, but through an existential alignment of the self to this truth, to the *Logos* in whom all things "live, move, and have their being" (Rom 17:28). Prayer makes this confession by performing its truth—by *being* receptive, surrendering, obedient. For Balthasar, prayer is metaphysical knowledge because it is the performance of the saint's union with the God who is the source and goal of creation, in whom lies the truth of all Being.[73] For Balthasar, to pray is to be in Christ, to be in the one who is the burning heart of all truth, the living exegesis of the Father, and the true metaphysic of the world.

We have seen that the truth of Being is ultimately the Trinitarian dynamic of love. This dynamic, Balthasar insists, "can only be one of prayer—be it adoration [*Anbetung*], thanksgiving, or intercession."[74] The Spirit brings about the necessary holiness of the saint by teaching them the Son's prayer. Through the Spirit the saint learns to pray with the Son: "Abba, Father." It is no coincidence that Balthasar uses familial language here. Prayer is the means through which the Spirit incorporates the sanctified into the family-love of Father and Son. The saints inhabit "all truth" through prayer, "which expresses the fact that we are admitted to this realm as children adopted by the Father."[75]

Nowhere is prayer more truthful, more metaphysical, and more epistemological than in the Eucharist. According to Balthasar, the Eucharist is the regular performance of the full drama of truth. In it heaven and earth meet in the form of Christ's mystical body. The truth of Christ is thus offered up to the Father by Christ, for whom the priest stands in, as sacrifice and as gift. This gift is received, and through it, the union of heaven and earth realized. The truth of Being is tasted on

---

73. Cf. Harrison, "*Homo Orans*," 285.
74. Ibid.
75. Ibid., 76. See also, Rom 8:15, 23; 9:4; Gal 4:5; Eph 1:5.

the tongue. This tasting yields understanding, *sapere* becomes *sapientia*, tasting becomes wisdom.[76] "To know much," Bonaventure once wrote, "and yet taste nothing—of what use is that?" Balthasar would agree.[77]

It may be easy at this point to see the connection between prayer and love in receptivity, surrender, and obedience. But what does prayer have to do with the mind, with understanding, with epistemology? What, in other words, is the difference between knowledge and love? The difference is that love is the perpetual source and goal of knowledge. Love as ground and end of knowledge is always the same—there is no difference in the *content*—but our human understanding of love grows, matures, and develops. We have to learn in order to understand. Through the increase of knowledge, our understanding of love infinitely deepens. We plunge further and further into the abyss of love's mystery from which our knowledge began in the first place. Human reason grows through its obedience to the call of love:

> Man is able, by his obedience, to make his mind a useful tool for the Holy Spirit; through obedience, pure contemplation guarantees the possibility of action, and only in this way can it be fully what God desires: something of benefit for all. . . . Man must pray until his mind is so seized by the Spirit that, like a twin sister, it follows the Spirit wherever it is required.[78]

Prayer surrenders the *entire* self, including the mind, in obedient receptivity to the Holy Spirit as the principle subject of knowledge. Prayer thus leads the mind as the proper form of the intellect. Contemplation is therefore the saintly form of knowledge. Like all knowledge, contemplation begins in wonder.[79] The drive to contemplate arises from the aesthetic shock that comes with the encounter with Being in its utter contingency and glorious non-necessity: "our astonishment at its 'being there' immediately moves on

---

76. See, Angel Mendez, O.P., *The Theology of Food: Eating and the Eucharist* (Oxford: Blackwell Publishing, 2009). See also, Pope Benedict XVI, *Jesus of Nazareth: Holy Week: From the Entrance into Jerusalem to the Resurrection*, trans. Libreria Editrice Vaticana (San Francisco: Ignatius Press, 2011), 152–62.
77. *Hexaem.*, XXIII, 21, quoted in *CM*, 52.
78. *TL* 3, 375–76.
79. *Prayer*, 156.

to our wonderment at it 'being thus.'"[80] We are overwhelmed by the beauty of existence and are thus drawn into the wonder and the love that fuel prayer.[81] Beauty is the saint's Virgil, bearing her forward from wonder to wonder toward divine vision. But only when beauty and wonder have handed themselves over to become love that the saint beholds the Love that moves the sun and the other stars.

Through his account of truth, Balthasar resets the epistemological playing field so that he can articulate a truly theological—a distinctively Catholic—way of knowing. The form of the saints is his way of doing this. The saints represent a way of truthfully being-in-the-world that fits the nature of Being: prayerfully, doxologically, and adoringly.[82] And so, for Balthasar, prayer is attunement [Gestimmtheit] to God, to Being.[83] The mind becomes "cosmoform"—that is, "Christoform." Prayer involves being in-formed by the archetype of all truth. Prayer is not simply a human act. It is Christ praying through the saint, insofar as the saint dwells in the life of Christ.[84] By surrendering to, and participating in, Christ's prayer, the saint is drawn into, and knows, the true heart of all things. For Balthasar, knowledge of truth

---

80. Ibid., 245.
81. This is the reason that Balthasar laments the loss of beauty from theology: for whoever is no longer enraptured by beauty, can no longer pray and will soon be unable to love. GL 1, 19.
82. Cf. Harrison, "Homo Orans," 292.
83. GL 1, 99: "This 'being attuned' means that man is encompassed and determined [that is, measured] by God. In so far as it passes over into consciousness, this state of being determined by God will then be seen to be a sensorium that perceives divine things, a living commerce between God and man, a real *spiritual equating* of the two, or a 'tuning' . . . This 'tuning' is . . . the living process whereby the tuner (der Bestimmende) and the tuned (der Bestimmte) are made equal. To be so tuned means, then, that the relationship of a thing to its element has been raised to the level of actuality and effectiveness. . . . So man has been tuned by God's breath to reflect and express the attunedness of matter and spirit, nature and God . . . All this reaches it perfection in the Christian revelation of the Trinity: 'The Father appears as the force that draws us, Christ as the medium, and the Spirit in us as God's very tuning of us itself.'" This, Balthasar claims, is one of the essential themes of all Catholic spirituality (100).
84. Here, we see Balthasar's dependence on the poetry of Charles Péguy whose art, Balthasar claims, flow more and more toward "prayer without one ever being able to say precisely whether this prayer is a dialogue or a monologue on God's part. It is a dialogue with God . . . but one which is constantly developing into a monologue of God the Father, addressed without distinction to his Son, to the men he has created and to himself. It is a form of 'theology as Trinitarian conversation' . . . which could only be risked by a poet using a simple and popular style of utterance that avoids any show of sublimity and yet does not for a moment degenerate into 'mateyness' and false familiarity. Only faith in the Holy Spirit can allow God to speak in such a way: in a meditation not only on the basic relationship of creation (analogia entis, of the ever-greater unlikeness of God in contrast to the world), but also on the basic relationship of the gospel and its analogia fidei—of the ever-greater unlikeness of the divine-human person of Jesus in contrast to sinners" (GL 3, 506).

comes by *being in* Truth, that is, Christ, through prayer, through the Spirit.

We must take care not to mistake Balthasar's point. Ignatius plays too formative a role in Balthasar's theology for us to think that prayer is primarily self-interested flight of the alone to the Alone. No, prayer and contemplative knowledge are missional. Contemplation is the saintly way of knowing *for the purpose of* sharing in Christ's mission of healing the world. In prayer, we see the saint in his "Janus-destiny: he is called to order and fashion the world according to his nature with its unity of body and soul; but at the same time he must look up to the God who is beyond the world, who he is to fear and love" and hand over (*tradere*) that shaped world to him.[85]

Contemplative knowledge is, for Balthasar, truly metaphysical, truly theological knowing. It means knowing the world through God and knowing God through the "sacred veils" of the world.[86] This contemplative knowing is the result of Christ who, "having dwelt among the forms of the world which are perceived by sense and intellect, returns to the Father, and in doing so he opens the real path of contemplation."[87] Contemplative prayer is the healing of Babel. Rather than attempting the ascent to God by our own means, we gratefully (that is, eucharistically) receive the *descending* God, who then *elevates* us—and the rest of creation—to the bosom of the Father. Thus, Idealism's goal of achieving absolute knowledge of Being is, in a sense, an appropriate impulse. This ascent, this union, is what humanity was created for. The downfall of Idealism is its titanism, its striving to achieve what can only be received.

Contemplation is not a purely "negative or apophatic mysticism which seeks to encounter God beyond the world."[88] Contemplation is *genuine* knowledge of truth as translated by Christ into "the multiplicity of time/space aspects, into the eloquent language of

---

85. *Prayer*, 265.
86. See Pseudo-Dionysius the Areopagite, *Cosmic Hierarchy*, 121D. See also Balthasar's account in *GL* 2, 173ff.
87. *Prayer*, 54.
88. Ibid.

human existence with its change, its growth, its strivings, undertakings, sufferings, its dying. . . ."[89]

For Balthasar, contemplation is the properly eschatological form of knowing because it sees and receives the world in its Christically transfigured reality. Contemplation sees the whole world "as co-creature, as a shared environment; it too becomes an object of prayerful contemplation."[90] Contemplation sees the form in the fragment; it beholds the flesh with the spiritual senses.[91] This is, again, a christological form of knowing. Christ is not, for Balthasar, an "isolated phenomenon," but the truth of all the world: "Just as he is inseparable from the world which he came to redeem, so the world cannot be separated from him in whom it 'subsists' and who thus provides its rationale."[92]

Prayer as Mission

Despite the possible reservation of some critics who think of prayer, and especially contemplative prayer, as detached from action in the world, Balthasar insists that saintly existence and the life of prayer are decidedly active. Unlike the ancient tradition that sees contemplation (*theoria*) as the apex of the Christian life, Balthasar sees it as its foundation. He derives this conclusion from Ignatius, especially the *Contemplation to Attain Love*. For Balthasar, the Son only *does* (acts) what

---

89. Ibid. And of course the task of the Pentecostal Spirit is to "gather all multiplicity into one" (*Prayer*, 74).
90. *Prayer*, 63.
91. Here again, we can see the influence of Ignatius on Balthasar's thought. In the *Exercises*, the participant is urged to sanctify the senses in order to contemplate the historical and divine action of Christ. For both Ignatius and Balthasar, divine truth is expressed *in* the world and *through* that world. This is why mystical theology is such an important concept for Balthasar. The mystical theologian understands divine truth precisely *in* the world, under the "sacred veils" that both reveal and hide the divine. Cf. *Prayer*, 266ff. Incidentally, the saints also serve as this kind of "sensible" and "intelligible" object of contemplation. Saints "forge the word of God in an intelligible form which the senses can grasp, so that the people of God, whether synagogue or Church, may hear it through them" (*Prayer*, 249). This is the objective dimension of Balthasar's theology of the saints to which the current project has not devoted much time. But we should not neglect to emphasize the importance of this objective dimension of the vocation of the saints, for it is through them that the truth of love is made known: "love alone is credible."
92. *Prayer*, 64.

he *sees* (contemplates) the Father doing (John 5:19). Action follows contemplation because contemplation commissions.

Prayer is the distinctively Catholic action that funds the mission of the saint—and thus, the Church—in the world. The mysteries probed by prayer are destined to be handed on to the world.[93] We must never "meditate on God's self-giving without recalling his self-giving to all ('the least of my brothers')."[94]

What, then, is this saintly mission in terms of truth as we have outlined it throughout this project? It is to join with the Spirit in the exposition of Christ's truth. The saints have a vocation to doxology, to glorifying God. But they also have a mission to the world: "To the extent that we who enjoy the peaceable grace of sonship, who have been addressed by the Word which is the Son, give the proper response of loving and living, we shall cause the whole creation to radiate with inner meaning . . . every creature will be given a share in the 'apocalyptic' (i.e., manifest) truth."[95] Contemplation receives and imparts meaning to the world, raising it to its true vocation to bear divine truth. Christian prayer includes the world in its meditation and contemplation and, by so doing, shares in the *raptus* of Christ and the Spirit that draws the world back to the Father. Prayer is the saints' performative sharing in the eschatological consummation of all things.

Balthasar insists that

> the Christian must not forget that the things of this world are also involved in the economy of salvation; they must not be thought of and dealt with in isolation from the truth of prayer. "For everything created by God is good, . . . it is consecrated by the word of God and prayer" (1 Tim 4:5). Therefore a prayerful contemplation of the sanctifying word is called for, so that we may be able to use God's good creatures according to his mind. And however much, in doing so, all our human powers come into play, our use of creatures must always be "of the truth" and "in the truth", in an attitude of prayer which has become habitual, an attitude of reverent worship of the divine truth, in which all the world's truth,

---

93. *CM*, 83.
94. Ibid., 85.
95. *Prayer*, 64. The "mysticism" of the saint's inner contemplation is "charismatic and missionary" (*Prayer*, 73).

even the most profane, is rooted. Hence the admonition to prayer without ceasing (1 Thess 5:25).[96]

Prayer is thus the "effective motivation for our own preoccupation with divine truth and with making it known to others."[97] It is the union of thought and will: "in 'thinking' about divine truth, [the believer] is inspired to further prayer, and . . . acts of the will (of surrender, of trust, of love)."[98] Prayer is the space in which knowledge of truth comes through the ecstasy of love, where the saint steps outside herself so as to be creatively receptive. The ecstasy implicit in the act of knowledge is here perfected in the ecstasy of prayer, the inspired act of saintly love. We find here Balthasar's reimagined epistemology of love.

This is the contemplative, prayerful mission of the saints. All creation groans, waiting for its fulfillment in the revelation of the sons of God (Rom 8:22). Perhaps these "sons of God" are the saints at prayer, who share in the mission of God to bring all creation back to its primal truth in the Trinity. Through her prayer, the saint conforms to truth, and her conformity makes her transparent to Truth's image. The saint is a living counterpart to Veronica's veil (the "true image"). Her life, her image becomes a knowable form through which the truth of God discloses itself. The saint's objective mission is thus to create in herself a dramatic space for the Trinity's theophany.[99]

Sainthood and Thought

We have seen how Balthasar frames the work of Christ and the Spirit in his *Theo-Logic* as re-establishing the possibility of analogical and participative knowledge. Such knowledge is possible, we know, within the descending truth of God in Christ. It falls to us now to articulate how the contemplative, prayerful form of the saints yields a distinctly Catholic way of thinking and understanding the mystery of Being.

We have so far considered the connection that Balthasar sees

---

96. *Prayer*, 80.
97. Ibid.
98. Ibid., 79.
99. This is what it means to say that the saint becomes "cosmoform" and "Christoform": she becomes transparent to God.

between love and knowledge. The ordering of these two is important, especially in light of his critique of Eckhart, for whom knowledge was more fundamental in God than love. But Balthasar re-establishes the ontological and theological priority of love over knowledge. One loves, and only thus does one know and understand the truth of the object known. Love unites subject and object, not confusing them, but holding them together in harmonious embrace.[100]

We must now turn to consider the two specific modes of saintly thought as Balthasar conceives them. The first is what we might call a "mystical theology," which is a way of reading the world in its relation to God. This is Balthasar's Ignatian way of seeing the world. The second is philosophical thought—the rational exploration of the logic of the world in its concrete existence.

The Saint as a Mystical, Ignatian Theologian

The saint is a mystical, or what Balthasar might call an "Ignatian" theologian, that is, a theologian of the mystery of divine truth that is revealed in and through the symbols of the world. She is the one who finds God in all things.[101] We have seen how Balthasar develops an account of truth in which mystery is not a problem to be solved, but rather the inner heart of truth. Mystical theology involves seeing a form (*Gestalt*) that results in the rapture of subject and object in the uprush of donation, receptivity, and love.

Such vision is the product of prayerful meditation. The *Spiritual Exercises* do not permit the direct contemplation of God, divorced from the world.[102] Instead, in meditation, the saints endeavor "to see the world through God's eyes . . . simultaneously in the alienation from God

---

100. Balthasar makes no attempt to dissolve the inner tension between subject and object, heaven and earth, Creator and creature. But he does reinterpret these tensions so that they are not conceived as dialectical antagonisms but symphonic harmonies—the beautiful balance and reciprocity of love. This is, in many ways, Balthasar's significant appropriation of Platonic cosmology. See Johnson, 23–24.
101. *CM*, 85ff.
102. Ibid., 30. Balthasar specifies that it is the work of the Spirit to make the infinite and invisible present in the finite and visible.

into which it attempts to flee and in its nearness to God through which God overtakes it in his work of mercy: the sending of his Son."[103]

The divinity of the invisible God radiates in and through all of the others forms in the world. This manifestation of the invisible in the visible is the *Herrlichkeit*, the glory of the Lord. For Balthasar, the relationship between the form of the Beautiful and earthly beauties is dialogical: Being manifests itself through visible forms which then respond by pointing *through themselves* back to Being.[104] This relationship is analogical because there is a non-identical proportion between the expressive forms of the world and the divine self-expression of the Son.

Nature as the intentional work of the Creator is intimately connected to that Creator; human existence, having been assumed in the incarnation, is intimately connected to the Son. This connection is always asymmetrical. The two forms are not mirror images of each other. Rather, "everything which is said of God—his divinity, his eternal might and glory, his power as Creator—consistently underscores the ever greater difference between him and creatures."[105] God and humanity do not stand on equal footing; man cannot peer over the wall of heaven on his own accord. Revelation must first *descend* to humanity. It is only by being open to the perception of Christ's form of revelation that humanity hopes to see the Reality hidden within the analogy. It is through the form of divine truth, beauty, and goodness in the world—especially as revealed in Christ—that the saint knows God. And it is by seeing the glory of God that the saint most truly knows the world.

The saints thus inhabit a sacramental world that is shot through with the glory of God. The saints know the world as the place of the eschatological in-breaking of the truth of God. Countering the cosmological and anthropological reductions of modernity, Balthasar posits that the saints live within the eschatological reduction that comes in the wake of Christ's ascension. The saint sees through worldly

---

103. *CM*, 85.
104. *Epilogue*, 55–57.
105. *GL* 1, 431.

Being to the divine *theologumena* undergirding it. It is the eschatological truth inaugurated by Christ and unveiled by the Spirit that renders the world transparent to the divine. This is how the saints know the truth of the world. The saint is the one who inhabits the world as we presented it at the end of chapter four:

> The mythical understanding of the world sees the whole world as a sacred theophany. In an eschatological sense, this is also what the world is for Christian faith. If the cosmos as a whole has been created in the image of God that appears—in the First-Born of creation, through him and for him—and if this First-Born indwells the world as its Head through the Church, then in the last analysis the world is a "body" of God, who represents and expresses himself in this body, on the basis of the principle not of pantheistic but of hypostatic union.[106]

As one who sees the world as a theophany, the saint is a mystical theologian.[107] She indwells the truth in such a way that her vision is elevated through the union of heaven and earth achieved by Christ and made accessible by the Spirit. The saint's understanding occurs *within* the perceived form of revelation.[108]

It is specifically from within the Christ-form that the saint trembles before the magnitude of the revelation of divine truth and is raptured upward into the presence of the Invisible God. The believer is enraptured when, "in a transcending manner, [she] abandons [herself] to the gravitational pull of its love for God (*amor pondus*), and, borne

---

106. Ibid., 679.
107. Mark A. McIntosh, *Christology from Within*, 63ff. See also Balthasar's account of Hopkins in *GL* 3, 390ff. Hopkins' poetry portrays the truth of the world, that "out of the glory of the Incarnate God there breaks forth the truest and most inward glory of forms both of natures and persons" (390). Indeed, "the mystery of God does not hold sway as something incomprehensible *behind* the forms of the world; rather, the divine Word was made flesh" (393). Hopkins, like Balthasar, emphasizes the mysterious of such a sacramental world: "Hopkins replied that mystery was not 'an interesting uncertainty' that held the mind only so long as one had not got to the bottom of it; he cited examples from the realm of the arts that prove that the delight—say of certain musical cadences—'is keenest when they are known and over'. . . . For an understanding of the way the mystery of God takes form in the world, the concept of the sacramental is at hand, which certainly contains within itself the power of the 'symbol', while it goes far beyond it; the form of the image is a likeness to the primordial form in that it has the 'stress' of the latter in itself: *sacramenta continent quae significant.* . . . The mystery of Christ is, on the one hand, of infinite depth, penetrating all the levels of being from flesh to spirit and beyond into the abyss of the Trinity; on the other, it is an infinitely dramatic event that in the kenotic descent into man and matter exalts and changes them, redeems and deifies them" (393–94).
108. *GL* 1, 151.

by God's grace, becomes perfected by the self-surrender to God of its loving faith."[109]

Here is Balthasar's form of a baptized Platonic mystical *eros*.[110] Following Pseudo-Dionysius, Balthasar argues that the Divine is drawn out of himself by *eros* for humanity into creation, revelation, and incarnation, and it is within the form of this revelation that the believer is enraptured, drawn like a magnet; human *eros* is drawn upwards by the descent of divine *eros*: "And the divine Eros also brings rapture, not allowing them that are touched by it to belong to themselves, but only to the objects of their love . . . not possessing a life of his own but the life of his Beloved. . . ."[111] The form of revelation that is perceived so enraptures the believer up into intimate union with God that it is no longer the believer's own life (this has been emptied through the kenosis of the self-will), but the life of God that dwells within him or her.[112] To use Balthasar's own construction: "The light of Being stems from the object, which, revealing itself to the subject, draws it out beyond itself (otherwise it would not be faith) into the sphere of the object."[113] The saint as a mystical theologian is shaped into the form of Jesus Christ, and as such, the saint understands the groundless mystery of the world as charged with the grandeur of God. She is drawn, through the world, to its source and goal in the divine life.[114]

The Saint as Philosopher

It would seem natural, in a theological project such as this, to limit

---

109. Ibid.
110. See Johnson, 23.
111. Ibid., 122.
112. "It is impossible to say where the natural perception of God in the world ceases and the supernatural, Christian perception begins, which presupposes a dogmatic knowledge. Faith is so deeply involved in flesh and blood (the Word indeed has become flesh), that the transfer of interpretation from sacramental signs to the indwelling grace of faith proceeds imperceptibly, ultimately indeed because the Christological . . . has been *understood* as the inner condition of the possibility of the whole natural order" (*GL* 3, 396–97).
113. Ibid., 181.
114. See, *GL* 3, 391: "His constant efforts and schooling in reading the forms of nature is therefore not 'aesthetic' in the usual sense nor 'mystical' nor one-sidedly 'exact and scientific,' but rather, it subsumes them all under the higher Christian law. It is, in a real sense, a 'learning to read'."

our understanding of the saints as lovers of God and as archetypal theologians. But were we to stop there, we would fail to capture one of the more controversial elements of Balthasar's theology of the saints. The saints' love does not make them theologians only; their love of God leads them into the love of wisdom. Saints are also philosophers.[115] This claim only makes sense given Balthasar's consistent emphasis that philosophy and theology both contemplate the mystery of Being. But herein lies Balthasar's controversial claim: the saints are philosophers only because they are first theologians. If *Theo-Logic* 1 insisted that without philosophy there could be no theology, Balthasar now adds that without theology, there can be no philosophy.[116]

What accounts for this difference? Simply this: philosophy does, to a certain extent, "prepare the way" for theology, just as John prepared the way for Christ. But even then, Christ also prepared the way for John, as we see when John proclaims Christ the one who "comes after me because he was before me" (John 1:30). By extension, theology is the condition of the possibility of philosophy. More precisely, it is the *subject* of theology, that is, God himself, that is the possibility of both theological and philosophical knowledge. Only by understanding the world *in relation to God*—theologically—does philosophy adequately apprehend truth. Balthasar, echoing Justin Martyr, insists that theology is the "true philosophy." For Balthasar, theology *is* the person of Christ, the primal "Word about God," and therefore, the Wisdom of creation (Prov 8:22).

> Because philosophy does not possess Christ, it cannot provide the final *resolutio* which would bring us to the true origins, or at most it can do so *semiplene*. Only one who knows the trinitarian mystery is a "true metaphysician", only one who knows Christ has the true *ethics generalis*. . . . On the other hand, whoever loves the Christian revelation loves philosophy also, through which he confirms the faith; but philosophy in

---

115. Balthasar cites Bonaventure at this point: "There is no secure passage from learning to wisdom—one must go through an intermediary, namely, holiness" (*GL* 2, 277). Holiness is necessary for growth in wisdom. Such a claim is grounded in Christ's identity as both the Holy One of Israel and the Wisdom of God.

116. *TL* 1, 29. Cf. Hans Urs von Balthasar, "On the Task of Catholic Philosophy in our Time," *Communio* vol. 20, no. 2 (1993): 154.

itself is the tree of the knowledge of good and evil—it remains ambivalent until it is polarized through true (that is to say, existential) theology.[117]

Both saint and philosopher are concerned with knowing and expressing the truth of Being, though, arguably, from different perspectives.[118] Because the saints know this truth intimately, at least in its divine dimension, they are necessarily connected to philosophy. Balthasar's own *discours de la méthode* on this point comes in his essay "On the Task of Catholic Philosophy in Our Time," in which he works out the relation between philosophy and theology and concludes that it is only the saint who can be a true philosopher in the fullest sense: a lover of wisdom, that is, Christ.[119]

He begins his exposition of philosophy by rooting the general relation of philosophy and theology in the ongoing debate on the relation between nature and grace.[120] As a creature, the human is a part of the world, and therefore subordinate to the laws of creation and of reason. Man thus may be a philosopher who studies the immanent logic of the world. But, like grace, divine truth is immanently present, through the Spirit, within this world, drawing the world to transcend

---

117. *GL* 2, 278.
118. At least, this is Balthasar's understanding of philosophy. He probably would not recognize the non-speculative, analytic thrust of Anglo-America philosophy as being genuinely philosophical. For Balthasar, philosophy is the speculative study of Being and existence. He would probably offer an exasperated sigh along with Blessed Pope John Paul II who, in his *Fides et Ratio*, bemoaned modern philosophy's "lack of confidence in reason." Cf. Balthasar's indictment of modern philosophy: "The result is that philosophy and theology lead increasingly separate lives. Philosophy dispenses with any sort of transcendence and, entrenched in the intra-worldly, quickly abandons all talk of undecodeable 'ciphers' or of 'shepherding being,' and contents itself more and more with varieties of a positivism à la Comte that dead-ends in sterile forms of functionalism, logicism, and linguistic analysis lacking any trace of truth as a transcendental property of Being" (*TL* 1, 14).
119. See Adrian Walker, "On 'Rephilosophizing' Theology," *Communio*, vol. 31, no. 1 (2004): 143–67. See especially Walker's insistence that "precisely in order to think with the 'mind' of Christ, the theologian has to assume the guardianship of human wonder—to enter into it, remain in it, and cultivate it" (143).
120. Vatican I granted the natural order and its areas of knowledge an autonomy in its attempt to offer a clear distinction between the order of nature and the order of grace: *duplex ordo cognitionis proprio objecto, propria methodo.* But this autonomy may be misinterpreted as placing Church authority and secular wisdom on an equal playing field where man must adjudicate between them: the anthropological totality in which divine revelation functions as partial element only (ibid., 148). Christianity cannot accept this kind of subordination (either of grace to nature or theology to philosophy): "Even if nature has its own regular laws and reason its own evidential character, still these laws and evidential character can never appear as a final authority over against grace and faith. Their autonomies remain relative and stand as such always at the disposal of the final authority which belongs to the divine revelation, and to its plans and directives" (149).

itself and come under the rule of Christ. Catholic philosophy must mediate between these two truths by being "*in* the world but not *of* the world" (John 17:16).

Balthasar identifies two unsatisfactory ways philosophy often attempts to overcome this dilemma. The first attempts an easy synthesis through the reckless adoption of secular philosophy (or its presuppositions). Balthasar sees this attitude at work in much of the Catholic fascination with German Idealism in his day. The second is an ahistorical extrinsicism that hides within the dusty corridors of repristinated medieval thought, as Balthasar saw among the neo-scholastics. Neither of these alternatives yields a satisfactorily Catholic philosophy. A truly Catholic philosophy exists within the structures of worldly logic while, at the same time, transcending them by opening them to the One who surpasses them because he was before them. Genuine philosophy does not occur outside of Christ, his cross and resurrection. These events cast their long shadow both forward and backward over the history of philosophy, bursting open its immanent logical seams that it may bear even a hint of that divine logic that is the truth of the world.

According to Balthasar, both philosophy and theology have the same formal object, namely, the mystery of Being. Yet even their material objects end up overlapping. "But if philosophy primarily contemplates the Being of this world, in order to press forward from this to the boundary of absolute Being as *principium et finis*, while theology primarily begins with God's self-utterance in the Logos—the two materially overlap. Supernatural light must necessarily also send its rays over onto the light of reason."[121] But disciplinary isolationism between "philosophy" and "theology" is not an option for Balthasar. The two confront each other and, through that confrontation, come into their own. Theology *theologizes* philosophy in order to make it more truly itself, analogous to the way Christ reveals truth to itself.

This confrontation has both a negative and a positive aspect. Put negatively, no truth that opposes the light of faith can be true on the

---

121. "On the Task," 151.

level of reason either. While philosophy and worldly Being do have *relative* autonomy from the supernatural, Balthasar is clear that there are not two different truths, nor two different schemas of truth.[122] But he does not dwell on this negative aspect for long. He focuses instead on the positive aspect of this confrontation, which is that "a reason which is illuminated by faith is able to know things of the natural world which a reason lacking this light—indeed, a reason deprived of this light by sin and weakened and obscured in itself—will necessarily overlook, or will recognize only in a disfigured form."[123] Whether disfigured or fragmented, Balthasar is clear that philosophy's understanding of Being needs theology in order for it to come to a fuller apprehension of truth. When studied in its concreteness, an account of Being cannot remain exclusively or immanently philosophical. It

> cannot in the least be separated from the reality of revelation—viz. of the grace which has gone out into nature and of the faith which has been given to reason and has been demanded by reason—only this perspective demonstrates the total interweaving of both spheres and justifies speaking of Catholic philosophy. In the light of faith, both a pure nature and a pure reason appear as abstractions which indeed need not be false as such, but which lack any corresponding detached and separate reality in the concrete world-order.[124]

In light of the preceding, we may say that Balthasar believes that *all* philosophy is potentially a *theo-logic*. It is the task of a Catholic philosophy to spoil the Egyptians, to recognize non-Christian philosophical achievements in understanding truth as *veiled* theology. This spoiling of Egyptians involves breaking open foreign forms of

---

122. Balthasar resists all forms of the infamous "two-tier" scheme of the relationship between God and world, nature and grace, theology and philosophy. This also evokes the thirteenth-century debate regarding the so-called radical Aristotelians—such as Siger of Brabant and Boethius of Dacia—and their belief in a theory of "double truth." See above for our summary of Balthasar's critique of this debate.
123. "On the Task," 151. Theology, Balthasar insists, sees the whole in the fragment. This is part and parcel of theology's uniquely aesthetic vocation to see the form that contemplates and interprets the fragments of truth that philosophy articulates. Philosophy, on the contrary, focuses quite intently on the fragment, because understanding that fragment of Being—the rational world—is philosophy's particular vocation.
124. "On the Task," 151.

thought, and theologically transposing their elements.[125] The Catholic philosopher, especially the saintly one, accomplishes this dual task through her christological hermeneutic of worldly truth.[126]

Infinite truth has been made worldly in Jesus Christ. Truth can no longer be considered an ungraspable transcendental. It is now something attainable, yet always surpassing human mind. Christ, the incarnate *Theologic*, descends on worldly logic, penetrating it to its core, making himself present within it in a way that no philosophy can anticipate.[127] Moreover, the *Logos* reveals worldly logic to itself:

> [Learn] to locate the essence of truth in general in this unique mystery of the love between the Father and the Son in the Holy Spirit, and one is able now to see all other truth as only a reflection of this innermost kernel of truth—then one will also have grasped that, just as the archetype of the revealed truth, the Son, is true because he eternally opens himself to the infinite Father, then *a fortiori* all the finite truth of this world can establish itself as truth only by opening onto the mystery of God.[128]

A genuinely Catholic philosophy focuses on the rational study of Being, but, just as created Being participates in divine love, so too does worldly logic participate in supernatural truth (the *Logos*), mirroring his absolute and eternal openness and receptivity. The logic that is the divine *Logos* opens worldly logic from created schools of thought that contradict and exclude each other. A distinctively Catholic theology is a gathering together of all things in, around, and for Christ.

For Balthasar, this gathering together is not syncretism or Hegelian synthesis. A genuinely Catholic philosophy does not attempt an artificial stitching together of various incompatible ideas. It attempts, instead, their harmonization through a theological, or more specifically christological and pneumatological, transposition: "[T]hey

---

125. Ibid., 154.
126. "If he is truly a Christian thinker, there is no other conclusive meaning which he can give to his thinking [than the truth of Christ]. But this produces in him a quite specific awareness of the truth. As a believer, he knows the word of the Lord, in which he calls himself the truth. He is the infinite truth as God, in his unity with the Father in the Holy Spirit; but in him, this infinite truth has appeared in the form of finite, worldly truth" ("On the Task," 154).
127. We will recall that, for Balthasar, *die unvordekliche der Liebe*: "love cannot be anticipated by thought."
128. "On the Task," 157.

[Catholic philosophers] are so deeply convinced of the all-embracing authority of Christ not only over all creatures in heaven, on earth, and under the earth, but also over all the forms of creaturely truth, that they cannot rest until they have brought all these forms into the service of the one truth."[129] This christological transposition, conducted through the creative agency of the saintly philosopher, is effected by the pentecostal Spirit that makes all words a single Word. Drawn by the Holy Spirit, "the true Christian thinker will discern and probe everywhere in order to test everything and to be able to retain what is good."[130]

The spiritual dimension of this philosophical transposition demands a particular intellectual disposition:

> [E]verything depends here on the disposition in which the synthesis is made: if the knowledge of the absoluteness of the truth of Christ stands at the abiding origin of such thought, and if the decision for him has been made with the entire purity of a loving soul, then it is legitimate and safe to adopt the intellectual mission to go out into all the world and to take captive all truth for Christ. "Test *everything* and retain what is good!" But "do not conform yourselves to the spirit of the world."[131]

The philosopher must spoil the Egyptians, but in a distinctively Catholic way.

Balthasar concludes that the one who wants to accomplish this transposition, this genuinely Catholic philosophy, must be a saint: "Thus the one who submits himself to this task ought to be a saint; and all the great figures who succeeded in the task were saints."[132] It is the saint who practices the discernment of spirits that can best perceive the potential (that is, openness) of any philosophy to become *theologic*.

We have seen that Balthasar is concerned that all speculation, whether philosophical or theological, focuses on the concrete world as it *actually* is. This means that all genuine philosophizing is done from

129. Ibid., 158.
130. Ibid., 162.
131. Ibid., 158.
132. Ibid., 159. We should note the Ignatian overtones of this passage. Balthasar adopts quite explicitly the Jesuit emphasis on the "discernment of spirits" for his project. Discernment is both a philosophical and theological task.

within the dynamic of the God–world relation, within the living *theo-logic* of the Trinity, Emmanuel, God-with-us.

Within this framework, the lives of the saints—their spirituality, their prayer, their contemplative affections—serve as the proper form of speculative knowledge. In other words, the saint acts as a modality of knowledge, of the apprehension of the truth of God found in the truth of the world. Holy *eros*, the longing for the Holy One, funds the love of wisdom.[133] This erotic holiness remains dissatisfied with any purely natural—*penultimate*—truth. Philosophical *eros* is discontent with worldly truth because it is a love that is fundamentally oriented to that which is ultimate. The saint is the one who also lives toward this ultimate truth, driven by her love to receive that which is the fulfillment of her soul. "Wherever Catholic philosophy is alive, the *eros* of thought propels it outward, over the penultimate sphere of the objects of philosophical thought, into the sphere of the personal divine *Logos*."[134] Even philosophy takes on a contemplative openness before God in love.

Love Itself is Understanding

And so, in conclusion, we return again to Balthasar's post-conciliar concern for the "distinctively Catholic." Balthasar saw the Church's *aggiornamento* and Rahner's "anonymous Christianity" as a capitulation to prevailing forms of intellectual culture that are deadly to the identity of Catholicism. Balthasar calls the Church to martyrdom, to become the saintly figures that will guide, enliven, and nourish the Church in the modern world. This enlivened Church in turn offers itself to the world, passing on the truth, beauty and goodness of the love that gives—and *is*—meaning to all things.

It is the prayer of the saints that feeds the Church's own meditation on revelation. The saints enlarge the side chapels of the Church, conforming her from within to the truth of Christ and thus funding her mission to the world. The Church of the saints is "God's instrument for

---

133. "On the Task," 152. For Balthasar, this *eros* is held in common by both philosophy and theology.
134. Ibid., 154.

the whole of his . . . creation."[135] This ecclesial mission of truth and love is the missional payoff of Balthasar's Ignatian theology of the saints.

As we have seen, Balthasar's account of truth cannot be separated from his concern over the separation of philosophy, theology, and spirituality, or the intellectual (philosopher and theologian) and the saint. For Balthasar, a faithful account of truth requires their reintegration. The intellectual, whether she be theologian or philosopher, if she wants to understand the heart of Being, must be holy. Her thought and her action must be adequated to that which she endeavors to know. She must be receptive and loving. She must be a saint.[136] To know that the truth is love, that Being is co-extensive with love, she must know as a lover knows, through union and conformity with what is known. And so, the saint knows the infinite mystery of divine love by contemplating, adoring in the Church, and hymning in the world.

Let us, by way of summary and conclusion, return to Ignatius and the *Spiritual Exercises*. The *Exercises* conclude with *The Contemplation to Attain Love*. This prayer holds together Balthasar's double-emphasis on contemplation (knowledge) and mission (service). Contemplation exposits Balthasar's metaphysics. This contemplation yields understanding by attuning the one at prayer to the nature of Being as dialogical receptivity, obedient participation, and love. Through the receptive dialogue of her contemplation, the saint performs metaphysical truth.

The Contemplation begins by seeing all of creation as the gift of divine surrender and as "God's intention to communicate himself to the utmost."[137] The sheer givenness of things discloses the reality of God as the "Father of lights" who gives freely from his divine plentitude. From this meditation, the one at prayer comes to see that "anyone who receives the gifts of being freed into existence and of being

---

135. *CM*, 83.

136. Again, this does not mean to imply that there is no knowledge available to anyone other than the saint. It simply means that the saints have a privileged grasp on truth in virtue of their conformity and participation with Christ.

137. *CM*, 88.

accompanied by God will in turn place his own creaturely space at God's disposal."[138] Just as the word "creation" means the creative receptivity of God's kenotic act of creating, so too is the one at prayer open in receptive surrender to God. From this, she sees "that everything created and released into its uniqueness can never dwell anywhere except in God."[139] To know truth is to know all Being as freely sheltered in the love of God. This love is, we have seen, the eternal dialogue of the Trinity; it is this dialogue of surrender, gift, receptivity, and love that we enter through the grace of the Spirit.

The result of *The Contemplation* as Balthasar articulates it is a metaphysical and theological understanding of created Being: "[i]n meditation we are to learn to see the existence of the world and all its values as something emanating from the origin, 'just as rays descend from the sun and water from its source.'"[140] What is attained through the world is God himself. But Balthasar makes a critical move in his interpretation of *The Contemplation* that safeguards this claim from being absorbed into the philosophical titanism of Idealism. The creature's yearning for God, he insists, rejects the temptation of a titanic will-to-power. She wills instead to surrender. This signals Balthasar's *agapeic* transformation of Platonic *eros*. The saints' knowledge comes in the surrender that allows God to grasp and enrapture them. The saint is "stamped with God's way of loving,"[141] and so, she offers up her intellectual *eros*, her human desire to know all things, in obedience through her contemplative, prayerful surrender. She chooses to receive truth, and by doing so enacts the truth of Being that gives and receives in love. This is what it means to say with Balthasar that love itself is understanding.

138. Ibid., 89.
139. Ibid.
140. Ibid., 92.
141. Ibid., 93.

8

Saintly Styles: A Case Study on Adrienne von Speyr

Despite the depth and complexity of Balthasar's *Theo-Logic* and the theology of the saints attendant to it, it remains incomplete. Balthasar's *Theo-Logic* gives his readers a mystagogical journey into the phenomenological, christological, and pneumatological dimensions of truth and knowledge. All of this reinforces the central thesis of the *Theo-Logic* that Being, truth, and love are co-extensive, and are revealed objectively as such in Jesus Christ, and known subjectively by the saints through the Holy Spirit.

Yet a significant problem remains. Balthasar's saints do not pray. Though presented as lovers of God, as partakers in the divine nature, as those who know by loving, Balthasar fails to offer a concrete model of his theology of the saints and its attendant epistemology of love, because he dedicates little time in the *Theo-Logic* to prayer. If knowledge and love, and therefore logic, arise from *dialogue*, then the absence of the archetypal dialogue of prayer is scandalous indeed. This penultimate chapter shall develop this critique further and identify resources in Balthasar's wider *oeuvre* to address this deficiency in his *Theo-Logic.*

Critiques of Balthasar

Though Balthasar's *Theo-Logic* works in accord with his theology of the saints to counter the titanic epistemologies of German Idealism, especially that of Hegel, Balthasar himself could be criticized as relying on an overly idealized metaphysic. That is to say, despite Balthasar's insistence on knowledge grounded in love as a particular form of life and action, his saints are primarily portrayed as *thinkers,* rather than as people in service and prayer. Karen Kilby recently leveled the accusation that Balthasar's theology falls into a Hegelian scheme, despite all of Balthasar's protestations to the contrary. While there may be some validity to Kilby's criticism, this chapter will show how there are nevertheless resources within Balthasar that can help address these problems.

We must admit that there is a notable *lacuna* in Balthasar's work at precisely this point, as noted above. A consideration of the actual *lives* of the saints is rare in his work. Balthasar's writing on the saints tends toward the systematic and intellectual far more than historical, existential, or even hagiographic.[1] Part of this problem is simply due to the limitations of the genre of Balthasar's writing, but since Balthasar styles himself as an agent for reintegrating saintly thought and life, his disproportionate favor toward the intellectual deserves critique. What Balthasar primarily draws from the saints is their theological insight, their teaching about God and the world. Reference to their actual lives seems too infrequent for us to validate Balthasar's claim to be writing kneeling theology.

It is this *lacuna* that gives Kilby the opportunity to critique

---

1. Contrast his books on Maximus Confessor and Gregory of Nyssa (or indeed any of his extended essays in the second and third volumes of *Glory of the Lord*) with his *Two Sisters in the Spirit* and, more controversially, his study of Adrienne von Speyr. Kilby suggests that Balthasar's "Theology and Sanctity" may have been written more as an *apologia* for his use of Speyr's mystical insight than as a programmatic call for a return to the saints more generally. See, Kilby, 157–60. To be fair, after raising the claim for three pages, Kilby does temper her accusation by admitting in a single line that this may not be the most charitable reading of Balthasar's intentions.

Balthasar's attempted reunion of theology and spirituality through the saints. We shall give a brief account of Kilby's critique, highlighting her three central criticisms: 1) Balthasar's conflation of "sanctity" and "spirituality"; 2) his "all seeing eye" into the inner lives of the saints; and 3) the failure of Balthasar's theology to be properly "prayerful." We should note from the outset that Kilby offers an important and penetrating critique on this point of Balthasar's work. Balthasar's *Theo-Logic* does fail to make room for the type of prayerful theology he calls for.[2] But as we shall show, he does provide resources for accomplishing the very thing at which he fails. But before we get there, we will consider Kilby's critique of the deficiency of Balthasar's "kneeling theology."[3]

Kilby's criticism of Balthasar's spirituality focuses on the essay "Theology and Sanctity." Kilby points out what she deems to be a problematic conflation in Balthasar's essay, namely, that he begins with an emphasis on "sanctity"—on the holiness of life—and then, abruptly shifts to calling for a reunification of "theology" (considered as a theoretical, dogmatic endeavor) and "spirituality" (which Kilby defines as "reflection on the nature of the Christian life").[4] She accuses Balthasar of reifying theology and spirituality, and then shifting focus from the actual life of the saint to a focus on that saint's *thought.*

Which is it, then? Is Balthasar calling for the reunification of the holiness of *life* for proper theologizing, or is he focusing, instead, on the content of saintly writings? Kilby suggests that Balthasar is calling more for a reintegration of dogmatic and spiritual *content* in

---

2. This is especially ironic—not to mention problematic—considering that his "Theology and Sanctity" is written in response to the negative consequences of the separation between theology and spirituality for Christian *truth*. One would expect his systematic treatment of truth in his *Theo-Logic* to give more space to prayer, the central action of saintly, even human, existence.

3. Kilby's book, by and large, fails to give a thorough and sustainable critique, especially because of its neglect of certain sections of Balthasar's thought—the *Theo-Logic* is entirely missing from her account. Kilby, then, does not make a good critique of Balthasar *in general* but a few of her criticisms, especially those noted below, do land. But even those criticisms that are valid do not, I think, fundamentally undermine the integrity of Balthasar's project. Balthasar's corpus is finite—though it often appears otherwise!—and he was not able to bring all of the diverse threads together. But Balthasar leaves behind a vast reservoir of resources for those who wish to take up his incomplete project and contribute to his theological and priestly legacy. It is one significant region of this reservoir that we shall consider in conclusion of this project.

4. See Kilby, 153.

contemporary theology. Perhaps he is gesturing to himself or to Adrienne von Speyr, justifying and endorsing their theological project. Both, after all, wrote both dogmatic *and* spiritual works throughout their lives.[5] Even if not, Kilby insists that Balthasar's programmatic essay ends up getting lost in flights of abstraction (even *spiritual* abstraction), rather than being properly grounded in the concrete lives and practices of the saints.

The problem with the easy separation that Kilby suggests here is that this kind of division between form and content is anathema to Balthasar. His idea of a theology of the saints cannot be reduced to a theology that talks about the kind of topics that the saints are interested in, as if "metaphysics" was meant only for dogmaticians and "prayer" only for saints. No, despite the messiness of such a claim, we must acknowledge that Balthasar posits the saints as both the form and the content of genuine theology. A proper theology of the saints will draw together all the dimensions of truth—philosophical, theological, *and* spiritual. A theology of the saints is at least meant to be a metaphysical, aesthetic, and epistemological approach to truth: a way of seeing and knowing by *being* a particular way.

This takes us to Kilby's second concern: what authority enables Balthasar to define the proper disposition of the saints? According to Kilby, Balthasar "makes some rather broad and confident assertions about the attitude of 'the saints.'"[6] Kilby is correct. Balthasar has a clear and definite vision of what saintly existence is like. He summarizes it in "Theology and Sanctity":

> The saints have always been on guard against such an attitude [of abstraction from historical revelation], and immersed themselves in the actual circumstances of the events of revelation. They desired to be present, when and where each thing happened. With Mary they sit at the

---

5. Kilby even notes that "quite serious difficulties" would emerge if we were to take Balthasar's first claim seriously: "One might want to ask questions, for instance, about factors that have contributed at one period or another to the Church's official recognition of saints; one might want to ask in particular whether some of the great patristic theologians were in fact *anything but* edifying exemplars of the Christian life; one might wonder whether Balthasar's language of the saints living what they taught so 'directly' and 'naively' is not suggestive of a degree of romanticizing nostalgia" (154n11).

6. Kilby, 157.

feet of Jesus, hearing from his own mouth the words of revelation. They want to know what the Lord says to them, and nothing else. They do not want to stop listening, not for a single moment, to what is being revealed . . . their dealings are with God and him exclusively. Everything, even what they know already, they wish to hear from him, as if they had never heard it before. They wish to have the world explained anew, interpreted afresh, in the light of revelation. . . . They are almost fanatically exclusivists, for they see this approach as the surest way to the universality and catholicity of the truth. They are not perturbed about how to reconcile the supernatural and natural orders, faith and reason, the secular and the ecclesiastical spheres, for they know that those whose standpoint is firmly fixed in Christ are relieved of concern for these.[7]

Balthasar is explicit: *this* is what a saint is. But where does Balthasar derive this penetrating insight into the inner (and universal) disposition of the saints? Kilby considers two possibilities. Balthasar may be generalizing and extrapolating from the saints' own public description of their experiences. Kilby quickly dismisses this possibility.[8] She prefers, instead, to see Balthasar as uncritically relying on the mystical insight of Adrienne von Speyr. According to Balthasar's hagiographic account of Speyr, one of her charisms was "insight into the prayer life of numerous saints."[9] She could "put herself in the place of individual saints or other faithful in order to see and describe their prayer, their whole attitude before God, from this interior viewpoint."[10] Kilby suggests that Balthasar's "all seeing eye" into the inner dispositions of the saints is derived from Speyr's mystically received revelation.

Kilby's suspicion here touches on the larger problem of Balthasar's theological relationship to Adrienne von Speyr.[11] There is certainly

7. Quoted in Kilby, 158.
8. "In this case one might feel there is a certain intellectual sloppiness involved. Balthasar makes broad generalizations, offers few examples, and writes with a kind of incautious directness about the dispositions, feelings, and inner attitudes of the saints that one would never find in a historian" (158). Balthasar himself also rejected in no uncertain the psychological study of the "inner states" of mystical experiences and dispositions in "Understanding Christian Mysticism," in *ET* 4, 330.
9. Hans Urs von Balthasar, *First Glance at Adrienne von Speyr*, trans. Antje Lawry and Sr. Sergia Englund, O.C.D. (San Francisco: Ignatius Press, 1981), 72. Cf. Adrienne von Speyr, *The Book of All Saints* (San Francisco: Ignatius Press, 2008).
10. Ibid. Also quoted in Kilby, 158.
11. On this relatively unexplored topic, see Matthew Lewis Sutton, "Hans Urs von Balthasar and Adrienne von Speyr's Ecclesial Relationship," *New Blackfriars*, vol. 94 (2012): 50–63.

room to question the integrity of Balthasar's reliance on her, especially for such central doctrinal *loci* as Holy Saturday and eschatology, both of which are significantly informed (if not outright determined) by Speyr's mystical thought. But Kilby neglects a less controversial, not to mention far more plausible, source for Balthasar's definition of saintly disposition: his own spiritual master, Ignatius of Loyola. As described at the beginning of this project, Ignatius provides the essential grammar of Balthasarian spirituality. It is primarily from Ignatius that Balthasar derives his emphasis on receptivity and obedience. Perhaps, then, we can understand Speyr's mystical insight into the inner lives of the saints as situated within the larger context of Balthasar's Ignatian spirituality. If we take it thus, we may say that Speyr's revelations serve as a kind of "experiential confirmation" of what Ignatius himself had taught about the nature of holiness.[12] Going even further, we can refer back to Balthasar's interpretation of the life of Christ as exemplifying just this disposition of the saints. Insofar as the saints are related back to Christ through the indwelling of the Spirit, their disposition is going to be the same as Christ. Indeed, how could the saints behave in a way other than according to the way of Christ? A saint whose disposition was not identical to that of Jesus Christ would not be a saint at all. The Christ that emerges in the *Spiritual Exercises*, spiritually and existentially confirmed by Speyr, is the most plausible source of Balthasar's insight into the nature of sainthood.

We might say that Kilby, though she is right to be concerned over some aspects of Balthasar's agenda in "Theology and Sancity," ends up asking the wrong question. She asks, "Which saints?" as if Balthasar were attempting historical expositions of *this* saint *or* that one. But Kilby is stuck on a purely canonical definition of sainthood. Canonical saints are not Balthasar's primary concern. And so the better question to ask of Balthasar is "How do *we* perform the theological task *as* saints?"[13] Balthasar is far less concerned with expositing the lives of

---

12. There are still a number of problems even with this way of understanding Speyr, as I will address at the conclusion of this chapter.

13. Rather than venerating the saints as Kilby seems to expect (and which an "ordinary" believer might be tempted to use as a way of avoiding her own call to holiness), Balthasar wants Christians

specific saints and far more with expositing *saintly existence* as such, insofar as it participates in the life of Christ. "Sainthood" is a *way of being*. Of course, the canonized saints of the Church are examples of the mode of being that Balthasar champions. But their very exemplarism presupposes the existence of a multitude of reflective images scattered throughout the world. For Balthasar, a saint is the one who loves God as Christ did, that is, with a radical, dis-possessive obedience to the mission of knowing and expressing truth. His theology of the saints is decidedly *not* a theology based in a historical account of the saints as Kilby seems to expect. It is, rather, a *drama* of the saints. Balthasar develops his account of the saintly form as an invitation to his readers to participate *in* that form. His concern is less that of a historian and more of a priestly theologian; he desires to develop a theology that draws his readers themselves into the divine reality the saints express. Saintliness is a vocation, a calling. It is a way of being that is open to all those who follow Christ.

But if saintliness is indeed an ontological way of being, then a theology of the saints will be metaphysical. What does this mean for the existential dimension of saintliness? Has Balthasar abstracted from the concrete lives of the saints a metaphysical or epistemological principle? Perhaps Balthasar has left the historical embodiment of truth behind in favor of an Idealist metaphysic in which the saints function merely as an instrument of epistemology.[14] This is Kilby's final

to *join* with the saints: "If we were to venerate this mystery [of the bridal union between God and humanity], the saints would have no objection, so to speak, to being venerated or honored. We would join them in gazing at the point that fascinates them, the point toward which, in self-forgetfulness, they transcend themselves. Far more is at stake here than feeling safe and protected by a powerful helper and advocate, feeling gratitude that the saint exists and admiration at his generosity: what is at issue here is the indivisibly theandric nature of the world, of which Christ is the radiant hub and the saints are those dedicated to him. Only in some such way as this can the veneration of ikons be justified: they refer not so much to the person depicted—Christ, angels, Mary, saints—as to the mystery that includes us, portrayed thus in archetypal situations and events. We look on from the periphery in veneration and lovingly draw near to them in prayer. For the rest, as far as the venerated saints themselves are concerned, we need not be surprised if they treat us with a certain element of humor. They will make light of the inevitable misunderstandings and, when we eventually see them face to face, refer us to the *Soli Deo Gloria*" (Hans Urs von Balthasar, *In the Fullness of Faith: On the Centrality of the Distinctively Catholic*, trans. Graham Harrison [San Francisco, Ignatius Press, 1988], 89).

14. The preceding should have alleviated a bit of the thrust of this final critique. If Balthasar is presenting a saintly way of being as an invitation to us to be, to know, and to understand *as* saints, then there is, of course, a necessary degree of abstraction and simplification that must attend

concern. For all of Balthasar's talk of writing a "kneeling theology" rather than a "theology at desk," she says it is "rare to find in Balthasar anything of the questing, wrestling, dialogical style of the classic works of theology in prayer of an Augustine or Anselm."[15]

Certainly, Kilby is correct. Balthasar's works are not dialogical in their form or exposition in the same way as Augustine's *Confessions* or Anselm's *Proslogion*.[16] Kilby goes on to say that the attitude we find in Balthasar's work is less that of one at prayer and more of that of a spiritual director, "speaking intimately, directly, confidently to his audience, working to bring them to the point of breaking down their barriers, of becoming open afresh to the gospel. Leading retreats seems in fact to have been a, if not the, staple activity of Balthasar's priestly ministry, and it is not hard to hear in some at least of his writings an extension of his activity."[17] Prayer, Kilby argues, is fundamentally an ongoing dialogue between God and humanity. If this is true, then the fact that Balthasar's style is (allegedly) that of a speculative monologue, then of course we cannot call his a theology at prayer.

Kilby's critique on this point is sound, although she perhaps does not make it as strongly as she should. Balthasar would agree with her thesis that prayer is dialogue. Indeed, as we have seen, dialogue

this. But this abstraction and simplification does not mean that he is reducing saintliness to a principle. Again, *Gestalt* is a central concept here. The historical and existential particularities of individual saints are images and reflections of a more general *Gestalt*. Balthasar would be surprised at being accused of imposing the centrality of receptivity, obedience, and surrender on the saints. He would, I believe, argue that this Ignatian interpretation of the saints is general enough to include all particularities of individual saints' lives.

15. Kilby, 160. Kilby points to Rahner's *Encounters with Silence* as embodying the dialogical characteristics of a kneeling theology that Balthasar's work lacks. Balthasar's theology is suspect for Kilby because it says too much and isn't properly agnostic. This is where Kilby's failure to engage Balthasar's *Theo-Logic* is especially problematic. For it is indeed in his account of truth that Balthasar develops his christological apophatic theology, derived from the silence of Christ before Pilate (cf. *TL* 2, 90ff).

16. The exception to this general statement would be Balthasar's grand theological hymn, *The Heart of the World*, a text noticeably absent from Kilby's critique. Andrew Louth makes a compelling case that *Heart of the World* plays a central role in the Balthasarian corpus in his "The Place of *The Heart of the World* in Balthasar's Writing" in *Analogy of Beauty*, ed. John Riches (London: T&T Clark 1986). In fact, one could make a fairly compelling case that all of Balthasar's subsequent dogmatic work is a working out of the theology prayed and sung in this lengthy hymn.

17. Kilby, 161. This is the heart of Kilby's general criticism of Balthasar's authorial voice. He writes assertions rather than arguments, demanding "a certain suspension of the argumentative and critical sides of one's intellect" so as to allow acceptance of his authorial, directorial authority. Kilby believes Balthasar's theology over-reaches, that he "presumes to know more than can be known."

is central to Balthasar's idea of prayer, his idea of truth, his idea of the God–world relationship, and even of the triune relations. By not adopting a dialogical style in his writing, he does not succeed in producing the type of kneeling theology for which he aims. But perhaps more scandalous is the ellision of the dialogicality of prayer from his account of truth in the *Theo-Logic*. I agree with Kilby that Balthasar does not always give due attention to the particular, historical lives of the saints, even though he *does* give a way of reading those lives well. Balthasar's theology is really a hermeneutical lens for reading the world and the faith. Despite Balthasar's probable protestations, I'd agree that the lack of the *per accidens* of particular saintly lives leaves his theology of the saints too abstracted, and too theoretical, to perform the re-integration of theology and spirituality at which he aims. His accounts of the saints are, for the most part, intellectual biographies or theological interpretations, rather than expositions of their lives at prayer. Balthasar does not, therefore, fully achieve the task for which he set out.

Yet, this is not to say that his project is doomed to failure. What Balthasar's *Theo-Logic*, and perhaps his Trilogy more generally, needs is one final volume. Just as Balthasar supplemented the first volume of *The Glory of the Lord* with volumes on clerical and lay styles, so too might we supplement his *Theo-Logic* with a volume on saintly styles that focuses on the way specific figures know and make known the truth of Being as divine love. The remainder of this chapter is a first attempt at doing just such a thing.

Adrienne von Speyr: A Case Study

The saint, as Balthasar understands her, lives the contemplative life. This life is both philosophical and theological insofar as it is a life of prayer. The charism that falls upon the saint charges them with the general Christian mission to know God and make God known. This saintly charism falls perfectly within the vocation of the Church, as Balthasar understands it. Balthasar's saints are never rogue agents, operating individually, apart from the structural authority of the

Church. The saint—or the mystic, the terms are virtually interchangeable for Balthasar—receives an *ecclesial* charism. She performs in her own knowledge and love the mystery of the Church's self-giving love, which itself is an image of the love of Father, Son, and Spirit.

Balthasar points continuously to his partner and spiritual directee, Adrienne von Speyr, as the most important mystic in the modern Catholic Church. She, in many ways, embodies for us both the subjective and the objective missions of the saint. Though Kilby sees Speyr as a problematic figure in Balthasar's theological project, it is perhaps better to say that Speyr best embodies and articulates Balthasar's theology of the saints. Rather than journeying backwards in a *ressourcement* of the saints of Tradition, Balthasar points his readers to the present, and to the contemporary action of the Spirit in the Church in this strange figure whose mystical insight could nourish the contemporary Church.

In this final section, I show how Balthasar's Ignatian spirituality, his concern with the philosophical titanism of his day, and his grounding of metaphysics and epistemology in the manifestation of divine love in Christ and illuminated by the Spirit, all come together in the mystical theology of Adrienne von Speyr.

Speyr's Theological Existence

Speyr herself was not inclined to draw attention to herself or her mystical experiences; she desired, above all, a kind of hiddenness and anonymity. While such traits are common among the saints and correspond to the way the Spirit works as the anonymous subject of theology, Balthasar nonetheless produced a great deal of biographical information about her. Part of the motivation behind this was Balthasar's desire to validate Speyr as a genuinely ecclesial mystic, despite the Church's ongoing suspicion.[18] But Balthasar is not motivated only by apologetic reasons. He is also convinced that Speyr's

---

18. Cf. Sutton, *Heaven Opens*, 27–36. Cf. *First Glance*, 33.

form of life is a fruitful model of a saintly disposition before God. Speyr's biography, her life, is a form of theological and metaphysical confession and revelation—in precisely the way we elucidated in the previous chapter—and, as such, deserves attention.

Under Balthasar's spiritual direction, Speyr composed a lengthy partial biography of her childhood that highlights especially her precocious sensitivity to the Spirit, her ardent desire for the Catholic faith despite being raised Protestant, and the first touch of mystical graces on her life. It was not until her confirmation as a Catholic on All Saints Day 1940 that a "veritable cataract of mystical graces" flooded her, increasing yearly until her death.[19] These graces included visions of saints, mystical transports to heaven, but most especially, Balthasar notes, graces in prayer. Despite all of the intrigue and controversy over Speyr's mystical experiences, the heart of her mission and work was her prayer. Her holiness and saintliness, Balthasar avers, is not seen in her mysticism, but in her humble surrender (*Gelassenheit*) in which she handed herself over to God.

It was not long after her conversion that Speyr reportedly heard a voice speak, telling her, "You shall live in heaven and earth," a clear portent of the mystical graces to come.[20] Speyr regularly underwent visions of the saints at prayer in heaven, learning from them the true nature of prayer as surrender, receptivity, and response to the Word (*Wort*) of God that comes through Christ.[21] There is an interesting reciprocal relationship between Speyr's prayer and her mystical visions, especially of the saints. Her mystical graces are funded solely by her contemplative openness to God. But her mystical experience is not an end in itself. Rather, it is through her experiences that her prayer was further nourished. Contemplation, mysticism, and prayer

---

19. *First Glance*, 33.
20. Ibid., 34.
21. Speyr eventually compiled these insights into the prayers of the saints in *The Book of All Saints* (San Francisco: Ignatius Press, 2008). It is a massive collection of brief studies of the saints, not in terms of the life or thought, but in terms of the way that they pray.

all intertwined, nourishing and giving rise to each other.[22] For Speyr, contemplative prayer and mystical vision are mutually fulfilling.[23]

Speyr's prayer and mysticism are ordered to one chief end, namely, the opening of heaven and earth to each other. Matthew Sutton has recently argued that Speyr's mysticism is a Trinitarian one in which the heavenly reality of divine love floods the world, enrapturing the Christian into its reality.[24] The chief biblical example of this is Christ's baptism. It is as Christ emerged from the waters of the Jordan that heaven opens and the world experiences the dialogue between Father and Son with the Holy Spirit. The Son responds to the Father's word with his surrendering "Let it be so now" (Matt 3:15). At the baptism, Christ's prayer of self-offering (Matt 3:15) results in the mystical opening of heaven (Matt 3:16). Christ is the archetypal saint.[25]

Speyr's mysticism is thus enfolded into the larger logic of a contemplative disposition of openness and receptivity to God. Mystical knowledge for Speyr is the fruit of contemplation. For Adrienne too, "the inner reality of Love can be known only by love."[26]

If the preceding is true, then the key to understanding Speyr (or at least Balthasar's fascination with her) has less to do with her mystical experiences and more to do with the saintly disposition of her life. Speyr's saintly life was fruit of her prior spiritual attitude or disposition. According to Speyr, the saints are all characterized by the attitude that she designated as "consent," or what Balthasar would call receptivity or *indiferencia*. The archetypal form of this consent is the *fiat* given by Mary at the annunciation.

Speyr herself first "met" Mary in a vision when Speyr was fifteen and received a small wound on her chest (which she called her "secret"). In this vision, Speyr witnessed Mary surrounded by both angels and saints

---

22. Speyr's *Book of All Saints* shows how the saints pray and, by so doing, invites the reader to pray as well (74). The saints do not live to point to themselves but their entire existence is to point beyond themselves to God (186).

23. It is interesting to note that Speyr's visions of the "saints" at prayer in heaven include not only canonical saints but also "customary" saints like artists (Péguy), kings, and not a few Protestants (74).

24. Sutton, *Heaven Opens*, 96.

25. Ibid., 67.

26. LA, 75.

in an image that was very much like a picture (as opposed to her later graces which were, in Balthasar's words, "total, intimate reality" in which she interacted with the saints). After this vision, Speyr humbly and openly knelt by her bedside until she was forced to leave in order to go to school. The fruit of this mystical vision was the way it infused all of Speyr's later mysticism with a "deeply Marian character."

Marian consent consists in being infinitely at the disposal of the Infinite. Marian openness leaves an empty space, a womb, for the incarnation of the Word. Mary submits to her vocation, receives the gift within herself, and brings it forth into the world in faithful obedience to her vocation. This is the maidenly service that Mary does by way of her *fiat*—a consent that is the absolute identity of love and obedience. And, just as Mary performs this "maidenly service" in her humble and obedient consent, so too does the mystic fulfill her vocation with the same attitude. Sanctity for Speyr is attentive openness to the call of God. Openness to God means forgetfulness of the self. Perfect receptivity of the Father's word is at the same time absolute surrender (*Gelassenheit*), or kenosis, of self-will.

It was her contemplative life that allowed Speyr this openness of consent to the Word. She prayed for personal anonymity and total transparency to the word of God. She prayed to become the open and receptive womb of Mary, ready to be filled with whatever God might will to be birthed. For Speyr, consent is the mark of genuine sanctity.

The critical point is that Speyr's *knowledge* of divine reality is the fruit of her living encounter with that divine reality in prayer. Nowhere is the explicitly Marian quality of the saintly life clearer than in Speyr's own prayers. In her prayer for the renewal of the spirit, Speyr is clear about the Marian origin of the saintly, contemplative life, yes, but she is also clear about the Marian origin of the Church. This prayer thus brings sanctity and ecclesiology together in inseparable union—a union intimately forged from the same Marian *fiat* and bearing the same Marian characteristics:

Dear Lord, you see how we become used to everything. Once, we gladly took up your service with the firm intent of being *wholly surrendered* to you. But, since every day brings nearly the same thing over and over again, it seems to us that our prayer has been circumscribed. We limit it to ourselves and to what seems necessary for just the task at hand so that in the end our spirit has assumed the size of this small task. We ask you not to allow us to narrow ourselves in this way; expand us again; bestow on us again some of the power of Mary's *consent*, which awaits in *readiness* to the entire divine will, which is always as all-embracing as when it was first pronounced and which is daily confirmed anew. She may have been glad or afraid or hopeful, weary of the daily work or led to the Cross: always she stood before you as at the first, *obeying* everything you said, hoping to do everything you wished. Behind every one of your wishes, even the smallest, she saw the great unlimited will of the Father which you, the Son, were fulfilling. . . . Grant that we contemplate and affirm you and your Church, carry out what our mission demands, in an ever new spirit, *in the spirit of the Mother's consent*. Grant also that we pray for this spirit. We know you yourself are where you send your Spirit. The Spirit brought you to your Mother; the Spirit enabled her to carry you, to give birth to you, to care for you; and because in her you found again your own Spirit, from her you formed your Church. And, since you have called us into this Church, make from each one of us a place where the Spirit of your Church blows, where the will of your Father, our Father, is done together with you and with the help of the Holy Spirit so that we may dare to pray together with you in all seriousness: *Our Father, who art in heaven . . . Amen.*[27]

These same themes are picked up in some of Speyr's other prayers, both those that she herself crafted and those mystically taught to her. In keeping with our emphasis on the manner in which the saints' performance of prayer funds their understanding of truth, let us consider one more of Speyr's prayers and highlight the way it draws out the sort of metaphysical and theological account we have developed in the preceding pages of this book.

The Ignatian character of Speyr's prayer is readily apparent in her prayer for indifference:

Lord, you know that I want to serve you but am always still hanging on to my work and opinion; that again and again I hastily crawl back into myself in order to consider everything from my point of view: that I do this, in order to avoid that, wish this and abhor that. But, in your whole life on earth and especially on the Cross, you have shown us what it means

27. Mary Ford-Grabowsky, ed., *Spiritual Writings on Mary: Annotated and Explained* (Woodstock, VT: Skylight Paths, 2005), 49.

to do the will of another. For you, this other person was the Father, a Father so perfect that, from the beginning and without forming your own opinion, you considered and accepted each of his decisions as perfect. You did this not through an insight which would have been the result each time of examination and deliberation, but out of love. Your love for the Father has once and for all taken the place of every personal examination. And this love you also bestowed on your saints; and your holy Ignatius has spoken and written about it. He has demonstrated how decisive the will of the superior, the will of the Father, the divine will itself is for the one who loves and no longer wants to know anything except the desire of the beloved. Give us your filial strength; grant that we become obedient by your perfect obedience, indifferent through your indifference. Grant that we no longer seek our own will in anything, but go directly to you, together with your holy Ignatius, and become indifferent down to the bottom of our hearts, not so as to become indifferent to you and the world, but to begin finally to love you and the Father in the Holy Spirit more than anything else. Amen.[28]

Speyr's prayer is for attunement to the disposition of Christ, sharing his obedience, indifference, surrender, and love for the Father. In Speyr's prayer, attunement to Christ is conformity through love to the Father, the source and goal of all things. Her prayer for obedience is an act of loving self-surrender, a kenotic or contemplative handing over of herself to the will of the Father. This surrender, we have seen, is the metaphysical act of love; it is an act that mirrors the self-surrender of the Father in the triune life and in the act of creation. Speyr's prayer of indifference is a prayer of metaphysical confession.

Discernment of Spirits

All of the preceding is fine and good in theory, but how is one to judge the validity of Speyr's insights? Is Speyr's mystical insight so fundamentally subjective and esoteric that it transcends the possibility of critical assessment? Both Balthasar and Speyr would deny such a claim. There must be a clear discernment of spirits involved when it comes to assessing the insights of the saints and mystics. The ecclesial

28. *First Glance*, 205–6.

standard of revealed truth must always measure the validity of saintly truth.

Discernment of spirits is a practice that informs both Speyr's mysticism and Balthasar's *Theo-Logic*. For Speyr, mysticism always serves an ecclesial and theological purpose. The content of all mysticism is the public revelation of the truth of God that has been disclosed to the Church. The mission of the mystic is to pour her private revelations into the well of the Church's truth, to disappear fully into the Church, "in order to deepen and enliven public revelation."[29] This disciplined obedience to the Church is what distinguishes the saintly figure of the mystic from the Gnostic. The mystic, like the saint, exists not for herself, but rather for her public mission. In that sense, the mystic is Marian, the handmaid of the objective revelation of truth as perfectly expressed in Christ.[30] Sutton helpfully distinguishes between mysticism and revelation with the illustration of a circle. The Church's revelation is the center of the circle, and mysticism is what fills out the periphery. According to Speyr, "everything that stands in the periphery is a supplement and a decoration and must always be read from the center."[31] While Speyr's experience may be *esoteric*, the fruit of that experience is essentially *exoteric*. It is private experience undergone for the sake of the public, that is, the *catholic*, good.

We return then to the interplay of the objective and subjective work of the Spirit that Balthasar discusses in *Theo-Logic* 3. Rather than a Hegelian account in which *Geist* comes to subjectivity through the unfolding of history, both Balthasar and Speyr highlight the positive and fruitful interplay of objectivity and subjectivity in the Spirit-led Church. Revelation and understanding, object and subject, *aletheia* and *emeth*, all of these are held together in the saint and the mystic.

Insofar as truth is theological *and* metaphysical, the wisdom of an ecclesial and saintly mystic such as Speyr will illumine both forms

---

29. Sutton, *Heaven Opens*, 75.
30. Ibid., 78.
31. Speyr, *Subjektive Mystik (Das Wort und die Mystik I): Nachlassband V*, 85, quoted in Sutton, *Heaven Opens*, 79.

of knowledge. Balthasar described Speyr's style as an "experiential dogmatics."[32] We can go a step further by saying that insofar as she contributes to dogmatic truth, Speyr's mysticism also yields an "experiential metaphysics." In the next section, we will examine Speyr's mystical theology of Christ's passion to see the metaphysical fruit that can be derived from it.

The Metaphysical Knowledge of Mystical Experience

Balthasar believed that the mission of the saints is to enlarge the cathedrals of Christian worship through their contemplative form of life and the insights that emerge from that life. The saints and mystics exist for the sake of "the central deepening and enlivening" of truth.[33] Insofar as truth has to do with Being (under both theological and metaphysical rubrics), we must see how the insights of a mystic—or "customary saint"—such as Speyr are fruitful for understanding truth in both its divine and metaphysical dimensions. First, let us consider the way Speyr's mysticism further complements Balthasar's own account of prayer as metaphysics in act.

All human prayer has its source in the Trinity.[34] Prayer has no beginning because Father, Son, and the Holy Spirit *are* the eternal dialogue of prayer. Speyr exposits the dynamic of love that the Trinity is under the rubric of prayer (similar to the way that Balthasar spells out Christ's existence as prayer). For her, love and prayer are co-extensive because both arise from divine vision:

> The eternal dialogue is prayer first and foremost because it is divine vision: vision as the core of contemplation, as a silent listening, a reciprocal beholding, being led, adjusting to the other and getting to know him more, a reciprocal expectation and response. This abundant life streams from one Person to another, since each one always stands in view of the others. There is no self-concealment or reserve between them, only a constant acceptable and surrender, self-opening and self-disclosure, showing and loving.[35]

32. *First Glance*, 85.
33. Ibid., 57.
34. Speyr, *The World of Prayer*, 28.
35. Ibid., 32.

We note here Speyr's language about the dynamic of prayer that constitutes the Trinity echoes the language Balthasar uses throughout the *Theo-Logic*: "dialogue," "self-concealment," "self-disclosure," "showing," and "loving." The dynamic of *truth* that the Trinity is for Balthasar is, at one and the same time, the dynamic of prayer for Speyr.

Speyr herself draws out the metaphysical and epistemological implications of her understanding of the Trinity by stressing the *fruitfulness* of Trinitarian prayer: it extends outward in the act of loving creation as the source of all created Being. Moreover, this dynamic of Trinitarian prayer also serves as the condition of the possibility of creation's participation in the eternal dialogue: "This eternal, amazing relationship of joy lays the foundation for the world and mankind to be taken up one day into the divine joy, just as the communion of true lovers is always a preparation for the adoption into this relationship of others who do not yet love."[36]

Prayer, therefore, is a metaphysical reality because it is the first cause of created Being *and* the possibility of participative understanding of this reality. Prayer, then, is the eternal movement of love in God and the ground of all things. Precisely as such, prayer is the truth of God and the truth of the world. The essential thing to note here is that Speyr's dogmatic understanding of the divine life emerged from her living encounter *with* that divine reality through prayer.

Perhaps the most significant of Speyr's mystical insights for Balthasar's theology centers around her experiential contemplation of Christ's passion. From her conversion, during Holy Week, Speyr underwent significant and severe episodes of mystical identification with Christ in his passion, gaining insight into the psychological states of Christ in his suffering and death.[37] Speyr's visceral experiences of Christ's passion, which she experienced from "within" Christ's own experience of suffering, are forms of Ignatian contemplation as Balthasar understands it. We might also hear the mystical realization of Ignatian "desolation" in Speyr's experience of Holy Saturday. If the

36. Ibid., 33.
37. Balthasar makes much of these insights, using them at great length in *TL* 2 and *TD* 4 and 5, especially.

goal of Ignatian spirituality is the contemplative understanding, even participation in, Christ's life and death, then Speyr, in her own semi-regular passions, *performed* that goal. She brought the stories of Christ's passion to life with existential and experiential vitality. Speyr identified herself with Christ's suffering so completely that during these episodes, her "I" became absolutely surrendered and transparent to Christ's "Thou" in an analogous way to Christ's own transparency to the will of the Father.

The passion of Christ is, as we have seen previously, the dramatic heart of history and the performative unveiling of the truth of Being. From Speyr's *agapeic* form of life—her openness, receptivity, and contemplation—comes an experiential insight and wisdom that rearranges and reorders both theological and metaphysical understanding. Speyr's mystical experience of Christ's passion granted her a mystical insight into the interior state of his suffering. She experienced what she understood as the subjective form of the objective reality of Christ's work. We have seen Balthasar's account of the objective work of Christ's death in *Theo-Logic 2*, as the confrontation between worldly mendacity and his divine truth. But Speyr's mystical experience draws the analytical and theological mind to contemplation of—and orantic participation in—the mystery of love as expressed in the Son's descent into hell.

Speyr's mysticism contributes three main insights into Christ's passion that critically inform Balthasar's theology: 1) the Son's perfect obedience; 2) the Trinitarian dimension of Holy Saturday; 3) the forsakenness of Christ under the objective weight of sin. While each of these elements is important for understanding both Speyr and Balthasar, we will focus only on the third.

Regarding the God-forsakenness of the dead Christ, we have already touched on it at several points. Christ's obedience of love to the Father is to will the acceptance of divine forsakenness. What Speyr's mystical experience allows her special access to is Christ's existential experience of the objective weight of sin that causes his God-forsakenness. Her dictation of this experience is worth quoting at length:

> In *hell* the Lord's bodily state becomes very different from what it was in life. . . . It is difficult to say; one cannot express in words all that one feels. It is something like this: in life, the Son of Man feels and experiences in his body wherever godlessness is hidden, be it in individual people with whom he deals or in the surrounding atmosphere. The power of evil appears to him as enmity with God. In hell, he experiences the power of evil, not in its relationship with God, but as a quality in itself . . . now the quality of evil is not related to anything. [Balthasar: How is this felt in the body?] As if the body had the possibility of existing without being related to God. As if it could be complete and cut off from everything, as sin is here. It is as if the body received so many possibilities of evil that the possibilities for good are nullified. . . .[38]

Hell, Speyr says, is where the reality of sin as a state of separation from God is fulfilled.[39] Speyr experiences from within Christ's encounter with the great metaphysical lie that hell is: that the God–world relationship can be torn asunder, dissolved and destroyed. Hell is the attempted annihilation of Being, the rejection of the analogical relationship between divine and creaturely truth, the triumph of the opaque "I" that is closed off to the "Thou."

Speyr understands hell as absolute abandonment and non-relational darkness.[40] This gives an existential weight to the speculative claims Balthasar makes in his Trilogy regarding the metaphysical mendacity of hell. In fact, we could parse the relationship between Speyr's mysticism and Balthasar's theology thus: the experience of Christ's passion undergone by Speyr enriches the distinctive, revelatory form (*Gestalt*) of Christ into which we are invited through dramatic participation. This participation results in the subjective apprehension of the objective truth of Christ.

Speyr's mystical insight is, thus, a performative meditation and

---

38. Speyr, *The Passion from Within*, trans. Sister Lucia Wiedenhöver, O.C.D. (San Francisco: Ignatius Press, 1998), 137–38.
39. Cf. Paul Griffiths, *Decreation* (Waco, TX: Baylor University Press, 2014), 191–214 for an account of sin that can achieve its perfection in annihilation. Without crossing into annihilationism, Speyr's theology of sin is similar to Griffiths.
40. Sutton, *Heaven Opens*, 184.

improvisation on the truth taught by the Church. Because the Church is always the Church *on mission* in the world, her insight cannot be locked up within the confines of esoteric or even ecclesial "spirituality." Sutton points out that the mystery of Holy Saturday, despite its difficulty for contemporary thinkers, is nevertheless useful for countering the nihilism of modernity.[41] Rather than granting the ultimacy of the abyss, Speyr's mysticism reveals the inviolable union of God and world in the incarnate, dead, resurrected, and ascended flesh of Christ, Emmanuel. Or, to put the same thing another way, Speyr shows that truth is stronger than mendacity just as life is stronger than death, precisely because Being is co-extensive with Love.

Experience, Obedience, and the Question of Authority

The theological relationship between Balthasar and Speyr has only recently begun receiving the attention it deserves. Though we could accept Kilby's argument that "Theology and Sanctity" is an *apologia* for Speyr, it is more plausible to read the essay as a part of Balthasar's Ignatian interpretation of metaphysics and epistemology in the light of the drama of Christ in which the saints participate.

But one final question remains. We know that Balthasar incorporates a great deal of Speyr's mystical knowledge into his theology; *Theo-Drama* 5 practically drips with references to her work. What grants Speyr this kind of authority? There is certainly the danger of ascribing theological authority to her experiences *qua* experiences. Denys Turner has criticized the over-emphasis on "experientialist" mysticism, as well as the assumption that subjective experience can itself arbitrate religious truth.[42] Is Balthasar guilty of this?

---

41. Ibid., 174n169.
42. Turner calls experientialist mysticism a kind of theological positivism: "For just as the philosophical positivists made a sharp division between the first-order experiential bedrock of 'sense experience' and the second-order theoretical reflection upon the language of experience, so there are those for whom there is, as it were, a 'mystical' equivalent to sense experience—equivalent in its 'immediacy' and subjectivity, equivalent in its foundational character, equivalent in its freedom from theoretical presupposition—in terms of which theological truth is capable of being verified or falsified. Such parallels are not, by any means, always made out explicitly. But insofar as the question can be raised as to whether 'mysticism' is in that way 'experientially immediate' that it can serve in the role of confirming or disconfirming

While it may be true that Balthasar appropriates Speyr's mystical experiences in a positivist way, it seems clear that Balthasar eschews the fascination with her experience *as* experience.[43] What is important in Speyr's mysticism is not her subjective experiences but the objective truth it discloses.[44] Moreover, the authority of Speyr's mysticism comes from her obedient receptivity to God, not from her experiences. By focusing on knowledge as the fruit of obedient openness to truth, Balthasar and Speyr relativize the role of experience. God may call the saint to experience divine plentitude, or to experience desolation, or to no experience at all. The height of authority lies not in the supernatural experiences of the mystic but in the obedience and receptivity of the saint.[45] What makes Speyr so significant is that her knowledge as a mystic is the fruit of her love as a saint.

Balthasar's appropriation of Speyr's mystical insight is simply Balthasar's attempt to do the very thing he laments *not being done* in "Theology and Sanctity": "What the prayer of the saints, their experience of God in the world, might have to contribute to this doctrine [that is, a Christological metaphysics] has hardly begun to be explored."[46] This claim takes our study full circle. We end as we began: with Balthasar's claim that the resources of Ignatian spirituality remained untapped in contemporary theology, but that in them lay hidden treasures of wisdom and love for a distinctively Catholic form of life, knowledge, and love.

---

religious belief-claims, the same general epistemic status is implied for the mystical in the theological as for sense experience in the scientific" (Denys Turner, *Darkness of God: Negativity in Christian Mysticism*" [Cambridge: Cambridge University Press, 1998], 262).

43. "Understanding Christian Mysticism" in *ET* 4, 324ff.

44. This is perhaps why Balthasar, as Speyr's spiritual director *and* publisher, devoted so much more time, energy, and money on her biblical commentaries, than on her chronicles of her experiences.

45. "This brings us to the decisive maxim that decides the issue: it is not the *experience* of union with God that represents the standard for perfection (the highest rung in the ladder of ascent) but *obedience* ("Understanding Christian Mysticism," in *ET* 4, 325).

46. "Theology and Sanctity," in *ET* 1, 198.

Conclusion: Theology and the Saints

It has been the task of this book to present Balthasar's meditation on the mystery of Being and his theology of the saints as organically linked in his account of truth, in both its metaphysical and theological dimensions. Metaphysical knowing, as I have presented it, is not an endeavor that is neutral to the pressures and concerns of either dogmatic theology or spirituality. Insofar as the object of knowledge is *truth*, its theological and metaphysical dimensions must be accounted for. And insofar as truth is that Being is co-extensive with divine love, then the form (*Gestalt*) of the saints signals the best way of understanding that truth. This is especially true of their loving and contemplative disposition of surrender, receptivity, and obedience.

Such was the core of my presentation. I have foregrounded this investigation of Balthasar's theology of the saints by emphasizing the Ignatian flavor of Balthasar's work, as one who engages critically and constructively with the prevailing intellectual culture of the day from a "distinctively Catholic" perspective. Balthasar's theology of the saints as presented in this essay stands as one dimension of such a perspective. The major achievement of Balthasar's theology of the saints is the way that it realizes the Ignatian dictum to "find God in all things." But countering the drive that funds Hegelian titanism, Balthasar offers the saints as those whose understanding of truth rises from the obedient receptivity of their love. The titanic will-to-power that aims for the intellectual mastery of Being is replaced by the saintly will-to-surrender that apprehends truth through the nuptial delight of contemplative union with God.

Balthasar does not see his theology of the saints as either a parochially Catholic option or a purely negative critique of culture. Despite the often antagonistic stance he takes toward cultural forms, Balthasar ultimately sees the saints as the *positive* fulfillment of the questions and concerns of modernity. Toward the end of his life, Balthasar published another assessment of his theological project. His work begins, he claims, with the situation of modern humans, confronted as they are with the metaphysical *real distinction*. The modern human, Balthasar claims, "exists as a limited being in a limited world, but his reason is open to the unlimited, to all of Being . . . I am, I could also, however, not be."[1] The mystery of Being runs right through the soul of history, even through the malaise of modernity. All philosophy has wrestled with this question, but without reaching a satisfying answer. Balthasar's constructive contribution to this metaphysical question of humanity's relationship to the whole of Being is, as he describes it, a dialogical anthropology that corresponds to the dialogicality of Being itself.[2] The saints, as Balthasar conceives them, perform this kind of dialogical interchange with God in an archetypal fashion. They thus function for Balthasar not only as a critique of modernity's egoism and titanism but also as the form of human existence that best fulfills and satisfies the longings of modern man for the mystery of Being and the revelation of divine love.

In a way, the argument of this book, focusing as it does on the subjective dimension of saintly existence, is incomplete. What is needed now is a follow-up project that turns to the objective dimension of the saints that exposits Balthasar's account not only of how saints *know,* but also, how saints *make known* the truth of Being. The understanding that arises from the contemplative disposition of the saint before God exists not for itself alone. Contemplation nourishes the dramatic mission of the saints in the Church and in the world.

1. *MW*, 112.
2. Ibid., 114–15.

Saintly contemplation unfolds within the missional dynamic of love that fuels petitionary prayer for the world: "Thy will be done on earth as it is in heaven" (Matt 6:10).

The previous sketch of Adrienne von Speyr was an overture to this kind of objective specification of Balthasar's theology of the saints. But illuminating as Speyr's life and insight might be for understanding Balthasar's own project, a study of her mysticism points to the undeniable fact that the needed "follow-up project" will be something more than another scholarly assessment of Balthasar's theology. Written theology necessarily falls short of theology proper. Theology, Balthasar never tires of saying, is a matter of life more than it is a matter of speculative or academic theorizing. Dogmatic theology, metaphysics, epistemology—all of these are good and important intellectual disciplines. But insofar as one can theorize about Being yet remain untransformed, theory's ability to capture the fullness of truth is limited. *Theoria* and *praktikē* are ordered to each other. Written theology aims toward its fulfillment in the practical, orantic performance of truth.[3]

Written theology in the Balthasarian framework is a kind of misnomer. More often than not, what we call "theology" is actually "theo-log-ology": words about words about God. And in a way, this is simply the nature of written theology. True theology is not found in a book, but in the person of Christ. Theology proper is dramatic and performative. Given Balthasar's account of Christ's life, theology is doxological and orantic. It is not an accident that Balthasar saves the *Theo-Logic* until the end of his Trilogy: theological understanding, though necessary for Theology proper, is always an *a posteriori* discipline. It is necessarily reflexive insofar as it is an understanding that arises *from* the contemplative participation in the form of Christ.

In his *Epilogue* to the Trilogy, Balthasar uses a cathedral as the image of the mystagogical nature of theology. This cathedral imagery

---

3. One way that this question might be considered in the academic context is through an analysis of the way the subjective dimension of Balthasar's theology of the saints expands into the structure, life, and mission of the lay Community of St. John that Balthasar and Speyr formed after Balthasar left the Jesuits.

structures the *Theo-Logic* as the movement into understanding the ever-greater mystery of truth. The most fitting language of this mystery is prayer, the language of love. Indeed, the cathedral itself as we have presented it is "the prayer of fleshly people, a glory, almost an impossibility, a miracle of prayer."[4] Prayer, then, is integral to Balthasar's account of the God–world relationship. This relationship is the truth of Being, which is to say, it is Christ, the mediator between heaven and earth. But Christ and his truth are *dramatic*, and can be known truly only by being dwelt within, and thus, *performed*. The mission of the saint is to participate in Christ, and by so doing, enlarge the chapels of his truth and his love. Prayer is the dramatic, existential, path *into* truth *by means of* truth: we run to God along the road of God; we come to Christ along the road of Christ; we pray through Christ's prayer. Thus prayer is the expressive language of the saint's drawing near *to*, being united *with*, and being commissioned *by* Christ in order to carry his truth in the world. Prayer is the heart of saintly existence; it is the saints' modality of *being-in-the-world* that has been transfigured by Christ. It is metaphysics in act, the expressive language of Balthasar's account of truth, his epistemology of love.

We might say, then, that written theology plays only a mediating role in the practice of theology. It arises from prayer and contemplation in order to further nourish prayer and contemplation. Though Kilby criticized Balthasar's theology for being insufficiently prayerful, written theology by itself *cannot be* properly prayerful. Written theology's mission, its *raison d'etre*, is not to *be* prayer, but to nourish the kneeling theology of prayer and the saintly form of life that arises from that prayer.

In this way, Balthasar's theology of the saints gestures toward the proper holism of theological truth that brings together dogmatic and metaphysical speculation with the practical form of the life of the saint. The loss of this integration is the driving concern of his essay "Theology and Sanctity" and the root of both the titanism and nihilism of the modern age. By re-integrating speculation and spirituality,

---

4. *GL* 3, 511.

Balthasar effectively out-narrates the Hegelian *Döppleganger* by representing truth in its fullness. In this way, Balthasar offers a theology of the saints in which theology fulfills metaphysics, prayer fulfills epistemology, and where truth is understood as love.

This is not to suggest that theology should forego its intellectual agenda in favor of sentimental fideism. Such a claim would only contribute to the "shattering of Christian truth" that Balthasar bemoans. Balthasar was no stranger to the intellectual, ecclesial, and cultural debates of his day. He wrestled over the nuances of theological language, the questions of metaphysics and epistemology, and the distinctiveness—or lack there of—of Catholic identity in the world. Balthasar's brilliant mind gives us much to wrestle with today as we face our own crises in ecclesiology, ethics, metaphysics, and so on. But in the midst of the relentless debates of intellectual and ecclesial controversy, Balthasar reminds us of the essential fact that, in the end, what matters is that we become saints.[5] It is as saints that we speculate and understand truth. For Balthasar, sanctity is the final mission of the Christian, the Church, and the discipline of theology. To be a saint is to be an agent of truth in the world, which is to say, an agent of love. God is love; and Being is co-extensive with love; the truth of all things is love, and love itself is understanding.

---

5. This is the insight of the poor whisky priest in Graham Greene's *The Power and the Glory* (New York: Penguin Classics, 2003), 211.

Selected Bibliography

Ackerman, Stephan. "The Church as Persons in the Theology of Hans Urs von Balthasar." *Communio* 29, no. 2 (2002): 238–49.

Babini, Ellero. "Jesus Christ: Form and Norm of Man According to Hans Urs Von Balthasar." In *Hans Urs Von Balthasar: His Life and Work.* Edited by David Schindler. San Francisco: Ignatius Press, 1991.

Balthasar, Hans Urs von. *Apokalypse der deutschen Seele, Band I: Der deutsche Idealismus.* Salzburg-Leipzig: Verlag Anton Pustet, 1937.

_____. "Beyond Contemplation and Action?" In *Explorations in Theology.* Vol. 4, *Spirit and Institution.* Translated by Edward T. Oakes. San Francisco: Ignatius Press, 1995.

_____. *Christian Meditation.* Translated by Sister Mary Theresilde Skerry. San Francisco: Ignatius Press, 1989

_____. *Christlicher Stand.* Einseideln: Johannes Verlag, 1977.

_____. *Cosmic Liturgy: The Universe According to Maximus the Confessor.* Translated by Brian E. Daley, S. J. San Francisco, Ignatius Press, 2003.

_____. "The Descent into Hell." In *Explorations in Theology.* Vol. 4, *Spirit and Institution.* Translated by Edward T. Oakes. San Francisco: Ignatius Press, 1995.

_____. "Earthly Beauty and Divine Glory." *Communio* 10, no. 2 (1983), 202–6.

_____. "Encountering God in Today's World." In *Explorations in Theology.* Vol. 3, *Creator Spirit.* Translated by Brian McNeil. San Francisco: Ignatius Press, 1993.

_____. *Epilogue.* Translated by Edward T. Oakes, S. J. San Francisco: Ignatius Press, 1987.

_____. "Eschatology in Outline." In *Explorations in Theology.* Vol. 4, *Spirit and Institution.* Translated by Edward T. Oakes. San Francisco: Ignatius Press, 1995.

_____. "The Fathers, the Scholastics and Ourselves." *Communio* 24, no. 2 (1997): 347–96.

_____. *First Glance at Adrienne Von Speyr.* San Francisco: Ignatius Press, 1981.

_____. *The Glory of the Lord.* Vol. 1, *Seeing the Form.* Translated by Erasmo Leiva-Merikakis. San Francisco: Ignatius Press, 1982.

_____. *The Glory of the Lord.* Vol. 2, *Studies in Theological Style: Clerical Styles.* Translated by Andrew Louth, Francis McDonagh, and Brian McNeil. San Francisco: Ignatius Press, 1984.

_____. *The Glory of the Lord.* Vol. 3, *Studies in Theological Style: Lay Styles.* Translated by Andrew Louth, John Saward, Martin Simon, and Rowan Williams. San Francisco: Ignatius Press, 1986.

_____. *The Glory of the Lord.* Vol. 4, *The Realm of Metaphysics in Antiquity.* Translated by Brian McNeil, Andrew Louth, John Saward, Rowan Williams, and Oliver Davies. San Francisco: Ignatius Press, 1989.

_____. *The Glory of the Lord.* Vol. 5, *The Realm of Metaphysics in the Modern Age.* Translated by Oliver Davies, Andrew Louth, Brian McNeil, John Saward, and Rowan Williams. San Francisco: Ignatius Press, 1991.

_____. *The Glory of the Lord.* Vol. 6, *Theology: The Old Covenant.* Translated by Brian McNeil and Erasmo Leiva-Merikakis. San Francisco: Ignatius Press, 1991.

_____. *The Glory of the Lord.* Vol. 7, *Theology: The New Covenant.* Translated by Brian McNeil. Edinburgh: T&T Clark, 1989.

_____. "God Speaks as Man." In *Explorations in Theology.* Vol. 1, *The Word Made Flesh.* Translated by A. V. Littledale. San Francisco: Ignatius Press, 1989.

_____. "The Holy Spirit as Love." In *Explorations in Theology.* Vol. 3, *Creator Spirit.* Translated by Brian McNeil. San Francisco: Ignatius Press, 1993.

_____. *Love Alone is Credible.* Translated by D. C. Schindler. San Francisco: Ignatius Press, 2004.

_____. "The Meaning of Christ's Saying, 'I am the Truth'." *Communio* 13, no. 2 (1986): 158–61.

_____. Hans Urs von Balthasar. *The Moment of Christian Witness*. Translated by Richard Beckley. San Francisco: Ignatius Press, 1994.

_____. "Movement toward God." In *Explorations in Theology*. Vol. 3, *Creator Spirit*. Translated by Brian McNeil. San Francisco: Ignatius Press, 1993.

_____. *Mysterium Paschale: The Mystery of Easter*. Translated by Aidan Nichols, O.P. San Francisco: Ignatius Press, 1990.

_____. "On the Tasks of Catholic Philosophy in Our Time." *Communio* 20, no. 1 (1993): 147–87.

_____. "On Vicarious Representation." In *Explorations in Theology*. Vol. 4, *Spirit and Institution*. Translated by Edward T. Oakes. San Francisco: Ignatius Press, 1995.

_____. *Our Task*. Translated by John Saward. San Francisco: Ignatius Press, 1994.

_____. "Philosophy, Christianity, Monasticism" in *Explorations in Theology*. Vol. 2, *Spouse of the Word*. San Francisco: Ignatius Press, 1991, 333–72.

_____. *Prayer*. Translated by A. V. Littledale. New York: Sheed & Ward, 1961.

_____. "Prayer for the Spirit." In *Explorations in Theology*. Vol. 3, *Creator Spirit*. Translated by Brian McNeil. San Francisco: Ignatius Press, 1993.

_____. *Razing the Bastions*. Translated by Brian McNeil. San Francisco: Ignatius Press, 1993.

_____. "Should Faith or Theology be the Basis of Catechesis?" *Communio* 10, no. 1 (1983), 10–16.

_____. "Spirit and Institution." In *Explorations in Theology*. Vol. 4, *Spirit and Institution*. Translated by Edward T. Oakes. San Francisco: Ignatius Press, 1995.

_____. "Spirit, Love, Contemplation." In *Explorations in Theology*. Vol. 3, *Creator Spirit*. Translated by Brian McNeil. San Francisco: Ignatius Press, 1993.

_____. "Spirituality." In *Explorations in Theology*. Vol. 1, *The Word Made Flesh*. Translated by A. V. Littledale. San Francisco: Ignatius Press, 1989.

_____. *Theo-Drama*. Vol. 3, *Dramatis Personae: Persons in Christ*. Translated by Graham Harrison. San Francisco: Ignatius Press, 1992.

———. *Theo-Logic*. Vol. 1, *Truth of the World*. Translated by Adrian J. Walker. San Francisco: Ignatius Press, 1985.

———. *Theo-Logic*. Vol. 2, *Truth of God*. Translated by Adrian J. Walker. San Francisco: Ignatius Press, 1985.

———. *Theo-Logic*. Vol. 3, *The Spirit of Truth*. Translated by Graham Harrison. San Francisco: Ignatius Press, 1987.

———. "*Theo-Logic*: On the Work as a Whole." *Communio* 20, no. 4 (1993): 623–38.

———. *Theologik, Band I: Wahrheit der Welt*. Einseideln: Johannes Verlag, 1985.

———. *Theologik, Band II: Wahrheit Gottes*. Einseideln: Johannes Verlag, 1986.

———. *Theologik, Band III: Der Geist der Wahrheit*. Einseideln: Johannes Verlag, 1987.

———. "Theology and Sanctity." In *Explorations in Theology*. Vol. 1, *The Word Made Flesh*. Translated by A. V. Littledale. San Francisco: Ignatius Press, 1989.

———. *A Theology of History*. San Francisco: Ignatius Press, 1994.

———. Hans Urs von Balthasar. *The Theology of Karl Barth: Exposition and Interpretation*. Translated by Edward T. Oakes, S. J. San Francisco: Ignatius Press, 1992.

———. "Truth and Life." In *Explorations in Theology*. Vol. 3, *Creator Spirit*. Translated by Brian McNeil. San Francisco: Ignatius Press, 1993.

———. *Truth is Symphonic: Aspects of Christian Pluralism*. Translated by Graham Harrison. San Francisco: Ignatius Press, 1987.

———. "Two Modes of Faith." In *Explorations in Theology*. Vol. 3, *Creator Spirit*. Translated by Brian McNeil. San Francisco: Ignatius Press, 1993.

———. *Two Sisters in the Spirit: Thérèse of Lisieux and Elizabeth of the Trinity*. Translated by Donald Nichols, Anne Elizabeth Englund, and Dennis Martin. San Francisco: Ignatius Press, 1992.

———. "Understanding Christian Mysticism." In *Explorations in Theology*. Vol. 4, *Spirit and Institution*. Translated by Edward T. Oakes. San Francisco: Ignatius Press, 1995.

———. "What Is Distinctively Christian in the Experience of God?" In *Explorations in Theology*. Vol. 4, *Spirit and Institution*. Translated by Edward T. Oakes. San Francisco: Ignatius Press, 1995.

_____. "The Word and Silence." In *Explorations in Theology*. Vol. 1, *The Word Made Flesh*. Translated by A. V. Littledale. San Francisco: Ignatius Press, 1989.

Bätzing, Georg. "Homesickness for God: Adrienne von Speyr's *Confession*." *Communio* 31, no. 4 (2004): 548–56.

Bauer, E. F. "Hans Urs Von Balthasar (1905-1988): Sein Philosophisches Werk." In *Christliche Philosophie Im Katholischen Denken Des 19. Und 20. Jahrhunderts, Iii Moderne Stromungen Im 20. Jahrhundert*, edited by W. M. Neidel, E. Coreth, and G. Pfligersdorffer, 285–304: Granz, 1990.

Beattie, Tina. *New Catholic Feminism: Theology and Theory*. London and New York: Routledge, 2006.

Bieler, Martin. "The Future of the Philosophy of Being." *Communio* 26, no. 3 (1999): 455–85.

_____. "Meta-anthropology and Christology: On the Philosophy of Hans Urs von Balthasar." *Communio* 20, no. 1 (1993): 129–46.

Blanchette, Oliva. *Maurice Blondel: A Philosophical Life*. Grand Rapids: Wm. Eerdmans Publishing Group, 2010.

Blätter, Peter. *Pneumatologia crucis: Das Kreuz in der Logik von Wahrheit und Freiheit: Ein phänomenologischer Zugang zur Theologik Hans Urs von Balthasars*. Würzburg: Echer Verlag GmbH, 2004.

Boersma, Hans. *Nouvelle Théologie and Sacramental Ontology: A Return to Mystery*. Oxford: Oxford University Press, 2010.

Botinovich, Kenneth M. "On the Death of Father Balthasar." *Communio* 16, no. 1 (1989): 152–54.

Carpenter, Anne Michelle. *Theo-Poetics: Hans Urs von Balthasar and the Risk of Art and Being*. Notre Dame: The University of Notre Dame Press, 2015.

Casarella, Peter J. "Experience as a Theological Category: Hans Urs Von Balthasar on the Christian Encounter with God's Image." *Communio* 20, no. 1 (1993): 118–28.

Casarella, Peter J. and Robin Young Darling. "Spirit and History: The Intelligence of Scripture." *Communio* 24, no. 4 (1997): 843–45.

Cavanaugh, William T. "Balthasar, Globalization, and the Problem of the One and the Many." *Communio* 28, no. 2 (2001): 324–47.

_____. *Being Consumed: Economics and Christian Desire*. Grand Rapids, Wm. Eerdmans Publishing Group, 2008.

Chantraine, Georges. "Exegesis and Contemplation in the Work of Hans Urs Von Balthasar." *Communio* 16, no. 3 (1989): 366–83.

_____. "Prayer within the Church." *Communio* 12, no. 3 (1985): 258–75.

Chapp, L. S. *The God Who Speaks: Hans Urs Von Balthasar's Theology of Revelation.* Bethesda, MD: International Scholars, 1997.

Chia, Roland. *Revelation and Theology: The Knowledge of God in Balthasar and Barth.* Berne: Peter Land Publishers, 1999.

_____. "Theological Aesthetics or Aesthetic Theology? Some Reflections on the Theology of Hans Urs Von Balthasar." *Scottish Journal of Theology* 49, no. 1 (1996): 75-95.

Clarke, W. Norris. *Explorations in Metaphysics: Being, God, Person.* Southbend: University of Notre Dame Press, 1994.

_____. "Metaphysics as Mediator Between Revelation and the Natural Sciences." *Communio* 28, no. 3 (2001): 464–87.

_____. *The One and the Many: A Contemporary Thomistic Metaphysics.* Southbend: University of Notre Dame Press, 2001.

_____. *Person and Being,* The Aquinas Lectures. Milwaukee: Marquette University Press, 1993.

Coda, Piero. "Reflections of Theological Knowledge from the Perspective of the Charism of Unity." *Communio* 28, no. 3 (2001): 533–48.

Darling, Robin Young. "Knowing the True One is Acting the Truth." *Communio* 27, no. 3 (2000): 609–11.

de Certaeu, Michel. *The Mystic Fable.* Translated by Michael B. Smith. Chicago: Chicago University Press, 1992.

de Lubac, Henri. *Mystery of the Supernatural.* New York: The Crossroads Publishing Group, 1998.

_____. "On Christian Philosophy." *Communio* 19, no. 3 (1992): 478–506.

_____. "A Witness of Christ in the Church: Hans Urs Von Balthasar." In *Hans Urs Von Balthasar: His Life and Work.* Edited by David Schindler. San Francisco: Ignatius Press, 1991.

de Schrijver, G. *Le Merveilleux Accord De L'homme Et De Dieu: Etude D L'analogie De L'entre Chez Hans Urs Von Balthasar.* Leuven: Peeters, 1983.

Del Nice, Augusto. "Thomism and the Critique of Rationalism: Gilson and Shestov." *Communio* 25, no. 3 (1998): 732–45.

Duffy, Stephen. *The Graced Horizon: Nature and Grace in Modern Catholic Thought.* Collegeville: Liturgical Press, 1992.

Dupré, Louis. "Christian Spirituality Confronts the Modern World." *Communio* 12, no. 3 (1985): 334–42.

_____. "From Silence to Speech: Negative Theology and Trinitarian Spirituality." *Communio* 11, no. 1 (1984): 28–34.

_____. "Ignatian Humanism and its Mystical Origins." *Communio* 18, no. 2 (1991): 164–82.

_____. *Passage to Modernity: An Essay in the Hermeneutics of Nature and Culture.* New Haven: Yale University Press, 1993.

Fields, Stephen. "Balthasar and Rahner on the Spiritual Senses." *Theological Studies* 57, no. 2 (1996): 223–41.

Figura, Michael. "Gnosis and Gnosticism: A Renewed Challenged to the Church." *Communio* 24, no. 4 (1997): 671–80.

Florensky, Pavel. "Truth is Intuition-Discursion." *Communio* 27, no. 2 (2000): 378–85.

Ford, David F., and Dan Hardy. *Jubilate: Theology in Praise.* London: Darton, Longman & Todd, 1984.

Franks, A. F. "Trinitarian *Analogia Entis* in Hans Urs Von Balthasar." *The Thomist* 62 (1998): 533–59.

Gabellieri, Emmanuel. "Ontologie de l'image et phénoménologie de la vérité (à la lumière de H.U. von Balthasar)". *Theophilyon* 93 (1971): 225–44.

Gardner, Lucy, and David Moss. "Something Like Time; Something Like the Sexes—an Essay in Reception." In *Balthasar at the End of Modernity.* Edinburgh: T&T Clark, 1999.

Gawronski, Raymond. *Word and Silence: Hans Urs Von Balthasar and the Spiritual Encounter between East and West.* Grand Rapids: Eerdmans Publishing Group, 1995.

Haas, Alois. "Hans Urs Von Balthasar's 'Apocalypse of the German Soul': At the Intersection of German Literature, Philosophy and Theology." In *Hans Urs Von Balthasar: His Life and Work.* Edited by David Schindler. San Francisco: Ignatius Press, 1991.

Harrison, Victoria. "Putnam's Internal Realism and von Balthasar's Religious

Epistemology." In *International Journal for Philosophy of Religion* 44 (1998), 67–92.

Haro, E. Perez. *El Misterio Del Ser: Una Mediacion Entre Filosofia Y Teologia En Hans Urs Von Balthasar*. Barcelona, 1994.

Henrici, Peter. "On Mystery in Philosophy." *Communio* 19, no. 3 (1992): 354–64.

_____. "The Philosophy of Hans Urs Von Balthasar." In *Hans Urs Von Balthasar: His Life and Work*. Edited by David Schindler, 149–68. San Francisco: Ignatius Press, 1991.

_____. "The Spiritual Dimension and its Form of Reason." *Communio* 20, no. 4 (1993): 638–51.

Holzer, Vincent. "Christologie De La Figure (Gestalt) Et Christologie De La Kénose Chez Hans Urs Von Balthasar." *Revue des sciences religieuses* 79, no. 2 (2005): 249–78.

Howsare, Rodney. "Why Begin with Love? *Eros*, *Agape*, and the Problem of Secularism." *Communio* 33, no. 3 (2006): 423–48.

Ide, Pascal. *Êntre et Mystère: La philosophie de Hans Urs von Balthasar*. Brussells: Culture et Vérité, 1995.

Imbelli, Robert. "The Unknown Beyond the Word: Pneumatological Foundations of Dialogue." *Communio* 24, no. 2 (1997): 326–35.

Johnson, Junius. *Christ and Analogy: The Christocentric Metaphysics of Hans Urs von Balthasar*. Minneapolis: Fortress Press, 2013.

Jordan, Mark. "The Terms of the Debate Over 'Christian Philosophy'." *Communio* 12, no. 3 (1985): 293–311.

Kannengiesser, Charles. "Listening to the Fathers." In *Hans Urs Von Balthasar: His Life and Work*. Edited by David Schindler. San Francisco: Ignatius Press, 1991.

Kereszty, Roch. "Theology and Spirituality: The Task of a Synthesis." *Communio* 10, no. 3 (1983): 314–31.

Kerr, Fergus. "Foreword: Assessing This 'Giddy Synthesis'." In *Balthasar at the End of Modernity*. Edinburgh: T&T Clark, 1999.

_____. *Twentieth Century Catholic Theologians*. Oxford: Blackwell Publishing, 2007.

Kevern, John R. "Form in Tragedy: Balthasar as a Correlational Theologian." *Communio* 21, no. 2 (1994): 311–30.

Kilby, Karen. *Balthasar: A (Very) Critical Introduction*. Grand Rapids: Wm. Eerdmans Publishing Group, 2012.

Lash, Nicholas. "Anselm Seeking." In *The Beginning and End of 'Religion.'* Cambridge: Cambridge University Press, 1996.

_____. "Performing the Scriptures: Interpretation through Living." *The Furrow* 33, no. 8 (1982), 467–74

Lee, Claudia. "The Role of Mysticism in the Church as Conceived by Hans Urs Von Balthasar." *Communio* 16, no. 1 (1989): 105–26.

Léna, Marguerite. "The Sanctity of Intelligence." *Communio* 19, no. 3 (1992): 342–53.

Long, D. Stephen. *Saving Karl Barth: Hans Urs von Balthasar's Preoccupation*. Minneapolis: Fortress Press, 2014.

Long, Stephen A. "Divine and Creaturely 'Receptivity': The Search for a Middle Term." *Communio* 21, no. 1 (1994): 151–61.

Löser, Werner. "The Ignation Exercises in the Work of Hans Urs Von Balthasar." In *Hans Urs Von Balthasar: His Life and Work*. Edited by David Schindler, 103–20. San Francisco: Ignatius Press, 1991.

_____. "Being Interpreted as Love: Reflections on the Theology of Hans Urs Von Balthasar." *Communio* 16, no. 3 (1989): 475–90.

Lubich, Chiara. "For a Philosophy that Stems from Christ." *Communio* 25, no. 4 (1998): 746–56.

Louth, Andrew. "The Place of *The Heart of the World* in Balthasar's Writing." In *Analogy of Beauty: The Theology of Hans Urs von Balthasar*. Edited by John Riches. London: T&T Clark, 1986, 147–63.

MacKinnon, Donald. "Some Reflections on Hans Urs Von Balthasar's Christology with Special Reference to Theodramatik Ii/2, Iii and Iv." In *Analogy of Beauty: The Theology of Hans Urs Von Balthasar*. Edited by John Riches. Edinburgh: T&T Clark, 1986.

Marion, Jean-Luc. "Christian Philosophy and Charity." *Communio* 19, no. 3 (1992): 465–73.

Martin, Jennifer Newsome. *Hans Urs von Balthasar and the Critical Appropriation of Russian Religious Thought*. Notre Dame: The University of Notre Dame Press, 2015.

McIntosh, Mark. *Christology from Within: Spirituality and Incarnation in Hans Urs*

Von Balthasar. Vol. 3, Studies in Spirituality and Theology. Southbend: University of Notre Dame Press, 2000.

_____. *Mystical Theology*. Oxford: Blackwell Publishers, 1998.

Mongrain, Kevin. *The Systematic Thought of Hans Urs Von Balthasar: An Irenaean Retrieval*. New York: The Crossroads Publishing Group, 2002.

Moss, David. "The Saints." In *The Cambridge Companion to Hans Urs von Balthasar*. Edited by Edward T. Oakes, S. J. and David Moss. Cambridge: Cambridge University Press, 2004.

Nichols, Aidan. "The Habit of Theology, and How to Acquire It." *The Downside Review* 105 (1987): 247–59.

_____. *Say It Is Pentecost*. Edinburgh: T&T Clark, 2001.

_____. *The Word Has Been Abroad*. Edinburgh: T&T Clark, 1998.

Oakes, Edward T. *Pattern of Redemption: The Theology of Hans Urs von Balthasar*. New York: Bloomsbury Academic, 1997.

O'Donnell, John. "Hans Urs Von Balthasar: The Form of His Theology." *Communio* 16, no. 3 (1989): 458–74.

O'Regan, Cyril. *The Anatomy of Misremembering: Balthasar's Critique of Philosophical Modernity. Volume 1: Hegel*. New York: Crossroads Publishing Group, 2014.

_____. "Balthasar and Eckhart: Theological Principles and Catholicity." *The Thomist* 60 (1996): 203–39.

_____. *Gnostic Return in Modernity*. Albany: State University of New York Press, 2001.

_____. "Newman and Von Balthasar: The Christological Contexting of the Numinous." *Eglise et Theologie* 26 (1995): 165–202.

_____. "Von Balthasar and Thick Retrieval: Post-Chalcedonian Symphonic Theology." *Gregorianum* 77, no. 2 (1996): 227–60.

_____. "Von Balthasar's Valorization and Critique of Heidegger's Genealogy of Modernity." In *Christian Spirituality and the Culture of Modernity*. Grand Rapids: Wm. Eerdmans Publishing Co., 1998.

Palakeel, J. *The Use of Analogy in Theological Discourse: An Investigation in Ecumenical Perspective*. Rome: Editrice Pontificia Universita Gregoriana, 1995.

Pitstick, Alyssa. *Light in the Darkness: Hans Urs von Balthasar and the Catholic*

Doctrine of Christ's Descent into Hell. Grand Rapids: Wm. Eerdmans Publishing Group, 2007.

Plaga-Kayser, U.. *Ich Bin Die Wahrheit: Die Theologische Dimension Der Christologie Hans Urs Von Balthasar.* Münster: Paulinus Press, 1998.

Polanyi, Michael. *Knowing and Being: Essays.* London: Routledge, 1969.

Ponnou-Delaffon, André-Marie. *Le chiffre trinitaire de la vérité chez Hans Urs von Balthasar: La Trinité comme principe d'intelligibilité de l'articulation de la philosophie et de la théologie dans La Théologique.* Paris: Parole et Silence, 2006.

Pope Benedict XVI. *God is Love.* San Francisco: Ignatius Press, 2006.

_____. *Jesus of Nazareth.* San Francisco: Ignatius Press, 2007.

Potworowski, Christophe. "Christian Experience in Hans Urs von Balthasar." *Communio* 20, no. 1 (1993): 107–17.

Proterra, Michael. "Another look at Christian spirituality." *Communio* 9, no. 2 (1982), 270–75.

Quash, Ben. *Theology and the Drama of History.* Cambridge: Cambridge University Press, 2005.

Ratzinger, Joseph Cardinal. "The Dignity of the Human Person." In *Commentary On the Documents of Vatican II.* Vol. 5, *Pastoral Constitution on the Church in the Modern World.* Edited by Herbert Vorgrimler. Translated by W. J. O'Hara. New York: The Crossroad Publishing Company, 1989), 159–63.

_____. "Faith, Philosophy and Theology." *Communio* 11, no. 4 (1984): 350–64.

_____. "Homily at the Funeral Liturgy of Hans Urs Von Balthasar." In *Hans Urs Von Balthasar: His Life and Work.* Edited by David L. Schindler. San Francisco: Ignatius Press, 1991.

_____. *The Theology of History in St. Bonaventure.* Translated by Zachary Hayes. Chicago: Franciscan Herald Press, 1971.

Riches, John. "Balthasar and the Analysis of Faith." In *Analogy of Beauty: The Theology of Hans Urs Von Balthasar.* Edited by John Riches. Edinburgh: T&T Clark, 1986.

Roten, Johann. "Hans Urs von Balthasar's Anthropology in Light of his Marian Thinking." *Communio* 20, no. 2 (1993): 306–33.

_____. "The Two Halves of the Moon: Marian Anthropological Dimensions in the Common Mission of Adrienne Von Speyr and Hans Urs Von Balthasar." *Communio* 16, no. 3 (1989): 419–45.

Sachs, Randall. "Spirit and Life: The Pneumatology and Spirituality of Hans Urs von Balthasar." PhD diss., Tübingen, 1982.

Sara, Juan. "Knowledge, the Transcendentals, and Communion." *Communio* 28, no. 3 (2001): 505–32.

Saward, John. "Mary and Peter in the Christological Constellation: Balthasar's Ecclesiology." In *Analogy of Beauty: The Theology of Hans Urs Von Balthasar.* Edited by John Riches. Edinburgh: T&T Clark, 1986.

Schindler, David L. "Catholicity and the State of Contemporary Theology: The Need for an Onto-logic of Holiness." *Communio* 14, no. 4 (1987): 426–50.

_____. "God and the End of Intelligence: Knowledge as Relationship." *Communio* 26, no. 3 (1999): 486–509.

_____. *Heart of the World, Center of the Church.* Edinburgh: T&T Clark, 1996.

_____. "Is Truth Ugly? Moralism and the Convertibility of Being and Love." *Communio* 27, no. 4 (2000): 701–28.

_____. "The Person: Philosophy, Theology, and Receptivity." *Communio* 20, no. 1 (1994): 172–91.

_____. "Sanctity and the Intellectual Life." *Communio* 20, no. 4 (1993): 652–72.

_____. "Trinity, Creation, and the Order of Intelligence in the Modern Academy." *Communio* 28, no. 3 (2001): 406–28.

Schindler, David C. *Hans Urs Von Balthasar and the Dramatic Structure of Truth: A Philosophical Investigation.* New York: Fordham University Press, 2004.

_____. "Reason in Mystery: Balthasar's *Gestalt* and the Augustinian Paradox." *Second Spring: An International Journal of Faith & Culture* 6 (2004): 23–33.

_____. "The Redemption of Eros: On Benedict XVI's First Encyclical." *Communio* 33, no. 3 (2006): 374–98.

_____. "Surprised by Truth: The Drama of Reason in Fundamental Theology." In *La Missione Teologica Di Hans Urs Von Balthasar: Atti Del Simposio Internazaionale Di Teologia in Occasione Del Centesimo Anniversario Della Nascita Di Hans Urs Von Balthasar, Lugano 2-4 Marzo 2005,* edited by A. and A. Tambolini Jerumanis, 131–50. Legano: Eupress FTL, 2005.

_____. "Toward a Non-Possessive Concept of Knowledge: On the Relation between Reason and Love in Aquinas and Balthasar." *Modern Theology* 22, no. 4 (2006): 577–67.

_____. "Truth and the Christian Imagination: The Reformation of Causality and the Iconoclasm of the Spirit." *Communio* 33, no. 4 (2006): 521–39.

_____. "Wer kommt der Mensch in die Theologie?: Heidegger, Hegel and the Stakes of Onto-Theo-Logy." *Communio* 32, no. 4 (2005): 637–68.

Schmitz, Kenneth L. "The Transfiguration of Gnosis in Late Enlightenment German Thought." *Communio* 24, no. 4 (1997).

Schaerr, Heinz. "Analogie und Geschichlichkeit der Wahrheit: Aspekte des Wahrheitproblems bei Hans Urs von Balthasar." *Annalen der Philosophischen Desellschaften Innerscheiz und Ostschweiz*, vol. 4 (1948): 105–22.

Scola, Antonio. "Christian Experience and Theology." *Communio* 23, no. 2 (1996): 203–6.

_____. *Hans Urs Von Balthasar: A Theological Style*. Grand Rapids: Eerdmans Publishing Group, 1995.

Servalis, Jacques. "Finding God in All Things." *Communio* 30, no. 2 (2003), 209–81.

_____. "Hans Urs von Balthasar and the Continuing Youthfulness of the Exercises." *Communio* 21, no. 2 (1994): 331–43.

_____. "The Lay Vocation in the World According to Hans Urs von Balthasar." *Communio* 23, no. 4 (1996), 656–76.

_____. "The *Ressourcement* of Contemporary Spirituality under the Guidance of Adrienne Von Speyr and Hans Urs Von Balthasar." *Communio* 23, no. 2 (1996): 300–321.

_____. "*Théologie des Exercices spirituels: H.U. von Balthasar interprète saint Ignace.* Paris: Culture et verite, 1996.

Sicari, Antonio. "Mary, Peter and John: Figures of the Church." *Communio*, 19, no. 2 (1999), 189–207.

Spaemann, Robert. "Rationality and Faith in God." *Communio* 32, no. 4 (2005): 618–36.

Strukelj, Anton. "Man and Woman under God: The Dignity of the Human Being according to Hans Urs von Balthasar." *Communio* 20, no. 2 (1993): 377–88.

_____. "The *Theo-Logic* of Hans Urs von Balthasar." *Communio* 20, no. 4 (1993): 616–22.

Sutton, Matthew Lewis. "Hans Urs von Balthasar and Adrienne von Speyr's Ecclesial Relationship." *New Blackfriars* 94 (2012), 50–63.

Sutton, Matthew Lewis. *Heaven Opens: The Trinitarian Mysticism of Adrienne von Speyr*. Minneapolis: Fortress Press, 2014.

Treitler, Wolfgang. "True Foundations of Authentic Theology." In *Hans Urs Von Balthasar: His Life and Work*. Edited by David Schindler. San Francisco: Ignatius Press, 1991.

Tugwell, Simon. "Scholarship, Sanctity and Spirituality." *Communio* 11, no. 1 (1984): 46–59.

Turner, Denys. *Darkness of God: Negativity in Christian Mysticism*. Cambridge: Cambridge University Press, 1995.

Van Erp, Stephen. *The Art of Theology: Hans Urs Von Balthasar's Theological Aesthetics and the Foundations of Faith*. Leuven: Peeters, 2004.

Walgrave, Jan-Hendrik. "Prayer and Mysticism". *Communio* 12, no. 3 (1985): 276–92.

Walker, Adrian. "Christ and Cosmology: Methodological Considerations for Catholic Educators." *Communio* 28, no. 3 (2001): 429–49.

_____. "Editorial: Fundamentalism and the Catholicity of Truth." *Communio* 29, no. 1 (2002): 5–27.

_____. "The Gift of Simplicity: Reflections on Obedience in the Work of Adrienne von Speyr." *Communio* 32, no. 4 (2007): 573–82.

_____. "Love Alone: Hans Urs von Balthasar as a Master of Theological Renewal." *Communio* 32, no. 3 (2005): 517–40.

_____. "On 'Rephilosophizing' Theology." *Communio* 31, no. 1 (2004): 143–67.

Wells, Samuel. *Improvisation: The Drama of Christian Ethics*. Grand Rapids: Baker Publishing Group, 2004.

Wilken, Robert Louis. "*In Dominico Eloquio*: Learning the Lord's Style of Language." *Communio* 24, no. 4 (1997): 846–66.

Williams, Rowan. "Balthasar and Rahner." In *Analogy of Beauty: The Theology of Hans Urs Von Balthasar*, edited by John Riches, 11–34. Edinburgh: T&T Clark, 1986.

Worgul, G. S. "M. Blondel and the Problem of Mysticism" in *Ephemerides Theologicae Lovanienses*, 61, no. 1 (1985), 100–122.

Young, Frances. *The Art of Performance: Towards a Theology of Holy Scripture*. London: Dartman, Longman and Todd, 1990.

Index